JOSEPH CONRAD

Books by Jeffrey Meyers

JOSEPH CONRAD

A Biography

Jeffrey Meyers

CHARLES SCRIBNER'S SONS
New York

Charles Scribner's Sons
Macmillan Publishing Company
866 Third Avenue
New York, NY 10022

Published by arrangement with John Murray (Publishers) Ltd.
50 Albemarle Street
London W1X 4BD
England

Grateful acknowledgment is made to the following for permission to reprint previously published material:
Doubleday: Excerpts from G. Jean-Aubry, *Joseph Conrad: Life and Letters*. Copyright 1927 by Doubleday.
Cambridge University Press: Excerpts from *The Collected Letters of Joseph Conrad*, volumes 1–3. Copyright 1983–88 by Cambridge University Press.

Library of Congress Cataloging-in-Publication Data
Meyers, Jeffrey.
  Joseph Conrad: a biography/Jeffrey Meyers.
    p. cm.
  Includes bibliographical references and index.
  ISBN 0-684-19230-6
  1. Conrad, Joseph, 1857–1924—Biography. 2. Novelists, English—20th century—Biography. I. Title.
PR6005.04Z778   1991
823'.912—dc20   90-19303
[B]

Macmillan books are available at special discounts for bulk purchases for sales promotions, premiums, fund-raising, or educational use. For details, contact:

Special Sales Director
Macmillan Publishing Company
866 Third Avenue
New York, NY 10022

DESIGNED BY ERICH HOBBING

10 9 8 7 6 5 4 3 2 1

Printed in the United States of America

For J. F. Powers

Contents

Illustrations

Maps

Preface

Conrad once observed: "I am not a personage for an orderly biography, either auto or otherwise," for he was shrewdly deceptive and often deliberately misleading about his own life. But he also had an apprehensive admiration for literary detection and told an acquaintance: "You are a terror for tracking people out!" Though Conrad's life and works have been intensively examined, my own research and the use of unpublished material has revealed new information about his Polish background, the Carlist war in Spain and Dutch colonial rule in the Malay Archipelago; Conrad's positive attitude toward the Jews and toward America; his suicide attempt; the questions asked on his three merchant marine examinations; his marriage; his gout; his close friendships with Perceval Gibbon and Sir Robert Jones; his little-known meeting with T. E. Lawrence; and, most importantly, his love affair in 1916 with the wild and beautiful American journalist Jane Anderson, who became a traitor in World War Two. I have found in Emin Pasha a new source for Kurtz in *Heart of Darkness*, in Sergei Nechaev for Razumov in *Under Western Eyes*, in Ford's wife and his friend Arthur Marwood for Flora de Barral and Captain Anthony in *Chance*. I reveal the pervasive influence of Jane Anderson on *The Arrow of Gold*; show the significance of music in Conrad's life and of opera in *The Rescue*; and discuss for the first time his unpublished film scenario, "The Strong Man."

Acknowledgments

I am pleased to acknowledge the generous assistance of a great many people and institutions. Frederick Karl and Laurence Davies sent xerox copies of a thousand pages of unpublished letters from volumes five to eight of their superb Cambridge Edition. Ian Watt sent unpublished typescripts of the valuable essay he wrote with John Halverson on Jane Anderson and of BBC interviews with friends of Conrad. My old friend Thomas Moser sent useful addresses, xeroxes and photographs. Leon Higdon, the editor of *Conradiana,* answered many detailed questions. Joan Givner, the biographer of Katherine Anne Porter, sent useful information and many valuable leads. Eugene Petriwsky of the University of Colorado clarified crucial problems about the Polish Ukraine. Ian Gibson, the biographer of Lorca, sent important material from Spain on the Marqués de Cienfuegos. The family of the late Kitty Barry Crawford sent seventy-five pages of unpublished material about Jane Anderson. Joan Kennedy Taylor, the daughter of the composer Deems Taylor, met me at her country house in Massachusetts and provided fascinating material about her father's marriage to Jane Anderson.

Though Conrad was born in 1857, I have interviewed five people who knew him: Philip Conrad, David Garnett, Sir John Rothenstein, George Seldes and Frank Swinnerton. And I have corresponded with three children of his close friends: Adam Curle, Conrad Russell and Veronica Wedgwood.

For other letters about Conrad I am deeply grateful to the late Jocelyn Baines, Basil Barlow, Michael Bolton, Ian Boyd, Morris Brownell, Keith Carabine, the late Borys Conrad, Dr. Sheldon Cooperman, H. M. Daleski, the Duke of Norfolk, John Edwards, Theodore Ehrsam, Hugh Epstein, Kevin Froggatt, James Gindin, Luis González-del-Valle, Eugene Goodheart, Stephen Gray, Donald Greene, Albert Guerard, Desmond Harmsworth, Eloise Hay, David Holmes, Mark Holloway, Douglas Hurd, Neill Joy, David Kenney, Jerzy Kosinski, Michael Markel, John McCarthy, Juliet McLauchlan, M. J. McLendon, Mario Menocal, Jr., the late Bernard Meyer, Michael Millgate, Paula Milone, Zdzislaw Najder, Beatrice Ogilvy, Felipe Orlando, Thomas Pinney, John Pomian, S. W. Reid, Donald Rude, Thorwald Sanchez, Timothy Seldes, Norman Sherry, William Shirer, Rowland Smith, Jon Stallworthy, the late Sondra Stang, Raymond Sutton, Jr., Bruce Teets, Hugh Thomas, the late Virgil Thomson, Hans van Marle, Cedric Watts, Randy Weinstein, Pieter Williams, A. N. Wilson, Senator Timothy Wirth.

I received useful material from the following institutions: American Academy and Institute of Arts and Letters, American Society of Composers, Authors and Publishers, Arizona Historical Society, Auswärtiges Amt, Boston College, British Library, Bundesarchiv, Colgate University, Department of the Army, Department of Transport: Marine Directorate, Deutsches Rundfunkarchiv, Federal Bureau of Investigation, Federal Communications Commission, General Register and Record Office of Shipping and Seamen, Georgia Department of Human Resources, German Embassy, Harvard University Alumni Office, Heffers Booksellers, Institut für Zeitgeschichte, Joseph Conrad Society (U.K.), Library of Congress, London Library, Ministerio de Justicia: Asuntos de Gracia (Madrid), National Maritime Museum, National Sound Archive, Netherlands Consulate, Netherlands Genealogy Office, New York City Municipal Archives, New York Public Library, the *Observer*, Piedmont College, St. Bernard's Convent School, Samuel French Ltd., Spanish Embassy, University of Colorado: Inter-Library Loan, University of Texas: Humanities Research Center, Yale University, Zentrales Staatsarchiv.

A grant from the University of Colorado paid part of my research expenses, and enabled me to visit libraries and conduct interviews in England and America. My wife, Valerie, scrutinized each chapter and compiled the index.

We live, as we dream—alone.

JOSEPH CONRAD

Conrad / bringer of the light of
a european point of view into
the black bog of britain.

EZRA POUND

JOSEPH
CONRAD

CHAPTER ONE

The Polish Heritage

I

Conrad's life and character were shaped by the troubled history of Poland and by the thwarted political idealism of his father. His patriotic and personal legacy was an anguished mixture of idealism, self-sacrifice, defeat, arrest, exile, bitterness and despair—leading to emigration, loneliness and guilt. Conrad's birthplace lacked natural frontiers and was surrounded by powerful neighbors. It had been a Roman Catholic kingdom since 1024, and had frequently been attacked and invaded by Swedes, Tartars, Hungarians, Turks and Russians. In 1772—when Poland was weakened and made powerless by internal dissension—Frederick the Great of Prussia and Maria Theresa of Austria, anxious to prevent Russia from controlling all of Poland, signed a treaty with Catherine the Great in St. Petersburg that divided 80,000 square miles (about thirty percent of the nation) among themselves. Austria obtained Galicia, a large section of southwest Poland; Prussia took Pomerania, in northwest Poland; and Russia got a strip of territory in eastern Poland.

Twenty years later, when the remnant of Poland adopted a new constitution and showed signs of national regeneration, it was invaded from the east and west by Russia and Prussia. In the second partition in 1793, Catherine took an enormous section of eastern Poland, including almost all of Lithuania, and Prussia seized most of Poland west of Warsaw as well as the Baltic port of Danzig. Poland became a landlocked nation, less than one-third the size it had been before the invasion, and its remaining central section came under Russian control. After the national uprising led by Tadeusz Kosciuszko (who had fought in the American Revolution) was defeated in 1795, the remainder of Poland was divided among the Great Powers. Catherine, who formally annexed the Baltic Duchy of Courland, took sixty-two percent of the territory, Prussia took the Warsaw region and Austria got the last eighteen percent of the land.

Norman Davies attributes the partitions not to deliberate policy, but to the Russians' brutal and blundering efforts to suppress political progress:

> By obstructing even moderate reform, they repeatedly drove the reformers into rebellion; whilst, by sending their armies into Poland to crush the rebellions, they threatened to upset the whole balance of power in eastern Europe. Hence, to have a free hand in Poland, they were obliged to calm the fears of the Prussians and Austrians by agreeing to territorial compensations. Essentially, the three Partitions of Poland in 1772, 1793, and 1795 were not planned in advance. They were made necessary by the Russians' compulsive desire to crush Reform at all costs, and they were sops to obtain the acquiescence of Berlin and Vienna.

After the third partition, Poland—transformed into the backward frontier regions of three dominant states and treated as a troublesome minority—disappeared from the map of Europe for 123 years. In 1897 the French playwright Alfred Jarry, creating an absurd scenario for an imaginary country, wrote the notorious stage direction: *"En Pologne, c'est-à-dire nulle part."*[1]

The history of Poland in the nineteenth century was a series of disastrous attempts to regain national independence. Conrad's family played a significant role in this history, sacrificing their fortune, liberty and life for an idealistic cause while maintaining no illusions about the possibility of success. Napoleon's victories in Europe and the establishment in 1806 of the Duchy of Warsaw, which had its own army, seemed to foreshadow the resurrection of the old Polish state in the new liberal order of Europe. Polish divisions fought alongside Napoleon in the Moscow campaign of 1812 and remained loyal to him until the very end. Conrad's paternal grandfather, Teodor Korzeniowski, was a cavalry lieutenant in Napoleon's armies in 1807 and 1809, and took part in the Russian campaign under Prince Jozef Poniatowski. After Napoleon's defeat at Waterloo in 1815, the Treaty of Vienna replaced the Duchy of Warsaw with the nominally independent Congress Kingdom of Poland, which had more extensive territory, but was unified with Russia and ruled by the Czar. The rest of Poland once again came under the complete—and apparently more final—control of the three reinstated partition powers.

Conrad owned more books on Napoleonic history, memoirs and campaigns than on any other subject. He remained a lifelong student of that era, and portrayed it in three stories and in his last two novels. *The Rover* (1923) takes place during Nelson's battles with Napoleon and the unfinished *Suspense* (1925) concerns Napoleon's escape from Elba. Though the Napoleonic legend lived on as part of the myth of Polish national-ism, Conrad, in his major political essay, "Autocracy and War" (1905), and in his autobiographical *A Personal Record* (1912), denied and disso-ciated himself from this myth. He condemned "the subtle and manifold influence for evil of the Napoleonic episode as a school of violence, as a sower of national hatreds, as the direct provocator of obscurantism and reaction, of political tyranny and injustice," which were restored throughout Europe after his defeat. Conrad was horrified by the immo-rality of the conqueror's ambition, expressed distaste for the character of Napoleon and blamed him for having raised in Poles "a false hope of national independence."[2]

Polish Romantic literature, especially Adam Mickiewicz's *Konrad Wal-lenrod* (1828), an exemplary tale of patriotic revenge and struggle for liberation, helped inspire the nationalist revival in 1830. His *Pan Tadeusz* (1834), the Polish national epic, nostalgically celebrated the glories of Polish country life and the hope of liberating the nation from the Rus-sians with the help of Napoleon's army. The Romantic literary tradition, in which Conrad's father wrote, "elevated sacrifice and sorrow to sub-lime heights. Poland was compared to the Christ among nations, re-deeming through suffering not only the Polish nation but mankind. Poland had a sacred mission to fulfill: to break the chains of absolutism and bring about universal freedom."

Inspired in part by nationalist poetry, the Poles rose up in November 1830, established a substantial army and had some initial success. But they were inevitably crushed the following year, when the Russians re-entered Warsaw. In reprisal, the enemy eliminated the separate Pol-ish army, closed the universities, suspended the constitution, abolished the parliament and made the Congress Kingdom an integral part of Russia.

Conrad's paternal grandfather, a captain in the Polish army, took part in the insurrection of 1830. He formed his own cavalry squadron, was wounded twice and was decorated with a medal for valor. Prince Roman Sanguszko, a greatly esteemed friend of the family whom the young Conrad met in 1867 and later made the hero of his only Polish story, also took part in this rising. After the death of his young wife, Roman, an officer in the Russian guards, resigned his commission, enlisted as a private soldier and joined the Polish revolt. When captured and ques-tioned by a sympathetic judge, who suggested that he was grief-stricken by his wife's death and had joined the rebels on a reckless impulse, Roman nobly stated that he had enlisted from conviction. He was con-

demned for life to the Siberian mines—a sentence of deferred death. In
Conrad's story of sacrificial patriotism, Roman's "religion of undying
hope resembles the mad cult of despair, of death, of annihilation."
Conrad pessimistically suggests that Poland, "which persists in thinking, breathing, speaking, hoping, and suffering in its grave, railed in by
a million of bayonets and triple-sealed with the seals of three great
empires," constantly demands such exemplary, if hopeless, martyrdom
in order to keep alive the patriotic flame.

After the failure of the rising, 10,000 leaders and soldiers, the majority
of the political and intellectual elite of the nation, left the country and
settled mainly in Paris, which became the center of Polish revolutionary
activities. Yet emigration was condemned even by those who had joined
the exodus: "The images of duty abandoned, of betrayal, and above
all—of desertion, had been common in Polish literature since the early
nineteenth century, since the loss of Polish national independence.
Adam Mickiewicz in his *Pan Tadeusz* wrote 'Woe to us, who fled at the
time of a plague, carrying our timorous heads abroad.' And the other
national poet-prophet, Juliusz Slowacki, was even more outspoken: 'I
have no dignity—I have fled from martyrdom.' And they both meant
voluntary exile."[3]

II

Conrad's homeland, the Polish Ukraine, that large fertile plain on the
borders of Poland and Russia, had four languages and four religions.
The governing class spoke Russian and belonged to the Orthodox
Church; the intellectuals, landowners and estate managers spoke Polish
and were Roman Catholics; the peasants and servants spoke Ukrainian
and were members of the Eastern Uniat Church; and the merchants
were mainly Yiddish-speaking Jews. This ethnically heterogeneous society gave Conrad a multi-lingual capacity and a cosmopolitan outlook
that enabled him to adapt to several different countries and cultures.

About ten percent of all Polish-speaking inhabitants of the Ukraine,
including Conrad's family, belonged to the *szlachta,* a hereditary class,
below the aristocracy, which combined the qualities of the gentry and
the nobility. After Conrad had left Poland, he idealized his country and
his class, praising its independence, morality and freedom, and stressing its historical connection to the philosophy and religion of the West.
In a letter of May 1917 to the novelist Hugh Walpole, he glorified the
Polish gentry and "those houses where, under a soul-crushing oppres-

sion, so much noble idealism, chivalrous traditions, the sanity and amenities of Western civilization were so valiantly preserved." And after Poland had finally regained independence in 1919, he apotheosized "the Polish temperament with its tradition of self-government, its chivalrous view of moral restraints and an exaggerated respect for individual rights: not to mention the important fact that the whole Polish mentality, Western in complexion, had received its training from Italy and France and, historically, had always remained, even in religious matters, in sympathy with the most liberal currents of European thought."

The reality, in fact, was quite different. In Poland, only the *szlachta* had political power and this proud but backward class was primarily responsible for the anarchy, weakness and degeneration of the country that had led to the partitions of the late eighteenth century. Though their ideals had been discredited, the noble ethos survived to inspire the hopeless rebellions of the nineteenth century. Davies observes:

> Of all the products of Polish life before the Partitions, the Polish nobility—the *szlachta* and all their works—might seem to have been the most discredited. The *szlachta's* knightly code had not helped them to fight and repel the Republic's enemies. Their peacock pride in a supposedly exclusive ancestry was grotesquely unsuited to their miserable decline. Their social ideals of brotherly love and equality ill fitted their continuing support for serfdom. The political philosophy of their "Golden Freedom" resulted in common anarchy. . . . The *szlachta* were the laughing-stock of Europe, the butt which every radical wit from Defoe to Cobden could mock. If, in Carlyle's cruel words, their noble Republic was "a beautifully phosphorescent rot-heap," then they were the parasites who swarmed upon it. One might have supposed that the ideals of the *szlachta* were supremely redundant, and would have been quietly forgotten at the first opportunity. In fact, though the legal status of the *szlachta* was annulled in 1795 by the partitioning powers, its ideals lived on. The *kultura szlachecka* (the noble ethos) has become one of the central features of the modern Polish outlook.[4]

Conrad's father, Apollo Korzeniowski (the name derives from the word *korzen,* or root), belonged to this impoverished landed gentry in the *gubernia* of Kiev, in the southeastern frontier of the Polish Ukraine. He was born into a family of Polish patriots in 1820 and educated at the local gymnasium at Zhitomir. At the age of twenty he entered St. Petersburg University, where he studied Oriental languages, literature and law. After six years, he seems to have learned very little Arabic and left without taking a degree. Physically unattractive, Apollo had an oversized head and a shrunken body, blunt features and thick hair, combed straight back from a wide Slavic forehead.

His brother-in-law Tadeusz Bobrowski, who had known Apollo since their schooldays, described his appearance and personality as well as the extremes of bitterness and kindness in his character:

> In our part of the country he had the reputation of being very ugly and sarcastic. In fact he was not beautiful, nor even handsome, but his eyes had a very kind expression and his sarcasm was only verbal, of the drawing-room type; for I have never detected any in his feeling or in his actions. Open-hearted and passionate, he had a sincere love of people. In his deeds he was impractical, often even helpless. Uncompromising in speech and writing, he was frequently over-tolerant in everyday life. . . . He also had two sets of measures: one for the weak and ignorant, the other for the mighty of this world.

Apollo's lack of social and political conformity, and his innate violence, were expressed in his writings as well as in his life. He had a fiery temperament and a powerful undercurrent of pessimism, tempered by "a special regard for the rights of the underprivileged of this earth."[5]

Conrad's mother, Eva Bobrowska, was, like Apollo, born on a country estate about 125 miles southwest of Kiev. Thirteen years younger than Apollo, she was the only surviving and much adored daughter in a family of six sons. Though Najder writes that she was "known for her beauty,"[6] contemporary photographs reveal that she was actually quite homely, with a low forehead, long nose, widely spaced eyes and mousy expression. In 1847, through his friend Tadeusz, Apollo met the adolescent Eva, who was immediately attracted to his poetic temperament, his passionate patriotism and his sympathy for the underdog. He, in turn, was drawn to her lively imagination and her warm heart.

Unlike the Korzeniowskis, the Bobrowskis had increased their wealth by remaining aloof from political rebellions. For both personal and political reasons, Eva's parents strongly disapproved of the courtship. Apollo had no occupation, owned nothing, seemed irresponsible and lazy. He was supported by his father, whose estate had been confiscated by the Russian authorities after the rising of 1830. Eva's father even tried to marry Apollo to someone else, but he resisted the rich young ladies and remained faithful to Eva, who also discouraged all other suitors. After her father's death, Eva, in poor health, was torn between his wishes and her love for Apollo. Finally, realizing that the strong-willed woman would never marry if she could not have the man she loved, the family acceded to her wishes, and they were married on May 4, 1856.

Apollo spent the first years of his marriage administering country estates. By 1860 he had lost all of his own money and some of his wife's
dowry of nine thousand silver rubles.

Apollo's soldier-father had written and privately printed a five-act
tragedy in verse, so extremely boring that no one had ever been able to
read it to the end. And Apollo—poet, dramatist, translator and
revolutionary—also devoted himself to literary and political activities
(which brought in very little money) rather than to his ostensible occupation: the management of agricultural estates. He published political,
social and literary articles; two volumes of poetry, including the patriotic-
religious *Purgatorial Songs;* and two plays, *A Comedy* (1854) and *For the
Love of Money* (1859), and wrote four other plays, including *No Hope*
(1866), whose title expressed his pessimistic philosophy.

A gifted linguist, Apollo had studied Russian, and translated German,
French and English works into Polish: Heine's poetry; Alfred de Vigny's
Chatterton (1857); Victor Hugo's *Toilers of the Sea, La Légende des siècles*
(1860), *Hernani* (1862) and *Marion Delorme* (1863); Shakespeare's early
comedies, *Much Ado About Nothing, The Two Gentlemen of Verona* and *The
Comedy of Errors* (of which only the latter was published, in 1866); and
Dickens' novel of social oppression in the coal mines, *Hard Times* (1866).
He also planned, but never wrote, "a great Polish novel" about Mus-
covy's corrupting and cynical influence on every aspect of Polish life.

Apollo's sharp social satire, *A Comedy*, shows the conflict between an
old and dishonest landowner and a poor but sympathetic proletarian,
who asks for the hand of his ward in marriage. *For the Love of Money*
attacks the *nouveau riche* and portrays a revolutionary idealist who has
turned into a cynic. Vigny's *Chatterton* dramatizes society's indifference,
even hostility, to poets; and Apollo's preface condemns the "time when
spiritual values are sacrificed to 'the circus of material interests.' " Apollo
had a caustic sense of humor and launched hysterical attacks on the
complacent, self-serving rich. A contemporary critic compared him to a
rabid animal: "His wit bites to the bone, his irony kills. His laughter is
a kind of snarl, followed by a deep bite." Modern Polish critics feel "his
verses often appear too exalted, too pathetic. There is a discrepancy
between the fairly simple ideas and the inflated form."[7] He was sceptical
about human nature and "obsessed by a somber vision of threatening
[Russian] forces which he saw rising up from a state of primeval chaos
to overshadow and overthrow civilized man." His poem "Before the
Thunderstorm," written after the failure of the Polish revolution of 1846
and the European revolutions of 1848, expresses his characteristic despair and patriotic grief:

So many days and so many years
have we groaned with the voice of orphans
on this our mother's grave,
accompanied by the music of thunder;
on our own soil—yet dispossessed,
in our own homes—yet homeless!
This once proud domain of our fathers
is now but a cemetery and a ruin.
Our fame and greatness have melted away
in a stream of blood and tears;
and our sole patrimony
is the dust and bones of our ancestors.[8]

Conrad was significantly influenced by his father's works. His translations first aroused Conrad's interest in French and English culture: in Hugo's *Toilers of the Sea* (written in political exile), which helped inspire Conrad's maritime career; in Shakespeare's plays, which he carried with him aboard ships and alluded to dozens of times in his fiction; and in Dickens' *Bleak House*, which affected his grim portrayal of London in *The Secret Agent*. Conrad's story "Because of the Dollars" (1914) echoed the title of Apollo's play. A proverbial phrase from Apollo's essay on Shakespeare: "Man fires, but God carries the bullet" is repeated in "Gaspar Ruiz": "Man discharges the piece, but God carries the bullet." The sacrifice of moral values to material interests, discussed in the Preface to *Chatterton*, is a dominant theme in *Nostromo*; the condemnation of the corrupting and cynical influence of Russia, in the unwritten novel, recurs powerfully in *Under Western Eyes*. Conrad certainly adopted his father's scepticism and pessimism, and he repeated the arguments of Apollo's polemic "Poland and Muscovy" in his own essay "Autocracy and War." Though Apollo died when Conrad was only eleven years old, they established an intense, even harrowing relationship, and the father had the profoundest impact on the son.

CHAPTER TWO

A Polish Childhood

1857–1874

I

In 1857, a year after her marriage, Eva became pregnant and the couple moved from a country estate to Berdichev, one hundred miles south-west of Kiev, to be near her mother. Seven years earlier, in March 1850, Honoré de Balzac had traveled through the countryside, "sandy tracts studded with clumps of pines," and had married Evelina Hanska in the Polish Roman Catholic church of Santa Barbara in Berdichev. In Conrad's fictional fragment, "The Sisters," the Ukrainian hero remembers scattered white huts with high thatched roofs and uneven windows, and the green cupola of a village church, topped by a gleaming cross. In "Prince Roman" Conrad also recalls his native landscape and portrays the great hedged fields, the dammed streams that made a chain of lakes set in the green meadows, the cold brilliant sun "above an undulating horizon of great folds of snow," the hidden villages of peasants and the region where wolves were to be found.

Berdichev, like nearby Zhitomir, where Conrad also lived as a young child, was typical of many towns in the Polish Ukraine. It had been fortified against invasions in the sixteenth century, but was later de-stroyed by Tartars and Cossacks. In 1630 a Polish Carmelite monastery was built and in 1739 a Roman Catholic church. The town prospered by supplying flour to Napoleon's troops during the invasion of 1812, be-came a major grain and cattle market, and began to manufacture shoes and clothing. Berdichev also became a place of pilgrimage and a center for publishing, though these were suppressed by the Russian govern-ment in 1866.

When Apollo and Eva married, Berdichev, the fourth-largest city in the Ukraine, was the second-largest Jewish community in Russia. Ever

9

since 1790, when Jews had been allowed to open shops, the Jews represented eighty to ninety percent of the total population. It had a Jewish
hospital and three Jewish schools, and was a major Hasidic center,
founded by the charismatic eighteenth-century leader, Rabbi Isaac ben
Levi.[1] Sholom Aleichem portrayed the town in *Gants Berdichev* (1908).
Conrad, who grew up among persecuted and patriotic Jews, was, for his
time and place, astonishingly free of anti-Semitic prejudice. For historical, familial and personal reasons, he was essentially sympathetic to the
Jews, and portrayed Hirsch in *Nostromo* and Yankel in "Prince Roman"
quite favorably.

Jozef Teodor Konrad Nalecz Korzeniowski was born in Berdichev on
December 3, 1857. Jozef was the name of his maternal grandfather,
Teodor of his paternal grandfather and Nalecz was the *szlachta* name.
Konrad, which he later anglicized and adopted as his surname, was the
name of two of Adam Mickiewicz's creations: Konrad Wallenrod, the
eponymous hero of that patriotic poem, and Konrad, the main character
of *Forefather's Eve*. To a Pole, the name symbolized an anti-Russian
fighter.

Conrad was born one year after the end of the Crimean War, when
Russia's defeat by Britain, France and Turkey had once again raised
hopes of Polish independence. Apollo celebrated his son's christening
with a characteristically patriotic-religious poem, "To my son born in the
85th year of Muscovite oppression." It alluded to the partition of 1772,
burdened the new-born child with overwhelming obligations and urged
him to sacrifice himself (as Apollo would do) for the good of his country:

> Bless you, my little son:
> Be a *Pole!* Though foes
> May spread before you
> A web of happiness
> Renounce it all: love your poverty. . . .
> Baby, son, tell yourself
> You are without land, without love,
> Without country, without people,
> While *Poland*—your *Mother* is in her grave.
> For only your *Mother* is dead—and yet
> She is your faith, your palm of martyrdom. . . .
> This thought will make your courage grow,
> Give Her and yourself immortality.

Andrzej Busza explains that Apollo's commitment to Polish patriotism, and scorn for those who rejected it, was absolute: "Conrad had

been brought up in an intensely patriotic atmosphere; amongst people who constantly thought in such categories as the national cause, duty to one's country, sacrifice for the nation; and, on the other hand, such [reprehensible] notions as the lack of patriotism, the neglect of patriotic duties, and, above all, *betrayal.*" There were four possible attitudes toward Russian rule in Poland: loyalism, conciliation, resistance and emigration. Uncle Tadeusz chose the second, Apollo the third and Conrad the fourth. Conrad's refusal to follow his father's exhortation and example, and his voluntary exile from Poland in 1874, were a source of lifelong guilt.

Conrad moved almost as frequently during his Polish childhood as he did during his years at sea, and he formed no close friendships in Poland. He lived in Berdichev, Zhitomir, Warsaw, Vologda, Chernikhov, Novofastov, Kiev, Lvov, Cracow and Krynica, and took holidays abroad in Odessa, Switzerland, Austria, Germany and Italy. At the beginning of 1859 the family moved thirty miles north to Zhitomir, where Apollo wrote, translated and worked in a short-lived publishing company. Conrad's first childhood recollection was of a scene that occurred early in 1861, just before the family's happiness was shattered forever. It concerned his mother and music; and was associated with a precious experience, a dramatic entrance and a benison of maternal love that focused exclusively on himself: "my earliest memory is of my mother at the piano; of being let into a room which to this day seems to me the very largest room which I was ever in, of the music suddenly stopping, and my mother, with her hands on the keyboard, turning her head to look at me."[2]

Apollo belonged to the revolutionary generation of Mazzini, Garibaldi, Herzen and Kossuth. But as the failed plotter of a failed insurrection, living amidst violence and catastrophe, he had to survive on his memories and his dreams. Roman Dmowski, a late-nineteenth-century right-wing nationalist, condemned the self-destructive legacy of Polish Romanticism, exemplified by Apollo, which built "political prospects on purely illusory grounds . . . [and embarked] on political activity with no specific aim in view and with no prior estimation of the means at disposal." Nevertheless, if the choice were between passive acceptance and reckless action, Apollo would certainly choose to act.

A. P. Coleman states that after the death of Czar Nicholas I in 1855, Apollo became the prime mover behind a secret society called The Trinity, which opposed conciliation and urged active resistance to Russian oppression: "At first its objective was purely spiritual: to nourish resistance to the idea then insinuating itself into the class from which most

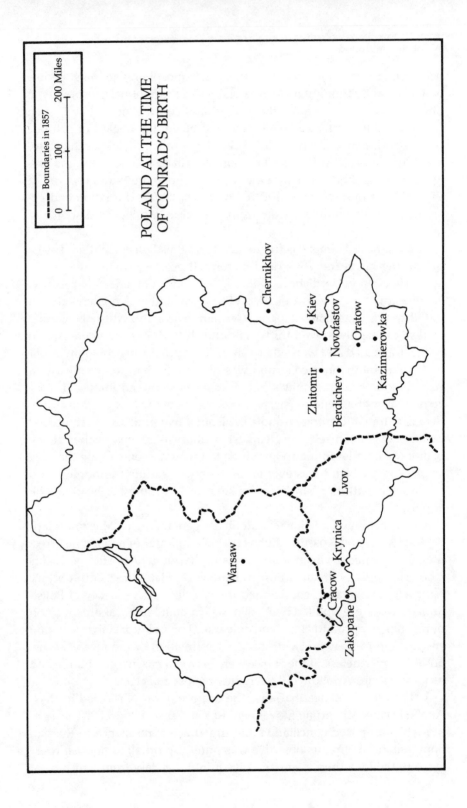

POLAND AT THE TIME
OF CONRAD'S BIRTH

Boundaries in 1857

0   100   200 Miles

of the [university] students came, that national emancipation could be achieved through political cooperation with Russia or with the Tsar. Its purpose was thus to keep alive the flame of Polish nationality and the conviction that, though the Powers considered Poland as dead, enough energy to save the nation still survived."[3]

In Warsaw, in the autumn of 1861, Apollo helped found a newspaper and the clandestine Committee of Action of the Red organization, which had developed from several conspiratorial groups. His extreme views were not generally accepted and he narrowly escaped death at the hands of a terrorist group, the Stilettists. Conrad later objected to a critic (probably the left-wing Edward Garnett) calling him "the son of a Revolutionist" and unconvincingly insisted that "No epithet could be more inapplicable to a man with such a strong sense of responsibility in the region of ideas and action." But Apollo, one of the most radical Red conspirators, clearly advocated violent revolt and national insurrection.

When the elections to the town and rural councils began in Warsaw on September 23, 1861, Apollo urged the electorate not to cast their votes. His leaflet "The Mandate of the People" "insisted that the electoral law was an attack on Polish national unity, both in the sense that the franchise was too narrow and that Lithuania and Russian Ruthenia [the Ukraine] were denied constitutional freedoms." Despite his extremely precarious position, Apollo was reckless about his own safety, and deliberately provoked the authorities by his outlandish dress and his public pronouncements: " 'An honourable but too ardent patriot, [he] went about Warsaw dressed in peasant fashion, in a peasant smock, frightful cap and knee-boots, attracting universal attention and exerting quite an influence on the youths gathered around him, by his intelligence, education, talent as a writer, and by his eloquence.' "[4]

II

Apollo paid dearly for his rash courage. Shortly after midnight on October 20, 1861, while he was writing and Eva reading in their flat on Nowy Swiat, a main street in the center of Warsaw, the doorbell suddenly rang. Apollo was arrested by the Russian police and was taken away in a matter of minutes. He spent seven months locked up in the Warsaw Citadel, suffering from rheumatism and scurvy, and waiting for the charges to be drawn up against him.

Under the "wide-browed, silent, protecting presence" of his mother, who was dressed in the black of national mourning in defiance of ferocious police regulations, the three-year-old Conrad remembered standing in the large prison courtyard and looking at his father's face staring at them through a barred window. Though Apollo's conspiratorial comrades offered to help him escape, he refused to consider this—ostensibly because he did not want them to risk their lives for his sake, but also because he wanted and welcomed this martyrdom for Poland.

Heightening the drama of his trial, Apollo later wrote that the Russian authorities were well aware that he "was not only a participant in but [also] the principal leader of the entire rebellious movement and the demonstrations designed to overthrow the government of our most gracious tzar." In fact, he was merely suspected of complicity in plotting the rebellion. If anything had been proved against him, he would either have been shot or sentenced to Siberia, where death would have been almost certain.

Since Apollo pleaded not guilty and no witnesses could be found to testify against him, the Russians, suspecting he was guilty, accused him of less serious charges: 1. that he had formed a committee which opposed elections to the Warsaw City Council, 2. that he had been the chief instigator of brawls in a confectionery shop, 3. that he had advocated an illegal union between Lithuania and Poland (a union had existed from 1569 to 1795), 4. that he had organized communal prayers for political martyrs. The court stated that "indirect evidence of his activities and of his alien way of thinking was found in the letters from his wife," foolishly written before she had joined him in Warsaw, which warned "him against returning to [Zhitomir] where he may be arrested."

Though Zdzislaw Najder speaks of Eva's "unshakable decision to participate in all his activities,"[5] she was actually forced into exile. Her letters had incriminated Apollo, and on May 9, 1862, she was convicted with him. Both were sentenced to indefinite exile in (as Apollo requested) the town of Perm. Sixteen years after leaving St. Petersburg, he was forced to return to the country where he had received his university education. His place of exile was changed, however, at the insistence of the Governor of Perm, who had once been a friend of Apollo in St. Petersburg. After traveling east for several weeks, the family was diverted to the more severe Vologda, 250 miles northeast of Moscow. Like many Polish patriots who remained faithful to their political principles and moral convictions, Apollo and Eva were thrown into the wilderness of penury and prison.

Conrad's friend and collaborator Ford Madox Ford later recorded an incident that took place in May 1862: "The oldest—the first—memory of his life was of being in a prison yard on the road to the Russian exile station of the Wologda. 'The Kossacks of the escort,' these are Conrad's exact words, repeated over and over again, 'were riding slowly up and down under the snowflakes that fell on women in furs and women in rags. The Russians had put the men into barracks the windows of which were tallowed. They fed them on red herrings and gave them no water to drink. My father was among them.' "

The family soon had to suffer far worse than cold and thirst, for both Conrad and Eva became seriously sick en route. When Conrad fell ill with pneumonia, near Moscow, the guards refused permission to break the journey. While the protesting parents refused to move, a sympathetic traveler sent a doctor from the city, who arrived in time to save the child. Apollo related that after the doctor had applied leeches and calomel (a purgative) and Conrad began to feel better, the guards started to harness the horses: "Naturally I protest against leaving, particularly as the doctor says openly that the child may die if we do so. My passive resistance postpones the departure but causes my guard to refer to the local authorities. The civilised oracle, after hearing the report, pronounces that we have to go at once—as children are born to die."

They were still traveling east toward Perm when Eva became ill at Nizhni Novgorod. The family asked permission to stay there until she recovered; though the request was refused, they gained a few days before turning north to Vologda. After a five-week journey, they arrived on June 16. In *Under Western Eyes,* Conrad described the vast, formless Russian landscape in which he had traveled and lived: "Under the sumptuous immensity of the sky, the snow covered the endless forests, the frozen rivers, the plains of an immense country, obliterating the landmarks, the accidents of the ground, levelling everything under its uniform whiteness, like a monstrous blank page awaiting the record of an inconceivable history."[6]

Though it is not clear why the Korzeniowskis took Conrad into exile instead of leaving him comfortably in Poland with his grandmother or his uncle, Eva probably could not bear to part from her frail only child and Apollo may have wanted him to experience the suffering that would turn him into a Polish patriot. Whatever their reasons, Conrad certainly shared their anxiety, grief, poverty, hardship and sickness. The governor of Vologda, Stanislaw Chominski, was a kindly man, able to fulfill the duties of his office and yet maintain a humanitarian attitude toward the twenty-one Poles, mostly priests, under his authority. Though his treatment of the prisoners was quite tolerable, the severe climate took its toll.

The penal town, east of St. Petersburg and north of Moscow, on the

Moscow–Siberia road, was spread out on both sides of the Vologda River. It had been founded in the twelfth century, when a monastery and a wooden church were constructed; a cathedral and Roman Catholic chapel were built later on. First defended by a wooden palisade and then by a stone fort, Vologda had traded furs and timber with England and Holland during the sixteenth century. Its large market-place sold hides, tobacco, eggs, grain and salt fish, and its factories made candles and furs. In 1861 the population was 16,500, including a number of Polish exiles from the revolutions of 1830 and 1846, who had been allowed to return home after the accession of Alexander II in 1855, but had married, become acclimatized and remained in northern Russia.

Apollo provided a personal and bitter description of the harsh and hostile physical conditions in a long letter of June 27, 1862:

> What is Vologda? A Christian is not required to know. Vologda is a huge quagmire stretching over three versts [two miles], cut up with parallel and intersecting lines of wooden foot-bridges, all rotten and shaky under one's feet: this is the only means of communication for the local people. . . . A year here has two seasons: white winter and green winter. The white winter lasts nine and a half months, the green winter two and a half. Now is the beginning of the green winter: it has been raining continually for twenty-one days and it will do so till the end.
>
> During the white winter the temperature falls to minus twenty-five or thirty degrees and the wind blows from the White Sea. . . .
>
> The air stinks of mud, birch tar and whale-oil: this is what we breathe. . . . All one does is pray with confidence and blind faith, although common sense says that prayers from here can never reach heaven and that God always looks another way, or else the view of the world would become too repugnant for Him. . . .
>
> Is it not better to die here? As a memory, exile and death will provide a better and more substantial evidence of service to the cause of truth and of one's beloved country than the return of someone driven to desperation by homesickness, rotten, and carrying that rottenness back home. . . . We do not regard exile as a punishment but as a new way of serving our country. There can be no punishment for us, since we are innocent.[7]

In October, after white winter had arrived, Apollo described the savage iciness and the difficulty of heating the crude, low-pitched log house: "We are bitterly cold here. For the last couple of days we have had plenty of snow. Firewood is as expensive as in Warsaw, and the number of stoves equals that of the windows, so we must heat furiously; but even when the stoves are red-hot, after several days of frost a white moss appears in the corners of the warmest of dwellings." The historian Edward Crankshaw, who visited Vologda in recent times, confirms the crude conditions and the insalubrious climate: "It was, and still largely is, a wooden town with streets and sidewalks of logs built on a swamp in the back of beyond, a station on the railway running east from St. Petersburg, or Leningrad, to the Urals. The people of the surrounding district are very poor indeed, and the summer climate is wretched and unhealthy into the bargain."[8]

The Korzeniowskis were supported in Vologda by remittances from Eva's brother Kazimierz. And Apollo's hot-house religious patriotism was the main consolation for shattered hopes in that remote penal settlement. His nationalistic sentiments led to one of Conrad's earliest pieces of writing (probably dictated by Apollo, who may also have guided his hand) on the back of a photograph taken in Vologda: "To my dear grandmother who helped me to send cakes to my poor father in prison—Pole, Catholic, gentleman. July 6th, 1863. Konrad." In *The Arrow of Gold,* Captain Blunt, a South Carolina supporter of the Confederacy, repeats this autobiographical description when he claims, *"Je suis Américain, catholique et gentilhomme."* Though Apollo was deadly serious in engendering these noble sentiments in his son, Conrad later classified them among the "absurd illusions common to all exiles," and deflated his father's ideals by declaring: "A class that has been under the ban for years lives on its passions and on prejudices whose growth stifles not only its sagacity but its visions of reality."[9]

III

Apollo could bear his martyrdom, an essential part of the Polish patriotic tradition, as long as he felt that his sacrifice had not been entirely in vain and that there was still some hope for the rebellion he had planned but failed to carry out. All the political disappointments that had tormented Poles for the last hundred years—the decline of the nation in the late eighteenth century, the three partitions, the false expectations raised by Napoleon's invasion of Russia in 1812, the reinstatement of Russian rule after the Congress of Vienna in 1815, the failures of the revolutions of 1830 and 1846, the defeat of Polish hopes after the European risings in 1848 and the Crimean War in 1856—could (Apollo felt) have finally been remedied by the rebellion that broke out in January 1863, while he was suffering arctic temperatures of thirty degrees below zero.

But—like the insurrections of 1794, 1830 and 1846—the revolt of 1863, which Coleman calls "the most heroic, if ill-advised, armed uprising in all Poland's history," was doomed to failure when it challenged the overwhelming might of absolutist Russia. According to a legend that began in the eighteenth century, most Polish men dreamed of dying in a hail of rifle fire while leading a cavalry charge in a hopeless attack on foreign invaders. Balzac, who was well acquainted with the Poles, confirmed their self-destructive courage when he wrote in *Cousin Bette* (1846): "Show a precipice to a Pole and he'll make the leap. As a nation they are like cavalrymen; they think they can overcome all obstacles and emerge victorious." (This daring tradition continued until September 1939, when Polish cavalry charged Nazi tanks during the *Blitzkrieg*.) Conrad, writing to his Russophile friend Edward Garnett and attempting, as always, to distinguish Poles from other Slavs, contrasted Poland's "delirium of the brave" with Britain's confident expectation of victory: "you seem to forget that I am a Pole. You forget that we have been used to go to battle without illusions. It's you Britishers that 'go in to win' only. We have been 'going in' these last hundred years repeatedly, to be knocked on the head only."[10]

The 1863 rising, which began on January 22, was defeated by internal dissension as well as by external repression, for there were two violently antithetical political parties in Warsaw: the Whites and the Reds. Both were opposed to conciliation with the Czarist government and wanted to re-establish the pre-partition boundaries of Poland. But while the Whites, protecting their material interests, tried to undermine revolutionary feeling and postpone the revolt to the indefinite future, the Reds—Apollo's party—advocated land reform, the abolition of serfdom and immediate revolutionary action. The Whites were supported by the gentry and the prosperous middle class; the Reds by students, intellectuals, clergymen, workers and the lower middle class. In *The Rainbow* (1915), D. H. Lawrence describes the political background of Lydia Lensky and her husband, who fled to England after the defeat in 1864: "They represented in Poland the new movement just begun in Russia. But they were very patriotic: and, at the same time, very 'European.' . . . Then came the great rebellion. Lensky, very ardent and full of words, went about inciting his countrymen. Little Poles flamed down the streets of Warsaw, on the way to shoot every Muscovite."

Vladimir Nabokov's grandfather Dimitri—aide-de-camp to the Czar's brother Constantine, who had been appointed viceroy of Poland in 1862—helped to suppress the rebellion that was incited by Conrad's father. Davies explains the immediate cause and eventual extent of the rising:

[The Russian viceroy could] smell a rebellion, but was unable to trace its source. He decided to force it into the open. His chosen instrument was the *Branka*, or "forced conscription." After saturating the Kingdom with 100,000 troops, he prepared to draft 30,000 young men into military service. . . . The *Branka* was timed for 14 January 1863. It was the immediate cause of open hostilities. . . .

[The Poles] did have a fully fledged political programme, an extensive financial organization which was already raising funds, and the cadres of an underground state. . . . He was faced from the start by a guerrilla war, which was master-minded by unseen hands from within his own capital, and which kept Europe's largest army at bay for sixteen months. . . .

Of the two hundred thousand Poles who were estimated to have carried arms during the Rising, there were never more than thirty thousand in the field at any one time. Most of them were scattered among hundreds of partisan bands operating in all the woods and wildernesses of the land. In the sixteen months that the Rising lasted, 1,229 engagements were fought—959 in the Kingdom, 237 in Lithuania, the rest in Byelorussia and the Ukraine.

In 1863 Ivan Turgenev, the only Russian writer Conrad admired, told a friend: "It is impossible not to wish for the speediest suppression of this senseless rebellion."[11] The Poles' hopes for foreign intervention were disappointed; Warsaw was paralyzed by dissension; and the partisan groups in the countryside dissolved and were eventually destroyed. The repression was severe, and all the leaders were captured and hanged. The uprising had been a costly failure that had destroyed the finest elements in the nation and provoked even greater repression.

In 1864 a policy of Russification was adopted: "the tsar and the bureaucracy took the decision to administer the Polish areas as occupied territory in which the inhabitants of Polish speech were to enjoy a minimum of civil rights." The rising left permanent scars in Poland, where a whole generation were deprived of their careers and their future. After 1864 there was no longer any hope for a successful revolution, and "the Franco-Prussian War and the Eastern crisis in the seventies finally removed the Polish question from the agenda of European diplomacy."[12]

The Korzeniowskis' immediate family suffered terribly from the defeat. Apollo's father died on the way to join the Partisans. His older brother, Robert, was killed during the insurrection. His younger brother, Hilary, a hunchback, was arrested just before the rising and died in Siberian exile in 1878. And the remnant of the Korzeniowski fortune was confiscated by the Russian government. His maternal uncle Tadeusz, fond of contrasting the cautious conservatism of the Bobrowskis with the reckless defiance of the Korzeniowskis, was opposed to the rising. He naïvely believed that Poles should place all their hopes in the "noble impulses" of Alexander II, thought there was absolutely no hope of defeating the Russians and wrote: "Without exaggeration it may be stated that the events of 1861–63 were begun in falsehood and that they ended in falsehood."

Yet his younger brothers Kazimierz and Stefan were as radical and as violent as Apollo. Kazimierz was imprisoned during the rising and Stefan, the underground commander in Warsaw, directed the revolutionary government and kept the struggle going. Najder asserts that Stefan "was killed on 12 April [1863] in a duel provoked by his right-wing opponents," but it was actually Stefan himself who provoked the duel. He called Count Grabowski (a leader of the Whites) a reactionary who had plotted against the revolution and wanted it to fail. Grabowski, cleared of the charge of treachery in a court of honor, asked Stefan to withdraw the accusation. When Stefan refused to do so and repeated the charge, the two men quarreled, a duel became inevitable and Stefan was mortally wounded.[13]

Apollo's response to the rising was a rambling and repetitive, passionate and prescient political essay, "Poland and Muscovy," which was smuggled out of Russia and published in an *émigré* journal in Leipzig in 1864. Its aim was to warn the European powers of the Russian threat to civilization. Apollo begins with a vitriolic account of his imprisonment and trial; he condemns Russia as the "terrible, depraved, destructive" embodiment of barbarism and chaos, as "the plague of humanity" and "negation of human progress"; he describes Russia's horrible oppression of Poland during the last century; and he concludes with the idea— repeated in Conrad's "Autocracy and War"—that the historical mission of humane, Catholic, democratic Poland is to protect their natural allies in western Europe from the destructive hordes of Moscow:

> The whole of Moscow is a prison. Beginning with the Ryryks [ninth-century founders of the Russian monarchy], and then with the Tartar thraldom, the oppression of Ivan, under the knouts of various tzars and empresses and so forth, Muscovy has been, is and always shall be a prison—otherwise it would cease to be itself. In that prison committed crimes and flourishing deceit copulate obscenely. The law and official religion sanctify these unions. Their offspring: the falseness and infamy of all religions, of all social, political, national and personal relations. . . .
>
> Ninety years ago the European governments and nations looked on

impassively as swarms of locusts descended on the most fertile fields, as the miasma of the most sordid and lethal plague spread, as seas of foul muck poured over the fruits of the earth, as barbarism, ignorance, renegation swallowed up civilization, light, faith in God and in the future of mankind; in short, it all happened when Muscovy seized Poland.

Apollo's frightening conception of Russia, "unrestrained, organized and ready to spew out millions of her criminals over Europe," was developed by Conrad in *The Secret Agent* and *Under Western Eyes*. And the idea of the barbaric "Tartar whip and tzarist knout" recurs in *The Magic Mountain* by Thomas Mann (a great admirer of Conrad) when the liberal Settembrini, alluding to the notorious prison in St. Petersburg, warns Hans Castorp: "Asia surrounds us. . . . Genghis Khan. Wolves of the steppes, snow, vodka, the knout, Schlüsselburg, Holy Russia. They ought to set up an altar to Pallas Athene, here in the vestibule—to ward off the evil spell."[14]

IV

In January 1863, the year of the fatal rising, Apollo was granted permission, on grounds of poor health, to move farther south to a less extreme climate. The family resettled in Chernikhov, eighty miles north of Kiev, where they remained for the next five years. In an atmosphere extremely hostile to Poles, Apollo continued to work on his translations. Despite the improved conditions, his wife's health began to deteriorate. In the summer of that year Eva's brother, who had served in the Russian Guards, used his influence to arrange a three-month "leave of absence" so that she and Conrad could get medical treatment and visit the family estate at Novofastov, between Berdichev and Kiev.

That summer—when Conrad played with his young cousins, first rode a pony and met his great-uncle Nicholas Bobrowski (who had fought with Napoleon and became the hero of Conrad's story "The Warrior's Soul")—seemed the happiest time in his life. Yet in *A Personal Record*, he recalled his mother's illness and connected it to the oppressive political conditions:

I did not understand the tragic significance of it all at the time, though indeed I remember that doctors also came. There were no signs of invalidism about her—but I think that already they had pronounced her doom unless perhaps the change to a southern climate could re-establish her declining strength. . . . Over all this hung the oppressive shadow of the great Russian Empire—the shadow lowering with the darkness of a new-born national hatred fostered by the Moscow school of journalists against the Poles after the ill-omened rising of 1863.

When the leave expired and Eva was too ill to return to exile, the provincial governor threatened to send her under escort to the prison hospital at Kiev. As they rode off in an open trap, harnessed with three horses, the tearful French governess who had taught him to read and speak his first foreign language, cried out: *"N'oublie pas ton français, mon chéri."*

In late February 1865, Apollo described his wife's terminal illness, which he ascribed to psychological suffering and to lack of proper medical treatment, and mentioned the disastrous effect this had on little Conrad:

> My poor wife, who these last two years has been destroyed by despair and by the repeated blows that fall on members of our joined families, for the last four months terribly—gravely ill, has barely the strength to look at me, to speak with a hollow voice. This state has been caused by the lack of everything for the body and the soul—no doctors, no medicines. Today she is allowed to go for treatment to Kiev but her lack of strength makes it impossible. . . . I am unable to satisfy, help or console my poor patient. Konradek is of course neglected.

Ten days later, when the crisis deepened, Apollo was more specific about her hemorrhages and mentioned "a sudden consuming fever, a lung condition and an inner tumour, caused by an irregular blood flow, requiring removal. . . . [The doctor] sees the operation as imperative but cannot perform it owing to her lack of strength. . . . The lung disease becomes more menacing. . . . There is a threat of death from every side."[15] On April 18, 1865, Eva died of tuberculosis in Chernikhov at the age of thirty-two. The seven-year-old Conrad, who witnessed her agonizing decline, was devastated by the loss. Apollo was also tormented by the guilty feeling that his arrest and exile had been largely responsible for Eva's death.

The death of his mother, the second great turning-point (after exile) in Conrad's childhood, weakened his own frail health and threw him into morbid conjunction with his father. As a boy, Conrad was pale, delicate, unstable and epileptic; as an adult, hypersensitive, intensely nervous and frequently ill. He had inflammation of the lungs in May 1862, en route to Vologda, and again in 1863. Three years later, he had a series of epileptic attacks. In June 1868 he suffered from what Apollo called a new onset of his old illness: urinary deposits in his bladder that caused constant stomach cramps. And in his early teens he had severe migraine headaches and nervous attacks.

Apollo gives a terribly depressing account of his solitary existence with Conrad. After the failure of the revolution and the death of his wife, his courage gave way to despair. He devoted himself to his son, but was not an effective teacher; he tried to protect Conrad from the pernicious Russian influence, but realized he was stifling the child by cutting him off from normal life; he tried to keep the memory of Eva alive, but was tormented by grief and guilt, which no penance, however harsh, could absolve:

> Poor child: he does not know what a contemporary playmate is; he looks at the decrepitude of my sadness and who knows if that sight does not make his young heart wrinkled or his awakening soul grizzled. These are important reasons for forcing me to tear the poor child away from my dejected heart. . . .
>
> Since last autumn my health has been declining badly and my dear little mite takes care of me. . . .
>
> My life is, at present, confined solely to Konradek. I teach him all I know myself—alas, it is not much; I guard him against the influence of the local atmosphere and the little mite is growing up as though in a cloister; the grave of our Unforgettable is our *memento mori* and so every letter . . . brings us fastings, hair-shirts and flogging.

Apollo taught his son at home, partly because he did not want the delicate child to be educated in Russian schools. But Apollo was too demanding and Conrad, living in almost complete isolation, burrowed "too deeply" into books. Though Apollo frequently asked friends to send him school materials, he mentioned in 1868 that Conrad's poor health, especially his epilepsy, had prevented him from studying during the past two years.

For a year and a half, from May 1866 until the autumn of 1867, Conrad was "torn" from Apollo while receiving medical treatment in Kiev, Zhitomir and Novofastov. In November 1866, Apollo wrote, with an element of self-pity: "I am lonely. Konradek is with his granny. . . . We both suffer equally: just imagine, the boy is so stupid that he misses his loneliness where all he saw was my clouded face and where the only diversions of his nine-year-old life were arduous lessons. . . . The boy pines away—he must be stupid, and, I fear, will remain so all his life!"[16]

Apollo was a poor estate administrator, a mediocre poet and a disastrous revolutionary—in short: a failure. These failures intensified his sacrificial patriotism, deepened his despairing mysticism and led to a morbid cult of his dead wife, all of which made life unbearably dreary for young Conrad. Apollo's religion—his only hope in life, apart from his son—"was based on a kind of Christian stoicism rather than on reasoned belief. 'Everything that surrounds me,' " he wrote from Chernikhov, " 'bids me doubt the existence of a divine omnipotence, in which I nonetheless place all my faith and to which I entrust the fate of my little one.' "

It is scarcely surprising that Conrad, from the age of thirteen (two years after Apollo's death) rejected the doctrines, ceremonies and festivals of his father's despairing religion. Later, he equated these beliefs and observances with Russians, especially with his *bête noire* Dostoyevsky, and dismissed them as "primitive natures fashioned by a Byzantine theological conception of life, with an inclination to perverted mysticism." Writing to the atheistic Garnett in 1914, and thinking of his deluded and long-suffering parents, Conrad condemned Christianity as "distasteful to me":

> I am not blind to its services but the absurd oriental fable from which it starts irritates me. Great, improving, softening, compassionate it may be but it has lent itself with amazing facility to cruel distortion and is the only religion which, with impossible standards, has brought an infinity of anguish to innumerable souls.[17]

In January 1868 Prince Gollitzen, the Governor of Chernikhov, declared that the dying Apollo, after five and a half years in Russia, was no longer dangerous, and released him from exile. Apollo received permission to travel to Algiers and Madeira, but—living frugally on Eva's inheritance, his modest literary earnings and handouts from the family—had neither the funds nor the energy to do so.

Austrian Poland, which recognized Polish nationality and allowed Poles civil rights if not political independence, was much freer than the parts of the country under German and Russian rule. In the Ukraine, for example, the school system had become thoroughly Russified after 1864; Polish, even in private conversation, was forbidden in school buildings. For these reasons, father and son moved west to Galicia, lived in Lvov, the provincial capital, for six weeks during January–February 1868, and then in the old royal and academic city of Cracow. In 1868 Apollo wrote that Conrad was having German lessons so that he could go to school. He passed the entrance examination for St. Anne's Gymnasium, but probably attended St. Jacek's school.

By the time they reached Cracow, Apollo was a desperately ill and mortally weary man—vanquished by disillusion, bereavement and gloom. Embittered by Galician indifference to the cause of Polish freedom, he told a friend: "I am broken, fit for nothing, too tired even to spit upon things." In "Poland Revisited" (1915), Conrad—who had witnessed his mother's slow death and now suffered the same experience with his father—gives a moving account of Apollo's final weeks.

The last time Apollo was seen out of bed, propped up with pillows in a deep armchair and attended by nursing nuns in white coifs, he supervised the burning of some of his manuscripts. The atmosphere around his deathbed was an uneasy mixture of pity, resignation and silence:

> My prep finished I would have had nothing to do but sit and watch the awful stillness of the sick room flow out through the closed door and coldly enclose my scared heart. . . .
>
> Later in the evening, but not always, I would be permitted to tip-toe into the sick room to say good-night to the figure prone on the bed, which often could not acknowledge my presence but by a slow movement of the eyes, put my lips dutifully to the nerveless hand lying on the coverlet, and tip-toe out again.

On May 23, 1869, Apollo, like Eva, died of tuberculosis. His funeral turned into a patriotic demonstration by several thousand people. Conrad, emotionally exhausted and no longer able to cry, led "the long procession [that] moved out of the narrow street, down a long street, past the Gothic front of St. Mary's under its unequal towers, towards the Florian Gate." The words cut into Apollo's gravestone were: "Victim of Muscovite Tyranny."

Thirty years later, Conrad gave Garnett an idealized yet essentially negative portrait of his father:

> A man of great sensibilities; of exalted and dreamy temperament; with a terrible gift of irony and of gloomy disposition; withal of strong religious feeling degenerating after the loss of his wife into mysticism touched with despair. His aspect was distinguished; his conversation very fascinating; his face in repose sombre, lighted all over when he [rarely] smiled. I remember him well. For the last two years of his life I lived alone with him.

Apollo was also the model for Heyst's father in *Victory*, a kind of third-rate Schopenhauer whose books were ignored by the world and whose only disciple was his unfortunate son.

Søren Kierkegaard's perceptive analysis of his own father's destructive love illuminates Conrad's final relation to Apollo as well as his portrayal of Apollo in *Victory*:

> Once upon a time there lived a father and a son. Both were very gifted, both witty, particularly the father. . . . On one rare occasion, when the father looking upon his son saw he was deeply troubled, he stood before him and said: poor child, you go about in silent despair. (But he never questioned him more closely, alas he could not, for he himself was in silent despair.) Otherwise, they never exchanged a word on the subject. Both father and son were, perhaps, two of the most melancholy men in the memory of man.
>
> And the father believed that he was the cause of the son's melancholy, and the son believed that he was the cause of the father's melancholy, and so they never discussed it. . . . And what is the meaning of this? The point precisely is that he made me unhappy—but out of love. His error did not consist in lack of love but in mistaking a child for an old man.

The pervasive gloom of the Kierkegaards and the Korzeniowskis was characterized by a melancholy atmosphere, mutual unhappiness, lack of understanding, poignant silence and bitter despair. "Conrad's father must have seemed to him at once awe-inspiring and absurd; his attitude towards him was a mixture of admiration and contemptuous pity. And he could never forgive his father the death of his mother."[18] Apollo's legacy to Conrad was a volatile temperament, an anguished patriotism, the bitterness of shattered hopes, the trauma of defeat and a deep-rooted pessimism.

V

After Apollo's death, Conrad became the ward of his uncle Tadeusz Bobrowski, who grew wheat and sugar beet on an estate at Kazi-mierowka, about thirty miles southeast of Zhitomir. Tadeusz was short and balding, with sharp Roman features and a bushy beard. A fussy, pedantic but essentially kind-hearted man, he was the temperamental antithesis of Apollo, and had the mind and cautious character of an accountant. He had married in 1857 and ten months later, when his wife died in childbirth, was left a widower and the father of a frail little girl. She had been treated in various spas and had died, at the age of thir-teen, in 1871. Tadeusz, who had a completely different set of values, replaced Apollo and became Conrad's surrogate father. He transferred all his affection to the orphaned child of his beloved sister, and looked after his education, moral progress and material welfare. At the end of a long financial account in 1876, Tadeusz wrote: "the upbringing of Master Conrad to manly status has cost (apart from the capital sum of 3,600 roubles given him) 17,454 roubles"—about $25,000. After Tadeusz's death, Conrad called him a distinguished man of powerful intelligence and great force of character, who had cared for several wards and had had an enormous influence among conservative landowners in the Ukraine.

Conrad remained in Cracow: during the first year in a pension for boys run by Ludwik Georgeon, a veteran of the 1863 rising, on Florianska Street; and during the next three years at his grandmother's flat on Szpitalna Street. During this time he was frequently in poor health, attended school irregularly and was tutored by a medical student at Jagiellonian University in Cracow, Adam Pulman. Conrad and his tutor spent the summers of 1870–72 at Krynica, in the Carpathian mountains, southeast of Cracow; and during the spring and summer of 1873 they traveled in Switzerland, Bavaria, Austria and northern Italy. In a Swiss boarding-house, Conrad first heard English spoken by some British engineers who were helping to build the St. Gotthard Tunnel. Though Conrad claimed that he had never seen the sea until he arrived in Venice with Pulman, he had actually visited Odessa, on the Black Sea, with Uncle Tadeusz in the summer of 1867. But in his memoirs, he wanted this crucial experience to be associated with the Mediterranean rather than with Russia. In 1881 Tadeusz wrote Conrad that Pulman had tricked many people out of money and refused all demands for repayment. But after Pulman's death, five years later, at the age of forty, Conrad recorded that all "the bereaved poor of the district, Christians and Jews alike, had mobbed the good doctor's coffin with sobs and lamentations at the very gate of the cemetery."[19]

During the Cracow years, the solitary, hypersensitive and well-read young Conrad impressed friends by memorizing and reciting long passages from Mickiewicz's *Pan Tadeusz* and by writing patriotic plays, like *The Eyes of Jan Sobieski*, in which Polish nationalists defeated the Muscovite enemy. Pleased with himself and accustomed to the undivided attention of his parents, Conrad once disturbed an adult conversation with the egoistic question: " 'And what do you think of me?' To which the reply was: 'You're a young fool who interrupts when his elders are talking.' " Conrad's distant cousin in Lvov, with whose family he lived in 1873–74, later described his intelligence, ambitions, Apollo-like sarcasm, desire for freedom, informal manners and ill health:

He stayed with us ten months while in the seventh class in the Gymnasium. Intellectually he was extremely advanced but disliked school routine, which he found tiring and dull; he used to say that he was very
talented and planned to become a great writer. Such declarations coupled
with a sarcastic expression on his face and with frequent critical remarks,
shocked his teachers and provoked laughter among his classmates. He
disliked all restrictions. At home, at school, or in the living room he would
sprawl unceremoniously. He used to suffer from severe headaches and
nervous attacks; the doctors thought that a stay at the seaside might cure
him.[20]

Conrad left high school early in 1874 without finishing the course. An
indifferent scholar, he had studied some Greek, Latin and German,
Polish Romantic literature, mathematics, history and his favorite subject, geography. But he had also read widely on his own, especially
books on distant voyages and exotic exploration. Hugo's *Toilers of the
Sea*, and adventure novels by Captain Marryat and Fenimore Cooper
inspired him to become a sailor. Like Lord Jim, he was attracted to the
adventurous aspects of nautical life and lived "in his mind the sea-life of
light literature. He saw himself saving people from sinking ships, cutting away masts in a hurricane . . . always an example of devotion to
duty, and as unflinching as a hero in a book." Conrad may also have
been drawn to Cooper who, in his appeal "To the American People,"
had nobly supported the Polish cause after the revolution of 1831:

The crime of Poland was too much liberty. Her independent existence, in
the vicinity of those who had reared their thrones on the foundation of
arbitrary will was not to be endured. Fellow Citizens, neither the ancient
institutions nor the ancient practices of Poland have been understood. The
former had, in common with all Europe, the inherited defects of feudal
opinions, but still were they among the freest of this hemisphere.[21]

VI

Though Conrad's motives for leaving Poland were extremely complex,
he had good political and personal reasons for going into voluntary
exile. He believed the 1863 rebellion had been a pointless and unquali-
fied disaster. When he left Russian Poland in 1874, his country had
suffered more than one hundred years of servitude and had absolutely
no prospects for independence. Like Apollo, Conrad found the enor-

mous Russian garrison, the despotism of petty officials and the extreme hostility to all things Polish oppressive and intolerable.

Conrad's sense of humiliation, his bitterness and anger, could never be extinguished. Speaking of Poland later in life, he told friends: "[I] spring from an oppressed race where oppression was not a matter of history but a crushing fact in the daily life of all individuals, made still more bitter by declared hatred and contempt. . . . I can't think of Poland often. It feels bad, bitter, painful. It would make life unbearable. . . . [The Russian] mentality and their emotionalism have always been repugnant to me, hereditarily and individually."[22] Conrad felt his family had suffered sufficiently; he wanted to escape from what he rightly considered a hopeless political situation. He loved Poland as a memory of the past, but her present frightened him and her future looked like a dark abyss. It is essential to emphasize and to remember the most crucial facts of Conrad's early life: the Russians had enslaved his country, forbidden his language, confiscated his inheritance, treated him as a convict, killed his parents and forced him into exile.

His motives for going to sea were both practical and romantic. A family physician, fearing that Conrad might die of the same tuberculosis that had stricken his parents, believed he could be saved by living near the sea and getting plenty of physical exercise. He had been thrilled by the Black Sea at Odessa and by the Adriatic at Venice. Inspired by reading fictional sea adventures, he had as a child wanted to enter the marine cadet school at Pola, across from Venice, in Austrian Croatia. He found Austria the most liberal and least antipathetic of the three powers ruling Poland, had some sympathy for the Hapsburg dynasty and wished to serve in the Austrian navy. But when his application for Austrian citizenship was refused, he was unable to enter the school.

Conrad's destiny was also determined by another practical consideration. As the son of a political convict, he was liable, when he reached military age, for conscription into the ranks of the Russian army for twenty-five years. Conrad *had* to leave Poland. His question, like Razumov's in *Under Western Eyes*, was: "Where to?"

Ever since Adam Mickiewicz and Frédéric Chopin had left the country after the rising of 1831, France, the enemy of Russia and Austria, had become the traditional, congenial refuge of Polish exiles. Conrad spoke French, his family had some useful contacts in Marseilles and he could join the French merchant marine in that pleasant Mediterranean seaport. So he decided to reject Apollo's sacrificial legacy ("Be a *Pole!*") and to cut himself off from the tragic past of his landlocked country. On October 13, 1874, the sixteen-year-old Conrad became one of the three

and a half million emigrants—including his close contemporaries Ignacy Paderewski and Marie Sklodowska Curie, as well as Guillaume Apollinaire (né Kostrowitsky), Lewis Namier and Bronislaw Malinowski—who left Poland between 1870 and 1914. Like Jasper Allen, the handsome hero of "Freya of the Seven Isles," Conrad, "an old man's child, having lost his mother early, [was] thrown out to sea out of the way while very young, [and] had not much experience of tenderness of any kind."[23]

tive, dark-haired young girls. Living near or on the sea, and freed from the psychological stress of his family and his country, Conrad's health, as the doctors predicted, showed a remarkable improvement.

The numerous allusions in *A Personal Record* create a lively picture of Marseilles. Conrad mentions two islands in the gulf, which housed the Planier lighthouse and the Château d'If, where Dumas's Count of Monte Cristo was imprisoned; the Old Town adjacent to the rectangular basin of the Old Port, guarded on both sides of the entrance by Fort St. Jean and Fort St. Nicolas; the Joliette breakwater near the Gare Maritime and the omnibus that rattled down the Quai de la Joliette toward the angular mass of the Fort; the wide and fashionable avenue du Prado, which runs east from the Old Port; and the white-and-red-striped pile of the Basilica of Notre Dame de la Garde, perched on a hill overlooking the ancient town. In 1878 Conrad lived in a lodging house owned by a Madame Fagot at 18 rue Sainte, a gently sloping street, close to the opera house, that runs parallel to one side of the Old Port.

The friends Conrad made in Marseilles belonged to three distinct classes—Royalists, bohemians and seamen—and reflected the social, intellectual and professional aspects of his character: his noble birth, his artistic interests and his desire to be a sailor. The wealthy shipowners, the Delestangs, were in their late seventies when he first became acquainted with them: "Madame Delestang, an imperious, handsome lady in a statuesque style, would carry me off now and then on the front seat of her carriage to the Prado, at the hour of fashionable airing." Observing his profligate habits, she kindly advised him not to spoil his life. Her husband, a "frozen-up, mummified Royalist" who favored the restoration of the Bourbon monarchy, had a "thin bony nose, a perfectly bloodless, narrow physiognomy clamped together as it were by short formal sidewhiskers." The Royalist circle gathered at the Café Bodoul on the rue St.-Ferréol, which ran east from the principal thoroughfare, La Canebière.

The bohemian friends of "Young Ulysses" or "Monsieur Georges," as Conrad was known in Marseilles, included his closest friend, Richard Fecht, a sober and sensible German from Württemberg, who acted as banker and liaison between Conrad and Uncle Tadeusz; Clovis Hugues, a journalist, poet and politician; the sculptor Frétigny, who became Prax in Conrad's Marseilles novel, *The Arrow of Gold*; and Henry Grand, Conrad's occasional English teacher, who became the model for the Professor of Languages in *Under Western Eyes* and of Mills in *The Arrow of Gold*.

With these friends the impressionable teenage apprentice first saw the plays of Victorien Sardou and Eugène Scribe, and heard the spectacular operas of Rossini and Verdi, which he still remembered with obvious pleasure at the end of his life. He would also have been attracted by the singing of a compatriot: "Theatrical life in Marseilles was flourishing at that time, particularly the opera, housed in the splendid building of the Grand Théâtre; from this period . . . date Conrad's memories of listening to Meyerbeer's works and to his favourite opera, *Carmen*. During Korzeniowski's stay in Marseilles the principal tenor of the opera, Wladyslaw Mierzwinski, sang the part of Don José."[2] By 1893 Conrad had seen this opera fourteen times.

Conrad's first maritime contact was Wiktor Chodzko, a Pole serving in the French merchant marine. Chodzko introduced him to Baptistin Solary, a cousin of the Delestangs and a ship's chandler, well connected to everyone in the nautical trade, who good-naturedly promised to help the young man get his start on a decent ship: "This Solary (Baptistin), when I beheld him in the flesh, turned out quite a young man, very good-looking, with a fine black, short beard, a fresh complexion, and soft, merry black eyes." He burst into Conrad's hotel room, just after he arrived, flung open the shutters to the sun of Provence, and urged him "to be up and off instantly for a three years' campaign in the South Seas." Conrad's connections with the Spanish rebels involved all three levels of Marseilles society: the Royalist friends who supported the cause, the bohemians who formed a syndicate to smuggle arms into Spain and the sailors who manned the *Tremolino* on this mission.

Conrad adapted remarkably well to maritime life. He began as an observer on pilot boats that guided ships into the harbor and took his first ocean voyage less than two months after arriving. In his memoirs, Conrad idealized the trusty sailors who welcomed him and initiated him into the craft:

> The very first whole day I ever spent on salt water was by invitation, in a big half-decked pilot-boat, cruising under close reefs on the lookout, in misty, blowing weather, for the sails of ships and the smoke of steamers rising out there, beyond the slim and tall Planier lighthouse cutting the line of the wind-swept horizon with a white perpendicular stroke. They were hospitable souls, these sturdy Provençal seamen. Under the general designation of *le petit ami de Baptistin* I was made the guest of the Corporation of Pilots, and had the freedom of their boats night or day.

Conrad also recalled the first time he came alongside an English ship and was addressed in the language in which he was destined to work and to write. When he rowed up in a dinghy to board the *James Westoll*, a big, powerfully rigged cargo steamer, a fat fellow growled huskily above his head: "Look out there!" And when he came alongside the strange ship, it seemed almost alive: "I bore against the smooth flank of the first English ship I ever touched in my life, [and] felt it already throbbing under my open palm."[3] Those first three words had the same magical, talismanic effect on Conrad as did the sound of English spoken by the engineers who were building the St. Gotthard Tunnel in Switzerland.

After six weeks on the pilot boats, Conrad took the first of three voyages on French ships, owned by the Delestangs, from Marseilles to the Caribbean. On the first, five-month voyage, he traveled as a passenger on the *Mont-Blanc*, an old three-masted, four-hundred-ton barque, built in 1852. The ship left on December 11, 1874, stayed six weeks in St. Pierre, Martinique—on the west coast, north of the capital, Fort de France—and returned on May 23, 1875. In *The Mirror of the Sea* (1906), he described the storm they encountered on the westward passage to the Straits of Gibraltar and paraphrased Milton's definition of fame in "Lycidas" ("that last infirmity of noble mind") when portraying the abundant leaks:

> The very first Christmas night I ever spent away from land was employed in running before a Gulf of Lyons gale, which made the old ship groan in every timber as she skipped between it over the short seas until we brought her to, battered and out of breath, under the lee of Majorca, where the smooth water was torn by fierce cat's-paws under a very stormy sky.
>
> We—or rather, they, for I had hardly had two glimpses of salt water in my life till then—kept her standing off and on all that day, while I listened for the first time with the curiosity of my tender years to the song of the wind in a ship's rigging. . . . The wind was fair, but that day we ran no more.
>
> The thing (I will not call her a ship twice in the same half-hour) leaked. She leaked fully, generously, overflowingly, all over—like a basket. I took an enthusiastic part in the excitement caused by that last infirmity of noble ships, without concerning myself much with the why or the wherefore.

On the second, six-month voyage to Martinique, from June 25, 1875, to December 23, 1875, Conrad sailed on the *Mont-Blanc* as an apprentice seaman. They stayed in St. Pierre for eight weeks and returned, with a cargo of timber and sugar, via St. Thomas (in the Danish Virgin Islands) and Haiti. The winter voyage back was very stormy and the ship was badly damaged by the time it reached Le Havre. Conrad, without waiting for repairs, disembarked in that port, where he lost his trunk, and returned to Marseilles by train, stopping for a few days in Paris on the way.

On his third and most significant voyage, Conrad earned thirty-five francs a month as a steward. The *Saint-Antoine*, a slightly larger but much newer three-masted barque, under Captain Escarras, left Marseilles on July 8, 1876, and returned on February 15, 1877. On the return journey, the ship went from St. Pierre to Cartagena in Colombia, to Puerto Cabello and La Guayra in Venezuela, to St. Thomas and to Haiti. His brief glimpse of the coast of South America became the germ of the setting of *Nostromo*. "If I ever mention 12 hours it must relate to P. Cabello where I was ashore at that time," he later told his young friend Richard Curle. "In La Guayra as I went up the hill and had a distant view of Caracas I must have been $2\frac{1}{2}$ to 3 days. It's such a long time ago! And there was a few hours in a few other places on that dreary coast of Ven'la."

The first mate on the ship was the forty-two-year-old Corsican, Dominic Cervoni, who became the model for Nostromo as well as for Peyrol in *The Rover* and Attilio in *Suspense*. In *The Mirror of the Sea*, Conrad portrays Dominic as tough, virile, capable and courageous:

> There was nothing in the world sudden enough to take Dominic unawares. His thick black moustaches, curled every morning with hot tongs by the barber at the corner of the quay, seemed to hide a perpetual smile. But nobody, I believe, had ever seen the true shape of his lips. From the slow, imperturbable gravity of that broad-chested man you would think he had never smiled in his life. In his eyes lurked a look of perfectly remorseless irony, as though he had been provided with an extremely experienced soul; and the slightest distension of his nostrils would give to his bronzed face a look of extraordinary boldness. This was the only play of feature of which he seemed capable, being a Southerner of a concentrated, deliberate type. His ebony hair curled slightly on the temples. He may have been forty years old, and he was a great voyager on the inland [Mediterranean] sea.[4]

Conrad, storing his experiences and using them twenty and thirty years later in his novels, also saw during this voyage the originals of Heyst, Jones and Ricardo in *Victory*. The realistic basis that provided the imaginative germ for Heyst, the Swedish baron and rescuer of Lena, derived, Conrad said, from "my visual impressions of the man in 1876; a couple of hours in a hotel in St. Thomas (West Indies). There was some talk of him the night after he had left our party; but—all I heard of him might have been written down on a cigarette-paper. Except for these hints he's altogether 'invented.' " Conrad's "Author's Note" to *Victory* reveals that the merest glimpse of a squalid man (or even of a country) was sufficient to stimulate his imagination and lead to the creation of his ghastly and ferocious villains: "It was in a little hotel on the Island of St.

Thomas . . . where we found [Jones] one hot afternoon extended on three chairs, all alone in the loud buzzing of flies to which his immobility and his cadaverous aspect gave a most gruesome significance. . . . It so happened that the very same year Ricardo—the physical Ricardo—was a fellow passenger of mine on board an extremely small and extremely dirty little schooner, during a four days' passage between two places in the Gulf of Mexico."[5]

The *Saint-Antoine* turned out to be the last French ship on which Conrad sailed. Three years later, at the request of Uncle Tadeusz, the owner sent Conrad a letter of recommendation:

> We the undersigned C. Delestang & Son, late shipowners, certify that Conrad de Korzeniowski, native of Poland, entered our service in the month of February, 1874, as midshipman on board our vessel the *Mont-Blanc*, then served as lieutenant on board our ship the *Saint-Antoine* and left this last-named vessel after 3 years' constant service in the West Indies and South America trade, on the 14th February, 1877, and that during that time he gave perfect satisfaction to his superior officers by his sobriety, general conduct and strict application in the discharge of his duties. Marseilles, 26th April, 1880. C. Delestang & Sons.[6]

This recommendation, very likely based on information supplied by Conrad and used as evidence to qualify for his second mate's examination in the British merchant service, was, like some of his other maritime documents, extremely inaccurate and misleading. This letter added the aristocratic particle "de," to which Conrad was not entitled; it began his service in February 1874, while he was still in school in Cracow, ten months before he actually set foot on the *Mont-Blanc*; it listed his positions as midshipman and lieutenant when, in fact, he was a passenger, an apprentice seaman and a steward; it credited him with service in South America, though he had been on the coast of that continent for only three days; and it awarded him "3 years' constant service," when his three voyages had lasted only thirteen months, with about five months in Caribbean ports.

II

Tired of bad food and bad weather, and perhaps somewhat disillusioned with the long periods of boredom and the dull companions on the ship after three consecutive voyages, Conrad spent the next year on land in Marseilles. Tadeusz had once observed that Conrad always behaved well at sea, but that "staying on land has always had an inauspicious influence upon you." From February 1877 to February 1878 Conrad spent money extravagantly, smuggled guns into Spain, fell ill for the first time, lost even more money in speculation and gambling, and then, deeply depressed, committed a desperate act.

Conrad returned from his voyage on the *Saint-Antoine* to find two admonitory letters from Uncle Tadeusz. In the first letter of October 9, 1876, written while Conrad was still in the Caribbean, Tadeusz adopted his characteristically nagging, preaching tone. In a series of rhetorical questions and answers, he treated his favorite nephew as if he were a small child: "Last year you lost a trunk full of things—and tell me—what else had you to remember and look after if not yourself and your things? Do you need a nanny—and am I cast in that role? Now again, you have lost a family photograph and some Polish books—and you ask me to replace them! Why? So that you should take the first opportunity of losing them again!? He who appreciates something looks after it." Tadeusz's "dressing down," however, did not prevent him "from loving you and blessing you, which I do with all my heart."

Conrad received a generous allowance of two thousand francs (or four hundred dollars) a year—the equivalent of the annual salary of a lieutenant in the French navy.[7] Yet he not only wildly overspent his allowance, but also had the irritating habit of telegraphing for additional money without bothering to explain why he needed it. This naturally produced a series of exasperated letters from the long-suffering Tadeusz. The letter of October 26, 1876, is representative. Starting with cool objectivity, Tadeusz suggested: "Let us . . . ask ourselves to what extent each of us has fulfilled his duties; for by answering this question, the recapitulation will enable us to correct any shortcomings that we may find in our conduct." Fair enough. But Tadeusz, who apparently did not have any shortcomings of his own, immediately launched into a detailed criticism of Conrad's fecklessness. He concluded that Conrad had spent, since leaving Poland, an extra 1,919 francs: "In short, during 2 years you have by your transgressions used up your *maintenance for the whole third year!!!* . . . Consider all that my dear—and you must admit that I am right—beat your breast—and swear to reform. . . . I would have refused my own son outright after so many warnings, but to you, the child of my Sister, grandson of my Mother . . . I, the victim of these absurdities, forgive you with all my heart, on condition, *that it is for the first and last time!*"[8] Conrad was willing to endure any number of long-distance lectures as long as he could continue his extravagant habits and have Tadeusz pay for them. He may have occasionally beaten his breast but, despite these avuncular admonitions, had no intention—now, or at any time in the future—of changing his spendthrift ways.

Conrad began his costly involvement with the Carlists—who led a revolution from the Right—through the Royalist Delestangs in polite society and through a *femme fatale* called Rita de Lastaola (who later became a model for the heroine of *The Arrow of Gold*) in the *demi-monde*. Rita, despite her improbable background, actually existed, but she was not, as Conrad later claimed, his mistress. As Conrad's worldly friend Joseph Retinger said of the Marseilles period: "I do not think that girls even then played a great rôle in his life."[9]

In Conrad's novel, Rita is born in the Basque country and spends her childhood tending goats in the hills near Tolosa. At the age of thirteen, she is sent from Spain to Paris by her uncle, a fanatical priest, to live with another uncle, an orange merchant. A few years later, Rita meets a rich painter, Allègre, becomes his model and mistress, and is transformed into a sophisticated society woman. After Allègre's death, she becomes the mistress of Don Carlos, pretender to the throne of Spain.

The immediate cause of the Carlist Wars was the dispute about whether the eldest daughter of King Ferdinand VII was entitled to succeed to the Spanish throne in 1833. Ferdinand had abrogated the Salic Law, which excluded females from succession to the crown, in favor of his daughter, who became Queen Isabella II. Ferdinand's brother Don Carlos refused to recognize Isabella and claimed the throne for himself. A civil war followed, in which the Basque provinces and Catalonia supported the ultra-reactionary and ultra-clerical Carlists, who were defeated in 1840.

Raymond Carr observes that Carlism was both reactionary and romantic:

> The Carlism of the [eighteen-]thirties was a negative creed, a crusade "for the elimination of the liberal *canaille*" . . . as the residual legatee of sixteenth-century heresy and eighteenth-century atheism. . . .
>
> It was a revolution of frustration, a revolution of the inadaptables, from the prince who had been pushed aside by court faction to the violent men who took to the hills in Catalonia and Aragon. Such men became the prisoners of an intransigent ideal: legitimacy and the Catholic unity of Spain. Against the court of Isabella stood the austere court of the true king, Charles V, regular in his habits and punctilious in his devotions, his army under the supreme command of the Virgin of the Sorrows. . . .
>
> Carlism, therefore, remained a romantic epic in which selfless devotion to an ideal was soiled by treason, desertion, and incapacity.[10]

In 1873, after the abdication of King Amadeus of Spain and the declaration of the Republic, the Carlists seized large parts of northeast Spain.
The Second Carlist War ended in 1876, a year after Alfonso XII, the son
of Isabella, was proclaimed king. Don Carlos was defeated and escaped
to France. But the Carlists, who later supported Franco in the Spanish
Civil War, remained a powerful force in Spanish politics until 1939.

Conrad sketches the historical background of the novel, and of his
own involvement in the cause, at the beginning of *The Arrow of Gold*.
Alluding to the proclamation of the two-year Republic in 1873 and the
rising in the Basque provinces, he declares that in "the middle years of
the seventies, Don Carlos de Bourbon, encouraged by the general reaction of all Europe against the excesses of communistic Republicanism
[after the Paris Commune of 1871], made his attempt for the throne of
Spain, arms in hand, amongst the hills and gorges of Guipuzcoa." The
supporters of the rising wanted "to organize a supply by sea of arms and
ammunition to the Carlist detachments in the South."

Conrad's rather naïve and romantic support of the Carlists in 1877
resembled Tennyson's involvement with the Spanish revolutionaries
who had opposed Ferdinand VII in 1830. Tennyson and his friend
Arthur Hallam took money and coded dispatches in invisible ink to the
revolutionaries gathering in the Pyrenees while his Cambridge friends
bought a ship to take the rebels to Spain and outfitted it with arms and
provisions. The venture ended disastrously when the rising was brutally
suppressed, and one of Tennyson's Cambridge friends was captured
and executed.[11]

Conrad's motives for joining the Carlists were an odd mixture of
expediency, opportunity, idealism and commitment. "We were all ardent Royalists of the snow-white Legitimist complexion—Heaven only
knows why!" wrote Conrad, with considerable irony. Busza suggests
that his (residual) Catholicism, which had led to an "Austrophil orientation," also aroused his sympathy for "such ultramontanist ventures as
the Carlist war." Ford, who knew Conrad well, stresses the romantic
and adventurous attraction: "The cause of the Carlists sufficiently appealed to Conrad: it was Legitimist; it was picturesque and was carried
on with at least some little efficiency."[12] Conrad had been painfully
familiar in Poland with the appeal of lost causes and still had an Apollo-
like devotion to an ideal—like that of the Polish rising of 1863—that
"was soiled by treason, desertion, and incapacity." The teenage Conrad
may also have engaged in the exciting venture for simpler reasons: his
friends urged him to join them, and he wanted to earn some money, to
please Rita and to help change the course of contemporary history.

Whatever his motives, Conrad formed a syndicate with three friends to buy the prettily named balancelle the *Tremolino*, whose name means "rustling of the wind," and to carry arms for the Carlists from hidden coves on the coast near Marseilles to the Gulf of Rosas in the northeast corner of Spain. The oldest partner, nearly thirty, was a Southern gentleman—*Américain, catholique et gentilhomme*—who claimed to live by the sword and eventually died by it in a Balkan squabble involving Serbs or Bulgarians. John Mason Key Blunt was "keen of face and elegantly slight of body, of distinguished aspect, with a fascinating drawing-room manner and with a dark, fatal glance." In *The Arrow of Gold* he also appears under his own name and is Monsieur George's villainous but unsuccessful rival for Doña Rita. At the end of the novel, he wounds George in a duel.

The second member, Henry Grand, the English teacher who lived a few doors down from Conrad on the rue Sainte, "had broken loose from the unyielding rigidity of his family, solidly rooted, if I remember rightly, in a well-to-do London suburb. . . . Narrow-chested, tall and short-sighted, he strode along the streets and the lanes, his long feet projecting far in advance of his body, and his white nose and gingery moustache buried in an open book: for he had the habit of reading as he walked." The third partner of the syndicate, who is briefly introduced and then disappears from Conrad's memoir, "was Roger P. de la S——, the most Scandinavian-looking of Provençal squires, fair, and six feet high, as became a descendant of sea-roving Northmen, authoritative, incisive, wittily scornful."

The captain of the ship would of course be the trusty Dominic Cervoni. When, Conrad says, he introduced Dominic to Rita and sought her approval, she was impressed by his massive mustache and his remorseless eyes: "he looked [suitably] piratical and monkish and darkly initiated into the most awful mysteries of the sea." And she immediately exclaimed, in her best *grande dame* manner: *"Mais il est parfait, cet homme."*

According to Conrad's account in *The Mirror of the Sea*, the *Tremolino*, officially known as a fruit and cork-wood trader but actually smuggling contraband arms, was betrayed by Dominic's nephew César Cervoni (the third member of the crew). When she is pursued by a Spanish patrol boat, Conrad exclaims: "She will never catch the *Tremolino*," but Dominic, observing that the roping stitches on the sail have been cut, realizes they have been treacherously sold. Dominic decides to destroy rather than surrender the boat by smashing it on the rocks and to escape with ten thousand francs he has hidden on board. Furious with César—who has also, unbeknownst to him, stolen the money—Dominic throws him overboard and César sinks with all the cash in a belt around his waist. "No ship ran so joyously to her death," Conrad writes of the dangerous venture. "At one moment the rush and the soaring swing of speed; the next a crash, and death, stillness. . . . The *Tremolino*, with her plucky heart crushed at one blow, had slipped off into deep water to her eternal rest."[13]

Conrad scholars have found no trace of a ship called the *Tremolino* in the Marseilles maritime records; they have discovered that César was not related to Dominic and, far from drowning with a money belt, survived to sail for many long years. Though the details of the story are suspect, the unpublished memoirs of one of Conrad's oldest English friends, G. F. W. Hope, who had extensive experience at sea and who met Conrad in 1880, long before he became a writer, confirms that some such incident actually happened. Conrad would have no reason to lie to a close friend and, in any case, could not have deceived him. In Hope's version of the story, the fourth partner was not French, but Spanish; the ship was not a balancelle, but a lateen (a similar Mediterranean ship, with a triangular sail set on a long sloping yard):

> Conrad told the story of when he was a youngster about eighteen, where he joined a party of four, an Englishman, an American, a Spaniard and himself, in Don Carlos's party when the Spaniards were trying to get up a revolution. They ran two cargoes but when running the third, a Spanish Revenue cruiser hove in sight and chased them, and finally they had to run their lateen ashore on the rocks and only just escaped with their lives.

In 1919 the older Conrad took a more practical and prosaic view of the affair, and emphasized the kind of peril and adventure that his father had experienced in Poland: "All this gun-running was a very dull, if dangerous business. . . . As to intrigues, if there were any, I didn't know anything of them. But, in truth, the Carlist invasion was a very straightforward adventure conducted with inconceivable stupidity and a foredoomed failure from the first."[14]

III

In a long and crucially important letter of March 24, 1879, to Stefan Buszczynski—Apollo's friend and biographer, and (for a short time) Conrad's former guardian—Tadeusz explained how Conrad's affairs had reached a crisis during the previous year. In March 1877, a month after returning to Marseilles on the *Saint-Antoine* and just before he planned to depart on his fourth voyage, for which Tadeusz had generously advanced him three thousand francs, Conrad became ill for four weeks with an anal abscess, which prevented him from sailing again with Captain Escarras. The captain expressed his regret in a letter to Tadeusz; and Conrad, his uncle explained, "not wishing to sign on under another captain, remained in Marseilles pursuing his theoretical studies and awaiting the return of his chief with whom he was to make a voyage round the world." Conrad's theoretical studies included some English and seamanship as well as idling, smuggling and gambling.

Though Conrad felt certain he would accompany Captain Escarras on his next voyage, in the autumn of 1877, the French Office of Military Conscription forbade him to go, Tadeusz said, "on the grounds of his being a 21-year-old alien who was under the obligation of doing [Russian] military service in his own country"—even though Conrad (who was actually nineteen and may have lied about his birth date to get better employment) would not reach the age of twenty-one until December 1878. The authorities discovered that Conrad had never obtained a permit to sail from the Russian consul; the Inspector of the Port of Marseilles, who had been persuaded (perhaps by the Delestangs, who seemed quite willing to bend the rules) to acknowledge officially the existence of such a permit, was severely reprimanded and nearly lost his job. After losing his temper and quarreling with Delestang, Conrad was forced to stay behind, with no hope of serving on French vessels.

Conrad's problems with the French authorities were followed by a financial catastrophe. While still in possession of the three thousand francs advanced by Tadeusz, Conrad met Captain Duteil of the *Mont-Blanc*, "who persuaded him to participate in some enterprise on the coasts of Spain—some kind of contraband! He invested 1,000 fr. in it and made over 400 which pleased them greatly so that on the second occasion he put in all he had—and lost the lot." It seems that Captain Duteil had urged him to join the *Tremolino* smugglers, and that the ship, after an initially successful foray, was wrecked sometime after October 14, 1877.

In early March 1878 Conrad, unable to work on a French ship, without any money and deeply in debt—for he had purchased equipment for his projected voyage and lived on credit while smuggling—borrowed eight hundred francs from his reliable friend Richard Fecht and unsuccessfully tried to join the American naval squadron at Villefranche. Then, attempting to recover his considerable losses, he risked everything at the casino in Monte Carlo and lost the eight hundred francs he had borrowed from Fecht.

Speaking of Conrad's previous misdemeanors in an earlier letter, Tadeusz had told him: "Certainly, there is no reason for one to take one's life . . . because of some folly one has committed." Yet that is what Conrad tried to do—and Tadeusz may later have felt guilty for having mentioned it. After losing his money in Monte Carlo, Conrad returned to Marseilles, invited Fecht to tea, left Tadeusz's address in a conspicuous place so that Fecht could instantly inform him of what had happened and, Tadeusz said, "before [Fecht's] arrival attempts to take his life with a revolver. . . . The bullet goes *durch und durch* [straight through] near his heart without damaging any vital organ."

Tadeusz, absolutely certain that Conrad was contentedly sailing somewhere in the Antipodes, suddenly, amidst all his agricultural business at the spring fair in Kiev, "received a telegram: '*Conrad blessé, envoyez argent—arrivez*' [Conrad wounded, send money—come]. . . . I set off at once from Kiev on [March 8], and arrived at Marseilles on [March 11]. I found Konrad already out of bed and having had a previous talk with his friend Mr. Richard Fecht, a most prudent and worthy young man [and notable contrast to Conrad], I saw the victim in person." After finding out what had happened and telling everyone that Conrad had been wounded in a duel, Tadeusz, "influenced by considerations of our national honour," paid Conrad's substantial debts.[15] These amounted to an additional three thousand francs: 1,700 to Fecht; 1,000 to another friend, Bonnard; 230 to his landlady, Madame Fagot; and 70 to the doctor.

"Suicide," Conrad later wrote in *Chance*, attributing it to enervation rather than to excitement, "is very often the outcome of mere mental weariness—not an act of savage energy but the final symptom of complete collapse." Apollo, who had suffered far more in Russia than Conrad did in Marseilles, never, even in his most pessimistic and despairing moments, succumbed to the temptation of suicide. Lacking the belief and the constraints of his father's faith, and far from his family and his homeland, Conrad felt desperately lonely. Brooding over the apparent wreck of his nautical career and the stupid squandering of a considerable fortune, he felt he had betrayed his uncle's trust and dishonored his name, and fell into a morbid depression.

But Conrad did not make a serious attempt at suicide. Later on, reflecting on his own experience, he wrote that he had been more frightened by the finality of death than by the awful circumstances of his life: "There are those who talk like that of suicide. And then there is always something lacking, sometimes strength, sometimes perseverance, sometimes courage. The courage to succeed or the courage to recognize one's impotence. What remains always cruel and ineradicable is the fear of finality. One temporizes with Fate, one seeks to deceive desire, one tries to play tricks with one's life. Men are always cowards. They are frightened of the expression 'nevermore.' "

His son John later reported that when he was "looking at some scars just below [Conrad's] left shoulder in the pectoral muscle, [he thought] the white weals looked as though they had been made with a sword or cutlass. There were two about an inch long, tapering together towards the top."[16] Though Conrad told John he had been wounded in a sword duel, he had actually been wounded by a bullet, near his shoulder rather than his heart, which went straight through his pectoral muscle without threatening his vital organs. Tadeusz heard by telegram, before he left Kiev, that Conrad was already better. Rescued by Fecht, he was out of bed by the time his uncle arrived in Marseilles. Conrad's rash, but not very dangerous, act was an extremely effective plea for help. It summoned Tadeusz from Russia, solved his financial problems in France and led to a new life in England.

Later, after returning to the Ukraine, Tadeusz repeated his necessary, if futile, admonitions: "You were idling for nearly a whole year—you fell into debt, you deliberately shot yourself. . . . Really, you have exceeded the limits of stupidity permitted to your age!"—though Tadeusz never defined precisely how stupid a teenager was allowed to be. The highly strung youth had been extremely foolish, selfish and irresponsible, but the generous Tadeusz—thankful that he was alive—was inclined to forgive him. After observing his behavior in Marseilles, Tadeusz told Buszczynski that Conrad had none of the common vices of a sailor. He did not drink, he did not gamble (apart from the one serious lapse in Monte Carlo), he had good manners, he was popular with both sailors and officers, and he was skilled in his profession: "He is not a bad boy, only one who is extremely sensitive, conceited, reserved, and in addition excitable. In short I found in him all the defects of the [Korzeniowski] family."[17]

Conrad urgently needed to change his nationality in order to free himself from military obligations in Russia. At various times in his early life he considered becoming a citizen of Austria, France, Switzerland and America—even of Japan or one of the South American republics. Finally, hoping to become a British citizen, he decided to join the largest fleet in the world, the British merchant marine, which did not require any of the French formalities for alien seamen. On April 24, 1878, less than two months after he had shot himself, Conrad signed on the *Mavis*,

a 764-ton English steamship, carrying coal from Marseilles to Constantinople. When re-ordering his life for his memoirs, Conrad tried to make
it appear as if he had always been predestined to serve on English ships:
"if a seaman, then an English seaman."[18] In fact, his life had been
radically changed—for the third time—by a series of events that began
with an infection between his buttocks.

CHAPTER FOUR

English Sailor
1878–1886

I

Conrad arrived in England in 1878, at the age of twenty, with only a few words of English, yet passed his examination for master within eight years. Though many foreigners worked on British ships, few aspired to become officers. And none had Conrad's noble-gentry heritage, cultured background, good education, refined manners, elegant dress, intellectual interests and rare sensitivity—all of which set him apart from both seamen and officers, and made him a lonely outsider.

During his twenty years at sea, he sought variety rather than consistency in the pursuit of his profession. He never sustained a successful career with any one firm or shipping line, and worked on eighteen different ships. He served during a period of transition from sail to steam and found it increasingly difficult to get suitable berths. He quarreled with several of his captains, and spent many long, frustrating periods ashore. Conrad had to serve as first mate after he had qualified as master. He had only one command—which he obtained by accident—and, after impulsively resigning, was never able to command another ship.

The unromantic steamer *Mavis* left Marseilles in April, with Conrad aboard as ordinary seaman, and stopped in Malta and Constantinople. Russia had just defeated Turkey in the war of 1878; as they approached the Bosporus, Conrad saw the pointed tents of the victorious army at San Stefano (now Yesilkoy, a village southwest of Istanbul, on the Sea of Marmara) where the peace treaty had been signed. The ship then entered Russian waters, docking at Kerch in the Crimea and Yeysk in the Sea of Azov, where she picked up a cargo of linseed. She then passed through the Mediterranean and returned to Lowestoft, on the

Norfolk coast. Having quarreled with the captain, William Munnings, Conrad forfeited part of his apprentice's deposit and left the ship. On June 18, 1878, he stepped onto English soil for the first time.

From July 11 to September 23, Conrad made three round-trip voyages between Lowestoft and Newcastle on a coal-carrying schooner, *The Skimmer of the Sea.* He may have recognized and been drawn to the schooner by its name, which was the subtitle of Fenimore Cooper's novel, *The Water-Witch* (1830). Though Conrad, known as "Polish Joe," earned only three shillings on his first English voyages, he got on well with the Norfolk sailors and later idealized them in his works.

Ignoring his two months on the *Mavis,* which had been unpleasant and could not be romanticized, Conrad said his voyages on *The Skimmer of the Sea* were his first experience on English ships. Writing to his close friend Cunninghame Graham in 1898, the small, dark Pole portrayed the sailors as hearty, high-colored Nordics: "In that craft I began to learn English from East Coast chaps each built as though to last forever, and coloured like a Christmas card. Tan and pink—gold hair and blue eyes with that Northern straight-away-there look! Twenty-two [actually, twenty] years ago! From Lowestoft to Newcastle and back again. Good school for a seaman."

In his speech to the Lifeboat Institution in 1923, he emphasized the sailors' amiability and their patience with the eager foreign apprentice who was trying to learn the essentials of seamanship and of English. And in "Poland Revisited" he also reminisced about his youthful experiences in the North Sea:

> That sea was to me something unforgettable, something much more than a name. It had been for some time the school-room of my trade. On it, I may safely say, I had learned, too, my first words of English. A wild and stormy abode, sometimes, was that confined, shallow-water academy of seamanship from which I launched myself on the wide oceans. My teachers had been the sailors of the Norfolk shore; coast men, with steady eyes, mighty limbs, and gentle voice; men of very few words, which at least were never bare of meaning.[1]

When he left *The Skimmer of the Sea,* after two months, to secure a berth sailing the wide oceans, he knew enough English to write (perhaps with some help) a letter to London inquiring about a job.

In a fascinating digression in "Poland Revisited," Conrad emphasized his loneliness and described his first visit to London as if he were penetrating the heart of darkness instead of the depths of the city:

I had come up from Lowestoft—my first long railway journey in England—
to "sign on" for an Antipodean voyage in a deep-water ship. Straight from
a railway carriage I had walked into the great city with something of the
feeling of a traveller penetrating into a vast and unexplored wilderness.
No explorer could have been more lonely. I did not know a single soul of
all these millions that all around me peopled the mysterious distances of
the streets.

Holding a folded map of London in his hand and placing the address of
the shipping agent in his pocket, he navigated the strange city without
asking anyone for help.

Finally, he found the Dickensian nook, under an inconspicuous arch-
way, where the office was hidden: "It was one o'clock in the afternoon,
but the day was gloomy. By the light of a single gas-jet depending from
the smoked ceiling I saw an elderly man, in a long coat of black broad-
cloth. . . . Standing up at a tall, shabby, slanting desk, his silver-rimmed
spectacles pushed up high on his forehead, he was eating a mutton-
chop." When Conrad muttered some phrases in broken English, James
Sutherland recognized him and exclaimed: "Oh it's you who wrote a
letter to me the other day from Lowestoft about getting a ship." The
agent informed Conrad that the law forbade him to procure ships for
sailors ("I had not been half an hour in London before I had run my
head against an Act of Parliament!"). But he extracted a sizable fee and,
circumventing the law, got Conrad a job as ordinary seaman on the *Duke
of Sutherland* for the derisory pay of one shilling a month.

The full-rigged, thousand-ton wooden wool clipper left London on
October 12, 1878, crossed the Equator, rounded the Cape of Good Hope,
took one hundred and nine days to reach Sydney, and returned home a
year and a week later. Noting the difference between the risk involved
and the skill required on sail and on steam ships, Conrad recalled during
an interview his agonizing time, high on the mainmast, struggling in the
darkness to unfurl the booming royals: "The conditions haven't changed
so much. It is the men who have changed. It's not that they are less
romantic, it's simply because they are of a different type. The man on a
steam vessel suffers less strain on the nerves. His work is easier." Conrad related how he had spent two terrible hours in the rigging, trying to
break the ice on the sails, accompanied by a terrified Australian boy who
cried out wildly, panicked by the flapping canvas. "The sailing ship
made men," said Conrad. "Sailors today are little more than factory
hands."[2]

While Conrad was acting as night-watchman aboard the *Duke of Sutherland* on Circular Quay in Sydney, a strange man begged for a night's shelter on the ship. When Conrad indignantly refused, the intruder suddenly knocked him down and gave him a black eye. Another problem during his five months in Sydney was helping A. G. Baker, the drunken chief mate, come on board every night. Ten years later, when Conrad was commanding the *Otago*, he met Baker, who had given up drink but was down and out. Conrad knew he would place himself in an impossible situation if he offered Baker a job under his command and, though sympathetic, was unable to help him.

Two months after returning from Sydney, and longing for the easier life on a Mediterranean voyage, Conrad sailed as an ordinary seaman on the 676-ton iron steamer *Europa*. The ship left London on December 12, 1879; called at Genoa, Livorno, Naples, at Patras in Greece, at Messina and Palermo in Sicily; and returned to London, after a seven-week voyage, on January 30, 1880.

Conrad's experience on the *Europa*, like that on the *Mavis*, was unpleasant. Since his letters to Uncle Tadeusz were lost when the family estate was destroyed during the Russian Revolution, and only six of his letters before 1889 have survived, our main—though indirect—source of information about Conrad's maritime years comes from Tadeusz's letters to him. Tadeusz's correspondence is concerned with money and filled with platitudes. Responding to Conrad's complaints on February 12, 1880, his uncle, like a Greek chorus, offered scant comfort to the resentful mariner. He felt harsh conditions were to be expected at sea and said that he—not Conrad—had foreseen them. He also expressed concern that the son of two parents who had died of tuberculosis was showing alarming symptoms, and commented rather too literally on the alleged insanity of the captain of the ship:

> I was not so much upset by the troubles you had on the *Europa*, though I realize you must have felt them keenly, for these are inseparable from life and getting to know people. They pain you, because you feel that you did not deserve them and that you are being exploited. I understand this and partly agree with you. But in your position, in which everything you gain must be won by work and endurance, in a profession where the conditions are extremely hard, what has happened was to be foreseen—and foreseen by me;—and probably now that you have had the first dose of experience they don't surprise although they hurt—and hurt they must! I am much more affected by the news that you "cough and sometimes have

fever," for these are symptoms which, if prolonged, may endanger your health and even your life. . . .

Your discomposure because of that madman Captain Munro worries me not less than it does you, although I don't understand English logic, since if the Captain is a madman his certificate and commission should be withdrawn.[3]

II

The glamour and romance which Conrad invested in sailing ships—in his fiction, autobiography and conversation—and his understandable reticence about the brutality and squalor on board, should not allow us to forget two crucial facts: that the merchant marine was a floating business whose main purpose was to make money; and that the conditions, as Tadeusz recognized, were extremely hard. There was a terrible stench aboard ship; the men suffered from damp, cold or heat; the quarters were cramped and primitive; there was no quiet and no privacy; the work was monotonous, exhausting and often hazardous. Robert Foulke observes that "during his twenty years of seafaring, a life not 'adventurous in itself' by his own report, Conrad suffered personal injury from a falling spar [on the *Highland Forest*], stranding, collision, fire, foundering [on the *Palestine*], and a survivor's voyage in an open boat."

The tainted food and sour water produced a high incidence of disease. When Conrad asked himself: "why should I . . . undertake the pursuit of fantastic meals of salt junk and hard tack upon the wide seas?," he could not give a satisfactory answer. In the East, when food was scarce, he had eaten shark, snake and trepang—worm-like aquatic animals, like mollusks, which the Chinese used to make soup. As Tadeusz told Stefan Buszczynski: Conrad "complains of the uncomfortable conditions on English ships [distinctly worse than the French] where no one is in the least concerned with the crew's comfort."[4]

Worse, perhaps, than the physical hardships, were the economic, social, psychological and intellectual difficulties. The pay was poor, promotion was slow, employment unsteady and insecure. Seamen, always abundant, were paid off in port and had to sign on again—months later—for the return journey. The caliber of shipmates, even among captains, was often quite poor. Donkin, in *The Nigger of the "Narcissus,"* represents the nadir among the sailors and shows how one man can spread his malign influence throughout the ship.

The social status of merchant seamen was dubious, and many sailors found it difficult to marry and have a family. (Conrad is amusing in "Typhoon" about how Mrs. MacWhirr dreaded the infrequent yet obtrusive visits of her strange husband.) "The most telling feature of voyages in sail," writes Foulke, "was almost complete isolation—an isolation which sealed off all contact with shore life and created a sense of estrangement. . . . They could not avoid the confinement and boredom of a microcosmic society." Joseph Retinger confirmed that Conrad felt the strain of isolation and *ennui*: "Not once but often he told me about his tremendous boredom at sea, when for months and months he had no congenial company, no books to read, no subject over which to meditate." The sea made Conrad "familiar with long silences," which, with the isolation, may have reminded him of the long, depressing months with his moribund father. The loneliness of Conrad's childhood was prolonged in his youth. As he realistically wrote in *Lord Jim*: "he had to bear the criticisms of men, the exactions of the sea, and the prosaic severity of the daily task that gives bread. . . . There is nothing more enticing, disenchanting, and enslaving than the life at sea."[5]

Conrad's time ashore, which became longer and longer between voyages, did not provide the necessary relief from the hardships at sea. He did not indulge in the customary sprees of drink and sex. He kept to the port; he did not travel inland, see the sights or explore the countries of Europe and Asia. He had no family to visit and knew almost no one in England. He had no social connections in Bangkok or Singapore, and felt they were not "very practicable for a seaman." He lived mostly in sailors' hostels and in seedy lodging houses in remote, unfashionable parts of London.

What did Conrad do on land? When he became an officer and lived aboard ship in port, he was occupied with his duties and responsibilities. He had to report to the owners, discharge the old cargo, find and stow the new one, pay off and hire the crew, oversee repairs, replenish stores and supplies, settle accounts with ship chandlers, deal with medical problems, attend to legal matters with the harbormaster and the consuls. "In Bangkok," Conrad wrote, "when I took command [of the *Otago*], I hardly ever left the ship except to go to my charterers. . . . I was really too busy ever to *hear* much about shore people."

When living ashore, he rested from the strenuous work, stretched his legs, bought a few books and tasted a change of cooking. The food, though better than trepang, could not have been very good in cheap London lodgings. He endured humiliating searches for employment with sailing agents and would go to the Shipmasters' Society at 60 Fenchurch Street, in east London, to see if they had managed to find him a berth. He prepared for his officer's exams, read extensively in English and French literature, and (as early as 1886) began his apprentice attempts at fiction. His future wife, Jessie, later summed it up by saying: "his days ashore were intervals of utter loneliness."[6]

During his long periods between voyages,[7] the increasingly disillusioned Conrad had ample opportunity to consider other ways of earning a living, and explored a great many possibilities that failed to eventuate. Unlike his father, who had taught him to despise money, Conrad was obsessed by it. He spent whatever he had, speculated to earn more, was always short of cash and counted on Tadeusz to supply the deficit. His annual allowance at the beginning of his career, about £80 or $400, was considerably more than he earned on ships until he became chief mate on the *Highland Forest*, at £8 a month (though not for every month of the year) in 1887. In 1881 Tadeusz reduced Conrad's allowance to £50 so he could support the numerous children of his impoverished brother Kazimierz (who had helped support Apollo in exile).

During his years at sea, Conrad's unrealistic projects to earn money outside the merchant marine included a whaling venture, piloting in the Suez Canal, Australian pearl fisheries, the Japanese navy, Canadian railroads, business in Newfoundland and work for an American politician. These projects, often inspired by gossip with casual acquaintances, were greeted by Tadeusz with great scepticism and caution: "You would not be a [Korzeniowski], dear boy, if you were steady in your enterprises and if you didn't chase after ever new projects." Yet, Conrad told a Polish friend in Cardiff in 1885: "It is not the desire of getting much money that prompts me. It is simply the wish to work for myself. I am sick and tired of sailing about for little money and less consideration." The only stints of shore work he actually did were to toil as a warehouseman and, for two months in the early 1890s, to work as a translator of Slavic languages. Sometimes his remuneration did not exceed ninepence per week.[8]

Conrad's business opportunities increased at the beginning of 1880. After leaving the *Europa* and renting a flat from William Ward in Tollington Park Street, Finsbury Park, north London, he met his first two English friends: G. F. W. Hope and Adolf Krieger. Hope, who became a lifelong companion, was born in 1854, the son of a solicitor. He had been trained as a boy on the *Conway*, had spent an adventurous year in the African diamond mines and was a former merchant marine officer. He had also served on the *Duke of Sutherland* and was a director of the South African Mercantile Company. A married man with a high forehead, trimmed beard and pointed mustache, Hope was fond of cigars and of yachting. He later took Conrad out on his cruising yawl *Nellie* and was the model for the director of companies mentioned at the beginning of *Heart of Darkness.*

Conrad met Hope in January 1880 through the sailing agent James Sutherland, whose office was frequented by men of the merchant marine. Hope later wrote: "I saw him several times before he found a berth and the more I saw him the more I liked him." When they went to the London Tavern for lunch, Hope had difficulty understanding Conrad's "very broken English." Richard Curle called Hope, who had no intellectual or artistic interests, "one of the simplest of men" and said that "Conrad rather bewildered him."[9] Hope introduced Conrad to his future wife. And Conrad maintained their friendship after he began to move in literary circles. In 1900, he dedicated *Lord Jim* to "Mr. and Mrs. G. F. W. Hope, with grateful affection after many years of friendship."

Adolf Krieger came from a German background and was born in Knox City, Indiana, in 1850. A rugged, good-looking man with thick hair and a drooping mustache, he also had rooms in Ward's house in Tollington Park Street. He married in 1881 and became a partner in a firm of shipping agents, Barr, Moering and Company, at 36 Camomile Street, near Liverpool Street Station. In the summer of 1883, after meeting Conrad in Marienbad, Tadeusz gave his nephew £350 to invest in Krieger's firm. Krieger often lent Conrad money and helped him find employment in the Congo. In 1898 Conrad dedicated his first collection of stories, *Tales of Unrest*, "To Adolf Krieger, for the sake of the old days." At the end of the century, however, Conrad got into financial difficulties with both friends. He lost his inheritance by speculating in South African gold shares with Hope, and quarreled with Krieger when he could not repay his loans.

III

On August 24, 1880, after seven months ashore, Conrad made his second voyage to Australia, on the *Loch Etive*, a full-rigged sailing ship of 1,287 tons, which could reach a speed of twelve knots. Though he passed his second mate's exam in 1880, Conrad had to sign on as third mate for wages of £3.10.0 a month.

The *Loch Etive*, a wool clipper known "for never losing steerage way as long as there was air enough to float a feather," was commanded by William Stuart. A tall, dark figure with a short white beard, he was famous for the quick, daredevil passages he had made on the sailing ship, the *Tweed*, which had once beaten the steam mail boat from Hong Kong to Singapore by a day and a half.

The chief mate, William Purdu, was rather deaf, could not hear how much wind there was and tended to carry too much sail. He had a "cheery temper, an admiration for jokes in *Punch*, [and] little oddities— like his strange passion for borrowing looking-glasses." Later, Purdu was washed overboard by a heavy sea during a rough passage from New Zealand to Cape Horn.

While crossing the mid-Atlantic, the *Loch Etive* took off the nine-man crew of a Danish brig that had been badly battered on her homeward passage from the West Indies. When the English crew sighted it, they first thought it was a water-logged derelict but soon realized that men were on board. As they lowered the boats, Captain Stuart warned Conrad: "You look out as you come alongside that she doesn't take you down with her" if she sinks. After the weirdly silent rescue, the Danish captain explained that they had lost their masts and sprung a leak in a hurricane, drifted for two weeks in bad weather, were not seen by passing ships and had nothing with which to make a raft. As they rowed back to the *Loch Etive*, the Danish brig sank behind them, marked only by an angry white stain undulating on the surface of the steely-grey waters.

The *Loch Etive* stayed in Sydney for seven weeks, took on a cargo of wool and arrived in London on April 24, 1881. On Christmas Day of the return voyage, they met an American whaler, the *Alaska*, two years out from New York. The English crew generously filled a wooden keg with old Australian newspapers and two boxes of figs, and flung it overboard as a holiday gift.[10]

Back in London, Conrad either speculated on credit with the sailing agent James Sutherland or, after the long confinement on ship, went on a spending spree. In any case, his half-yearly allowance disappeared. In order to recover his money, he concocted, in a letter to Tadeusz, a fantastic story about costly losses during an accident that had wrecked his ship, the *Annie Frost*, and put him into the hospital.

Though Conrad had absolutely no connection with this ship, the kind-hearted and gullible Tadeusz, relieved "that you had the uncommon luck to emerge safely from that ill-fated adventure," immediately sent a remittance to the "mariner in distress." He also told Conrad that news of the latest calamity had given him diarrhea and warned him, as a Korzeniowski, to "beware of risky speculations based only on hope." Tadeusz concluded with the suggestion that Conrad assist a certain

Professor Kopernicki in an unusual way: "He earnestly requests you to collect during your voyages skulls of natives, writing on each one whose skull it is and the place of origin. When you have collected a dozen or so of such skulls, write to me and I will obtain from him information as to the best way of dispatching them to Cracow where there is a special Museum devoted to Craniology." A macabre collection of skulls turns up on Kurtz's fence post in *Heart of Darkness* and Cesare Lombroso's theory of cranial types appears in *The Secret Agent*.

Before Conrad departed on his most disastrous journey—his first voyage to the Far East—Tadeusz made a sentimental appeal for a more practical project (which Conrad also ignored): as "a tribute to the memory of your father who always wanted to and did serve his country by his pen . . . [you should] collect some reminiscences from the voyage and send them as a sample [to] the address of *Wedrowiec* [*The Wanderer*, a Warsaw weekly]. . . . Six reports sent from different parts of the world during the year would not take much of your time: they would bring you some benefit and provide you with a pleasant recreation, while giving pleasure to others."[11]

IV

The *Palestine*, a wooden barque of 427 tons, with Conrad as second mate at £4 a month, left London for Bangkok on September 21, 1881. In "Youth" (1898) he gave a fairly accurate account of the adventurous though ill-fated voyage. The ship (called the *Judea* in the story) "was all rust, dust, grime—soot aloft, dirt on deck." She experienced heavy gales on the way up to Newcastle, where she took on a new crew and a full cargo of coal. During another gale, when she was three hundred miles from England, the ship lost her sails and sprang a leak—"Boats gone, decks swept clean, cabin gutted, men without a stitch but what they stood in, stores spoiled, ship stranded"—and put back to Falmouth, where they spent eight months undergoing repairs. While waiting in Cornwall, Conrad took a brief leave and squandered all his money in London: "It took me a day to get there and pretty well another to come back—but three months' pay went all the same. I don't know what I did with it. I went to a music-hall, I believe, lunched, dined, and supped in a swell place in Regent Street, and was back to time, with nothing but a complete set of Byron's works and a new railway rug to show for three months' work."

The *Palestine* finally left Falmouth, a year after its original departure and with a fourth new crew, on September 17, 1882. Six months later, the dangerous cargo of coal caught fire by spontaneous combustion. The crew fought the fire with water and then had to pump water out of the hold in order to save the ship from sinking. On March 14, the coal gas exploded, blowing up the decks and burning Conrad: "I did not know that I had no hair, no eyebrows, no eyelashes, that my young moustache was burnt off, that my face was black, one cheek laid open, my nose cut, and my chin bleeding."

The fiery ship was then taken into tow by the *Somerset*, which had to cut the tow rope when the fire threatened to spread to their own ship. The crew, forced to abandon the *Palestine*, lowered the boats; and Conrad's "first command" was a fourteen-foot rowboat with a crew of three. As they pulled away, the ship suddenly went down, head first, in a great hiss of steam. After rowing for twelve hours, they reached Mentok, on Bangka Island, off the southeast coast of Sumatra, where Conrad, his romantic illusions shattered, got his first view of the exotic Orient.

In a fine passage in "Youth," he describes how the burnt and blackened sailors were greeted by those on shore:

> Then I saw the men of the East—they were looking at me. The whole length of the jetty was full of people. I saw brown, bronze, yellow faces, the black eyes, the glitter, the colour of an Eastern crowd. And all these beings stared without a murmur, without a sigh, without a movement. They stared down at the boats, at the sleeping men who at night had come to them from the sea. Nothing moved. The fronds of palms stood still against the sky. Not a branch stirred along the shore, and the brown roofs of the hidden houses peeped through the green foliage, through the big leaves that hung shining and still like leaves forged of heavy metal.[12]

When Richard Curle was writing an essay on Conrad, the novelist, arguing for suggestiveness rather than specificity, objected to Curle mentioning the name of the place where he had landed: "The paragraph you quote of the East meeting the narrator is all right in itself; whereas directly it's connected to Muntok [now, Mentok] it becomes nothing at all. Muntok is a damned hole without any beach and without any glamour. . . . Therefore the paragraph, when pinned to a particular spot, must appear diminished—a fake. And yet it is true."

Conrad stayed in Mentok for six days; took the *Sissie* to Singapore, where he remained for a month; returned to London, via Port Said, as a passenger on a steamer; and arrived in early June 1883. Though Conrad was attracted to women of mixed blood, and some of the heroines of his Malayan novels are Eurasian, he was never seriously tempted by Eastern women in Singapore, Bangkok or Borneo. "A dash of Orientalism on white is very fascinating, at least for me," Conrad confessed; then primly added: "though I must say that the genuine Eastern had never the power to lead me away from the path of rectitude; to any serious extent—that is."[13]

The Court of Enquiry on the *Palestine* took place in Singapore on April 2, 1883, while Conrad was following the path of rectitude, and exonerated the officers and the crew. The detailed report describes the facts that Conrad later intensified and transformed into fiction. In the story, conditions are worse than they were in reality. The fictional *Judea*, between gales, was rammed in the dark by a steamer; the open boat knocked about for "nights and days" instead of reaching Mentok in twelve hours. On the *Palestine*,

> the passage was tedious owing to persistent light winds, but nothing unusual occurred until noon of the 11th March, when a strong smell resembling paraffin oil was perceived; at this time the vessel's position was . . . [in the] Bangka Strait. Next day smoke was discovered issuing from the coals on the port side of the main hatch. Water was thrown over them until the smoke abated, the boats were lowered, water placed in them. On the 13th some coals were thrown overboard, about 4 tons, and more water poured down the hold. On the 14th, the hatches being on but not battened down, the decks blew up fore and aft as far as the poop. The boats were then provisioned and the vessel headed for the Sumatra shore. About 3 p.m. the S.S. *Somerset* came alongside in answer to signals and about 6 p.m. she took the vessel in tow. Shortly afterwards the fire rapidly increased and the master of the *Palestine* requested the master of the *Somerset* to tow the barque on shore. This being refused, the tow-rope was slipped and about 11 p.m. the vessel was a mass of fire, and all hands got into the boats, 3 in number. The mate and 4 seamen in one boat, the 2nd mate with 3 hands in another and the master in the long boat with 3 men. The boats remained by the vessel until 8.30 a.m. on the 15th. She was still above water, but inside appeared a mass of fire. The boats arrived at Mintok at 10 p.m. on the 15th, and the master reported the casualty to the harbour master. The officers and crew came on to Singapore in the British steamer *Sissie* arriving on 22nd March.

Conrad behaved admirably during the series of disasters. After he had left the ship the chief mate, H. Mahon, told G. F. W. Hope that he was an "excellent fellow, good officer, the best second mate I ever sailed with."[14]

V

In 1881 Tadeusz had planned a crankish "grape cure" with Conrad in Wiesbaden. During July and August 1883, five years after their unfortunate encounter in Marseilles, Conrad finally arranged to stay with his uncle for a month—first in Marienbad and then in Töplitz [now, Teplice], in Bohemia, south of Dresden. The visit with Tadeusz provided a welcome and luxurious relief from the austere life at sea. It gave him an opportunity to speak his own language, to catch up on news and to reminisce about the past with the closest and best-loved member of his family, who was deeply concerned with Conrad's welfare and also paid all the bills. Uncle and nephew enjoyed the continental cuisine, the comfortable surroundings, the relaxing and well-regulated routine of hydrotherapy, massage and mineral waters as well as modest gambling in the casino, listening to the evening concerts, taking carriage rides and strolling amidst good society in the well-manicured *Kurort*.

After Conrad returned to London, Tadeusz, spending another week at the spa, wrote that he had enjoyed their holiday and was grateful for Conrad's unusually considerate letter: "You were right in supposing that on returning to Toeplitz I was sad and melancholy, sitting down alone to my evening cup of tea, opposite the empty chair of my Admiral!!! . . . I noticed immediately that you had gone out of your way to give me pleasure, and this small fact gave me a far deeper joy than the most eloquent words." While at Töplitz, Conrad wrote to his father's friend Stefan Buszczynski about his recent difficulties and dangers on the *Palestine*, and made a pious declaration of loyalty to his country: "I have not been too happy on my journeyings. I was nearly drowned, nearly got burned. . . . I always remember what you said when I was leaving Cracow: 'Remember . . . wherever you may sail you are sailing towards Poland!' That I have never forgotten, and never will forget!"[15] In fact, Conrad was always sailing *away* from Poland—which was filled with so many sad memories and hopeless prospects. He returned there only three times after leaving in 1874: to see Tadeusz in 1890 and 1893; and, after a hiatus of twenty years, to show his family Cracow in 1914.

On September 10, 1883, Conrad signed on the *Riversdale* as second mate at five guineas a month. The full-rigged sailing ship of 1,490 tons went round the Cape of Good Hope and arrived in Madras on April 8, 1884. During the voyage the captain, Lawrence McDonald, behaved like a despot. The officers were kept at a distance and treated "as machines, to be worked by himself when and as he pleased." When they reached

Madras, McDonald had some kind of convulsive fit and Conrad was sent ashore with a friend of the captain to fetch a doctor. When the doctor inquired about the captain's condition, Conrad rashly remarked that he was suffering from the effects of drink, and the doctor expected to find him in a state of delirium tremens. After the doctor had examined the captain and found no evidence of alcoholism, the friend told McDonald what Conrad had said. The captain was naturally furious at his insubordination. Though Conrad wrote an insincere letter of apology (which he later regretted), withdrawing his charges, expressing regret and assuring the captain that "there was never any intention to cast even the shadow of a suspicion on Captain McDonald's personal or professional character," he was dismissed by the captain on April 17. By agreeing to pay 60 rupees for the expenses involved in replacing him, Conrad admitted a certain responsibility.

McDonald also gave Conrad, for the only time in his career, a harmful "Decline [to answer]" mark for conduct on his Certificate of Discharge. R. L. Cornewall-Jones explains that the negative evaluation was quite clear: "It is by law, however, competent to the seaman who would have B. [Bad] stamped on his discharge to decline to have anything put upon it; but as nobody would object to G. [Good] or V.G. [Very Good], the absence of any marking is perfectly intelligible."

On April 28, twenty-four hours after leaving Madras, without Conrad, the *Riversdale*, sixty miles off course in fine weather, ran aground on the coast of India. McDonald's negligent and reckless navigation were blamed for the wreck and his certificate was suspended for a year. During the Court of Enquiry, McDonald accused Conrad of falling asleep three times during his watch, but admitted he had discharged him "for making certain statements to Dr. Thompson." Conrad was eventually cleared of these serious charges and allowed to take his chief mate's exam. In 1919, he joked about the incident and gave the novelist Hugh Walpole "a wonderful account about his time with the drunken captain on the *Riversdale*."[16] But in 1884, this incident could have destroyed his career. It is not clear exactly why Conrad would make—and then attempt to withdraw—this reckless accusation. But it seems that McDonald, though not drunk when examined by Dr. Thompson, was often intoxicated and that Conrad had wrongly assumed that alcohol had caused his fit.

Eager to get another ship and clear his name, Conrad crossed India by land from Madras in the southeast to Bombay on the west coast. Once there, he was struck by the sight of a graceful, full-rigged iron sailing

ship, which had left Wales without a second mate and had had serious
trouble with the crew throughout the voyage:

> One evening he was sitting with other officers of the Mercantile Marine on
> the veranda of the Sailors' Home in Bombay, which overlooks the port,
> when he saw a lovely ship, with all the graces of a yacht, come sailing into
> the harbour. She was the *Narcissus*, of 1,300 tons, built by a sugar refiner
> of Greenock nine years before. Her owner had originally intended her for
> some undertaking in connection with the Brazilian sugar trade. This had
> not come off, and subsequently he had decided to employ her in the
> Indian Ocean and the Far East.

On June 3, 1884, Conrad sailed from Bombay as second mate at £5 a
month and reached Dunkirk, on the Channel coast of France, on October 16. The *Narcissus*, the only actual ship's name he used in his fiction,
had a rough passage home and inspired his first great work, *The Nigger
of the "Narcissus."* In August, on the edge of the Agulhas Bank off
Capetown, the seas, driven by a westerly gale, became terribly precip-
itous. The *Narcissus* "went on her beam ends and remained lying thus
on her side for thirty hours among these steep seas, whose menacing
aspect and vicious rush are not to be forgotten."

Most of the characters portrayed in the novel—including Archie, Bel-
fast, Donkin and Singleton (whose real name was Sullivan)—belonged
to the real *Narcissus*. Conrad later told his first biographer that the eponymous hero was a thirty-five-year-old American named Joseph Barron,
who died in the North Atlantic on September 24:

> I remember, as if it had occurred but yesterday, the last occasion I saw the
> Nigger. That morning I was quarter officer, and about five o'clock I en-
> tered the double-bedded cabin where he was lying full length. On the
> lower bunk, ropes, fids [tapered wooden pins] and pieces of cloth had
> been deposited, so as not to have to take them down into the sail-room if
> they should be wanted at once. I asked him how he felt, but he hardly
> made me any answer. A little later a man brought some coffee in a cup
> provided with a hook to suspend it on the edge of the bunk. At about six
> o'clock the officer-in-charge came to tell me that he was dead. We had just
> experienced an awful gale in the vicinity of Needles, south of the Cape.[17]

Conrad, like conventional sailors, brought back a pet monkey from
India. But he could not keep it in his boarding-house and did not know
what to do with it. He was not terribly attached to it and when the
monkey tore up the papers in Krieger's office, it had to be sold.

VI

Conrad then spent two months ashore studying for his chief mate's exam, which he passed in December 1884. But ships were hard to find and he had to accept a berth on the *Tilkhurst* as second mate at the same wages, £5 a month, that he had earned on the *Narcissus*. The *Tilkhurst*, a full-rigged iron sailing ship of 1,527 tons (Conrad's largest sailing ship) left Hull on April 27, 1885, and picked up a cargo of coal in Cardiff, where it remained for a month before leaving for Singapore.

A Polish sailor had asked Conrad to deliver some money he owed to a watchmaker in Cardiff, Spiridion Kliszczewski, who had emigrated to Britain after the insurrection of 1830. Conrad received an enthusiastic welcome and formed a close friendship with the watchmaker's son Joseph, who was his contemporary. Joseph's young son noted how strange Conrad seemed in England and "was struck by their guest's unusual attire—a frock coat with a flat felt hat, the traditional headgear of the Anglican clergy—his strong foreign accent and refined manners." When Conrad reached Calcutta, he wrote Spiridion his earliest surviving letters on politics, repudiating Apollo's liberal ideas and expressing his lifelong pessimism: "The present has, you easily understand, but few charms for me. I look with the serenity of despair and the indifference of contempt upon the passing events. Disestablishment, Land Reform, Universal Brotherhood are but like milestones on the road to ruin. The end will be awful, no doubt!"[18]

The night before sailing from Singapore to Calcutta, a drunken brawl broke out on the *Tilkhurst* and an able seaman, William Cummings, was severely struck on the head. He became delirious and, though watched by the sailors, committed suicide by jumping overboard in the Andaman Sea. It was probably on the *Tilkhurst* that Conrad received an unexpected compliment about his seamanship. "One day [Conrad] had ordered the men working at the sail on deck to put it away, for he saw the weather would change, and, his order being heard by the captain below through the open skylight, Conrad heard him growl to the mate: 'That second officer knows the weather.' 'That cheered me up,' he explained. 'For he was a silent man, and I had never known before how he took me.'"

The master of the *Tilkhurst*, E. J. Blake, was a Plymouth man, well over fifty years old, short, stout, dignified and a bit pompous. When they docked in Dundee with a full cargo of jute from Calcutta, Blake inquired about Conrad's plans. He then complimented him by saying: "If you happen to be in want of employment, remember that as long as

I have a ship you have a ship, too."[19] But soon after this conversation, Blake fell ill and was forced to retire. Conrad visited the captain in his home, but never sailed with him again.

When Conrad was still in Marseilles, Tadeusz, on the lookout for opportunities to make money, had asked his nephew to inquire about the price and transport cost of a case of local *Liqueurs des Îles* and of 10,000 Havana cigars (which Conrad had fancied in Cracow), so he could import them into Russia. And after leaving the *Tilkhurst* on June 17, 1886, Conrad began negotiations to import flour and sugar, through Krieger's Barr, Moering and Company, with Tadeusz as his Russian agent. But this project, like all the earlier attempts to escape from the sea, came to nothing.

Conrad was busier and more successful than usual during his next eight months ashore. In the summer he responded to an advertisement in the May 1, 1886, number of the magazine *Tit-Bits*, which offered a "SPECIAL PRIZE FOR SAILORS. . . . We will give the sum of Twenty Guineas [more than four months' wages on the *Tilkhurst*] for the best article entitled 'My Experiences as a Sailor.' " Conrad did not win the prize and the original of his first story has been lost; but a revised version appeared in the *London Magazine* in 1908 and was collected in the posthumous *Tales of Hearsay* (1925). "The Black Mate," one of Conrad's weakest tales, turns on a trick and appeals to the spiritualism that was fashionable at that time. After being rejected as an oldster during a heart-breaking search for a berth, the chief mate Bunter dyes his hair raven black. During a storm at sea, he loses his hair dye and then slips on some brass-plated steps. In order to disguise the natural growth of his white hair, so disliked by the irritating and gullible spiritualist, Captain Jones, Bunter claims that he fell on the stairs after being frightened by a ghost, which suddenly changed the color of his hair.

On August 18, Conrad finally escaped from the clutches of Russia and became a British citizen. A police sergeant reported that the "Applicant, who is about 30 years old, stated that he left Russia when he was 12 years old. He had been 10 years in the British Merchant Service, and now holds an appointment as chief mate." In fact, the twenty-eight-year-old Conrad was ten years old when he left Russia, had served for only eight years and had never been a chief mate.

In November Conrad achieved his long-held ambition. He passed his master's exam and became the only Polish-born captain in the merchant marine of the most powerful country in the world. Uncle Tadeusz, who had first opposed and then supported Conrad's nautical career, was ecstatic that his investment had paid off: "Dear boy! Long live the 'Ordin[ary] Master in the British Merchant Service'!! May he live long! May he be healthy and may every success attend him in every enterprise both on sea and on land! You have really delighted me with the news of the 'Red Seal' on your certificate. Not being an Admiral I have no right to give orders to a newly created Master. . . . As the humble provider of the means for this enterprise I can only rejoice that my groats have not been wasted but have led you to the peak of your chosen profession."[20]

CHAPTER FIVE

From Second Mate
to Master
1880–1886

In the 1880s Conrad took three examinations for the rank of second mate, chief mate and master. The practical knowledge he needed for these difficult and often protracted tests, both written and oral, he acquired from experience at sea as well as from crammer's courses on land. The questions give a vivid idea of what Conrad knew and did—his responsibilities, duties and dangers—aboard ships. These exams also illuminate the cause of a back injury Conrad suffered on the *Highland Forest* in 1887, the technical expertise he exhibits in "The End of the Tether" and *Lord Jim*, his attitude toward training apprentices, and the contrast he was fond of making between sail and steam.

Conrad described his ordeals not only in Chapter VI of *A Personal Record* (1912), but also in the opening pages of *Chance* (1913) and in "Outside Literature" (December 1922); and he parodied an exam in "Some Reflections on the Loss of the *Titanic*" (1912). His exams in the Port of London were administered by the Marine Department of the Board of Trade and took place at St. Katharine's Dock House on Tower Hill. Though he kept his head during the tests, he twice mentions that "many good men had lost their heads" on Tower Hill.

In order to distinguish the three-exam episodes in his writing, Conrad gave each examiner a different physical appearance, distinct personality and method of inquiry. During the first exam (for second mate) on May 28, 1880, Conrad respectfully described the (unnamed) Captain James Rankin as "tall, spare, with a perfectly white head and moustache, a quiet, kindly manner, and an air of benign intelligence. . . . His old thin hands loosely clasped resting on crossed legs, he began by an elementary question in a mild voice, and went on, went on. . . ."[1] Ignoring the content of the test, Conrad subjectively described the intense and interminable scrutiny he endured. Captain Rankin seemed unfavorably impressed with his appearance and though Conrad was not afraid of failing, he was lightheaded, thought his brain was becoming addled and felt like a squeezed lemon when the grave old gentleman silently handed him the blue pass slip. During a brief exchange with the doorkeeper, whom he gratefully tipped a shilling, Conrad learned the ordeal had lasted just under three hours. Only after he had stepped outside the building did he experience euphoric relief and the feeling of walking on air.

Conrad repeated this scene, with slight variations, in *Chance*. Powell's trial (which lasts only an hour and a half) is fiercer than Conrad's. He has "the hottest time of his life with Captain R——, the most dreaded of the three seamanship examiners. . . . We all who were preparing [in a course] to pass . . . used to shake in our shoes at the idea of going before him." In contrast to the silent old man in *A Personal Record*, the taciturn Captain R. growls out nine whole words: "You will do! . . . Good morning, good luck to you." Powell gives a half-crown to the doorkeeper, who comments on the unusual length of time the exam had taken and informs him that two men had failed the second mate's exam, in less than twenty minutes each, that very morning. Powell floats down the staircase and feels it is "the finest day of my life. The day you get your first command is nothing to it. . . . That day I wouldn't have called the Queen my cousin."[2]

Conrad's exam for the chief mate's certificate took place four years later on November 28, 1884. In contrast to the tall, white-haired and gentle Captain Rankin (who began with an easy question), Captain P. Thompson was short and sturdy, with a sallow, unamiable face, and was clad in a brown morning suit. He leaned on his elbow, shaded his eyes and turned away from Conrad. The practical and familiar paraphernalia of the same room Conrad now described for the first time: "models of ships and tackle, a board for signals on the wall; a big long table covered with official forms, and having an unrigged mast fixed to the edge." The rather affected, theatrical Captain Thompson—"Motionless, mysterious, remote, enigmatical"—lived up to his execrable and even fiendish reputation by trying to make Conrad talk nonsense. Thompson then tested Conrad's resourcefulness with a substantial question that involved a series of imaginary catastrophes:

placing me in a ship of a certain size at sea, under certain conditions of weather, season, locality, etc., etc.—all very clear and precise—[he] ordered me to execute a certain manoeuvre. Before I was half through with it he did some material damage to the ship. Directly I had grappled with the difficulty he caused another to present itself, and when that too was met he stuck another ship before me, creating a very dangerous situation.

Thompson then threw in, for good measure, some thick fog, a lee-shore with outlying sandbanks and a lost anchor cable. Conrad, exasperated by the endless misfortunes, explained: "I would back [the bow anchors], if I could, and tail the heaviest hawser on board on the end of the chain before letting go, and if she parted from that, which is quite likely, I would just do nothing. She would have to go."[3] After a few more perfunctory questions about lights and signals, Conrad passed the exam—in only forty minutes.

In "Outside Literature" Conrad added some interesting details about the written part of this exam. He endangered his maritime career by making a trivial mistake and

writing the letter W instead of the letter E at the bottom of a page full of figures. It was an examination and I ought to have been plucked mercilessly. But in consideration, I believe, of all my other answers being correct I was handed that azimuth [astronomical navigation] paper back by the examiner's assistant, with the calm remark, "You have fourteen minutes yet."[4]

Conrad at first thought the examiner was a sarcastic brute, for there was no hope of going over all his calculations in only fourteen minutes. But he soon picked up the hint, changed "West" to "East" and handed in his sheet of blue paper with a shaky hand.

During his third ordeal, for his master's certificate, on October 29, 1886, the Dickensian examiner was "short, plump, with a round, soft face in grey, fluffy whiskers, and fresh, loquacious lips." Conrad specified only two questions: "tell me all you know of charter-parties" and "what's your idea of a jury-[temporary] rudder?" He dutifully replied to the last query by giving "two classical examples of make-shifts out of a text-book." This genial captain then described his own inventions and experiences, which dated back to the Crimean War, inquired about how Conrad came into the merchant service from a landlocked, agricultural country and soundly advised him to go into steam. Hans van Marle states that, contrary to *A Personal Record*, "the examiner's signature on the 1884 and 1886 applications proves beyond doubt that Conrad had to face the *same man twice."* But in November 1916 Conrad confirmed what he said in *A Personal Record*—which suggests van Marle may be wrong in his assertion—by telling Captain Sutherland that "when sitting for his Master's Certificate before Mr. Sterry [not Mr. Thompson], a London Board of Trade Examiner, he was asked by him how he would 'rig a jury-rudder.' "[5]

In "Typhoon" Conrad wrote of the unimaginative Captain Mac-Whirr, who cannot believe the typhoon exists because he has never actually experienced one. "Before he could be considered as fit to take charge of a ship he should be able to answer certain simple questions on the subject of circular storms such as hurricanes, cyclones, typhoons; and apparently he had answered them." Unfortunately, MacWhirr's theoretical knowledge of how to escape storms does him absolutely no good, for he steams into a deadly typhoon and nearly destroys his ship.

In "Some Reflections on the Loss of the *Titanic*," Conrad caustically contradicted the builders' arrogant notion that the *Titanic* was unsinkable "if only handled in accordance with the new seamanship." And he imagined an exam for the masters and mates of the future:

> Enter to the grizzled examiner a young man of modest aspect: "Are you well up in modern seamanship?" "I hope so, sir." "H'm, let's see. You are at night on the bridge in charge of a 150,000-ton ship, with a motor track, organ-loft, etc., etc., with a full cargo of passengers, a full crew of 1,500 café waiters, two sailors and a boy, three collapsible boats as per Board of Trade regulations, and going at your three-quarter speed of, say, about forty knots. You perceive suddenly right ahead, and close to, something that looks like a large ice-floe. What would you do?" "Put the helm amidships." "Very well. Why?" "In order to hit end on." "On what grounds should you endeavor to hit end on?" "Because we are taught by our builders and masters that the heavier the smash, the smaller the damage, and because the requirements of material should be attended to."
>
> And so on and so on. The new seamanship: when in doubt try to ram fairly—whatever's before you. Very simple.[6]

Despite the monstrous size of the ship, the satirically disproportionate number of waiters to crew and three boats for a full cargo of thousands of transatlantic passengers, Conrad's criticism (as the war approached) of the modern trust in mere material and in the new seamanship ("ram fairly") was both prophetic and deadly serious.

Information from the *Notice of Examinations of Masters and Mates and*

Engineers under the Merchant Shipping Act of 1854 (1870) and Alfred Henry Alston's *Seamanship* (1860) throw considerable light on Conrad's account of his ordeals. Compulsory exams for officers in the merchant service were first instituted by an act of Parliament in 1851. According to the *Notice of Examinations*, the tests were given in London every Monday and once or twice a month in other major ports in Great Britain. Officers were encouraged to study for them while in port and to attend schools of instruction. Conrad was tutored by John Newton, who ran a navigation school in Dock Street,[7] east London, and was the author of standard books on this subject. The exam fees were £1 for a second and chief mate, £2 for master. The penalty for sailing without a certificate was £50.

The experience at sea required by the Board of Trade regulations was four years for second mate, five for chief and six for master; and the minimum ages needed for certificates seem very low: seventeen for second mate, nineteen for first mate and only twenty-one for master. (A young man taking the exam for second mate at the minimum age would have left school when he was only thirteen and found the ordeal extremely taxing.) Service in the coasting trade was allowed to count, so Conrad could include his ten weeks' sailing between Lowestoft and Newcastle on the *Skimmer of the Sea*. As Najder points out, "the entire duration of his service [on French ships] amounted to thirteen months and five days, not [as he said] three years" and Conrad "took his first step on the [professional] ladder by means of deceit."

Conrad's remark in *A Personal Record*: "By its regulations issued under the first Merchant Shipping Act, the very word SOBER must be written, or a whole sackful, a ton, a mountain of the most enthusiastic appreciation will avail you nothing" is precisely confirmed by the *Notice*, which emphatically states: "Testimonials of character, and of sobriety, experience, ability, and good conduct on board ship will be required of all applicants, and without producing them no person will be examined."[8]

Candidates were examined in both navigation and seamanship. If they failed the latter, they not only forfeited their fees, but had to go to sea for six months before they could present themselves again for questioning. The candidates had five long hours to complete the written problems. Hans van Marle, an expert sleuth, has shown that Conrad failed the Day's Work section of the navigation test (a twenty-four-hour reckoning based on all the entries in the log book: the ship's position, speed and so on) in his chief mate's and master's exams, a fact which he does not mention in *A Personal Record*. He passed the chief mate's exam eleven days and his master's exam three months after his initial failures. If the applicant passed, he received the blue slip (mentioned by Conrad) from the examiner, which entitled him to receive his Certificate of Competency from the Superintendent of the Merchant Marine Office at any port he requested. This would allow him to take a new berth immediately and at his new rank, and have the certificate forwarded to his next destination.

The *Notice* also provides precise details about the knowledge required for each rank. In navigation, the second mate had to understand arithmetic and logarithms, work bearings and distance of the port he is bound to, find latitude by meridian altitude of the sun and be able to use the sextant. In seamanship, he had to give satisfactory answers about rigging and unrigging ships, stowing of holds, measurement of the log-line, glass and lead-line, rules of the road, light and fog signals, and code of signals.

In his "Memorandum" (written in 1920) for fitting out a sailing ship to train merchant service officers, Conrad takes up one of these points and states: "The proper stowage of a sailing ship was an extremely important part of her preparation for sea, affecting her sailing powers, the comfort of everybody on board, and even her absolute safety."[9] As chief mate of the *Highland Forest*, sailing from Amsterdam to Semarang in 1887, Conrad was responsible for the stowage. In *The Mirror of the Sea* he described the results of his error. When the former chief mate asked: "You have got her pretty well in her fore and aft trim. Now, what about your weights?," and Conrad told him "I had managed to keep the weight sufficiently well up, as I thought, one third of the whole being in the upper part 'above the beams,' " he smiled in vexed disbelief and predicted: "Well, we shall have a lively time of it this passage." Because of Conrad's system of loading, the ship rolled madly and he paid the penalty for his mistake: "A piece of one of the minor spars that did carry away flew against the chief mate's [i.e., Conrad's] back, and sent him sliding on his face for quite a considerable distance along the main deck." This severe back injury sent him into hospital as soon as he reached Singapore.

The chief mate's and master's certificates required an increasingly demanding knowledge of seamanship, the rigging of vessels, the stowing of holds, and of navigation and nautical astronomy. In navigation, the chief mate had to observe azimuths and compute the variation, compare chronometers and keep their rates, find longitude and latitude by the sun, and use the sextant by the sun. In seamanship, he had to be able to shift large spars and sails, manage a ship in stormy weather, take in and make sail, shift yards and masts, get heavy weights and anchors in and out, cast a ship on a lee-shore and secure masts in the event of an accident.

In addition to this, the master had to be able to find latitude by a star, know the nature of the attraction of the ship's iron on the compass, be able to shape a course and compare soundings with depths on charts, construct jury rudders and rafts, and preserve the crew in the event of a wreck. He also had to know the law concerning the management of his crew, know how to prevent scurvy, and understand invoices and charters, the nature of bottomry and channel lights.

The nature of the attraction of iron on the ship's compass plays a crucial part in Conrad's moving story, "The End of the Tether" (1902). Old Captain Whalley, a nautical Père Goriot, in order to provide for his distant and rather rapacious daughter, sells his ship, invests £500 and becomes a partner in a steamer with the villainous Massy. He employs a loyal Malay helmsman to disguise his blindness so he can complete the term of his contract and recover his investment. But Massy, discovering Whalley's blindness, deflects the magnetic needle of the ship's compass by filling his coat with pieces of soft iron in order to wreck the ship and collect the insurance money. Whalley discovers the plot as the coat loop breaks and it falls to the deck, but it is too late to save the vessel, which swings off course and hits a reef. In despair, Whalley puts the iron in his own pockets and goes down with his ship.[10]

There was also a voluntary Extra Master's Examination, which Conrad (after his two failures) did not take. It was "intended for such persons as wish to prove their superior qualifications, and are desirous of having certificates for the highest grade granted by the Board of Trade." For this certificate, the masters needed a much more sophisticated understanding of navigation and nautical astronomy, including geometry and trigonometry, and of Mercator's charts, as well as a more extensive knowledge of accidents in seamanship. In 1897, Edward Blackmore observed that the English exams were, nevertheless, much easier than the French: "In the standard of education as proved by examinations we are far behind those other nations whose example we professed to follow. . . . Out of the *thirteen subjects* which continental European maritime nations deem necessary to form component parts of a master mariner's education, the Board of Trade deem *five* only necessary." England required tests in winds and currents, navigation, nautical astronomy, instruments and observations while France, in addition, required algebra, geometry, trigonometry, mechanics, physics, steam engine, languages and nautical survey.[11]

Alston's *Seamanship* usefully lists 530 questions (with explanations) under the headings: "Fitting Out" (sails, ropes, knotting and splicing) and "At Sea" (emergencies). Many of these questions involved an extremely specialized vocabulary.[12] Though Conrad absorbed his technical terms directly, rather than learning the English equivalents of Polish words, it must have been extremely difficult, for a man who had known English for only two years and gave his answers in a strong foreign accent, when asked how to "rig a nun-boy" (channel marker) or "pass a nipper" (a short braided cord for securing a hemp cable). The question: "How is the lacing rove on the lower part of the luff of a spanker?"[13] (i.e., how is the cord passed through the hole on the lower part of the forward edge of a fore-and-aft sail of the aftermost lower mast?) could easily be misunderstood and Conrad might have associated "lacing" and "spanker" with sex rather than with seamanship.

Eight complex but representative questions (like the catastrophic one he was asked on his chief mate's exam) give some idea of the difficulties of the tests:

Prepare your ship, a frigate, for rounding the Horn in the winter months. (P. 29)

You foul another ship as you are getting under weigh, and carry away your boomkin and cat-head flush with the bows:—how will you secure the anchor for sea, and work the foresail? (P. 34)

You are totally dismasted, and consequently quite unmanageable: what will you do to keep the ship from foundering by the sea striking her astern or amidships? (P. 24)

You discover your mainmast to be decayed; dispose of the old one, and get a new one in, having no spars on board suitable for sheers, and being unable to procure any. (P. 39)

In command of boats you have been employed towing a ship out of harbour; but, before you part company, a thick fog comes on:—how will you find your way back, having no compass? (P. 36)

Two ships are drifting towards each other in a calm; they lower their boats, and endeavour to tow each other in contrary directions, but they still close: what should they do? (P. 25)

Two ships, each with the wind a point abaft the beam are standing towards each other, and will inevitably come into collision if they continue their course. One is steering E. by S., and the other W. by S., with the wind at North:—what is the duty of each? (P. 16)

You are taking your ship up a river, and are forced by an ebb-tide on a reef of rocks. All attempt to get spars over, as shores, are rendered futile by the rapidity of the current, and, in defiance of all efforts to the contrary, the ship falls over 22°. The usual preparations are made by battening down the hatchways; but, owing to a defect in the chain-pumps, the water gains upon the ship, and she falls over, and remains at an angle of 45°:—how will you endeavour to raise her? (P. 30)

Conrad's preparation enhanced his ability to deal with such disasters when they actually occurred on the *Palestine* and on the *Narcissus*. It also increased the technical expertise that informed so many of his works. In a brilliant moment in *Lord Jim*, for example, the officers who have abandoned the *Patna* see no lights, though they are quite close to the vessel, and naturally assume the ship has gone down. Conrad's explanation reveals the truth of the matter. The ship's stern was "canted high and her bows brought down low in the water through the filling of the fore-compartment. Being thus out of trim, when the squall struck her a little on the quarter, she swung head to the wind as sharply as though she had been at anchor. By this change in her position all her lights were in a very few moments shut off from the boat to leeward."[14]

In 1917 Conrad was gratified to receive a letter from a former apprentice who had sailed with him on the *Highland Forest*. He praised Conrad's gentleness and his desire to instruct the young men so they would be as well (or better) prepared for the exams than he was: "I have loved you more than any man I ever knew except my own father and I revere the memory that was made upon the most irresponsible of human beings, the schoolboy, because I had only just left school when I had the honour of being your boy. I remember so distinctly the trouble you took in the silent watches of a tropical night to teach me the different ropes."[15] Conrad was justly proud of the extraordinary achievement of rising to master in the British merchant service, and it was especially important to him to have "proved to the English that a gentleman from the Ukraine can be as good a sailor as they."[16]

CHAPTER SIX

Eastern Voyages
1886–1889

I

On December 28, 1886, two months after passing his master's examination, Conrad took his shortest voyage—five days from London to Cardiff—as second mate, at £5 a month, on the 2,000-ton iron sailing ship, the *Falconhurst*. When he reached Cardiff, his London agent told him of a 1,000-ton iron barque, in Amsterdam, that needed a chief mate. As he had not yet signed on for a second voyage on the *Falconhurst*, he left her in Cardiff, came up to London and met Hope at Holborn station. They dined together and Conrad "was in very good spirits at having got the berth of chief mate of the *Highland Forest*" at £7 a month.[1]

Conrad crossed over to Amsterdam, where he found conditions that resembled Vologda. The ship was frozen, the canals solid and the cargo delayed—with no prospect of a thaw until late spring. In *The Mirror of the Sea*, he described his frustration, his discomfort and—as always—his loneliness; and recalled how he sought refuge in the luxurious surroundings of the Grand Hotel Krasnopolsky (founded by a Polish *émigré*) on the Warmoesstraat in the center of town:

I was . . . biting my fists with impatience for that cargo frozen up-country; with rage at that canal set fast, at the wintry and deserted aspect of all those ships that seemed to decay in grim depression for want of the open water. I was chief mate, and very much alone. . . .

Notwithstanding the little iron stove, the ink froze on the swing-table in the cabin, and I found it more convenient to go ashore stumbling over the Arctic waste land and shivering in glazed tramcars in order to write my evening letter to my owners in a gorgeous café. . . . It was an immense place, lofty and gilt, upholstered in red plush, full of electric lights, and so thoroughly warmed that even the marble tables felt tepid to the touch. The waiter who brought me my cup of coffee bore, by comparison with my utter isolation, the dear aspect of an intimate friend.

When the owners ordered him to threaten the charterers with penalties and insisted that the cargo should immediately be sent by rail, Conrad would visit the cozy office of Mynheer Jan Hudig, "a big, swarthy Netherlander, with black moustaches and a bold glance," who amiably assured him that nothing could be done. Finally, after a month in Amsterdam, the thaw set in and the cargo arrived. But Conrad (as we have seen) miscalculated the stowage; and the ship rolled constantly and furiously all the way to Semarang in Java, "with an awful dislodging jerk and that dizzily fast sweep of her masts on every swing."[2]

After being hit in the back by the flying spar, Conrad suffered inexplicable periods of listlessness and sudden spurts of mysterious pain. His lameness, like Lord Jim's, persisted. When the ship arrived in Semarang on June 20, he was ordered to remain quiet for three months and signed off the *Highland Forest*. He left Semarang aboard the steamship *Celestial* on July 2, reached Singapore four days later, went straight into the great airy ward of the European hospital and surrendered himself to the sensual ease of the Orient:

> [The hospital] stood on a hill, and a gentle breeze entering through the windows, always flung wide open, brought into the bare room the softness of the sky, the languor of the earth, the bewitching breath of the Eastern waters. There were perfumes in it, suggestions of infinite repose, the gift of endless dreams. . . .
>
> Lying on my back, I had plenty of leisure to remember the dreadful cold and snow of Amsterdam, while looking at the fronds of the palm trees tossing and rustling at the height of the window.[3]

Conrad recovered within a month, and sought an undemanding ship that would allow him to regain his strength and to see more of the East. James Craig, the captain of the *Vidar*, a 300-ton iron steamer, recalled: "The first time I met Conrad was at the Shipping Office of Singapore about the middle of August, 1887. He pleased me at once by his manners, which were distinguished and reserved. One of the first things he told me was that he was a foreigner by birth, which I had already guessed by his accent. I replied that that did not matter in the least as he had his certificate. (It was quite difficult at that time to find officers in the East who were not over fond of the bottle.)"

Conrad signed on as chief mate on August 20. During the next four and a half months he made four round-trip voyages between Singapore and the east coast of Borneo: "She was an eastern ship. . . . She traded among dark islands on a blue reef-scarred sea, with the Red Ensign over the taffrail and at her masthead a house-flag, also red, but with a green border and with a white crescent in it. For an Arab [in Singapore] owned her." The *Vidar* steamed southeast through the Karimata Strait (between Sumatra and Borneo) to Banjarmasin on the south coast of Borneo, to the island of Laut to take on coal, across the Macassar Strait to Donggala on the west coast of Celebes, back to the east coast of Borneo to Tanjung Redeb on the Berau River and to Tanjung Selor in the north. The *Vidar* then returned to Singapore, stopping at the same ports on the way back. These brief voyages through the Malay archipelago during the last half of 1887 gave Conrad his richest literary material and provided the inspiration for "The End of the Tether" and four early novels: *Almayer's Folly, An Outcast of the Islands, Lord Jim* and *The Rescue* (begun in 1896 but not finished until 1919).

One night the *Vidar*, steaming along a badly charted coast, got inside a ledge of reefs that she should have cleared, on her familiar track, by a mile and a half. In the midst of fierce rain squalls and blinding lightning, Conrad had just enough time to snatch the telegraph handle, change the course and escape the tangle of rocks without wrecking the ship. He did not fully realize the extreme danger until their position was revealed at daybreak.[4]

Conrad later told his publisher that he was extremely busy in port while on the *Vidar* and knew very little about shore people: "And anyway I would not have cared to form social connections, even if I had had time and opportunity." But at least one man, at a trading station up the Berau River, made a tremendous impression on Conrad. William Charles Olmeijer—the model for Kaspar Almayer in Conrad's first two Malayan novels—was a Dutch half-caste, born in the East Indies in 1848. He arrived in Berau in 1870, married a Malay four years later, and had five sons and six daughters. He maintained close relations with the head-hunting Land Dyaks, which aroused the suspicions of the Dutch authorities, and he did construct an oversized house locally known as The Folly.

Conrad first saw Olmeijer's incongruous figure when the *Vidar* tied up to a "rickety little wharf forty miles up, more or less, a Bornean river. . . . He was clad simply in flapping pyjamas of cretonne pattern (enormous flowers with yellow petals on a disagreeable blue ground) and a thin cotton singlet with short sleeves." Olmeijer boasted that he owned the only flock of geese on the east coast of Borneo and revealed

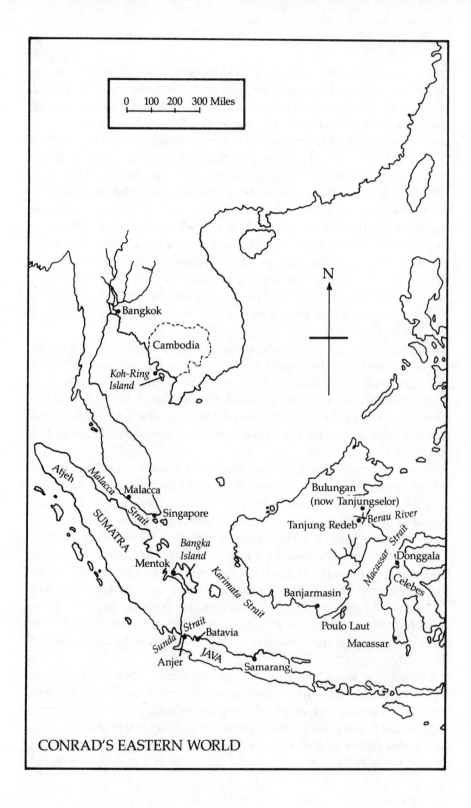

N

Bangkok

Cambodia

Koh-Ring Island

Atjeh

Malacca

Malacca

SUMATRA

Singapore

Bangka Island

Mentok

Karimata Strait

Macassar Strait

Bulungan
(now Tanjungselor)

Tanjung Redeb

Berau River

Donggala

Celebes

Banjarmasin

Poulo Laut

Macassar

Sunda Strait

Batavia

Anjer

JAVA

Samarang

CONRAD'S EASTERN WORLD

his grandiose ambitions by importing a pony (which Conrad had diffi-culty landing and which immediately ran off into the jungle), although the settlement had only one quarter-mile path that was suitable for such an animal.

Olmeijer traded in gutta-percha, rattan and rubber, and shipped his products through his benefactor, Captain William Lingard, an important trader who owned a schooner and had good business connections in Singapore. Lingard was married to Olmeijer's sister and had helped establish his nephew Jim Lingard as a trader in Olmeijer's settlement. Known as Rajah Laut, or King of the Seas, Lingard had made his fortune by discovering a secret passage that enabled him to sail up the Berau River. A contemporary described William Lingard—the model for Tom Lingard in Conrad's Malayan novels—as "a personage of almost myth-ical renown, a sort of ubiquitous sea-hero, perhaps at times a sort of terror to evildoers, all over Eastern waters from Singapore to Torres Straits, and from Timor to Mindanao. [He] was a well-set-up man of perhaps fifty-two when I saw him [in 1887]. Alert, decisive in his move-ments, just above middle height, with grizzled hair, moustache and beard, cut short after the naval style."[5]

Conrad's voyages to Borneo provided his first significant experience with Dutch colonial rule in the East Indies. Most of the country, apart from the rivers, was inhospitable to human settlement. And the interior was (then, as now) only partially explored: "Tropical, covered in dense rain forest, often mountainous, fringed by mangrove swamp, its soils leached by heat and torrential rain, the area offered little encouragement to extensive habitation. Only the rivers, with which the coastlines were deeply and frequently incised, made it possible . . . to develop complex polities." The population was composed of the indigenous pagan Dyaks of the interior, the Malay and Arab Moslems on the coast, and the precariously placed European adventurers—often in a state of advanced decay—in the riverine trading stations.

The Dutch had struggled with the Portuguese and the English for control of the vast archipelago, and had emerged as the dominant power, after a series of Anglo-Dutch conflicts, in 1623. Throughout the seventeenth and eighteenth centuries, the Dutch East India Company steadily expanded its control over the entire region. When it was liqui-dated in 1798, the Dutch government took over its holdings. Dutch power collapsed during their defeats by the French in the Napoleonic wars, and the British, under Sir Stamford Raffles, occupied all their possessions in southeast Asia. But during the nineteenth century, the Dutch revived and began the serious work of establishing an empire. By the Anglo-Dutch treaty of 1824, the Dutch gained freedom of action in Sumatra and the British in the Malay peninsula. The extension of Dutch political power in Java, Sumatra, Celebes, the Moluccas and Borneo involved several wars with native states. Atjeh, the wealthiest and most powerful sultanate, in northern Sumatra, fought the Dutch from 1873 until 1904. The Dutch began their incursions by trading and by signing treaties with sultans who ceded their sovereignty; they concluded by occupying territory and by establishing political control.

The Dutch government returned to Borneo (the third-largest island in the world) in 1817. Graham Irwin describes the uncertainty of their rule:

> By virtue of contracts negotiated between 1817 and 1826, the Dutch had acquired from Bandjermasin full sovereign powers over the greater part of the territory which later became South and Eastern Division. The areas surrendered comprised the south-west and east coasts and certain provinces in the interior, none of which had actually been subject to the [Moslem] Sultanate when the contracts were signed, and over which the Dutch, at least until the 1840's, exercised no more than nominal rule themselves. . . .
>
> In the mid-nineteenth century the East Coast of Borneo was ruled by a number of more or less independent native princes. . . . The Sultanate of Berouw [i.e., Berau, was] an ancient kingdom which had been partitioned in 1770 after a civil war; suzerainty over Berouw was claimed by the Sultan of Sulu as well as by the Sultan of Bandjermasin.

The Dutch retained loose sovereignty but generally neglected their recently restored possessions until James Brooke appeared on the northwest coast in 1839 and the British renewed their political rivalry. The next forty years "saw a steady increase of the influence and dominion of both powers, until by 1888 [the year after Conrad reached Borneo] the island had been partitioned between the two."[6]

The liberal rule of the Dutch did not fulfill its early promise. After the severe economic crisis of 1883–85, initial progress was followed by stagnation and collapse. Both English and Dutch critics have attacked Dutch colonial rule. J. S. Furnivall argued that the Malay population suffered social derangement without corresponding economic benefits: "the European element grew rapidly in numbers and wealth, and so, in even larger measure, did the Chinese element, whereas the natives, hemmed in ever more narrowly within a contracting economic frontier, saw their own social life disorganized without gaining enfranchisement in any more comprehensive social order." And Amry Vandenbosch, in a more severe condemnation, charged the Dutch with gross violation of their traditional policy: indirect rule through the powerful sultans and local chiefs: "The Dutch East Indies Government is accused of having played fast and loose with the native states and of having ruthlessly forced its will upon them. Intervention in the internal affairs of the native states by the right of 'paramountcy' . . . has been used to justify all manner of intervention."[7]

Conrad, with his Polish sympathy for the underdog, disliked Dutch rule in the East Indies almost as much as he was to hate Belgian colonialism in the Congo. He often portrayed Dutch authorities as incompetent, belligerent and oppressive. In 1899, his patriotism inflamed by the war against the Boers, he told his Polish cousin: it is "a fact that they have no idea of liberty, which can only be found under the British flag all over the world. C'est un peuple essentiellement despotique, like by the way all the Dutch." And in "Freya of the Seven Isles" (1912), he created the vile Dutch naval lieutenant, Heemskirk, who uses his official power to terrorize Freya's father, to destroy her fiancé's ship and to exploit her sexually. Freya's father, old Nielsen, "was not so horrified at the Dutch as he was at the Spaniards [in the Philippines], but he was even more mistrustful of them. Very mistrustful indeed. The Dutch, in his view, were capable of 'playing any ugly trick on a man' who had the misfortune to displease them. There were their laws and their regulations, but they had no notion of fair-play in applying them."[8]

After four and a half months on the Vidar, Conrad had regained his health (he was never again troubled by his back injury) and had acquired precious literary material from an unknown part of the world. In January 1888, although he knew that berths would be difficult to find, he gave up his position as chief mate. In The Shadow-Line, he attributes this impulsive decision to "moments of boredom, of weariness, of dissatisfaction. Rash moments. I mean moments when the still young [Conrad was then thirty] are inclined to commit rash actions, such as getting married suddenly or else throwing up a job for no reason."

Despite Conrad's claim that his decision was purely irrational, there were several reasons for his impulsive behavior. He felt no loyalty to the steamship, had learned what he could from these voyages, and was bored by the remoteness and the routine on a ship that seemed to have no future. At the beginning of Lord Jim, he expresses strong disapproval of sailors who had renounced the harsher conditions and severer duties of stormy oceans, and had become hedonistically "attuned to the eternal peace of Eastern sky and sea. They loved short passages, good deck-chairs, large native crews [the Vidar carried a dozen Malays and eighty-two Chinese to land cargo in the up-river ports], and the distinction of being white." They led precariously easy lives, "serving Chinamen, Arabs, half-castes." Conrad feared he would become accustomed to this soft, decadent life and sternly resisted the temptation "to lounge safely through existence."

When Conrad left the ship in Singapore on January 5, 1888, the thirty-three-year-old English captain, exaggerating Conrad's period of service, gave him a solid recommendation: "This is to certify that Mr. C. Korzeniowski has sailed with me as Chief Officer on the S.S. *Vidar* for a period of seven months, and during that time I found him a steady, sober and attentive officer at all times. I can recommend him to any Owner or Master to look after their interests, and [as] a good seaman, James Craig, Master."

In 1909, when Captain Carlos Marris visited him in England, he told Conrad that his novels were read by sailors of the Eastern seas and that Joshua Lingard (William's other nephew), perceiving the strange Pole's difference from the other merchant officers, guessed that *he* was the author of those books: "It must have been the fellow who was mate in the *Vidar* with Craig."[9]

II

On January 9, 1888, while staying in the Officers' Home in Singapore, Conrad heard from the harbor master, Henry Ellis, that the British Consul in Bangkok had asked for a competent master to replace the captain who had died on board the *Otago*. That evening, Conrad took the steamer *Melita* and reached Bangkok four days later.

In *The Shadow-Line*, he vividly described his first impressions of the glittering and decrepit buildings (including the nineteenth-century Grand Palace), as well as the fragile houses (which still exist in the torrid, sinking city), as he snaked up the Menam River and into the capital of independent Siam:

> We steamed up the innumerable bends, passed under the shadow of the great gilt pagoda, and reached the outskirts of the town.
>
> There it was, spread largely on both banks, the Oriental capital which had as yet suffered no white conqueror; an expanse of brown houses of bamboo, of mats, of leaves, of a vegetable-matter style of architecture, sprung out of the brown soil on the banks of the muddy river. It was amazing to think that in those miles of human habitations there was not probably half a dozen pounds of nails. Some of those houses of sticks and

grass, like the nests of an aquatic race, clung to the low shores. Others seemed to grow out of the water; others again floated in long anchored rows in the very middle of the stream. Here and there in the distance, above the crowded mob of low, brown roof ridges, towered great piles of masonry, King's Palace, temples, gorgeous and dilapidated, crumbling under the vertical sunlight, tremendous, overpowering, almost palpable, which seemed to enter one's breast with the breath of one's nostrils and soak into one's limbs through every pore of one's skin.

Inside the city he saw more disintegrating houses, and "the broad main thoroughfare ruinous and gay, running away, away between stretches of decaying masonry, bamboo fences, ranges of arcades of brick and plaster, hovels of lath and mud, lofty temple gates of carved timber, huts of rattan mats—an immensely wide thoroughfare, loosely packed as far as the eye could reach with a barefooted and brown multitude paddling ankle deep in the dust."[10]

As soon as he arrived, Conrad gave the Consul the letter from Ellis stating the terms of his employment:

> The person I have engaged is Mr. Conrad Korzeniowski, who holds a certificate of Competency as Master from the Board of Trade. He bears a good character from the several vessels he has sailed out of this Port. I have agreed with him that his wages at £14 per month to count from the date of arrival at Bangkok, ship to provide him with food and all necessary articles for the navigation of the vessel. His passage from Singapore to Bangkok to be paid by the ship, also on his arrival at Melbourne if his services be dispensed with, the owner to provide him with a cabin passage back to Singapore.

Within fourteen months of passing his master's exam, Conrad had progressed to higher ranks on smaller ships: from second mate of the 2,000-ton *Falconhurst*, to chief mate of the 1,000-ton *Highland Forest*, to master of the 345-ton iron sailing barque *Otago*. Conrad's first command (named after a province on the South Island of New Zealand) provided the inspiration for "Falk," "A Smile of Fortune" and *The Shadow-Line*.

In Poland, the serfs and servants called the owner of an estate "The Master"; on the *Otago*, the sailors and officers addressed the Polish captain with the same respectful phrase. Cornewall-Jones, defining the master's duties and powers, explains: "His word is law, which nobody must dispute, and which permits of no argument. . . . He stands no watch, comes and goes when he pleases, and is accountable to no one except to his owners. He has entire control of the discipline of the ship;

so much so that none of the officers under him have any authority to punish a seaman, or to use any force without the master's order, except only in cases of urgent necessity that admit of no delay."[11]

On the *Otago*, Conrad was immediately faced with several serious problems. The crew was suffering severely from tropical fever, dysentery and cholera; but Conrad, delayed by the charterers, was unable to leave port for sixteen days. The new steward, recommended perhaps by a local hotelier, was an ageless "Chinaman of the death's-head type of face. . . . Before the end of the third day he had revealed himself as a confirmed opium-smoker, a gambler, a most audacious thief, and a first-class sprinter"—and had made off with Conrad's entire savings: £32 in gold sovereigns. The robbery, as well as the stealthy character of the steward, made a deep impression on Conrad, who twice referred to them in later conversations. He compared the duplicitous behavior of his son's dog to "that of the Chinaman who stole all my money. All smiles to your face but snatch anything behind your back." And, referring to a town southeast of Bangkok, Conrad told Bertrand Russell, who had recently returned from the Orient: "I have always liked the Chinese, even those that tried to kill me (and some other people) in the yard of a private house in Chantabun, even (but not so much) the fellow who stole all my money one night in Bangkok, but brushed and folded my clothes neatly for me to dress in the morning, before vanishing into the depths of Siam."[12]

Conrad later discovered that the former captain of the *Otago*, John Snadden, had sold the ship's supply of quinine and had replaced it with worthless powder. And he had spent most of his time during the last voyage locked in his cabin, playing the violin. The German chief mate, Charles Born, had taken the ship to Bangkok (instead of to Singapore, where there were many qualified masters) and had expected, from the lack of suitable candidates, to be put in temporary command. Conrad's arrival ruined his plans and aroused his resentment.

The *Otago* finally left, with a cargo of teakwood and seven sick crew (only the captain and the cook were healthy), on February 9, 1888. With no strong winds to carry her south, she took twenty-one days to sail back to Singapore. Most of the crew were hospitalized there with fever and six new seamen signed on. The ship passed between Java and Sumatra and on May 7 reached Sydney, where Conrad had previously sailed on the *Duke of Sutherland* and the *Loch Etive*.

On August 7, after several voyages between Sydney and Melbourne, the *Otago* sailed to Mauritius with a cargo of fertilizer, soap and tallow. In a late essay, Conrad explained that he was inspired by the adventurous explorers of the Pacific and decided to take the faster but longer and more dangerous route, between New Guinea and the northern tip of Australia. He may also have been prompted by the desire to test himself in his first command. "Almost without reflection," he recalled, "I sat down and wrote a letter to my owners [in Adelaide] suggesting that, instead of the usual southern route, I should take the ship to Mauritius by way of the Torres Strait." When the owners unexpectedly agreed, Conrad "insisted on leaving Sydney during a heavy southeast gale. Both the pilot and the tug-master were scandalised by my obstinacy, and they hastened to leave me to my own devices while still inside Sydney Heads. The fierce southeaster caught me up on its wings, and no later than the ninth day I was outside the entrance of Torres Strait." Passing through the Strait, he saw two vessels that had been wrecked on the reefs, but brought his own ship through safely.

Mauritius, a tropical island in the Indian Ocean, east of Madagascar, is rich in sugar cane, surrounded by coral reefs and crossed with volcanic ranges. Originally settled by the French in 1721, it was taken by the British, during the Napoleonic wars, in 1810. Conrad arrived in Port Louis on September 30 and, while waiting for jute sacks (which had been destroyed in a fire and which he needed to hold his cargo of sugar and potatoes), remained in the English colony for two months. With his cultured background, distinguished manners and elegant appearance, Conrad felt entirely at ease in the Catholic, French-speaking society on the island. It was the only port, apart from Marseilles in the mid-1870s, where he had a pleasant social life, and the only place (if we discount his fanciful connection with Doña Rita) where he showed any interest in women.

The description of the thirty-one-year-old Conrad in Mauritius by Paul Langlois, his local charterer, is the earliest account (apart from Tadeusz's) of the young mariner, who was known as "the Russian count." However irritating and ironic this title may have been, it was a considerable improvement on the familiar and perhaps condescending "Polish Joe."

> He had vigorous, extremely mobile features which would change very quickly from gentleness to an excitability bordering on anger; large black eyes which were as a rule melancholy and dreamy, and gentle, too, except in his quite frequent moments of irritation; a determined chin, a well-shaped handsome mouth, and a thick, well trimmed dark-brown moustache. . . .
>
> In contrast to his colleagues Captain Korzeniowski was always dressed like a dandy. I can still see him (and just because of this contrast with the

other sailors my memory is precise) arriving almost every day in my office dressed in a black or dark coat, a waistcoat, usually of a light colour, and "fancy" trousers, all well cut and of great elegance; he would be wearing a black or grey bowler tilted slightly to one side, would always wear gloves and carried a cane with a gold knob. . . .

As to his character, he had a perfect education, and a varied and interesting fund of conversation when he was in the mood—which was not always. He who was to become famous under the name of Joseph Conrad was often enough very taciturn and irritable. On such days he would have a nervous tic in the shoulder and eyes: anything unexpected, something falling on the floor or the slam of a door, would make him jump. He was what one would call a "neurasthenic"; in those days one spoke of "nerves."[13]

To Langlois, Conrad was very different from, and therefore more welcome than, the unpolished, hard-drinking officers of the merchant marine. His dress had improved and was now elegant, rather than awkward, as it had been in Cardiff in 1885. His incomplete high school education, augmented by his studious reading, appeared "perfect." And his extreme (almost shell-shocked) nervousness, a lifelong characteristic, seemed a dangerous liability for a master who frequently had to deal with sudden emergencies.

In "A Smile of Fortune," Conrad was retrospectively critical of Mauritian society, which had unintentionally wounded his feelings and which may have aroused mournful emotions by reminding him, in its essential traits, of the *szlachta* families of the Ukraine: "the old French families [are] descendants of the old colonists; all noble, all impoverished, and living a narrow domestic life in dull, dignified decay. The men, as a rule, occupy inferior posts in Government offices or in business houses. The girls are almost always pretty, ignorant of the world, kind and agreeable and generally bilingual; they prattle innocently both in French and English. The emptiness of their existence passes belief."

In a sudden access of passion, Conrad courted two young ladies on the island. The first was the sulky Alice Shaw, the seventeen-year-old daughter of a shipping agent, who cultivated a famous rose garden. "I cared for the girl in a particular way," Conrad wrote in his Mauritius story, "seduced by the moody expression of her face, by her obstinate silences, her rare, scornful words."[14] In the story, as in reality, Alice's father forced a cargo of potatoes on the unwilling captain, who made a huge profit on it when he arrived in Melbourne to find that a potato famine had suddenly increased its value.

His second, more serious and livelier lady friend was the twenty-six-year-old Eugénie Renouf, the daughter of an officer in the French merchant service. Conrad would invite the Renouf family for tea and show them around the *Otago*, take them for an open-carriage ride to an elegant café in the country or visit their home, carrying his gold-topped cane and charming them in perfectly spoken French with accounts of his exciting adventures at sea. Eugénie would amuse herself and flirt with Conrad by asking him to respond to the questions in her "Album of Confessions." Though the questions (like the conversations) were in French, Conrad answered flippantly, evasively and more formally in English: "Que préférez vous, les brunes ou les blondes?" *"Both."* A few of his answers, however, were quite revealing:

> Quel est le principal trait de votre caractère?
> *Laziness.* . . .
> Quelle est la qualité que vous préférez chez la femme?
> *Beauty.* . . .
> Quel est le don de la nature dont vous voudriez être doué?
> *Self-confidence.* . . .
> Que détestez-vous le plus?
> *False pretences.*

Toward the end of November, in a moment of self-confidence, the young captain, having made his way up the nautical ladder and impressed the provincial family with his odd mixture of charm and courage, proposed marriage to Eugénie—and discovered that she had flirted with him under false pretences. He looked and felt like a complete fool for believing he had won her heart when she was, in fact, engaged to a local pharmacist whom she married two months later, in January 1889. The humiliated suitor, unwilling to pay a farewell visit, wrote her father, with wounded pride, that he would never return to Mauritius. In "A Smile of Fortune" he explained: "The Pearl of the Ocean had in a few short hours grown odious to me. And I did not want to meet any one. My reputation had suffered. I knew I was the object of unkind and sarcastic comments."[15]

Having finally secured the jute sacks, Conrad left Port Louis on November 22 and arrived in Melbourne on January 5, 1889. For the next three months he carried cargoes of wheat between Melbourne and Port Adelaide. And on March 26 he resigned his command of the *Otago*—as suddenly and as inexplicably as he had left the *Vidar*. The owners of the Black Diamond Line, like Captain Craig, gave him a strong recommendation: "we entertain a high opinion of your ability in the capacity you now vacate, of your attainments generally, and should be glad to learn of your future success."

The ostensible reason for resigning was that he wanted to sail in the China Seas instead of returning, as the owners wished, to Mauritius. But he probably thought, after his experience on the *Otago*, that he could gain command of a larger and more important ship. Finally, he wanted to return to Europe, after more than two years in the East, and to see Uncle Tadeusz, whose health was beginning to fail: "You didn't tell me in your letters," Tadeusz wrote, "how long you think you will stay in Australian waters, but this nevertheless is of great interest to me. I do not wish to influence you either to prolong or to shorten your stay, if you are satisfied with it, but for an old man [he was fifty-nine] who has not long to live, time is a matter of some interest as it is also to know that he may possibly see again those who are dear to him—in this particular case: you!"[16] Conrad left Adelaide on the German steamer *Nürnberg*, passed through the Suez Canal as he had when returning from his fiery voyage on the *Palestine* in 1883, reached Southampton on May 14, and rented a modest and more centrally located room in Bessborough Gardens, Pimlico, where Vauxhall Bridge Road meets the Thames.

III

In the summer of 1889 Conrad began the crucial transition from sailor to writer by starting his first novel, *Almayer's Folly*, based on his brief acquaintance with the seedy Eurasian trader in Borneo. In *A Personal Record*, he states that he began the book in idleness as a holiday task; that he had until then written nothing but a few letters, had never kept a notebook or diary, had never planned to become an author: "the conception of a planned book was entirely outside my mental range when I sat down to write." Though he claimed "the necessity which impelled me was a hidden, obscure necessity, a completely masked and unaccountable phenomenon," his motives were not quite so murky. He had written patriotic plays as a boy and had entered a competition with "The Black Mate." And the powerful example of his father certainly inspired his creative impulse. He had spent his lonely childhood watching Apollo pour out his poems, plays, tracts and translations; and he was a great reader in the literature of three nations. In a subtle tribute to his background, he named Berau, in the novel, Sambir—a variant of

Sambor, the town in Galicia where his old tutor, Adam Pulman, had practiced medicine.

The decision to write a novel, if not to become a writer, raises two important questions. First, why did he begin with the subject of *Almayer's Folly*? Conrad knew some Malay, had closely observed the riverine Dyaks and Arabs, and found them culturally accessible. He wanted to follow the popular success of Kipling's works on India and Stevenson's on the South Seas, and to carve out a territory—an unknown river on the east coast of Borneo—that had not been used in fiction. He was strongly attracted to the theme of the degeneration of the white man in the tropics, and found it safer, for social and political reasons, to write about the Dutch rather than the English imperialists.

Second, why did Conrad write in English? He came from a mixed ethnic society in the Ukraine, which had a considerable tradition of multilingual authors writing in several languages. When asked by a Pole, ten years later, why he did not write in Polish, Conrad evaded the issue with an insincere deprecation of himself as well as of the English literary tradition: "Sir, I value our beautiful literature too highly to introduce into it my inept fumbling. But for the English my abilities are sufficient and secure my daily bread." Though he took Flaubert and Maupassant as his literary models, his written French was far from perfect.[17]

Conrad had been thinking in English for eleven years, had lived his Eastern experience in English and did not hesitate about which language to use in his nautical novels. As Thomas Mann noted, English is "the classical tongue of the sea-faring man." More unusual than his choice of language was the fact that Conrad, as an adult, had learned literary English from reading Shakespeare and Byron at the same time that he had learned colloquial English from the fishermen and sailors of Lowestoft. He later said that when he "came to England, he did not know anything of the language, and it was in a little inn at Lowestoft, frequented by sailors, at which he stayed between his voyages, that he puzzled out in the articles of the *Standard*—the only English literature to be found there—his first lessons in English."

At that time, his choice of an alien language was unique. Later, Vladimir Nabokov, Arthur Koestler, Isak Dinesen as well as Samuel Beckett and Eugène Ionesco also achieved distinction while writing in a foreign tongue. Conrad clarified this issue in 1918 by telling Hugh Walpole: "When I wrote the first words of *Almayer's Folly*, I had been already for years and years *thinking* in English. I began to think in English long before I mastered, I won't say the style (I haven't done that yet), but the mere uttered speech. . . . You may take it from me that if I had not known English I wouldn't have written a line for print, in my life."[18] Conrad's choice of English showed his commitment to England.

CHAPTER SEVEN

Into the Congo

1890

I

During the seventeen long months on land between leaving the *Otago* in Adelaide and boarding the *Roi des Belges* in Kinshasa (March 1889–August 1890), Conrad had ample time to reflect on the unsuccessful course of his maritime service. The "Polish nobleman, cased in British tar" had, by extraordinary effort, worked his way up from ordinary seaman to captain. But his career was stagnant and he found it extremely hard to get a job. It was difficult to have the right connections and the right luck, to be on the scene when the appropriate ship was available, to have the necessary qualifications and to make the right impression.

The struggle to find a berth was often followed by bad experiences on board. The *Tremolino* had been wrecked near Marseilles; he had been excluded, for political reasons, from service on French ships; had quarreled with the master of the *Mavis* and lost his deposit; had been exploited by the mad captain of the *Europa*. He had not completed the round-trip voyages on the *Palestine* or on the *Riversdale*. He had a series of disasters—including an explosion and fire—on the former; and had been dismissed with a bad recommendation by the drunken master of the latter. He had been injured by a flying spar on the *Highland Forest*; had resigned from the *Vidar* and from the *Otago*. Conrad had commanded an ocean-going vessel in Eastern waters. But now, under adverse conditions, he had to seek humble employment as captain of a decrepit, fifteen-ton, fresh-water steamer—which he called "a sluggish beetle"—on an uncharted and perilous river in the middle of Africa.

In boyhood Conrad's favorite subject was geography. He was thrilled by poring over maps and reading about the African expeditions of

Mungo Park on the Niger, James Bruce in Abyssinia, Richard Burton and John Speke in Central Africa. At ten years old, he had looked at a map of Africa, put his finger on the blank space that represented "the unsolved mystery of that continent" and vowed to himself "with absolute assurance and an amazing audacity . . . When I grow up I shall go *there*."

The enormous publicity generated by the more recent adventures of the British explorer and journalist, Henry Morton Stanley, continued to stimulate Conrad's interest in the heart of darkness. In 1871 Stanley had found Dr. Livingstone in the center of the continent. Five years later, he penetrated Africa from the east coast and traced the course of the Congo River. In 1889 he found and brought back the German Emin Pasha, governor of the Equatoria province of the southern Sudan, who had been isolated by the Mahdi Revolt in 1882. During 1879–84 Stanley had worked for the Belgian King Leopold II as an explorer and administrator, and had bolstered the king's prestige with his propagandistic report, *The Congo and the Founding of its Free State: A Story of Work and Exploration* (1885), which had been translated into seventeen languages.

Conrad said that in *Heart of Darkness* "experience [is] pushed a little (and only very little) beyond the actual facts of the case." In that novella, the autobiographical hero, Charlie Marlow, describes his search for a job after coming back from the Orient: "I had . . . just returned to London after a lot of Indian Ocean, Pacific, China Seas—a regular dose of the East—six years or so, and I was loafing about, hindering you fellows in your work and invading your homes, just as though I had got a heavenly mission to civilise you. It was very fine for a time, but after a bit I did get tired of resting. Then I began to look for a ship—I should think the hardest work on earth. But the ships wouldn't even look at me. And I got tired of that game, too."[1]

Adolf Krieger's firm, Barr Moering, put Conrad in touch with ship brokers in Ghent. They recommended him, as a man with excellent testimonials, a superior education and the manners of a perfect gentleman, to Albert Thys, the powerful director of the Société Belge pour le Commerce du Haut-Congo. In November 1889 Thys, who gave Conrad the impression of "pale plumpness in a frock coat," interviewed him in Brussels, tested his French (an important qualification for this position) and held out vague possibilities for the future. The following month, having been invited by Tadeusz to visit his estate in the Ukraine, Conrad asked Thys whether he had sufficient time to make this long and expensive journey, before being summoned to the Congo.

Since Thys was in no great hurry for his services, Conrad went ahead with his plans for a trip to Poland. Though he had obtained British citizenship in August 1886 and been released as a Russian subject—after a tedious struggle with the Ministry of Home Affairs—in March 1889, he still needed a visa. This involved many visits to the Russian Embassy in Belgrave Square (the basis of Verloc's visits to Mr. Vladimir in *The Secret Agent*) before he could safely return to Poland, after an absence of sixteen years.

Meanwhile, in order to help Conrad secure a post with the Belgian authorities, Tadeusz put him in touch with a distant relative, Alexander Poradowski (his maternal grandmother's first cousin), who lived in Brussels with his influential French-born wife, Marguerite. Alexander, who had been an officer in the Russian army, had commanded a Polish company in the disastrous rising of 1863. He was taken prisoner and condemned to death, but escaped with the aid of a fellow Russian officer. After living for a few years in Lvov, he spent the rest of his life in exile. In Brussels, he had founded a charitable organization to assist Polish refugees.

His wife Marguerite (*née* Gachet), nine years older than Conrad, was the daughter of a medieval scholar who worked in the Royal Archives of Belgium. Her uncle Paul Gachet—a country doctor, friend of Cézanne and Pissarro, and amateur painter—agreed to look after Van Gogh in May 1890. A faithful and sympathetic friend, Gachet admired and collected Van Gogh's work. Van Gogh's portrait of the tilted and tormented doctor, whom he described as "a very nervous man himself and very queer in his behaviour," revealed the "heart-broken expression of our times." When Van Gogh shot himself in July 1890, Gachet had to break the news of his death to his family. A year later, when Conrad saw the disturbing paintings by Van Gogh owned by Gachet, he compared Gachet's flat to a famous lunatic asylum near Paris and declared: "It had a nightmarish atmosphere, with its paintings of the Charenton school."[2]

Marguerite was a witty, intelligent, cultured, sophisticated and sympathetic woman. She was connected to Conrad's family and to his past, had lived with her husband in Galicia and knew the torments of exile. Most important, perhaps, for Conrad as an aspiring writer, she had published two novels about Galician life, *Yaga* (1888) and *Demoiselle Micia* (1889)—both of which had been serialized in the prestigious *Revue des Deux Mondes*. Marguerite looked astonishingly like Alexander's niece by marriage, Aniela Zagorska, with whose family Conrad remained close until the end of his life. Jessie Conrad later said that Marguerite "was, I think, the most beautiful woman I had ever seen."[3]

On January 16, 1890, in a letter addressing Alexander as "My Dear

Uncle," Conrad recalled his great kindness during Conrad's boyhood in Cracow and suggested a visit to Brussels on the way to the Ukraine. Alexander welcomed him, but replied that he was seriously ill and about to have an operation. Delayed by the Russian authorities, Conrad did not reach Brussels until February 5, two days before Alexander died. Conrad and Marguerite were undoubtedly drawn together by this tragic event. During the next five years his "Aunt" (as he fondly called her) became his closest correspondent, confidante and friend.

In *Heart of Darkness*, Marlow describes how, after appealing in vain to his male friends for help in securing a berth, he desperately sought the assistance of a female relative:

> The men said "My dear fellow," and did nothing. Then—would you believe it?—I tried the women. I, Charlie Marlow, set the women to work— to get a job. Heavens! Well, you see, the notion drove me. I had an aunt, a dear enthusiastic soul. She wrote: "It will be delightful. I am ready to do anything, anything for you. It is a glorious idea. I know the wife of a very high personage in the Administration, and also a man who has lots of influence with," etc., etc. She was determined to make no end of fuss to get me appointed skipper of a river steamboat.

Conrad was deeply grateful for Marguerite's help and for her love; she became his emotional lifeline when he was in Africa—and afterward. "You have endowed my life with new interest, new affection; I am very grateful to you for this," he told her. "I know that there is in the world someone who takes an interest in me, whose heart is open to me, who makes me happy."[4] Conrad's visit to Marguerite on the way back from the Congo, the basis of Marlow's visit to Kurtz's Intended, suggests that he was considering Marguerite as his own Intended bride as early as January 1891.

After a few days in Brussels, Conrad traveled via Berlin to Warsaw and to Lublin, where he visited friends and family. He then took a train southeast to Koziatin, near Berdichev, waited a few hours, changed to a slower goods and passenger train, and reached Oratow, the closest station—twenty-eight miles away—to Tadeusz's country estate at Kazimierowka. Tadeusz's servant—wearing a sheepskin cap, short coat bound with a leather belt and high boots—was surprised that the "foreign" visitor spoke Polish. He gave Conrad an enormous bearskin overcoat to keep him warm during the eight-hour drive and bundled him into the traveling carriage with sleigh-runners, drawn by four big bays. During the cold but pleasant ride, Conrad studied the familiar countryside, "a kindly, bread-giving land of low, rounded ridges, all white now, with black patches of timber nestling in the hollows." On February 16, deeply moved by Conrad's appearance, Tadeusz embraced him and welcomed him into the great stone-paved hall, warmed by a huge stove of white tiles. "You won't have many hours to yourself while you are staying with me," Tadeusz warned, in a moment of affectionate elation. "I shall always be coming in for a chat."

Two contemporaries recorded their impressions of Conrad's visit to the remote province in the early months of 1890. A lady in Novofastov, where Conrad had stayed with his sickly mother in 1863, was fascinated by the stories of the adventurer, who had come from Australia and was bound for the Congo: "Those were unforgettable days—gathered round a blazing fire we spent long hours listening to Conrad who was talking about his voyages and impressions; he talked in Polish but occasionally lacking a word, he would replace it with an English or French expression." A male acquaintance was more critical of Conrad's coldness and indifference, which may have masked his uneasy feelings about returning to his homeland: "All the gentlemen were obviously ready to make friends with Conrad but his manner cast a chill. He answered all questions with a strained politeness, he spoke with concentration and listened carefully but one could not fail to notice his extreme boredom. . . . He spoke with a hint of a foreign accent and occasional bursts of our characteristic borderland intonation."[5]

II

Conrad left the Ukraine, after a two-month visit, on April 18. Eleven days later he reached Brussels and found that a chance event (as well as Marguerite's efforts on his behalf) required his immediate presence in the Congo. A Danish captain Johannes Freiesleben had, during a trivial quarrel, been murdered by Africans, and Conrad was hired to replace him—as he had been hired in Bangkok to replace the dead master of the *Otago*. In July 1891, the *Official Bulletin* of the Congo reported Freiesleben's death and promised harsh retaliation: "The only really troubled situation was in the region of Tchumbiri, at Bolobo [north of Kinshasa]. In the face of the persistent ill-will and acts of aggression culminating in the assassination of the captain of one of the steamers of the Société du Haut-Congo, over a year ago, it has been necessary to make an example. The security of the white man demands that outrages of this kind be vigorously repressed."

Conrad described his frantic rush back and forth across the Channel in an effort to gather his equipment and say goodbye to his friends before leaving for Africa on May 10:

> If you only knew the devilish haste I had to make! From London to Brussels, and back again to London! And then again I dashed full tilt to Brussels! If you had only seen all the tin boxes and revolvers, the high boots and the tender farewells; just another handshake and just another pair of trousers!—and if you knew all the bottles of medicine and all the affectionate wishes I took away with me, you would understand in what a typhoon, cyclone, hurricane, earthquake—no!—in what a universal cataclysm, in what a fantastic atmosphere of mixed shopping, business, and affecting scenes, I passed two whole weeks.[6]

Conrad signed a three-year contract—his longest commitment to any job—and took the manuscript of *Almayer's Folly* with him to the Congo, but conditions there were not conducive to literary composition.

From 1865 until 1908 the Congo was not a possession of the state of Belgium, but the private property of King Leopold II. Eager for work and inexperienced in Africa, Conrad at first believed the high-minded progaganda about bringing the benevolent light of civilization to the dark continent. Only after he had reached the Congo and seen the brutal exploitation of the resources and the people did he realize it was "the vilest scramble for loot that ever disfigured the history of human conscience and geographical exploration." *The Inheritors* (1901), a novel Conrad wrote with Ford Madox Hueffer (who later changed his surname, and is best known as Ford Madox Ford), satirized Leopold II as the greedy and unscrupulous Duc de Mersch. Referring to Leopold's diplomatic success in acquiring the Congo and to the railroad that was being built from Matadi to Kinshasa when Conrad was there, they wrote:

> [He] was by way of being a philanthropist on megalomaniac lines. For some international reason he had been allowed to possess himself of the pleasant land of Greenland [the Congo]. There was gold in it and train-oil in it and other things that paid. . . . No one of the great powers would let any other of the great powers possess the country, so it had been handed over to the Duc de Mersch. . . .
>
> [He] wanted money, and he wanted to run a railway across Greenland. . . . [So he started a newspaper whose purpose] was to extol the Duc de Mersch's moral purpose; to pat the Government's back; influence public opinion; and generally advance the cause of the System for the Regeneration of the Arctic [African] Regions.[7]

On May 10 Conrad left Bordeaux on the *Ville de Maceio* (named for a town on the coast of Brazil). It went first to Tenerife in the Canary Islands and then traveled south along the west coast of Africa, stopping at Dakar in (what is now) Senegal; Conakry, Guinea; Freetown, Sierra Leone; Grand Bassam, Ivory Coast; Cotonou, Benin; Libreville, Gabon; Loango, French Congo; in Banana, at the mouth of the Congo River, and in Boma, since 1886 the seat of the government of the Congo. After talking to some old Africa hands on the ship, Conrad sent a letter from Freetown, filled with statistics that revealed the alarming rate of casualties: "What makes me rather uneasy is the information that 60 per cent. of our Company's employees return to Europe before they have completed even six months' service. Fever and dysentery! There are others who are sent home in a hurry at the end of a year, so that they shouldn't die in the Congo. . . . In a word, there are only 7 per cent. who can do their three years' service."[8] The "incomprehensible" French man-of-war that Conrad saw anchored off the coast and firing tiny projectiles into the continent, actually marked the beginning of the campaign against the powerful African kingdom of Dahomey, which was conquered by the French in 1893.

After a month's voyage, Conrad reached Boma on June 12. The next day he steamed up to Matadi, the farthest navigable point of the Lower Congo, and met the extraordinary Roger Casement, the only man in Africa he was to like and respect. Casement was born in Dublin in 1864. Like Conrad's, his parents died when he was a child; he was brought up by an uncle in northern Ireland, and educated at Ballymena Academy. He became a clerk in a Liverpool trading company when he was eighteen; two years later, in 1884, he sailed for Africa and served King Leopold's Congo Free State as a hunter, explorer, surveyor and administrator. He returned to England after five years of service, but was sent out again the following year to arrange transport for the Belgian authorities on the Lower Congo. In his diary of June 13, Conrad recorded with considerable enthusiasm his meeting with the cultured and experienced Casement: "Made the acquaintance of Mr. Roger Casement, which I should consider as a great pleasure under any circumstances and now it becomes a positive piece of luck. Thinks, speaks well, most intelligent and very sympathetic."

Casement was a tall, extremely handsome man, with fine bearing, a muscle and bone thinness, wrinkled forehead, face deeply tanned from long tropical service, thick, curly black hair, full and long pointed beard, and brilliant blue eyes. He was idealistic and unselfish, and had con-

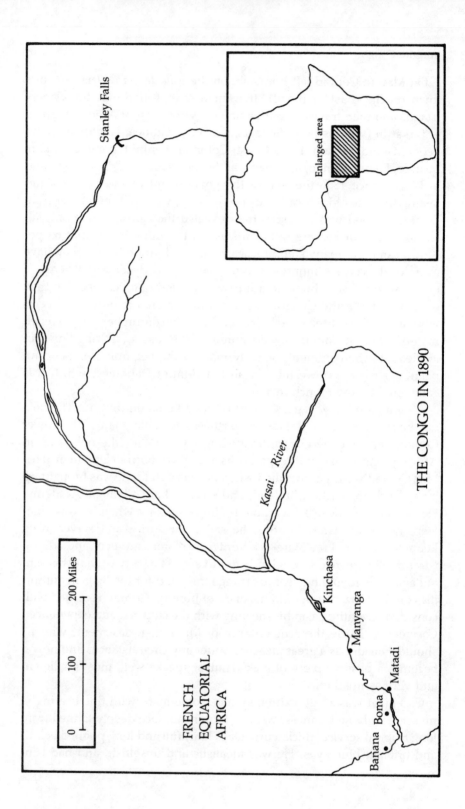

Stanley Falls

Enlarged area

FRENCH
EQUATORIAL
AFRICA

Kasai River

Kinchasa

Manyanga

Matadi

Boma

Banana

0   100   200 Miles

THE CONGO IN 1890

siderable charm, but was also high-strung and unstable, subject to periods of intense melancholy and self-pity. He appears in *The Inheritors* as the physically impressive Soane, the son of an Irish peer, who opposes the Duc de Mersch: "He had magnificent features—a little blurred nowadays—and a remainder of the grand manner. His nose was a marvel of classic workmanship, but the floods of time had reddened and speckled it—not offensively but ironically; his hair was turning gray, his eyes were bloodshot, his heavy moustache rather ragged. He inspired one with the respect that one feels for a man who has lived and does not care a curse. He had a weird intermittent genius."[9]

Conrad shared a room with Casement, who was considered a rather enigmatic personality, for two weeks and soon became very friendly with him. "He knew the coast languages well," Conrad told the Irish-American patron of the arts, John Quinn. "I went with him several times on short expeditions to hold 'palavers' with neighbouring village-chiefs. The object of them was procuring porters for the company's caravans from Matadi to . . . Kinchassa." Writing in 1903 to his swashbuckling anti-imperialist friend, Cunninghame Graham, Conrad described Casement's careless courage and his habit of traveling unarmed and unattended through the dangerous jungle:

> He's a Protestant Irishman, pious too. But so was Pizarro. For the rest I can assure you that he is a limpid personality. There is a touch of the Conquistador in him too; for I've seen him start off into an unspeakable wilderness swinging a crookhandled stick for all weapons, with two bulldogs: Paddy (white) and Biddy (brindle) at his heels and a Loanda [i.e., Luanda] boy carrying a bundle for all company. A few months afterwards it so happened that I saw him come out again, a little leaner, a little browner, with his stick, dogs, and Loanda boy, and quietly serene as though he had been for a stroll in a park. . . . He could tell you things! Things I've tried to forget; things I never did know. He has had as many years of Africa as I had months—almost.

Conrad's amazed account of Casement's serene stroll through the unspeakable wilderness suggests that he may have been the model for the elusive and inexplicable Russian in motley in *Heart of Darkness*. On June 28 Conrad trekked up-river to take command of his "tin-pot steamboat" and "parted with Casement in a very friendly manner."[10] They did not meet again until 1896, at a dinner of the Johnson Society in London, which had been founded by Conrad's publisher Fisher Unwin. But Casement had a profound impact on Conrad's attitude toward the Congo and on his fictional portrayal of his grim experience in Africa.

In 1895 Casement joined the British Consular Service, and held positions in Mozambique, Angola and Capetown. Five years later Casement was appointed Consul at Boma. In 1903 his investigation of the treatment of the rubber workers in the Upper Congo brought him worldwide fame. Casement's long, factual, excruciating report documented the atrocities committed upon what he called "the poor, the naked, the fugitive, the hunted, the tortured, the dying men and women of the Congo."

Casement reported that Africans, bound with thongs that contracted in the rain and cut to the bone, had their swollen hands beaten with rifle butts until they fell off. Chained slaves were forced to drink the white man's defecations, hands and feet were chopped off for their rings, men were lined up behind each other and shot with one cartridge, wounded prisoners were eaten by maggots till they died and were then thrown to starving pye-dogs or devoured by cannibal tribes. One girl carried the bones of her parents clinking in a ragged canvas sack, and testified that starving people ate peeling whitewash torn from old buildings and then vomited up a green bile filled with leeches. Another boy described to Casement how during a raid on his village he was wounded and "fell down, presumably insensible, but came to his senses while his hand was being hacked off at the wrist. I asked him how it was he could possibly lie silent and give no sign. He answered that he felt the cutting, but was afraid to move, knowing that he would be killed, if he showed any sign of life."[11]

Though he had official sanction from the king's government in Brussels, Casement suffered daily obstructions by the officials of the Free State whose very existence was threatened by his inquiries. His detailed record of the atrocities achieved great force through its moderate tone and objective style, which expressed Casement's passionate commitment to the oppressed. In 1908, after the creation of the Congo Reform Association, Casement finally triumphed. World opinion, stirred by his revelations, forced King Leopold to surrender his personal ownership of the Congo, which became a colony of Belgium. A grateful nation paid the King fifty million francs; Casement was rewarded by the British government and made a Commander of the Order of St. Michael and St. George.

Casement's investigation, which helped to extinguish the cruel and exploitative colonialism in the Congo, stands as one of the great humanitarian achievements of this century. Like Conrad, who shared his feeling of moral outrage, Casement was one of the first men to question the Western notion of progress, a dominant idea in Europe from the

Renaissance to the Great War, to attack the hypocritical justification of colonialism and to reveal in documentary form the savage degradation of the white man in Africa.

Casement's "Congo Diary" substantiated the accuracy of the conditions described in *Heart of Darkness*: the chain gangs, the grove of death, the payment in brass rods, the cannibalism and the human skulls on the fence posts. Casement confirms that Conrad did not exaggerate or invent the horrors that provided the political and humanitarian basis for his attack on colonialism.

In Coquilhatville, half-way between Kinshasa and Stanley Falls, Casement reported that "two men were chained together and made to carry heavy loads of bricks and water, and were frequently beaten by the soldiers in charge of them," and that many Africans, including chiefs, died in their chains. In a grove of death similar to Conrad's, Casement "found seventeen sleeping sickness patients, male and female, lying about in the utmost dirt. Most of them were lying on the bare ground— several out in the pathway in front of the houses, and one, a woman, had fallen into the fire. . . . All the seventeen people I saw were near their end."

In *Heart of Darkness*, Marlow's starving cannibalistic crew are paid in brass rods instead of money or even food. Casement wrote that "in most parts of the Upper Congo the recognized currency consists of lengths varying according to the district. At one period the recognised length of a brass rod was 18 inches, but today the average length of a rod cannot be more than 8 or 9 inches. . . . Such as it is, clumsy and dirty, this is the principal form of currency known on the Upper Congo."

Though the cannibals on Marlow's ship have their rations of rotten hippo meat thrown overboard, they show a surprising and unexpected restraint. But during the Belgian pacification of the Congo in the 1880s and 1890s—which was not subject to moral, legal or political control— troops from more impulsive cannibal tribes fought on both sides, and the captured prisoners as well as the enemy dead were carved and eaten on the spot. As late as 1903 Casement authenticated incidents of mercenary soldiers who "took a woman and cut her throat, and divided her and ate her." Just as Marlow is horrified to see human skulls decorating a European's fence, so a shocked Casement "saw lying about in the grass surrounding the [state rubber] post, which is built on the site of several large towns, human bones, skulls and in some cases complete skeletons."[12]

While noting that "the trade in ivory today has entirely passed from the hands of the natives of the Upper Congo," Casement reported on

the fanatical and unscrupulous Europeans who could have been prototypes of Kurtz: "The praiseworthy official would be he whose district
yielded the best and biggest supply of the commodity; and, succeeding
in this, the means whereby he brought about the enhanced value of that
yield would not, it may be believed, be too closely scrutinized." But it
was Casement's (as well as Conrad's) purpose to make a close scrutiny,
and Casement wrote to his friend Edmund Morel, the great Congo
reformer, that he had decided "if I got home again I should go to all
lengths to let my countrymen know what a hell upon earth our own
white race has made, and was daily making, of the homes of the black
people it was our duty to protect." In one of his last letters, Casement
questioned the value of European civilization in terms that echo one of
the most important ideas in *Heart of Darkness*. He juxtaposed the brutal
colonists with their "savage" victims just as Conrad contrasted the restrained cannibals and the predatory white "pilgrims": Africa "has been
'opened up' (as if it were an oyster) and the Civilizers are now busy
developing it with blood and slaying each other, and burning with hatred against me because I think their work is organized murder, far
worse than anything the savages did before them."[13]

III

The conversations with Casement at Matadi fortified Conrad's well-
founded doubts about the Congo. And his first impressions of the country foreshadowed his difficulties with the Belgian colonists. On June 13,
the day after he arrived in the country, he noted: "Feel considerably in
doubt about the future. Think just now that my life amongst the people
(white) around here cannot be very comfortable. Intend avoid acquaintances as much as possible." Eleven days later, when he had been engaged in the "idiotic" and humiliating task of packing ivory in casks, he
observed that the chief social activity among the hundred Europeans of
the trading station was backbiting.

In 1888, two years before Conrad arrived, Albert Thys himself had
gloomily declared: "On arriving at Matadi one seems to have reached an
accursed land, set there as a barrier by Nature herself, to impede all
progress."[14] Because of the violent cataracts, the stretch of river between
Matadi and Kinshasa was not navigable. Since the railway had not yet
been completed, Conrad had to cover this strenuous 230-mile passage
on foot.

He left Matadi on June 28, rested in Manyanga (the half-way point) from July 8 to 25, and reached Kinshasa on August 2. His "Congo Diary" covered this period and was, thus far, his most extensive piece of writing in English. Conrad recorded hot, gloomy days and cold, sleepless nights; long, steep climbs up chilly ravines; stabbing mosquitoes, foul drinking water and menacing drums beating in the dark. On the way up-river he passed a skeleton tied up to a post, a putrefying corpse, "another dead body lying by the path in an attitude of meditative repose." He had to nurse his feverish companion, Prosper Harou, who had sailed with him from Bordeaux and seemed destined to join the others in the stations of the dead. As they approached Kinshasa on August 1, Conrad recorded: "Harou not very well. Mosquitoes. Frogs. Beastly. Glad to see the end of this stupid tramp. Feel rather seedy." Conrad alludes to Harou when Marlow says, with his habitual understated irony: "I had a white companion, too, not a bad chap, but rather too fleshy and with the exasperating habit of fainting on the hot hillsides, miles away from the least bit of shade and water. . . . Then he got a fever, and had to be carried in a hammock slung under a pole. As he weighed sixteen stone [224 pounds] I had no end of rows with the carriers."[15]

When he reached Kinshasa, after this exhausting eighteen days' march, Conrad had a contentious encounter with Camille Delcommune, the Société Belge's manager and his immediate superior. He was two years younger than the thirty-two-year-old Conrad and had been in the Congo since 1883. "My first interview with the manager was curious," Marlow recounts in *Heart of Darkness*. "He did not ask me to sit down after my twenty-mile walk that morning. He was commonplace in complexion, in feature, in manners, and in voice. He was of middle size and of ordinary build. His eyes, of the usual blue, were perhaps remarkably cold, and he certainly could make his glance fall on one as trenchant and heavy as an axe." Impatient and irritated, Delcommune criticized Conrad for taking so long on his journey from Matadi, and informed him that the *Florida*, which he was supposed to command, had been damaged on the treacherous river and towed to Kinshasa for extensive repairs.

Since Conrad had to learn to navigate the swift and ever-changing river (he kept a second, very detailed and technical diary for this purpose), Delcommune assigned him to the *Roi des Belges*. It was commanded by a young Dane, Ludvig Koch, and went up-river to Stanley Falls on August 4. The grandly named ship was a decrepit two-story affair, both decks lined with fragile wooden railings and covered by rectangular iron roofs, propped up by wobbly posts. The wood-burning, stern-wheel steamer carried, in addition to a Belgian mechanic, four passengers, including Delcommune. It towed two wood-filled scows and stopped at night so that trees could be chopped down for fuel. The crew of thirty Africans included a number of certified cannibals. When Conrad was still in Matadi, Tadeusz had jokingly remarked: "I feel confident that sooner or later I shall hear from you, provided that you have not been already cooked on a spit and eaten as a roast." Though Conrad's up-river trip was not as dangerous as Marlow's fictional journey into the unknown, the cannibals were a real threat. One African, "when asked if he ate human flesh, answered, 'Ah! I wish I could eat everybody on earth.' "[16]

On the up-river journey Conrad, like Casement, was able to observe the disastrous effects of Belgian rule. As Casement's friend Edmund Morel wrote in 1904: "The country is ruined. Passengers in the steamer *Roi des Belges* have been able to see for themselves that from Bontya, half a day's journey below our factory at Upoto [about 200 miles] inclusive, there is not an inhabited village left—that is to say four days' steaming through a country formerly so rich, today entirely ruined."

Conrad reached Stanley Falls, the farthest point of his penetration into Africa, nearly one thousand miles from the Atlantic, on September 1. He later mentioned his close proximity to the Arab slave-traders and recalled: "The subdued thundering mutter of the Stanley Falls hung in the heavy night air of the last navigable reach of the Upper Congo, while no more than ten miles away, in Reshid's camp just above the Falls, the yet unbroken powers of the Congo Arabs slumbered uneasily."[17]

On September 6 Delcommune ordered Conrad to take command of the *Roi des Belges* as Captain Koch had become ill. The following day the steamer, with the ailing Koch and the cannibal crew, left Stanley Falls for the faster down-river trip to Kinshasa. By September 15 Koch had recovered and taken charge of the ship again. Georges Antoine Klein, a commercial agent at Stanley Falls who was severely ill with dysentery, died on the down-river trip. Though Klein was clearly a model for Kurtz, his life did not match the sensational aspects of Kurtz's career. These were inspired by another agent, Arthur Hodister, who had been tortured as Kurtz had tortured others. On December 8, 1892, *The Times* reported that Hodister "and his comrades were seized and put to death, and their heads were stuck on poles and their bodies eaten."

When the ship reached Kinshasa on September 24, Conrad had also come down with a serious attack of malarial fever and dysentery, which caused severe vomiting and bloody diarrhea. This illness plagued him during the rest of his time in the Congo and provided the excuse for terminating his contract—like sixty percent of the employees—after spending only six months in Africa. His debilitating illness certainly influenced his poor relations with Delcommune. It also provoked a long lament to Marguerite that bore a striking resemblance to Arthur Rimbaud's complaints about his unbearable solitude and degradation in Abyssinia in 1888. Rimbaud wrote:

> I am lonely and bored. I have never known anyone as lonely and bored as I. Is it not wretched, this life I lead, without family, without friends, without any intellectual companionship or occupation, lost in the midst of these negroes, whose lot one would like to improve and who try, for their part, to exploit you? . . . Obliged to chatter their gibberish, to eat their filthy messes, to endure a thousand and one annoyances that come from their idleness, their treachery, and their stupidity. But that is not the worst. The worst thing is the fear of becoming doltish oneself, isolated as one is, and cut off from any intellectual companionship.[18]

In a similar fashion, Conrad told Marguerite that he had made a terrible mistake by coming to the Congo, that he had quarreled with Delcommune, that he had no future prospects and that his health had broken down. (His illness made everything seem even worse than it actually was.) Conrad, who had suffered as a Pole in Russia, was now blamed for being an Englishman in the Congo. He also informed Marguerite that, lacking a ship, he was doing the work of a lumberjack in the depths of the forest:

> My days here are dreary. No use deluding oneself! Decidedly I regret having come here. I even regret it bitterly. . . .
> Everything here is repellent to me. Men and things, but men above all. And I am repellent to them, also. From the manager in Africa who has taken the trouble to tell one and all that I offend him supremely, down to the lowest mechanic, they all have the gift of irritating my nerves—so that I am not as agreeable to them perhaps as I should be. The manager is a common ivory dealer with base instincts who considers himself a merchant although he is only a kind of African shop-keeper. His name is Delcommune. He detests the English, and out here I am naturally regarded as such. I cannot hope for either promotion or salary increases while he is here. Besides, he has said that promises made in Europe carry no weight here if they are not in the contract. Those made to me by M. Wauters [an important figure in the Brussels Company] are not. In addition, I cannot look forward to anything because I don't have a ship to command. The new boat will not be completed until June of next year,

perhaps. Meanwhile, my position here is unclear and I am troubled by
that. So there you are! As crowning joy, my health is far from good. . . .
In going up the river I suffered from fever four times in two months, and
then at the Falls (which is its home territory), I suffered an attack of
dysentery lasting five days. I feel somewhat weak physically and not a
little demoralized. . . .

I leave within an hour for Bamou, by canoe, to select trees and have
them felled for building operations at the station here. I shall remain
encamped in the forest for two or three weeks, unless ill. I like the prospects well enough. I can doubtless have a shot at some buffaloes or ele-
phants.

Conrad's most important letter from Africa rehearses his grievances
and his reasons for wanting to leave. His only hope was to obtain command of a Belgian ocean-going vessel. He again asked Marguerite to
help him get this job ("would you believe it?—I tried the women") and
promised to visit her when the ship returned to port in Antwerp. Conrad refers to this aborted plan, which depended on surviving the fever
of the Congo, when Marlow says of the Roman trireme commander in
ancient Britain: "perhaps he was cheered by keeping his eye on a chance
of promotion to the fleet at Ravenna [Antwerp] by and by, if he had
good friends in Rome [Brussels] and survived the awful climate."[19]

Though we do not know the precise reasons for Conrad's unfortunate
quarrel with Delcommune, it is clear that Conrad was offended by his
rudeness in Kinshasa, considered him an inferior with "base instincts"
and resented his absolute authority. Exhausted that day by his twenty-
mile walk through the bush, Conrad (who had been made to pack ivory)
may have tactlessly emphasized his social superiority, stressed his importance as a captain and failed to show sufficient respect for his chief.
He may even, after talking to Casement and seeing the Belgian depre-
dations, mentioned their hypocrisy and criticized their colonialism.
Whatever the details, Delcommune told Conrad with brutal honesty
that he had no prospects as long as he remained in the Congo. When
Conrad discovered that he would not be given command of one of the
steamers (including the newly repaired *Florida*) intended to carry the
exploring expedition of Camille's older brother Alexandre up the Lo-
mami River, near Stanley Falls, he realized his situation was intolerable,
abandoned his plans for the Congo and decided to return home.

Conrad wrote the same despondent letter to Tadeusz and to his Lublin cousins, Karol and Aniela Zagorski, as he had to Marguerite. His
uncle responded to Conrad's charges against Delcommune of "exploi-

tation," which were similar to those Conrad had made ten years earlier against the captain of the *Europa*, with his characteristic caution and his "I told you so" advice. Forgetting that death would also hurt Conrad's future career, he urged his touchy nephew to fulfill his contractual obligations:

> I see from your last letter that you feel a deep resentment towards the Belgians for exploiting you so mercilessly! In general there is no love in your heart for the Latin races, but this time, you must admit, nothing forced you to put yourself into Belgian hands. . . . If you had paid any attention to my opinion on the subject when discussing it with me, you would have certainly detected a lack of enthusiasm. . . .
>
> Let me observe that by breaking your agreement you would expose yourself to considerable financial loss, and you certainly lay yourself open to an accusation of irresponsibility which may be harmful to your future career.

That same November, as Conrad was dragging his sick body on land from Kinshasa to Matadi (he left on October 19 and arrived on December 4), his Lublin cousin wrote a paternal, indignant but ultimately futile complaint to the Société du Haut-Congo. He repeated Conrad's suggestion that he be given command of a steamer running between Antwerp and Banana, and concluded: "It is sad to think that a capable man such as Mr. Conrad Korzeniowski, who has been used to commanding steamers for fifteen years [in fact, he had commanded the *Roi des Belges* for only one week], should be reduced to this subordinate position, and should be exposed [like everyone else in the Congo] to such fatal disease."[20]

On October 23, four days after Conrad left Kinshasa, the Danish Captain Duhst recorded in his diary: "Camped in a negro town, which is called Fumemba. I am in company with an English captain Conrad from the Kinshasa Company: he is continually sick with dysentery and fever." In *A Personal Record*, confusing Kinshasa and Leopoldville (which are African and Belgian names for the same place), Conrad described the terrible illness that made him quite indifferent to the possible loss of his precious manuscript and to the considerable dangers of the river. He was nearly drowned in

> a specially awkward turn of the Congo between Kinchassa and Leopoldville—more particularly when one had to take it at night in a big canoe, with only half the proper number of paddlers. . . . I got round the turn more or less alive, though I was too sick to care whether I did or not,

and, always with *Almayer's Folly* amongst my diminishing baggage, I arrived at the delectable capital Boma, where, before the departure of the steamer which was to take me home I had the time to wish myself dead over and over again with perfect sincerity.[21]

Conrad left Boma for Belgium during the second week in December. After stopping for a few days to see Marguerite in Brussels, he reached London on February 1, 1891, and began his dismal convalescence. "When he arrived," Hope recalled, "he looked half dead with fever, so Krieger, who knew the Doctor at the German Hospital at Dalston [in northeast London], got him in there, and he and I used to go see him frequently. The Nurse said she thought he would die, but he pulled round, and in a few weeks was able to go to his rooms, Gillingham Street, near Victoria Station"[22]—his London base for the next six years.

Tadeusz noticed that Conrad's handwriting had greatly changed, and expressed concern about the weakening and exhausting effects of his fever and dysentery. And from the German Hospital, where he spent late February and most of March, Conrad mentioned rheumatism in his left leg, neuralgia in his right arm, swollen veins and legs, thinning hair, as well as disordered nerves, debilitating palpitations of the heart and painful attacks of breathlessness. From May 21 to June 14 he stayed in Champel, a suburb of Geneva, at the Hôtel de la Roseraie—a square, four-story building, set in a tree-filled park on the banks of the Arve, with shuttered windows and a balcony with a stone balustrade above the pillared entrance. Here Conrad completed his nervous cure at the Hydropathic Institute by submitting to high-pressure hosings with ice-cold water.

The malarial fever Conrad contracted in the Congo permanently damaged his health. But the psychological effects went even deeper. The long months spent in hospitals and spas allowed him to meditate on his tragic experience and think about how he might transform it into literature. Conrad saw this experience as the turning-point of his intellectual development and once told Edward Garnett: before the Congo, "I was a perfect animal." Afterward, his new insights into the nature of evil turned his innate pessimism into a tragic vision: "I see everything with such despondency—all in black."[23]

CHAPTER EIGHT

Sailor to Writer

1891–1894

I

Conrad felt he had lost a year of his life in the Congo and was desperately eager to recover his health and resume his career. But it took fourteen months to find a new berth. During that time, suffering humiliation and rejection, Conrad grew increasingly despondent. His pessimism, gloom and depression were caused not only by the human frailty, baseness and greed he had witnessed in the Congo, but also by his melancholy disposition, the effects of his illness and his inability to find work. In *The Mirror of the Sea* he ironically described searching for a berth as "an occupation as engrossing as gambling, and as little favourable to the free exchange of ideas, besides being destructive of the kindly temper needed for casual intercourse with one's fellow-creatures."

Tadeusz, upset by Conrad's melancholic letters and by his chasing after chimerical projects, tactlessly mentioned that his nephew's maritime career had not been a great success. He warned Conrad about the futility of pessimism and—in a typical homily—related his defects to the pernicious Korzeniowski strain: "you have always lacked endurance and perseverance in decisions, which is the result of your instability in your aims and desires. . . . You let your imagination run away with you—you become an optimist; but when you encounter disappointments you fall easily into pessimism—and as you have a lot of pride, you suffer more as the result of disappointments than somebody would who had a more moderate imagination but was endowed with greater endurance." As if to substantiate Tadeusz's accusation, the thin-skinned Conrad told Marguerite Poradowska: "A transaction full of promise fell through at the last moment. I ate the bread of bitterness for an entire week."[1]

He tried, through Marguerite's influence, to fulfill an ambition he had conceived in the Congo to get a job with the Prince shipping company, which operated a fleet of vessels between Antwerp and Africa. When this, and many other prospects, failed to materialize, he continued his snail's progress on *Almayer's Folly*, did some ill-paid commercial translations for a firm in London and managed the dusty waterside warehouse of Barr, Moering and Company at 95 Upper Thames Street. He compared this boring job to penal servitude—without the pleasure of having committed a crime.

Finally, on November 19, 1891, an old acquaintance, Captain W. H. Cope, offered Conrad the position of chief mate on the *Torrens*. Still in poor health, Conrad confessed his doubts about his physical fitness for the post. But when Cope said moping ashore would be futile, and was very encouraging about work on the *Torrens*, Conrad gladly accepted the job. His culture and refinement would be a distinct advantage on a ship that carried passengers. The *Torrens*, a full-rigged clipper of 1,334 tons, built in 1875, was one of the fastest and most famous ships of her time. Basil Lubbock writes in *The Colonial Clippers*: "In easting weather she would drive along as dry as a bone, making 300 miles a day without wetting her decks. . . . Her biggest run in the 24 hours was 336 miles; and her fastest speed through the water by the log was 14 knots." Conrad confirms that the *Torrens* was attractive, "known to handle easily and to be a good sea boat in heavy weather."

Between November 1891 and July 1893 Conrad made two round-trip voyages to Adelaide on the *Torrens*. On the first outbound voyage he became friendly with one of the sixty passengers, the attractive, reserved and sympathetic twenty-two-year-old W. H. Jacques, who had just come down from Cambridge and was traveling to recover his health. His terminal illness was reflected in his sallow, sunken face and in his thoughtful, introspective look. While sailing off the Cape of Good Hope, Conrad asked Jacques—the first educated Englishman he had ever met—to look at the incomplete manuscript of *Almayer's Folly*. Jacques "had the patience to read with the very shadows of Eternity gathering already in the hollows of his kind, steadfast eyes."

If the laconic, moribund Englishman had been negative and discouraging, he might well have terminated Conrad's literary career at its inception. But his positive response to the author's queries gave Conrad the courage to complete his first book:

"Well, what do you say?" I asked at last. "Is it worth finishing?" This question expressed exactly the whole of my thoughts.

"Distinctly," he answered in his sedate veiled voice, and then coughed a little.

"Were you interested?" I inquired further, almost in a whisper.

"Very much!" . . .

"Now let me ask you one more thing: Is the story quite clear to you as it stands?"

He raised his dark, gentle eyes to my face and seemed surprised.

"Yes! Perfectly."[2]

In *A Personal Record* Conrad states that Jacques "died rather suddenly in the end, either in Australia or it may be on the passage while going home through the Suez Canal." In fact, Jacques returned to England and died there of tuberculosis in 1893. On the first return voyage the *Torrens* stopped for four days on the island of Saint Helena; but it is not clear whether Conrad had time to investigate the Napoleonic history which so absorbed him toward the end of his life.

On the second return voyage from Adelaide (which Conrad had visited on the *Otago* in 1889) he formed important friendships with two young Englishmen who had been companions at Harrow and Oxford. They had gone to the South Seas in search of Robert Louis Stevenson but, unable to get a boat to Samoa, had never found him. The tall, handsome, bearded Ted Sanderson—a prototype of Lord Jim—was the son of the Headmaster of the Elstree Preparatory School in Hertfordshire. The oldest of thirteen surviving children in a lively, intellectual and socially unpretentious family, which constantly invited friends for a meal or a weekend, he would later fight against the Boers, spend ten years in East Africa and succeed his father as headmaster.

John Galsworthy, born (like Sanderson) in 1867 and ten years younger than Conrad, was the son of a prosperous solicitor. Educated at New College, Oxford, he was called to the Bar, but had no desire to practice law. He was completing his education by traveling around the world, was supposed to be studying navigation for the Admiralty Bar and faithfully worked out the daily position of the ship with the captain. "Tall, austere looking, with a Roman profile and tightly closed lips, always correctly dressed," writes William Rothenstein, "Galsworthy would not have looked out of place in Downing Street." And his manners were as severely correct as his dress. In contrast to the easy-going Sanderson, Galsworthy was rather formal and stiff.

On March 18, 1893, Sanderson and Galsworthy boarded the *Torrens* with fifteen other passengers in Adelaide, met Conrad and sailed with him for fifty-six days, until Galsworthy disembarked to visit the mines at Capetown. Confinement and intimacy aboard ship enabled their friendship, which might not have been possible in England, to ripen quickly. In a letter to his family, Galsworthy noted Conrad's strangeness and commented on the marvellous stories that always fascinated his friends: "The first mate is a Pole called Conrad and is a capital chap, though queer to look at; he is a man of travel and experience in many parts of the world, and has a fund of yarns on which I draw freely. He has been right up the Congo and all around Malacca and Borneo and other out of the way parts, to say nothing of a little smuggling in the days of his youth."[3]

In "The Doldrums" (1897), a story that appeared in his first book and that offended Conrad's wife, Jessie, Galsworthy portrayed him as the first mate Armand, emphasized the mournful Slavic qualities that made him queer to look at and attempted to convey Conrad's peculiar pronunciation of the English language:

> "Dosé fallows, you know" (he pronounced it "gnau"), said the mate in his slightly nasal, foreign accent, evidently resuming, "it's very curious you know, day [Chinamen] rraally haven't any feelings." . . .
>
> The mate looked up sharply, and with his brown, almond-shaped Slav eyes scrutinised keenly the dim figure of the speaker; and his mouth, between the close-trimmed, pointed beard and drooping moustaches, took a more than usually cynical and mournful curve. . . .
>
> His mournful eyes [were] the eyes of a man who has been to the edge of the world many times, and looking over—come back again. . . .
>
> The melancholy fatalism of his face, that outcome of his Slav blood, was veiled by a look of sorrowful concern.

Galsworthy's reminiscences of Conrad, written after his friend's death, give a vivid sense of his heavy-lidded, long-armed appearance, his nervous energy, his poor health and his duties at sea:

> Very dark he looked in the burning sunlight—tanned, with a peaked brown beard, almost black hair, and dark brown eyes, over which the lids were deeply folded. He was thin, not tall, his arms very long, his shoulders broad, his head set rather forward. . . .
>
> I never saw Conrad quite in repose. His hands, his feet, his knees, his lips—sensitive, expressive, and ironical—something was always in motion. . . .

His subordinate position [as first mate] on the *Torrens* was only due to
the fact that he was then still convalescent from the Congo experience
which had nearly killed him. . . .

All the first night he was fighting a fire in the hold. . . . He was a good
seaman, watchful of the weather, quick in handling the ship; considerate
with the apprentices.[4]

After their return to England, Conrad and Galsworthy frequently met
at the Sandersons' home and, despite differences in art and in temperament, became lifelong friends. Conrad gave Galsworthy good advice
about his early work and sent characteristically flattering appraisals of
his thin but popular novels; Galsworthy gave the hard-pressed Conrad
many generous loans and gifts, and dedicated *Jocelyn* (1898) and *In
Chancery* (1920) to Conrad, who, in turn, dedicated *Nostromo* (1904) to
him.

Conrad was successful, content and fortunate in the friends he met on
the *Torrens,* the classiest of all his ships. But the ship was laid up for a
while after the second voyage; Captain Cope left and Conrad was once
more without a berth. He therefore decided to make his second visit to
the Ukraine to see his ailing uncle Tadeusz. Though Tadeusz did not
want Conrad to damage his career by leaving the *Torrens* if he had a
chance of succeeding Cope and getting command of the ship, he also
did not want to forgo the pleasure of a last meeting: "as always, I wish
for and await your visit, my dear lad—for at my age any postponement
might mean final defeat!!" Yielding to family piety, to his uncle's wishes
and to his own inclinations, Conrad traveled to the Ukraine via Holland
and Berlin (where he nearly lost the manuscript of *Almayer's Folly* in the
Friedrichstrasse railway station), and spent about a month there during
September–October 1893. "This is a good place to be ill (if one must be
ill)," he told Marguerite. "My uncle has cared for me as if I were a little
child."[5]

II

Conrad was unable to regain his position on the *Torrens* and took thirteen months to secure a lowly berth as second mate—a position he had
held on the *Palestine* as long ago as 1881!—on a steamship that never
sailed. The *Adowa* (named after the town where the Ethiopians were
to defeat the Italians in 1896) was a 2,097-ton English-owned steamer
that had been chartered by the Franco-Canadian Transport Company

and was supposed to carry French emigrants on fortnightly sailings to Montreal and Quebec. Conrad got the job through Captain Froud of the Shipmasters' Society in Fenchurch Street, who needed an officer with fluent French.

He joined the ship in London on November 26, 1893. Four hundred and sixty bunks had been put together between decks by industrious carpenters in the Victoria Dock and "some gentlemen from Paris . . . turned up indeed and went from end to end of the ship, knocking their silk hats cruelly against the deck-beams. . . . Their faces as they went ashore wore a cheerfully inconclusive expression." Conrad crossed to Rouen on December 4 and remained on board the moored ship, first in the center and then in the outskirts of town, for six weeks. In the old part of the city, as night-watchman of the ship, he would lean his elbows on the rail, gaze at the shop windows and at the brilliant cafés, watch the audience enter and leave the opera house, and think of Flaubert's *Madame Bovary*, which was set in Rouen. In the suburbs of the city, he was gripped by inclement weather along the quay—as he had been on the *Highland Forest* in Amsterdam in 1887. Staring through the brass-rimmed porthole, he saw "a row of casks ranged on the frozen ground and the tail-end of a great cart. A red-nosed carter in a blouse and a woollen nightcap leaned against the wheel."[6]

In early December he expected to sail for La Rochelle and Halifax, Nova Scotia, but not a single emigrant turned up in Rouen. The Franco-Canadian Company broke its agreement with the shipowner, the sailing was postponed and then cancelled. The venture was a complete disaster and they never left for Canada. The *Adowa* eventually returned to London, Conrad signed off on January 18, 1894, and—though he did not know it at the time—ingloriously concluded his maritime career, which had progressed until he left for the Congo and had then gone into a steep decline.

Conrad clung to the romance of clippers and always preferred sail to steam. But in the 1890s there were eight hundred new certified masters each year for a decreasing number of berths. At the end of 1897 there were forty-two fewer British ships than there had been in 1892. Steamers, which were replacing sailing ships, carried larger cargoes and smaller crews. Frank Bullen writes that all captains believed "that the position of master of even a fifth-rate steamship marks a step upward from the same position on board of the finest sailing ship afloat. . . . The mate of a steamer is so much better paid as a rule, that he naturally regards his status as much higher than the mate of a 'wind-jammer.' " And Edward Blackmore observes that though foreigners intensified the competition for jobs, they were not at a disadvantage. Shipowners frequently felt the alien " 'is a better shipmaster' and understands his business; is more attentive, more docile, and altogether *better educated* and *better mannered*" than English officers.

Despite this supposed advantage, Conrad was never able to secure another berth. Though he tried strenuously to get a command in Glasgow as late as September 1898, he finally realized that he had spent twenty years of his life mastering an art that was no longer needed. By that date, as Captain David Bone observed: "He had been away from the sea for a long time and much had changed: not many sailing ships remained under British registry at that date and those that lingered were ill-found and 'parish-rigged' [with worn or bad gear] alow and aloft."[7]

Though the termination of Conrad's maritime career was essentially involuntary, the longer he stayed ashore and tried to be a writer, the more difficult it was to return to the sea. The beginning of his writing career coincided with the onset of the extraordinarily painful gout that often crippled his hands and feet. He frequently became despondent about his literary work, but felt poor health made it dishonorable for him to accept a command. When John Sutherland asked Conrad what induced him to become a writer, "he was silent for some minutes, and then said, as if he had considered my question: 'Well, Commander, I was a long time on shore.' " Conrad replaced the impecunious life of a sailor with the equally precarious life of an invalid writer.

Ford Madox Ford, who knew Conrad extremely well, pointed out a crucial but often neglected fact: that Conrad *hated* the isolation, tedium, drudgery and hardship of the sea:

> His whole existence [was] passed in a series of ninety-day passages, in labouring ships, beneath appalling weathers, amongst duties and work too heavy, in continual discomfort and acute physical pain—with, in between each voyage, a few days spent as Jack-ashore. And that, in effect, was the life of Conrad. . . .
>
> He detested the sea as a man detests a cast-off mistress, and with the hatred of a small man who has had, on freezing nights of gales, to wrestle with immense yards and dripping cordage; his passion became to live out of sight of the sea and all its memories.

Unlike many old sailors, Conrad never owned a boat; he preferred to travel on land and by car. Sea life for Conrad, who spent half his time ashore, had often been a boring failure. He liked the sea much better when he remembered it than when he was actually experiencing it. As he wrote of Captain Marryat: "He loved his country first, the Service next, the sea perhaps not at all."[8] Conrad's years at sea prepared him for a literary career by giving him technical expertise, exposing him to exotic experience, trusting him with immense responsibilities, forming his character and providing him with an honorable code of conduct.

Attempting to connect his two apparently disparate lives, Conrad was fond of drawing parallels between deck and desk. He claimed that he went to sea and began to write for the same inexplicable reasons: "The necessity which impelled me was a hidden, obscure necessity, a completely masked and unaccountable phenomenon." His nautical and literary careers both led to an immense, oppressive and often intolerable solitude. To Conrad, both isolated occupations made intense physical demands, and he compared the anguished creation of a work of art to a dangerously turbulent voyage: "the strain of a creative effort in which mind and will and conscience are engaged to the full, hour after hour, day after day, away from the world, and to the exclusion of all that makes life really lovable and gentle—[is] something for which a material parallel can only be found in the everlasting sombre stress of the westward winter passage round Cape Horn."

In his essay on the much-admired Henry James, Conrad likened the imaginative re-creation of experience to salvage work at sea, for both saved what otherwise might have been lost: "Action in its essence, the creative art of a writer of fiction may be compared to rescue work carried out in darkness against cross gusts of wind swaying the action of a great multitude. It is rescue work, this snatching of vanishing phrases of turbulence, disguised in fair words, out of the native obscurity into . . . light." As the sociable and sedentary Henry James told Conrad, with acute perception, after reading *The Mirror of the Sea* in 1906: "No one has *known*—for intellectual use—the things you know, and you have, as the artist of the whole matter, an authority that no one has approached."[9]

Another crucial phase of Conrad's life also came to an end in 1894. On January 28 (ten days after Conrad left the *Adowa*) Tadeusz went to bed in apparently good health, woke up the next morning feeling short of breath, called his manservant to rub him with alcohol and then, at seven o'clock in the morning, pronounced the word: "Attack!" and suddenly expired at the age of sixty-four. "It seems as if everything has died in me," the grief-stricken Conrad told Marguerite. "He seems to have carried my soul away with him." Though Conrad did not attend his uncle's funeral, he dedicated *Almayer's Folly* "To the memory of T. B." and paid tribute to Tadeusz's kindness and generosity in *A Personal Record*: he "had been for a quarter of a century the wisest, the firmest, the most indulgent of guardians, extending over me a paternal care and affection, a moral support which I seemed to feel always near me in the most distant parts of the earth."[10] Tadeusz's death severed Conrad's ties with Poland for the next twenty years; his legacy of 15,000 rubles [£4,000 or $20,000], which Conrad received a year after his death, gave him the financial security to begin his career as a writer.

After Tadeusz's death Conrad became even closer to Marguerite, the last intimate member of his family, despite previous warnings from his uncle about the dangers of getting emotionally involved with her. In many respects Marguerite was the ideal woman for Conrad. She was attractive, intelligent and cultured; had money, social position and a literary reputation. His frequent letters to her in French contain intimate revelations about his health, maritime career and literary work as well as cries of despair, affectionate teasing and declarations (albeit in the *vous* rather than in the *tu* form) of his esteem. On July 8, 1891, for example, he wrote: "I admire you and love you more and more. I kiss your hands." Ten days later Tadeusz, who said Marguerite was "as romantic as a girl of sixteen," referred to the fact that she was past childbearing age, suggested she would make a more suitable alliance with her long-time suitor, the *Burgomeister* of Brussels, and told Conrad that he would not be able to support her: "I advise you to give up this game, which will end in nothing sensible. A worn-out female, and if she is to join up with somebody, it will be with Buls who would give her a position and love—of which he has given proof. It would be a stone round your neck for you—and for her as well. If you are wise you will leave this amusement alone and part simply as friends: if not, however, you have been warned!" When Conrad was visiting the Ukraine in September 1893, Marguerite heard a rumor that he was going to marry a local girl. She became deeply distressed and forced Conrad to make an emotional denial: "It is perfectly true that Marysienka is getting married; but in the name of all the follies, what have I to do with this matrimonial affair! However, I can hardly believe that you could speak seriously of the matter in your letter, for it must have seemed strange to you to see someone suddenly rush from the depths of Australia, without warning anyone, to the depths of the Ukraine in order to throw himself into the arms of—the whole idea is ludicrous."[11]

The first six years of Conrad's relations with Marguerite were marked by his constant attempts to establish intimacy, beginning by calling her aunt and ending with proposals for literary collaboration. He visited her frequently, begged for her sympathy and her help, expressed his pes-

simistic philosophy and grossly flattered her competent but commonplace novels. Though Marguerite refused Charles Buls, Conrad, as
Tadeusz's letters reveal, seriously considered marrying her. But he was
inhibited by the difference in age, social position and wealth. He may
not have had the courage to propose to her or may have done so and
been rejected. (If he *had* married her, he might have moved to Paris and
become a French instead of an English writer.) In any case, their correspondence broke off for five years in June 1895, while he was courting
Jessie, his future wife, because either she or Marguerite became jealous.

III

Almayer's Folly had grown line by line, rather than page by page. His
shortest novel took five years to write—in London, the Congo, Australia, the Ukraine, Switzerland and France—and earned only £20 (which
Conrad had made in two and a half months as chief mate of the *Torrens*).
But in the early months of 1894, to compensate for unemployment, he
pressed on to the conclusion of the novel. Conrad's main literary model,
if not direct influence, was Gustave Flaubert. He admired Flaubert's
unworldly, almost ascetic devotion to his art, his literary technique and
good craftsmanship, his ability to render concrete reality and visual impressions. "One never questions for a moment either his characters or
his incidents," Conrad told Marguerite; "one would rather doubt one's
own existence." Flaubert, with his friends Ivan Turgenev and Henry
James, were the three writers Conrad most admired.

Marguerite also received confidential revelations about his method of
composition and—as he would lament to friends throughout his life—
his agonies of creation. As Conrad stared at the blank sheet of paper, the
characters that existed in his imagination gradually took solid form and
could be described in words: "I begrudge each minute I spend away
from the page. I do not say from the pen, for I have written very little,
but inspiration comes to me while gazing at the paper. Then there are
vistas that extend out of sight; my mind goes wandering through great
spaces filled with vague forms. Everything is still chaos, but slowly,
ghosts are transformed into living flesh, floating vapours turn solid,
and—who knows?—perhaps something will be born from the collision
of indistinct ideas." Proust's technique was similar to Conrad's—
recovery of the past through memory. The French novelist compared
the creation of characters, who "take on colour and distinctive shape,
become . . . permanent and recognisable . . . [and] taking their proper

shapes and growing solid, spring into being," to the little crumbs of paper that assume form when the Japanese steep them in porcelain bowls of water.[12]

When things were not going well and the characters did not spring into being, Conrad became tormented by neurasthenia, which crippled his attempts to write: "My nervous disorder tortures me, makes me wretched, and paralyses action, thought, everything! I ask myself why I exist. It is a frightful condition. Even in the intervals, when I am supposed to be well, I live in fear of the return of this tormenting malady. . . . I no longer have the courage to do anything. I hardly have enough to write to you. It is an effort, a sudden rush to finish before the pen falls from my hand in the depression of complete discouragement."

In April 1894 Conrad spent a weekend with the Sandersons at Elstree. Galsworthy's sister remembered "that both Ted and his mother . . . took a hand, and considerable trouble, in editing the already amazingly excellent English of their Polish friend's *Almayer* manuscript, and in generally screwing up Conrad's courage to the sticking-point of publication." Conrad expressed his gratitude by dedicating his next book, *An Outcast of the Islands* (1896), to Ted Sanderson and *The Mirror of the Sea* to Ted's mother, Katherine. On April 24 Conrad, whose fictional characters had become real people, was—as his creations faded and resumed their ghostly shapes—finally able to announce to Marguerite the completion of the novel: "I regret to inform you of the death of Mr. Kaspar Almayer, which occurred this morning at 3 o'clock. It's finished! A scratching of the pen writing the final word, and suddenly this entire company of people who have spoken into my ear, gesticulated before my eyes, lived with me for so many years, becomes a band of phantoms who retreat, fade and dissolve."[13]

Once the novel was completed, he had to get it published. Conrad had no great confidence in its merits and tried to improve his prospects during July and August 1894 with two peculiar proposals to Marguerite. He first suggested that she translate *Almayer's Folly* into French and that they publish it as a collaboration in the prestigious *Revue des Deux Mondes*, where her novels had been serialized. "Haven't I any amount of cheek to speak to you like this, dear Teacher!" he wrote with ingratiating irony. The following month, having adopted *kemudi* (the Malay word for "rudder") as his pseudonym, he proposed that Marguerite's name appear as author on the title page with an explanatory note to say that *kemudi* (the real author) had merely collaborated on the book.

Conrad submitted the novel to Fisher Unwin on July 4 and, as he often did after completing a major work, took a holiday on the Continent. He returned to the hydropathic establishment and spent August in Champel, outside Geneva. Perhaps because of her unwillingness to collaborate on his novel, Conrad did not stop to see Marguerite on his way to and from Switzerland.

When he returned to London in early September and found no response from the publisher, Conrad wrote a fatuous letter to Fisher Unwin, in his most stilted and awkward English, which was bound to make a bad impression on the man he hoped would bring out his work. After an elaborate but pointless description of how the parcel had been wrapped and tied, he said (with mock modesty) that though the worthless book did not deserve to be read, he had neglected to make a duplicate of the precious work and was (like all authors) absurdly attached to his only copy: "I venture now upon the liberty of asking You whether there is the slightest likelihood of the MS. (Malay life, about 64,000 words) being read at some future time? If not, it would be—probably—not worse fate than it deserves, yet, in that case, I am sure you will not take it amiss if I remind you that, however worthless for the purpose of publication, it is very dear to me. A ridiculous feeling—no doubt—but not unprecedented I believe. In this instance it is intensified by the accident that I do not possess another copy, either written or typed."

When Fisher Unwin finally accepted the novel in early October, he said Conrad could either subsidize the publication with his own money and share in the profits or retain French rights and sell the copyright for £20. When Conrad chose the latter, the notoriously tight-fisted publisher explained: "We are paying you very little . . . but, remember, dear Sir, that you are unknown and your book will appeal to a very limited public. . . . Write something shorter—same type of thing—for our Pseudonym Library, and if it suits us, we shall be very happy to be able to give you a much better cheque."[14]

Fisher Unwin's first reader, W. H. Cheeson, alerted Edward Garnett to the merits of *Almayer's Folly*. Garnett, a sympathetic and worldly bohemian, "most beautifully free of the world's conventions" (according to D. H. Lawrence), understood Conrad's feelings as well as his novels. After recommending the book for publication, he became a close friend and adviser, a literary mentor and a replacement for Uncle Tadeusz.

The tall and mildly eccentric Edward, born in 1868, was the son of the Keeper of Printed Books in the British Museum. Conrad's son John said Edward's "face lacked colour, and his dark eyes and dark-grey unruly hair gave him the appearance of rugged untidiness." Garnett's son,

David, observed that "Edward was intuitive, illogical and in many ways ill-educated. . . . He arrived at his opinions, especially his aesthetic ones, by instinct and by sympathy."[15] Edward had critical rather than imaginative ability. He was a notoriously unsuccessful poet, playwright and novelist, but a brilliantly perceptive publisher's reader, who discovered Galsworthy and Lawrence, and also helped W. H. Hudson and H. E. Bates.

Edward's wife, Constance, six years his senior, was a prolific and influential translator of Russian novels into English. She had won a scholarship to Newnham College, Cambridge, where she took a first-class degree in Greek, and had learned Russian from exiles and during a short visit to Russia, where she met Tolstoy. She maintained an adulterous liaison with the anarchist and assassin Sergei Stepniak, as Edward did with Nellie Heath, who painted the first portrait of Conrad in 1898. The Garnetts lived with their small son at the Cearne, a country house in Surrey that Conrad frequently visited.

Garnett, struck by the unusual setting and style of *Almayer's Folly*, was particularly captivated by "Babalatchi, the aged one-eyed statesman and [by] the night scene at the river's edge between Mrs. Almayer and her daughter [Nina]. The strangeness of the tropical atmosphere, the poetic 'realism' of this romantic narrative excited my curiosity about the author, who I fancied might have Eastern blood in his veins." When they first met at the National Liberal Club in November 1894, Garnett noted the complex and contradictory aspects of Conrad's character. He was "a dark-haired man, short but extremely graceful in his nervous gestures, with brilliant eyes, now narrow and penetrating, now soft and warm, with a manner alert yet caressing, whose speech was ingratiating, guarded, or brusk turn by turn. I have never seen before a man so masculinely keen yet so femininely sensitive." Late in life, Conrad recalled that Garnett had encouraged him—when he was still torn between the life of art or of action—by praising *Almayer's Folly* and insisting that he had the style and temperament to become a professional novelist: "If he had said to me, 'Why not go on writing?' I should have been paralysed. I could not have done it. But he said to me, 'You have written one book. It is very good. Why not *write another*?' Do you see what a difference that made? Another? Yes, I would do that. *I* could do that. Many others I could not. Another I could. That is how Edward made me go on writing. That is what made me an author."

The two friends also met at Conrad's snug bachelor quarters at 17 Gillingham Street, which contained a tall screen, an easy chair, a cozy fire, a row of French novels and, on the mantelpiece, family photographs and engravings. Conrad fascinated Garnett (as he had fascinated Galsworthy) with stories of his adventures and told him about the time he "had to keep an enraged negro armed with a razor from coming aboard, along a ten-inch plank, and drive him back to the wharf with only a short stick in [my] hands." When Conrad read aloud to Garnett from the early chapters of his second novel, *An Outcast of the Islands,* he mispronounced so many words—which he had learned from books but never heard spoken—that Edward could scarcely understand him. When Garnett, anticipating a crucial problem in Conrad's career, urged him to follow his own artistic ideals and to disregard the public's taste, the thirty-seven-year-old novelist became alarmed and upset, and declared: "I *won't* live in an attic. . . . I'm past that, you understand? I *won't* live in an attic."[16] Conrad's works (as Garnett predicted) did not appeal to a wide public; though never forced into an attic, he was extremely hard-pressed for money during his first twenty years as a writer.

Garnett and Cunninghame Graham, whom Conrad met in 1897, were the only correspondents with whom he was completely honest and sincere. Garnett read all of Conrad's early works in manuscript: not only his first two Malayan novels but also *Tales of Unrest, The Nigger of the "Narcissus"* (dedicated to Edward), the first part of *The Rescue* and the unfinished draft of "The Sisters." Conrad was grateful for Garnett's frankness, criticism, appreciation, encouragement and friendship. He valued the younger man's good opinion, used him (as he had used Tadeusz) as a moral touchstone and apologized when Garnett's expectations were disappointed: "I feel to you like a son who has gone wrong and what with shame and recklessness remains silent—and yet nourishes the hope of rehabilitation and keeps his eye fixed steadily on some distant day of pardon and embraces." Conrad paid his finest tribute to Garnett when he portrayed him as Lea in *The Inheritors,* praised his generosity and insight, and expressed uneasiness about his inability to repay his friend:

> Lea had helped me a good deal in the old days—he had helped everybody, for that matter. You would probably find traces of Lea's influence in the beginnings of every writer of about my decade; of everybody who ever did anything decent, and of some who never got beyond the stage of burgeoning decently. He had given me the material help that a publisher's reader could give, until his professional reputation was endangered, and

he had given me the more valuable help that so few can give. I had grown ashamed of this one-sided friendship.[17]

IV

Though Garnett, an extremely sophisticated reader, found *Almayer's Folly* so authentic that he believed Conrad had Eastern blood in his veins, other authorities questioned the authenticity of the work. In the *Singapore Free Press* of September 6, 1898, Hugh Clifford, an author with long experience in the Malayan Colonial Service, praised the atmospheric power of the river and jungle, but claimed the novel was flawed by ignorance: "a real Nina would not go back to native ways, a real Babalatchi would never dare to yawn and scratch himself in the royal presence." Clifford, who later became Conrad's friend, repeated these charges in a lecture he gave in Colombo: "the author had none but a superficial acquaintance with the Malayan customs, language and character. Hardly a proper name, or a Malayan word, from one end of the book to the other, was not misspelt."[18]

Having spent only twelve days or so on land in Borneo, Conrad could not, with all his perception, have learned very much about the native population during that time. (He had, however, observed Malays in Malacca and in Singapore, and worked with them aboard the *Vidar*: a trusty *serang* steers the ship for the blind Captain Whalley in "The End of the Tether.") But he compensated for his lack of extensive knowledge by using "dull, wise" source books for the Malay names (including the improbable-sounding Babalatchi), language, characters and customs.[19] Since Conrad took considerable trouble to make his novels accurate, he was surprisingly (and too readily) deferential—in letters and in print—when editors and critics challenged his authority. Responding to Clifford's review—"Extremely laudatory but in fact telling me I don't know anything about it"—he told William Blackwood, who published "Karain" and other Malayan stories: "Well I never did set up as an authority on Malaysia," and he repeated this in his Author's Note to *A Personal Record*. Deferring to Clifford's authority when writing to him, Conrad suspected that "my assumption of Malay colouring for my fiction must be exasperating to those who *know*."[20] Yet Conrad was not writing for a select audience of old Malaya hands. Since the English reader could not differentiate Clifford's accuracy from Conrad's, the essential point was how realistically and effectively the Malays were portrayed in fiction. Clifford's characters were perhaps expertly drawn, and had all the pedantically proper diacritical marks attached to their names. But they were also terribly dull. Conrad's Malays, though sententious, were convincing and alive.

Almayer's Folly portrays not only the indigenous Malays, Dyaks, Arabs (and their slaves), but also suggests the political hierarchy in the local rajah, the remote sultan on the far side of the island and the Dutch rulers in distant Batavia, whose gunboats show the flag on occasional visits. Starting with the character of the real Charles Olmeijer, Conrad significantly changed the details of his life: he gave him a tragic fate and a single disloyal daughter instead of a brood of eleven children. The title of the novel refers to Almayer's megalomanic dreams about Tom Lingard's patronage, his own prosperous marriage to a Eurasian woman, a great future for Nina, fabulous wealth, escape from Borneo and a prominent social position in Amsterdam (which he has never seen) as well as to his grandiose but decrepit house.

The plot of the novel—filled with suspicion, deception and intrigue—revolves around Almayer's futile hope of discovering gold treasure, his illegal trading in gunpowder and his attempt to redeem himself through his beautiful half-caste daughter. Despite her Dutch father and her convent education in Singapore, Nina reverts to the race of her primitive mother, chooses to be a Malay and, in an operatic scene, remains loyal to her princely lover, Dain Maroola, rather than to her father. It is significant that Dain Maroola is the romantic hero of the novel; that Almayer and all the other Dutchmen are portrayed as foolish and mercenary. When writing the novel Conrad imagined what might have happened to him if he had given in to his irresponsible impulses, remained on the *Vidar* and become enthralled by a native woman. His theme is the destruction of a man by the East and by his own corrupt ambition.

Two scenes in this first novel are especially memorable and strikingly Conradian, the first for its pathos, the second for its sardonic humor. After Almayer has been abandoned by Nina and has accepted the tragic insight that "No two human beings understand each other," Conrad reverses the famous scene in which Robinson Crusoe first discovers Friday and shows Almayer creating a pathetic and morbid memorial to his loss. To the dismay of his servant, Almayer "fell on his hands and knees, and, creeping along the sand, erased carefully with his hand all traces of Nina's footsteps. He piled up small heaps of sand, leaving behind him a line of miniature graves right down to the water."

In the second scene Conrad wittily juxtaposes the evil plots of Lakamba, the Malay rajah, with the lament of Manrico, the hero of Verdi's *Il Trovatore*. After Lakamba tells his pock-marked factotum and adviser, Babalatchi, that he must poison Almayer to prevent him from revealing to the Dutch the secret of his gold, Lakamba demands music. And Babalatchi must reluctantly and incongruously provide it. Nearly falling asleep while he turns the hand-organ, Babalatchi fills the unresponsive jungle with alien yet soothing sounds. As Lakamba dozes comfortably in his armchair, and the music plays, Manrico, captured in battle and about to be beheaded, sings (in the first scene of the final act of *Trovatore*) his farewell to life and to Leonora:

> Through the open shutter the notes of Verdi's music floated out on the great silence over the river and forest. Lakamba listened with closed eyes and a delighted smile; Babalatchi turned, at times dozing off and swaying over, then catching himself up in a great fright with a few quick turns of the handle. Nature slept in an exhausted repose after the fierce turmoil, while under the unsteady hand of the statesman of Sambir the Trovatore fitfully wept, wailed, and bade good-bye to his Leonore again and again in a mournful round of tearful and endless iteration.[21]

The crucial events of 1894 proved as important in Conrad's life as his departure from Poland in 1874. In mid-January he had signed off the *Adowa* and ended his career at sea. In late January the death of Tadeusz had broken his ties with Poland. In April he had finished *Almayer's Folly*. In October his first novel had been accepted for publication and he became a professional writer. And in November he had met Edward Garnett, his lifelong friend, and Jessie George, his future wife.

CHAPTER NINE

Courtship and Marriage
1894–1896

I

In November 1894, when Conrad first met Jessie George, he was nearly thirty-seven and she was twenty-one. The numerous descriptions of his appearance agree about his essential characteristics. On his application for the master's examination, Conrad stretched his shorter than average height to five feet, nine and a half inches and said his complexion was dark, his hair dark brown and his eyes hazel. By 1883, when he met Tadeusz in Marienbad, Conrad had grown a dark nautical beard that followed the curve of his jaw. By 1896, when he married, his wiry black beard had become pointed at the chin, and the ends of his mustache twisted into points that projected from his face.

Conrad's most striking features were his short neck, high shoulders and broad chest, which conveyed the impression of compact strength. He had a sallow, weather-beaten, powerfully sculpted triangular face, with a wide forehead, dark shaggy eyebrows, clear flashing eyes, high Slavic cheekbones, aquiline nose, thin mobile lips and firm jutting jaw. He made sudden, convulsive gestures, and had a habit of tilting his head backward when he laughed. The critic Desmond MacCarthy emphasized Conrad's hawkish aspect and the reflective expression of his half-obscured eyes:

> The length of his head from chin to crown struck me, and this was accentuated by a pointed greyish beard, which a backward carriage of his head on high shoulders projected forwards. Black eyebrows, hooked nose, hunched shoulders gave him a more hawk-like look than even his photograph had suggested. His eyes were very bright and dark when he opened them wide, but unless lit and expanded by enthusiasm or indignation,

they remained half-hidden, and as though filmed in a kind of abstruse slumberous meditation.

And his French translator Henry-Durand Davray also stressed the play of light on Conrad's luminous eyes:

> He is slightly less than average in height; his head is sunken between large bulging shoulders which seem to shorten his torso, lengthening his legs. But the head is unforgettable and one looks at nothing besides. His high open forehead, large aquiline nose, on both sides deep lines disappearing in a pointed beard which elongate even more the perfect oval of his face. His brown eyes beneath two black lines of his thick brows draw our attention. When he happens to open his eyes wide they shine with a strange expression but more often they remain half covered by the lids as if to filter part of the light, or of the sunglare on the waves. When he looks at his interlocutor, his gaze becomes sharp, penetrating and deep; then suddenly it loses its intensity as if he saw what he had been seeking.[1]

Ford wrote that Conrad's "ambition was to be taken for—to be!—a [mid-Victorian] English country gentleman of the time of Lord Palmerston," but he remained indelibly foreign in appearance, manners, gestures, speech and dress. His checked suit, habitual havelock overcoat, bowler hat pressed down on his head and single eyeglass—to aid his right eye, which had been injured in childhood by a whip—were his only English attributes. The American sculptor Jo Davidson, like many other friends, found him "curiously dressed. Under his overcoat you spotted riding breeches, and his legs were clothed in puttees [though Conrad never rode or shot]. He wore a bowler hat. He thought he was being very English."[2]

Though no recording of Conrad's voice was ever made, it is possible to reconstruct his way of speaking from many accounts by his friends. Ford agreed with Galsworthy and Garnett that Conrad's pronunciation was so faulty that he was often very difficult to understand. His use of adverbs, and of "shall" and "will," was eccentric and arbitrary. He found the English "th" sound troublesome and—like so many foreigners—would say "dis" and "dat." He transposed "v" and "w" so that "vowel" became "wowvel"; said "used a sword" as "úsit a súword." "Iodine" he pronounced "uredyne," which his young son once took to mean "you are dying." Hugh Clifford, who believed Conrad spoke French more fluently and perfectly than English (he always included many French expressions in his spoken English), heard him describe an editor as a *"Horréeble* Personalitee! *Horréeble* Personalitee!"

He would also say: "I thought he was afraïd (as in Port Saïd), so I askèd him, but I was ütterly [ooterly] wrong" and "It is uncomfortable. On komm for tarble for them!" And he frequently corrected himself when remarking: "I buyed it—I bought it." Adam Curle, the son of Conrad's friend Richard Curle, recalled an incident that occurred at Capel House: "His pronunciation was extremely foreign. Once when they were looking at the view from his house, which my mother admired, he disagreed, saying obscurely, 'too many awks.' He meant, of course, oaks, which interrupted the long view which, as a sailor, he preferred." And H. G. Wells explained: "He had learnt to read English long before he spoke it and he had formed wrong sound impressions of many familiar words; he had for example acquired an incurable tendency to pronounce the last e in these and those. He would say, 'Wat shall we do with thesa things?' . . . When he talked of seafaring his terminology was excellent but when he turned to less familiar topics he was often at a loss for phrases." Yet when Conrad asked Jessie to read aloud some pages from the manuscript of An Outcast of the Islands and had difficulty following her pronunciation, he exclaimed: "Speak distinctly . . . don't eat your words. You English are all alike, you make the same sound for every letter."[3] Conrad's Polish accent became stronger as he grew older, and he always ranted in Polish when delirious and ill.

Acutely sensitive about his faulty accent, Conrad parodied his own way of speaking English in his fiction. He wrote of the half-caste captain of the ship that takes Lord Jim to Patusan: "His flowing English seemed to be derived from a dictionary compiled by a lunatic." In "Falk," the English pronunciation of the German merchant Mr. Siegers "was so extravagant that I can't even attempt to reproduce it. For instance, he said 'Fferie strantch.' " And in The Rescue, a German commercial agent has many of the characteristics of Conrad's own speech. He pronounces English words in the German way; includes German words in his English sentences (Hase and Monat, with an English plural), substitutes "d" for "th" and "v" for "w," and even uses pidgin English ("first chop"): " 'Nefer mind him, shentlemens, he's matt, matt as a Marsh Hase. Dree monats ago I call on board his prig to talk pizness. And he says like dis—"Glear oudt." "Vat for?" I say. "Glear oudt before I shuck you oferboard." Gott-for-dam! Iss dat the vay to talk pizness? I vant sell him ein liddle case first chop grockery for trade and—.' " As Conrad told Joseph de Smet, one of his French translators: "My pronunciation is rather defective to this day. Having unluckily no ear, my accentuation is uncertain, especially when in the course of a conversation I become self-conscious."[4]

After twenty years at sea Conrad's tastes, habits and character were fully—and rather rigidly—formed. He drank tea, Slavic style, in tall glasses, with lemon and quantities of sugar. His favorite fruits were cherries and raspberries. John Conrad described his other tastes in food, formed in Marseilles and in India, and fully satisfied by Jessie, who became an excellent cook: "He had a strong preference for French cooking, more especially for the traditional dishes of the Mediterranean coast. He was very fond of hot dishes, hot curry that made one perspire over the eyelids, horseradish sauce made rather sweet, tabasco and pimentoes, and any other hot substances; and heaven help anyone who served soggy rice. He had a weakness for ravioli, gnocchi, and mushroom omelettes."[5] But he had the bad habit (acquired during the more informal dining at sea) of making bread pellets and, when annoyed at mealtimes, even in restaurants and among strangers, flinging them about the room.

Conrad liked to go sailing during the 1890s with his friend G. F. W. Hope, but he did not know how to swim. As a cultivated European, he hated the English passion for open windows, cold baths, long walks and outdoor sports. He had no interest in gardening, farming or country life. Though he retained a romantic attachment to sailing ships rather than steamers, he preferred to travel on land as fast as possible in a mechanical car rather than in a horse-drawn vehicle. He acquired a series of cars early in the century and membership of his club—the RAC in Pall Mall— was based solely on ownership of automobiles rather than on commonly shared personal, educational, social, artistic, political or professional interests.

Conrad was high-strung, sensitive and passionate. He had a mercurial temperament and a neurasthenic personality; was a chronic hypochondriac and often maniacally depressed; and had several nervous breakdowns during his marriage. There were also radical contradictions in his character. He loved adventure, but cultivated order; he had a great capacity for affection, but great difficulty in expressing it. As a captain, Conrad had responsibility for all the legal, medical and commercial aspects of his job as well as for the lives of his crew, the safety of his ship and the care of his cargo. Yet he found it difficult to cope with the problems of everyday life. Moody, irritable, absent-minded, indolent and impractical, he was deeply dependent on his wife and friends, and utterly helpless when suffering from his frequent attacks of gout.

Conrad protected his inner self behind a mask of inscrutable politeness. Few visitors were able to penetrate his elaborately courteous demeanor; many interviews and memoirs provide little more than a record of his trivial conversation mixed with the adoration and flattery of his interlocutors. Arnold Bennett, who admired Conrad's work and met him at the end of the century, was probably the first to describe his politeness, tact, conversation, style and gesticulation as "Oriental"; and this epithet was repeated by Ford, Curle, Henry Newbolt and even by Jessie. Wells also observed: "At first he impressed me, as he impressed Henry James, as the strangest of creatures. . . . [He had] a trouble-wrinkled forehead and very troubled dark eyes, and the gestures of his hands and arms were from the shoulders and very Oriental indeed."[6]

Conrad sometimes attributed his unstable personality and emotional outbursts to the anti-romantic romanticism, the curious mixture of patriotism and scepticism in his Polish heritage. "We Poles are poor specimens," he told Cunninghame Graham in 1898. "The strain of national worry has weakened the moral fibre. . . . It is not a fault; it is a misfortune. . . . I don't repine at the nature of my inheritance but now and then it is too heavy not to let out a groan." He certainly took pleasure in detailing his disasters. And his agonized, sometimes self-pitying letters—bulletins of despair mixed with poignant pleas for visits, sympathy and money—resembled those of his father in exile.

His depression was usually caused by difficulty in writing. He struggled with the elusive foreign language, tested himself against the work of his literary masters and strove to satisfy his compulsive perfectionism. He complained to Marguerite: "when I'm not well I have attacks of melancholy which paralyse my thought and will." And in the summer of 1896, while grappling with the first version of *The Rescue*, he told Garnett (who had succeeded Marguerite, who in turn had succeeded Tadeusz, as the recipient of Conrad's howls of distress): "I have long fits of depression, that in a lunatic asylum would be called madness. I do not know what it is. It springs from nothing. It is ghastly. It lasts an hour or a day; and when it departs it leaves a fear. . . . I suspect I am getting through a severe mental illness."[7]

In 1905, when he was trying to help Conrad through one of his recurrent financial crises, the painter William Rothenstein told Edmund Gosse, an influential man of letters, that Conrad's irrational outbursts drained the emotions of his friends: "Of course he is terribly hysterical—indeed last year I feared for his reason." Rothenstein referred to Conrad's "morbid excitable mind" and then added: "I am terribly sorry for him, but it is very hard at times to be patient—natures like his demand as a right, if once one gives affection, a very great deal of one's time and energy."

When Conrad lost his temper and "chattered and screamed like a monkey," he would calm himself by compulsively brushing his hair. He portrayed this habit in two early stories. In "Falk," the harbor-bound captain, irrationally detained by the master of the only tugboat, believes he will finally be able to sail from Bangkok: "Greatly cheered by the idea, I seized the hair-brushes and looking at myself in the glass began to use them." And in "The Return," when Alvan Hervey discovers that his apparently devoted wife has deserted him for another man, he attempts to calm himself in a similar fashion: "Only his hair was slightly ruffled, and that disorder, somehow, was so suggestive of trouble that he went quickly to the table, and began to use the brushes, in an anxious desire to obliterate the compromising trace, that only vestige of his emotion."[8]

Though Conrad was sometimes able to establish, with friends like Richard Curle, "one of those decisive silences that alone establish a perfect communion between creatures gifted with speech," he remained—in marriage, with friends and as a writer—in the same inextricably lonely state that had characterized his previous lives as an orphan in Poland and as an officer at sea. "Through my fault—or is it simply Fate?—I have missed all along the chances of closer contacts," he told a young American friend. But, like Lord Jim's, "his loneliness added to his stature."[9]

II

Conrad had been seeing Jessie George since November 1894. But in May 1895 he interrupted his courtship and made his third visit to Champel in Switzerland, in the hope that mountain air and being sprayed twice a day by a high-pressure fire hose (he took the waters in both senses) would somehow improve his health and his work. In Champel he met Émilie Briquel, the daughter of a rich, cultured bourgeois family from Lunéville in Lorraine, who was on holiday with her mother and brother. The twenty-year-old Émilie, just young enough to be Conrad's daughter, was two years younger than Jessie George, six years younger than Eugénie Renouf had been when Conrad met her in Mauritius in 1888 and twenty-seven years younger than Marguerite Poradowska.

Like Henry James' Winterbourne and Daisy Miller, Conrad and Émilie (accompanied by her *Maman*) dined together at the pension, took excursions to the local beauty spots and sailed in a rented boat, skillfully manned by Captain Conrad, around Lake Geneva. Despite Émilie's rather coarse features—thick lips, snouted nose, fleshy ears and high frizzy hair—they soon became intimate and began a serious flirtation. Conrad escorted her to the local lending library and taught her to play billiards; she sang for him and played both the piano and violin.

At the end of May a grateful Conrad, cheered by their company, told Émilie's brother Paul that "Fate has favoured me in a quite special way by allowing me to meet your mother and Mademoiselle Émilie here." Their meeting would later inspire Razumov's Geneva encounter with Nathalie Haldin and her mother in *Under Western Eyes*. At Champel, Conrad gave her a copy of the newly published *Almayer's Folly*, with a flattering inscription: "To Miss Emily Briquel—whose charming musical gift and everbright presence has cheered for him the dull life of Champel, this book is presented by her most humble, grateful and obedient servant—the Author." The presentation of his first novel not only substantiated his credentials as a writer, but also stimulated her interest in translating the book into French. Conrad told Émilie, with characteristic hyperbole, that her interest in his book has "given me one of the greatest pleasures I have ever experienced in my life" and that her "gift for mastering a foreign language leaves me dumbfounded and full of admiration."[10] But her knowledge of English could not have been very good, for she mistook Conrad for an Englishman.

When Conrad left in late May, he agreed to visit Lunéville in the autumn and she promised to get on with the translation of his novel. Émilie, sad to lose her cultured and courteous companion, felt "as if I was losing a true friend, the likes of whom I shall never find again." She distinguished her friendship for Conrad from her love for her family and her future husband; and in her diary of July 20, 1895, revealed that the attentive, diverting captain (who had no ship) had inspired fondness rather than passion in her ultra-conventional heart: "This year in Champel, I met Mr. Conrad, I speak about him often and at length, I write to him and I think that I am very fond of him! Perhaps, but I am fond of him as a friend, as an agreeable acquaintance, which cannot be compared to love! I dream of a quiet little nest, of a secluded happiness for two, of the supreme happiness of married love."

During July and August 1895 the old salt, assuming a jaunty, daredevil persona, first told the impressionable Émilie that he was leaving for Norway with Hope on the *Ildegonde*; and then said that he had sailed round the Shetland and Orkney Islands (north of Scotland) and had "spent entire days without trysails [used for keeping a vessel headed into the wind], amidst the fog and heavy seas of the Atlantic. The little

Ildegonde (which is a twenty-three-ton cutter) danced on top of the high waves like a nutshell." In fact, the prosaic voyage went only as far as Holland. Trying to impress Émilie, Conrad clearly wanted to ask for her hand—and for the rest of her as well. But her dreams of a "quiet little nest"—impossible with the tempestuous Conrad, even if they had lived on her money in Lorraine—was not to be. According to Najder, who closely studied this romantic episode, "Conrad apparently had been made to understand that, because of the age gap between them [not unusual in those days] and his nomadic life style [though he had left the sea], he could not hope to win the girl's hand."[11] He sighed as a lover and obeyed like a man.

III

By the autumn of 1895 Conrad had been rejected by several French women: by Eugénie Renouf in Mauritius, by Émilie Briquel in Champel and, quite possibly, by Marguerite Poradowska in Paris. These humiliating rejections not only intensified his lifelong misogyny and fear of women, but also turned his attention to Jessie George. She was the homespun antithesis not only of these exotic, cultivated and artistic women, but also of his feminine ideal: the sultry and passionate Rita de Lastaola of Marseilles. If Marguerite was much older, widowed, intellectual, sophisticated, beautiful and related to Conrad by marriage and by her experience in the Ukraine, Jessie was much younger, virginal, uneducated, provincial, plain and completely alien to his background and interests. As he observed in *Lord Jim*: "The marital relations of seamen would make an interesting subject."

The man who had adopted the pseudonym of Monsieur George in Marseilles had met Jessie George through his old friends the Hopes in November 1894. Born on February 22, 1873, the second of nine children, she worked as a typist and was living a quiet, circumscribed life at 10 Shepherd's Place, Kennington Lane, a short walk across the Thames on Vauxhall Bridge from Bessborough Gardens, where Conrad began *Almayer's Folly* in 1889. Jessie's deceased father had been a warehouseman (Conrad's sometime occupation) whose status was elevated, on her marriage certificate and for snobbish reasons, to "bookseller." Her mother, Jane, had little formal education and was, according to her grandson Borys, who found it impossible to feel affection for her, "a grim-featured old lady who habitually wore an expression of disgust and disapproval." Torn between a desire to unload one of her five dowerless daughters and a strong distaste for Conrad's strange behavior, she soon became anathema to her future son-in-law. A few years after his marriage, she was permanently banned from his house.

Conrad combined an orphan's attraction to the solidarity of a large family with a horror of getting entangled in it. Jessie's young sister Dolly, whom Conrad described as "a young person with her hair down her back, and of extreme docility"[12] (the girls were made that way in the George family), sometimes served with another sister, Ethel, as maid and nanny in the Conrad household. They were the only siblings of Jessie's to become significantly involved in his family life. Between 1900 and 1904 Conrad helped pay the fees of Dolly and Nelly George at St. Bernard's Convent School in Slough; and he supported Jessie's mother during the war when her sons were away at the front.

Jessie was about five feet two inches tall and very dark, with a wide mouth, thin upper lip and slightly protruding ears. She appears to have been reasonably attractive in her early photographs; foreign, even Slavic-looking in her middle years; grotesquely obese—loaded, like a Gypsy fortune-teller, with rings, bangles and beads—in her late years. Her dominant and most valuable trait was a calm, placid temperament and a self-control that withstood all provocations. Ford's mistress Violet Hunt, describing a heated political argument with Conrad, said, with some irony: "Mrs. Conrad had not turned a hair. She never did. The perfect wife for an author." And Borys, who admired his mother, thought her temperament was unnatural and unnerving: "Complete imperturbability and apparent lack of emotion under any circumstances, in spite of almost constant pain and physical discomfort [from a knee injury in 1904], remained with her throughout her life. This unassailable placidity was almost frightening at times."

When Conrad introduced Jessie to Edward Garnett, his adviser was immediately struck by the disparity in their education and breeding, by her inability to understand his intellectual existence, his imaginative life and his intense devotion to his work. Tactfully arguing Conrad's un-suitability for domestic life, Garnett tried to dissuade him from marrying her. Later on, Garnett (who was not a snob) wrote a savage letter to Cunninghame Graham, expecting Graham to agree with his estimate of their friend's wife: "Jessie ought to have been the manageress of a fourth-rate hotel or home for Barmaids. I knew that from the first & Conrad having no knowledge of the social shades of Englishwomen &

wanting a Housekeeper has had to pay at long last, for his experiment."[13]

IV

Jocelyn Baines rather surprisingly remarks: "there is nothing to show what prompted his desire to marry at this moment nor why his choice fell on Jessie," though there is considerable evidence to explain his motivation. Uncle Tadeusz died the year Conrad met Jessie, and he virtually severed relations with Marguerite while he was courting his future wife in 1895. Cut off from his country, his family and his profession; sickly, strange and lonely; approaching the age of forty, with few friends in England and uncertain prospects as an author, Conrad desperately needed the security and affection of marriage and children. He knew no other girls, she had no other suitors. The Polish sailor and the suburban typist satisfied each other's needs in a strange sort of way. Jessie's class and background were appropriate to Conrad's meager income and to the style of life he could then afford to give her. She was skilled in precisely the domestic arts (cooking and typewriting) that he required, and could give him the maternal care and the secure middle-class home he had always lacked. Most importantly, unlike the frivolous French girls who seemed to have led him on and then rejected his proposals, Jessie was completely dominated by and subservient to Conrad's age, authority and experience.

Conrad was not only the first foreigner Jessie had ever known, but also the first adult male who had ever taken an emotional interest in her. His mode of courtship was surely one of the most bizarre in literary history. Jessie was startled by the noticeable strangeness, heavy accent and extravagant gestures of the fastidious and (she too used the word) "almost oriental" aristocrat. Despite his long years at sea and in Asian ports, and his inflexible habits, they were essentially sympathetic. She rightly believed she could "be happy in constant contact with a nature so charming, yet often hyper-sensitive and broodingly reserved."

They had infrequent but agreeable meetings during their leisurely fifteen-month courtship. Chaperoned by one of her numerous siblings, they would hire a carriage, drive into the center of London and take in the sights. In February 1896 they met at Victoria Station, and Conrad immediately criticized Jessie's clothes and appearance. They then took a cab to the National Gallery in Trafalgar Square and climbed the steps to the entrance. Glancing around to make certain they were alone, Conrad suddenly blurted out his awkward proposal: "Look here, my dear, we had better get married and out of this. Look at the weather. We will get married at once and get over to France. How soon can you be ready? In a week—a fortnight?" After intimidating Jessie, Conrad cited his desire to escape the prevailing English climate as the cause of his urgency, and ordered her rather than asked her to marry him. Another reason for his impatience, he told Jessie, was "that he had not very long to live and no intention of having children; but such as his life was (his [French] shrug was very characteristic) he thought we might spend a few happy years together."

Their lunch at a small café gave them food poisoning and made them desperately ill. Jessie heard absolutely nothing from Conrad for three days after his proposal and was not at all sure he had been serious. After interviewing Conrad, her mother (who was strongly prejudiced against foreigners) quite sensibly said she did not quite see why he wished to get married. Jessie did not quite see either but, despite his discouraging prognosis, accepted his proposal.

There could also have been another important reason for Conrad's pressing haste to marry. In Ford's satiric novel *The Simple Life Limited*, published in 1911 shortly after his break with Conrad, he portrayed his old friend as the lazy, improvident writer Simon Bransdon, who hires a young typist, works late into the night with her and soon seduces her. She becomes his mistress and they marry so he no longer has to pay her wages. Conrad's "we had better get married and out of this" may therefore refer to his fear that Jessie might be pregnant. As he wrote in an unpublished fragment on marriage: "I can imagine that correct young man perfectly capable of setting himself deliberately to worry a distracted girl into surrender."[14]

When Eugénie Renouf asked Conrad what quality he preferred in a woman, he answered: "Beauty." But he also emphasized the erratic and paradoxical nature of human emotions, and wrote in "Because of the Dollars": "Women are loved for all sorts of reasons and even for characteristics which one would think repellent." On March 10, 1896, he wrote a strange and important letter—in the convoluted style he adopted when discussing his deepest feelings—announcing his imminent marriage. Describing it as a dangerous adventure and finding it difficult to justify his odd choice to his cousin and closest surviving relative, Karol Zagorski, he ironically stressed Jessie's lack of physical attraction, humble background, virtuous (though unpleasant) mother and teeming family—as well as his own foolishness:

> No one can be more surprised at it than myself. However, I am not fright-
> ened at all, for as you know, I am accustomed to an adventurous life and
> to facing terrible dangers. Moreover, I have to avow that my betrothed
> does not give the impression of being at all dangerous. Jessie is her name;
> George her surname. She is a small, not at all striking-looking person (to
> tell the truth alas—rather plain!) who nevertheless is very dear to me.
> When I met her a year and a half ago she was earning her living in the City
> as a 'Typewriter' in an American business office of the 'Caligraph' com-
> pany. Her father died three years ago. There are nine children in the
> family. The mother is a very decent woman (and I do not doubt very
> virtuous as well). However, I must confess that it is all the same to me, as
> *vous comprenez?*—I am not marrying the whole family. The wedding will
> take place on the 24th of this month and we shall leave London immedi-
> ately so as to conceal from people's eyes our happiness (or our stupidity)
> amidst the wilderness and beauty of the coast of Brittany where I intend
> to rent a small house in some fishing village.

Conrad's admission of Jessie's plainness and his own stupidity seemed to prove that he, at least, had not been duped by love. His morbid proposal, his need to apologize for normal feelings, and his self-consciously ironic attitude to Jessie and to marriage, suggest grave misgivings about his transformation from an adventurous to a domestic life. To further conceal his moderate though unusual display of passion, Conrad insisted that Jessie burn the love letters he had sent her during their courtship. Jessie complacently wrote that "a really timid and col-ourless wife will lose all attraction for her husband once she has lost her own individuality." But this was not true of Conrad, who wanted pre-cisely such a wife and who described Jessie, in "The End of the Tether," when portraying Captain Whalley's dead wife: "Most likely common-place with domestic instincts, utterly insignificant."[15]

While Conrad was courting Jessie he was also seeking command or even ownership of a vessel, which he planned to take on a two to three year voyage in order to provide a secure foundation for his marriage. To this end, he negotiated in Liverpool for the "pretty little ship," the *Primera*, in October 1894, traveled to Antwerp in November 1894, planned a trip to Newfoundland in February 1895 and considered a Southern whaler in October 1895. In March 1896, the month of his marriage, he was offered command of the *Windermere* and went up to

Grangemouth, on the Firth of Forth, west of Edinburgh, with Hope, Jessie and her sister, to inspect the ship. Jessie, who "liked the sea" though she had no experience with it, planned to accompany him on the voyage. But it was also quite possible, since Conrad felt wives aboard ship were always troublesome, that he intended to return to the sea alone and (like Captain Whalley) keep Jessie as a part-time and safely distant wife. However, the brooding old hulk had an air of ill omen, and the terms of the *Windermere* were so unsatisfactory that he refused the command and was thrown back on literature as his means of support.

Like Conrad, Jessie was nominally a Catholic but actually an atheist. So they were married at St. George's Registry Office, Hanover Square, rather than in a church, on March 24, 1896, with only Hope, Krieger and Jessie's mother in attendance. Conrad's marriage connected him not only to Jessie, but also to England, the English, a writing career, domestic life and children.

Conrad's wedding night and honeymoon were as strange as his courtship and proposal. His sexual life during his first thirty-seven years is extremely obscure. His inexperience, dignity and reserve would not permit him to go whoring in foreign ports or parts, and he preferred to idealize rather than sleep with women like Rita de Lastaola. He seemed frightened by Orientals and Eurasians, who were readily available in the East, and was always chaperoned with the girls he courted in Mauritius and in Europe. Though he may well have had sexual relations before he met Jessie, there is no evidence about this.

On his wedding night Conrad was either indifferent about sex with Jessie or anxious about deflowering his bride. In any case, he felt the need to delay consummation and was more interested in catching up with his correspondence than in sleeping with his wife. He stayed up until 2 a.m. writing inconsequential letters (none dated March 24/25 have survived) and then went out to post them in the middle of the night—though they could not possibly be collected until morning. His anxiety continued the next day when they crossed the Channel to Saint-Malo and Conrad, as well as Jessie, became seasick.

Conrad made it more difficult for Jessie to adjust on her honeymoon by removing her from her family, country and culture for six months, and by taking her to a strange place where he knew the language—but she did not—in order to dominate the situation completely. In April 1896 he described, in letters to Ted Sanderson and Edward Garnett, the bleak landscape around Lannion, in north Brittany, and the peasant's cottage, the first house he ever had, on Île-Grande, which was connected to the coast by a narrow causeway:

The coast is rocky, sandy, wild and full of mournful expressiveness. But the land at the back of the wide stretches of the sea enclosed by the barren archipelago, is green and smiling and sunny. . . . The people that inhabits these shores is a people of women—black-clad and white-capped. . . .

We have got a small house, all kitchen downstairs and all bedroom upstairs, on as rocky and barren an island as the heart of (right thinking) man would wish to have. And the people! They are dirty and delightful and very Catholic. And most of them are women. The men fish in Iceland [and] on the Great banks of Newfoundland.

They hired a four-ton cutter, *La Pervenche* (the periwinkle flower), and sailed along the coast. But Conrad became indignant when Jessie was mistaken for his daughter by a Frenchman, who asked permission to court her. Their fifteen-year difference in age disturbed Conrad, who did not like anyone to remember—let alone celebrate—his birthday. During his honeymoon he wrote "The Idiots," a story about a woman who has produced four mentally defective children and kills her husband with scissors while repelling his sexual advances.

Conrad's honeymoon, far from idyllic, was, like the rest of his married life, characterized by frequent crises, acute anxiety, serious sickness and a desperate lack of money. Within two weeks of reaching Lannion, Jessie, who was subject to fainting fits, terrified Conrad with a three-day illness. "Unaccustomed as I am to matrimonial possibilities," he archly wrote to Ted's mother, "I was alarmed,—not to say horribly scared! However she had convincing proofs of my nursing qualifications: and no doubt in a year or two I will be disposed to take things with much more composure."[16]

Conrad retaliated—and placed himself in the passively dependent role—with a violent attack of fever and gout. The former was a recurrence of the blackwater fever (a form of malaria that turns urine black) that had poisoned his system in the Congo. The latter was precipitated by the malarial infection. Conrad's chronic gout may have originated in the sandy urinary deposits in his bladder, which had caused severe stomach cramps when he was ten years old. Gout is caused by sodium deposits in the joints that come from an excess of uric acid. The effect is hypertension and acute inflammatory arthritis in the toe, ankle, knee, wrist or elbow: "The initial attack may be sudden, waking the patient from sleep. The affected joint becomes hot, red, and swollen with shiny overlying skin and is extremely painful and tender. . . . Very acute attacks may be accompanied by . . . a change in mood."

Conrad's attacks of gout were partly psychological in origin. He did not seriously suffer from this disease, which crippled his hands, until he had to support himself and his wife as a writer. Jessie witnessed his first attack of gout on the Île-Grande in May 1896, when he ran a high fever, raved and had shivering fits for an entire week: "for most of the time Conrad was delirious. To see him lying in the white canopied bed, dark-faced, with gleaming teeth and shining eyes, was sufficiently alarming, but to hear him muttering to himself in a strange tongue (he must have been speaking Polish), to be unable to penetrate the clouded mind or catch one intelligible word, was for a young, inexperienced girl truly awful."[17]

Gout is now easily treatable by drugs that reduce the level of uric acid in the body. But in Conrad's time there was no cure for his agonizing illness, and he was reduced to the pathetic remedies of painting his hands and wrists with iodine and wearing woolen gout gloves (with the fingers cut off) for extra warmth. He consulted many doctors in England, France, Italy and Switzerland, tried all kinds of treatment and diet, and discovered that—like a vine clinging to a dying tree—it could not be driven off by "Medicine-man incantations." His attacks were often accompanied by angry explosions that provided a necessary—but unpleasant—release from excruciating pain.

Conrad's medical crisis was intensified by a financial disaster in July, while he was still on his honeymoon. In February 1895 he had received his inheritance from Uncle Tadeusz—15,000 rubles plus 1,200 rubles interest—and had lost all but a few hundred pounds of it through the bankruptcy of a South African gold mining company that belonged to Hope's brother-in-law. This loss, the failure of his bank in 1904 and his long years of arduous work for low wages as a writer, influenced his bitter satire on material interests in *Nostromo* and on financial speculation in *Chance*.

V

The financial crisis hastened the Conrads' departure for England at the end of September 1896. They wanted to live near the Hopes and found an all-too-modest house in the dreary hamlet of Stanford-le-Hope. It was about an hour by rail from London and a few miles inland from the north shore of the Thames estuary, amidst the Essex mud flats. The setting was similar to the watery landscape described in the opening pages of *Great Expectations*: "Ours was the marsh country, down by the river, within, as the river wound, twenty miles of the sea. . . . The dark flat wilderness beyond the churchyard, intersected with dykes and mounds and gates, with scattered cattle feeding on it, was the marshes; and the low leaden line beyond was the river; and the distant savage lair from which the wind was rushing, was the sea." Conrad also described this riverine setting in the second paragraph of *Heart of Darkness* and in *The Mirror of the Sea*, where he wrote, rather negatively: "The estuary of the Thames is not beautiful; it has no noble features, no romantic grandeur of aspect, no smiling geniality; but it is wide open, spacious, inviting, hospitable at the first glance, with a strange air of mysteriousness."

The best house they could find was a recently built semi-detached villa at the end of Victoria Street, which ran down from the railroad station. Conrad remained in his Gillingham Street lodgings while Jessie, with the help of her mother, prepared the cottage. "I have ordered her to get everything ready for work there in a week's time," he told Garnett, defining their characteristic roles. "Her efforts are superhuman. I sit still and grumble." Jessie described the theatrical role that Conrad had given her, which was designed to convey the impression of domestic perfection: "He had written the most minute instructions. I was to be ready dressed for the evening and taking my ease in the drawing-room three days after the arrival of the furniture; the new maid was to be instructed to answer his ring and show him into the room; the meal was to appear; he was to be shown to his study." But when the moment of his entrance arrived, Jessie spoiled the effect by her "childish impetuosity": "unable to restrain myself, I dashed to the door to receive him. . . . He received me coldly, and began to reproach me with concentrated bitterness. . . . There followed some really painful criticisms, sweeping condemnations, indeed, of all or nearly all I had done."

Garnett, an early visitor, remembered "the creaking boards, flimsy staircase and pokiness of that temporary dwelling place which stood indistinguishable from its fellows in a genteelish row."[18] Though Conrad was used to close confinement on a ship, his response to the admittedly hideous house was: "Damned jerry-built rabbit hutch. . . . Not room in this blamed hole to swing a cat." The five months on Victoria Street permanently cured him of living in a village or a town. From then on, he always remained isolated in the country.

This incident seems to confirm Jessie's and her sons' portraits of Conrad as a domestic tyrant—compulsive, rigid, demanding, severe—who issued orders to his "crew." Even Richard Curle, who adored Conrad, declared: "He never really lost the sea captain's attitude of thinking that orders were given to be obeyed, and that the work of a house ought to function as smoothly as that of a ship at sea."

Like Captain Shotover in Shaw's *Heartbreak House*, Conrad retained his maritime habits and habitually used nautical terminology at home. Borys reported that he kept the custom of four-hour rest periods, the result of his watches at sea, and would sleep in his wing-chair at odd hours of the day. He sometimes chided his sons for their "lubberly manner" and urged them to be "smart and seamanlike." He referred to Jessie's crutches as her "outriggers," and rather obscurely called a frock coat and top hat "a square-mainsail coat and gaff topsail-hat." John noted that "my father did not like his plate to be overloaded and 'looking like the deck cargo of a tramp steamer.' He maintained that in order to enjoy food one should always have 'a little bit of stowage space left,' which was far better than getting up from the table 'loaded to the gunnels.' "[19]

From the very beginning of their marriage Jessie developed a maternal as well as a wifely relationship with the lonely orphan and wanderer, who had little experience of a mother's care and a settled home, and he soon became extremely dependent upon her. Conrad, who wanted and needed a sacrificial wife and surrogate mother, wrote to an editor, after his first son was born: "I really ought to have a nurse—since my wife must also look after the other child." In a revealing and representative incident, recorded by Jessie, which took place during their holiday on Capri in 1905, Conrad (who had recurrent problems with his teeth but, terrified of dentists, did nothing about them) behaved like a child whose health and sanity were preserved by her care: "One night he lay with his poor head on my shoulder and his mouth full of water (I keeping awake and holding the glass ready to pass to him as he wanted it). He would fill his mouth, hand me the glass, and fall asleep, and the water would run all over me. I was soaked before the morning. When he finally roused himself sufficiently to be aware that he was uncomfortable, he declared we had been sleeping in a damp bed."[20]

Their way of addressing each other, in speech and in script, reinforced their mother-son relations. Jessie, who called her sons by their names, never called her husband "Joseph" or "Conrad" but—like Uncle Tadeusz—always addressed the older man as "Dear Boy." He called Jessie "Chica" (Spanish for "girl") or "Mrs. C."—both of which defined her relation to him. And he sometimes affectionately addressed her as "you old image"—as Kayerts does to the African Gobila in "Outpost of Progress." Conrad's letters to Jessie were solicitous but extremely stilted and oddly impersonal, as if he were writing to a stranger rather than a wife. Even late in life he tenderly wrote to her as "Dearest, Best of Girls," "Kit," "Kita," "Kitty," "Kittywick" and "Treasure, Heart, Dearest of All Dear Girls That Ever Were," and defined her as charming, precious, sweet, delightful and ever-so-good. Though well aware of her limitations, he was deeply attached to his wife.

Most of Conrad's friends found Jessie boring and could offer her little more than polite toleration. Ford, Lady Ottoline Morrell, Ellen Glasgow and (as we have seen) Edward Garnett were scathing about her gluttony and ignorance. Yet Jessie, denying reality or perhaps unaware of his true feelings, rashly claimed that Garnett "accepted me without question. . . . All [Conrad's] friends accepted me on indisputable terms. . . . I never had the slightest doubt about the sincerity of their feelings towards me." Her relations with the Garnetts, in fact, went from bad to worse. Their son, David, recalled that after Conrad had spent the night at the Cearne drinking a bottle of wine with Edward, Jessie—waiting in their lodgings, jealous of his friends and prone to take offense—"made a scene with Constance. There was nothing my mother hated more than a scene. So I believe that Jessie never came to our house again."[21]

H. G. Wells, alluding to the Conrads' marshy residence in Essex and to Jessie's dull, phlegmatic nature, called her "a Flemish thing from the mud flats." And Bloomsbury was no kinder. The svelte Virginia Woolf referred to her as Conrad's "lump of a wife." The grand Lady Ottoline, who had the greatest difficulty in making herself polite but knew she had to treat Jessie with proper respect, recognized her good qualities and was perceptive about her marriage to Conrad: "she seemed a nice and good-looking fat creature, an excellent cook . . . and was indeed a good and reposeful mattress for this hypersensitive, nerve-wrecked man, who did not ask from his wife high intelligence, only an assuagement of life's vibrations." And Dame Veronica Wedgwood realized, even as a child, "that my parents found her a bore but Conrad treated her with tremendous and rather formal protective courtesy and expected everyone who came to see him to do the same."[22] William Rothenstein and Conrad's disciple Richard Curle agreed about Conrad's gallantry and solicitude toward Jessie. Though self-centered, he was always concerned for her welfare. He gave serious thought to the presents and the holidays that would please her, had a touching fondness for her company and did not like to be invited anywhere without her.

The warm-hearted Jessie put up with poverty and tolerated his tantrums. But her companionship did little to alleviate his loneliness, and he preserved within his marriage his solitary inner life. Like Marlow with Kurtz's Intended, Conrad believed he had to protect Jessie when "darkness descends upon the stage" and to isolate himself within his anguish. After nineteen months of marriage, he felt a little more lonely than before and, using a favorite nautical metaphor, lamented: "I live so alone that I often fancy myself clinging stupidly to a derelict planet abandoned by its precious crew." As Conrad, who married at thirty-eight, poignantly and self-reflectively wrote in *Chance*: "Captain Anthony of the *Ferndale* must have had his loneliness brought home to his bosom for the first time of his life, at an age, thirty-five or thereabouts, when one is mature enough to feel the pang of such a discovery."[23]

VI

Conrad portrayed his hostility to marriage and fear of abandonment in *Victory*, "Amy Foster" (1903) and (as we shall see later on) in *The Secret Agent*. Axel Heyst, Yanko Goorall and Adolf Verloc are all isolated from society yet doomed by the need to form contacts with other people. In these three works, a young English wife (or mistress) is responsible for the death of her older, foreign husband.

Victory portrays Heyst's conflict between a desire for solitude and a need for emotional commitment. Lena's self-sacrificial desire to protect him merely intensifies his lack of feeling and inability to respond to her. Jessie dressed up as Lena and read her part aloud when the novel was dramatized; Conrad's exotic fantasy about the painful relations of a brooding intellectual and a humble, uneducated and grateful girl was partly based on his marriage.

Jessie refused to recognize the resemblance between herself and the biographical heroine of "Amy Foster," a dismal story that emphasized the radical gulf between the Poles and the English. She was even deliberately misleading and insisted that "the actual character, Amy Foster, was for many years in our service, and it was her animal-like capacity for sheer uncomplaining endurance that inspired Conrad. That and nothing else."

"Amy Foster," Conrad's most personal story, portrays Jessie's negative qualities, their intellectual estrangement and the fierce undercurrent of his isolation, loneliness and despair, his fear of being used and then abandoned by a woman—just as his mother had "abandoned" him when she died in exile. In the story, Yanko Goorall, whose Slavic surname means "mountain man," is completely out of his element while at sea. Emigrating to America, he is shipwrecked (Conrad's greatest professional fear) on the south coast of England, and washed ashore in an unknown country. He knows no English, is inarticulate and illiterate, and arouses suspicion, dislike and fear. He "finds himself a lost stranger, helpless, incomprehensible, and of a mysterious origin, in some obscure corner of the earth." The savage treatment of the castaway by the ordinary Kentish people helps to explain Conrad's desire to marry, to acclimatize himself and (despite his strong accent and exotic manners) to become an English gentleman.

Amy Foster, a plain, passive and stupid creature, the eldest of a large family, was put into service at the age of fifteen. The desperate Yanko courts her because she was the only person who pitied his isolation and saved him from suicide. Yet "it's enough to look at the red hands hanging at the end of those short arms, at those slow, prominent brown eyes, to know the inertness of her mind." Though Amy's father (like Jessie's mother) mistrusts foreigners, who sometimes behave very queerly to women and might want "to carry her off somewhere—or run off himself" (as Conrad himself did after his marriage and after his proposal), Yanko eventually marries the gentle and loving Amy.

Jessie wrote that during the malaria attack on their honeymoon, Conrad

> raved in grim earnest, speaking only in his native tongue and betraying no knowledge of who I might be. For hours I remained by his side watching the feverish glitter of his eyes . . . and listening to the meaningless phrases and lengthy speeches, not a word of which I could understand.

And during the fever attack in "Amy Foster," Yanko

> tossed, moaned, and now and then muttered a complaint. And she sat with the table between her and the couch, watching every movement and every sound, with the terror, the unreasonable terror, of that man she could not understand.

Both passages describe the delirious foreigner, watched over by a frightened English wife, who cannot help him or even understand his Slavic rantings.

Though Conrad, who was accused of abandoning his native country, regretted that Borys, despite his Slavic name, did not know the language, Yanko maintains contact with his culture by speaking to his son in a "disturbing, passionate and bizarre" tongue. Yanko gradually alienates Amy, who is repelled and frightened by the strangeness that first attracted her, and whose ignorance makes her behave in a cruel and inhuman way. When she finally abandons Yanko during his fever and runs off with their child, the innocent man is left to die in misery: thirsty, sick, helpless. His son has stolen his wife's love, and he is "cast out mysteriously by the sea to perish in the supreme disaster of loneliness and despair."[24]

VII

During his courtship and honeymoon Conrad not only searched for a ship but also, more successfully, continued his literary career. *Almayer's Folly* had been published under the pseudonym of Joseph Conrad in April 1895 in an edition of about 2,000 copies. And Conrad was gratified by the excellent reviews of his first novel. The *Daily News* said he had "annexed the island of Borneo." *T. P.'s Weekly* enthusiastically exclaimed: "under the magic of the writer of genius who has told its story—and he is a writer of genius—I learned almost the entire mystery and heart of this strange, far-off region." Most significantly, an anonymous reviewer in Frank Harris' prestigious *Saturday Review* declared, with considerable certainty: "*Almayer's Folly* is a very powerful story indeed, with effects that will certainly capture the imagination and haunt the memory of the reader. . . . It is exceedingly well imagined and well written, and it will certainly secure Mr. Conrad a high place among contemporary story-tellers."[25]

After Garnett had read *Almayer's Folly* in typescript and encouraged Conrad to write another book, they took a long night walk through the streets of London. When Conrad returned to his lodgings at eleven o'clock, tired but stimulated by their conversation, he sat down and wrote half a page of *An Outcast of the Islands* before going to sleep. This, he felt, committed him to another book, if not to another life. In his retrospective Author's Note to the novel, he described his first encounter with the model for Peter Willems and his curiosity about the paradoxical status of a man who was morally and physically isolated on a remote river in eastern Borneo:

The man who suggested Willems to me was not particularly interesting in himself. My interest was aroused by his dependent position, his strange, dubious status of a mistrusted, disliked, worn-out European living on the reluctant toleration of that Settlement hidden in the heart of the forest-

land, up that sombre stream which our ship was the only white man's ship
to visit. With his hollow, clean-shaved cheeks, a heavy grey moustache
and eyes without any expression whatever, clad always in a spotless sleeping suit much befrogged in front, which left his lean neck wholly uncov-
ered, and with his bare feet in a pair of straw slippers, he wandered
silently amongst the houses in daylight, almost as dumb as an animal and
apparently much more homeless.

Conrad was told that this familiar pariah had betrayed the Europeans
and brought the Arabs into the river. And yet the first time Conrad
dined with Olmeijer, there was the man who became the fictional
Willems "sitting at table with us in the manner of the skeleton at the
feast, obviously shunned by everybody, never addressed by anyone."
Faced with a situation that he himself feared (and which partly explained his decision to leave the *Vidar*), Conrad created the novel by
imagining the circumstances that would account for Willems' treachery
and disaster.

He did not begin serious work on the book (originally entitled *Two
Vagabonds*) until mid-August 1894, when he wrote Marguerite about his
original conception, his search for a dramatic conclusion and—
anticipating a critical problem—the difficulty of writing a novel without
women:

> I want to describe in broad strokes, without shading or details, two human
> outcasts such as one finds in the lost corners of the world. A white man
> and a Malay. You see how Malays cling to me! I am devoted to Borneo.
> What bothers me most is that my characters are so true. I know them so
> well that they shackle the imagination. The white is a friend of Almayer—
> the Malay is our old friend Babalatchi before he arrived at the dignity of
> prime minister and confidential adviser to the Rajah. There they are. But
> I can't find a dramatic climax. My head is empty, and even the beginning
> is heavy going. I won't inflict more on you. I already feel like letting
> everything drop. Do you think one can make something interesting with-
> out any women?!

Two and a half months later he told Marguerite that he had clarified his
theme, planned a climactic suicide and introduced Aissa: "First, the
theme is the unrestrained, fierce vanity of an ignorant man who has had
some success but neither principles nor any other line of conduct than
the satisfaction of his vanity. In addition, he is not even faithful to
himself. Whence a fall, a sudden descent to physical enslavement by an
absolutely untamed woman. I have seen that! The catastrophe will be

brought about by the intrigues of a little Malay state where poisoning has the last word. The *dénouement* is: suicide, again because of vanity."

In April 1894 Conrad had announced the death of the fictional Almayer in a letter to Marguerite; in September 1895, after thirteen months of work, he told Garnett, with mock-funereal diction: "It is my painful duty to inform you of the sad death of Mr. Peter Willems late of Rotterdam and Macassar [in the Celebes] who has been murdered on the 16th inst. at 4 p.m." Conrad would continue this habit by telling Garnett that the Nigger of the *Narcissus* "died on the 7th at 6 p.m." And he shouted out the window: " 'She's dead, Jess!' 'Who?' [Jessie] asked, suddenly feeling sick. 'Why, Lena, of course, and I have got the title: it is *Victory.*' "[26]

An Outcast of the Islands, twice as long and half as interesting as *Almayer's Folly,* takes place in Sambir twenty years before his first novel. It contains many of the same characters (Lingard, Almayer, Babalatchi and Lakamba) and portrays the themes of betrayal and retribution. Though the novel is overwritten and portentous, and has too much indirect narration instead of vivid rendering of direct experience, the heavy, convoluted style effectively suggests the claustrophobic jungle. Willems, caught stealing, is sent by the compassionate Lingard to Borneo to assist Almayer, whom he comes to despise. Married to a half-caste woman, overwhelmed by the tropical environment and by his sense of isolation, Willems becomes enslaved by Aissa, his Malay mistress. He reveals the valuable secret of Lingard's hidden river to his rivals, the Arab traders; and is finally shot by the embittered and vengeful Aissa.

The theme of the novel, which recurs throughout Conrad's life and works, is "the indestructible loneliness that surrounds, envelops, clothes every human soul from the cradle to the grave, and, perhaps, beyond." Conrad, who changed the conclusion from suicide to murder, told Garnett how he established a tranquil mood that contrasted to the violent ending, provoked when Willems' wife, Joanna, slaps Aissa in the face. Willems rushes toward Aissa and is shot by her, but he cannot accept the reality of his own extinction. Conrad portrays his last deranged thoughts through fragmented interior monologue: "His mouth was full of something salt and warm. He tried to cough; spat out. . . . Who shrieks: In the name of God, he dies!—he dies!—Who dies?—Must pick up—Night!—What? . . . Night already. . . ."

For copyright reasons the novel had to be published on the same day in both England and the United States. So when a fire in New York destroyed the entire American edition, the English publishers were forced to wait for a reprint. The book was finally brought out by Fisher

Unwin, in an edition of 3,000 copies, on Monday March 16, 1896—eight days before Conrad's marriage. The mostly unsigned reviews of *An Outcast of the Islands*, though not as enthusiastic as those of *Almayer's Folly*, praised "his marvellous power of depicting a painful situation," and conceded: "much is forgiven to genius, and there is genius in this novel." Other critics were troubled by the repulsive nature of the hero and by the verbosity of the book: "Mr. Conrad is wordy: his story is not so much told as seen intermittently through a haze of sentences. His style is like a river-mist."

After criticizing Conrad's murky style, the anonymous notice in the *Saturday Review* paradoxically concluded: "*An Outcast of the Islands* is, perhaps, the finest piece of fiction that has been published this year, as *Almayer's Folly* was one of the finest that was published in 1895. . . . Only greatness could make books of which the detailed workmanship was so copiously bad, so well worth reading, so convincing, and so stimulating."[27]

Conrad, then in Brittany, humbly wrote to thank the reviewer for his praise as well as for his criticism: "in the twilight of my ignorance, I have yet seen dimly the very shortcomings of which You point with a hand so fine and yet so friendly"—and was astonished and gratified to discover it had been written by H. G. Wells. "May I be cremated alive like a miserable moth if I suspected it!" he jubilantly told Garnett. "Anyway he descended from his 'Time Machine' to be as kind as he knew how." In his reply to Conrad, Wells wrote, with a tinge of superiority: "I really don't see why you should think gratitude necessary when a reviewer gives you your deserts. . . . If I have indeed put my finger on a weak point in your armour of technique, so that you may be able to strengthen it against your next occasion, I shall have done the best a reviewer can do. You have everything for the making of a splendid novelist except dexterity, and that is attainable by drill."[28]

This friendly exchange led to further correspondence and, early in 1899, after Conrad had moved to Pent Farm in Kent and become a neighbor, to meeting Wells through Ford. D. H. Lawrence perceptively described Wells, the self-made son of a shopkeeper and a lady's maid, apprenticed to a draper and then trained as a scientist, as "a funny little chap: his conversation is a continual squirting of thin little jets of weak acid: amusing, but not expansive." Nine years younger than Conrad, Wells had just established his reputation with two innovative novels, written in a clear, straightforward manner: *The Time Machine* (1895) and *The Island of Dr. Moreau* (1896). Conrad admired Wells' honesty and intelligence, called him a "Realist of the Fantastic" and told his Polish cousin that he was "a very original writer, *romancier du fantastique*, with a very individualistic judgment in all things and an astonishing imagination." In *Chance*, Conrad alluded to Wells' short stature and predilection for hiking as well as to his adulterous love affairs when he called Fyne "a serious-faced, broad-chested, little man," an "enthusiastic pedestrian," who "held very solemn views as to the destiny of women on this earth, the nature of our sublunary love, the obligations of this transient life."

Wells was one of the few people who did not seem to like Conrad. In his autobiography, he wrote that Conrad's implacable foreignness, their fundamentally different personalities and outlooks on life, created an unbridgeable chasm between them.

> [We had a] long, fairly friendly but always rather strained acquaintance. Conrad with Mrs. Conrad and his small blond haired bright-eyed boy [Borys], would come over to Sandgate, cracking a whip along the road, driving a little black pony carriage as though it was a droshky and encouraging a puzzled little Kentish pony with loud cries and endearments in Polish, to the dismay of all beholders. We never really "got on" together. I was perhaps more sympathetic and incomprehensible to Conrad than he was to me. I think he found me Philistine, stupid and intensely English; he was incredulous that I could take social and political issues seriously.[29]

Conrad later expressed his pessimistic philosophy and defined their fundamental difference: "You don't care for humanity," he told Wells, "but think they are to be improved. I love humanity but know they are not!" But he retained his affection for Wells and dedicated his darkest political novel, *The Secret Agent*, to him in 1907.

Conrad revealed his alienation from English culture when, wringing his hands and wrinkling his forehead, he would ask: "What is all this about Jane Austen? What is there *in* her? What is it all *about*?" Wells also ridiculed Conrad's noble persona (which others found sincere and attractive): "a romantic adventurous un-mercenary intensely artistic European gentleman carrying an exquisite code of unblemished honour through a universe of baseness." The hero of Wells' satiric novel *Boon* (1915), who "could not endure" Conrad, sneers at Americans for preferring Conrad to Crane and adoring his "florid mental gestures. . . . Conrad 'writes.' It shows." When Wells met the war poet Siegfried Sassoon in 1925, Wells repeated his early criticism and said "Conrad's books are very much *over-written*." Sassoon agreed, but noted: "I wish H.G. took as much trouble in finishing his own books, all the same."[30]

VIII

After the encouraging reviews—by Wells and others—and the relative ease with which he had completed *An Outcast of the Islands*, Conrad might well have expected to continue his critical success. Instead, he hit a bad patch and made two false starts. In the fall of 1895, after completing his second book, he wrote thirty-five pages of "The Sisters," a novel about a Ukrainian painter and a young Basque girl named Rita, who are both living in Paris. Conrad realized the novel was a failure and, following the sound advice of Garnett, abandoned it. Rita reappeared twenty years later in *The Arrow of Gold*.

In 1896, after asking Fisher Unwin to send him a Malay dictionary, Conrad began his third Malayan novel, *The Rescuer*. But he became blocked by doubts during the summer in Brittany and complained to Garnett about the difficulty of summoning up—like a demented medium—the plot of his novel:

> Now I've got all my people together I don't know what to do with them. The progressive episodes of the story *will* not emerge from the chaos of my sensations. I feel nothing clearly. And I am frightened when I remember that I have to drag it all out of myself. . . .
>
> There is 12 pages written and I sit before them every morning, day after day, for the last 2 months and can not add a sentence, add a word! I am paralyzed by doubt and have just sense enough to feel the agony but am powerless to invent a way out of it. This is sober truth. I had bad moments with the *Outcast* but never anything so ghastly—nothing half so hopeless. When I face that fatal manuscript it seems to me that I have forgotten how to think—worse! how to write.

He worked on it fitfully and fretfully between March 1896 and February 1899, progressed a short way into Part IV (nearly halfway through the novel), rescued the abandoned work in 1918, completed it the following year and finally published it as *The Rescue* in 1920.

As relief from *The Rescuer*, and while still on his honeymoon, Conrad began to write (and Jessie to type) his earliest short stories. He first wrote "The Idiots," influenced by Maupassant and set in Brittany; then "The Lagoon," a Malayan tale, which he described as "a tricky thing with the usual forests, river—stars—wind, sunrise, and so on—and lots of secondhand Conradese in it." He could, even at that early date, be ironic about his over-elaborate style, which Max Beerbohm wittily parodied in "The Feast," published in *The Christmas Garland* in 1912: "The roofs of the congested trees, writhing in some kind of agony private and eternal, made tenebrous and shifty silhouettes against the sky."[31]

Conrad conceded that the motif of "Karain," which he wrote in 1897, was almost identical with the motif of betrayal in "The Lagoon." Both are stories within a story, with similar Malay settings and themes. In "The Lagoon," Arsat steals the rajah's girl, is pursued, betrays his brother and leaves him behind to die. In "Karain," a Dutchman steals a native girl and is pursued by Karain, who accidentally shoots his loyal friend. In both tales, nature is hostile to man and indifferent to human suffering. "Karain" was the first story Conrad published in the magisterial *Blackwood's Magazine*, which paid the handsome sum of £40 and later serialized "Youth," *Heart of Darkness* and *Lord Jim*.

The ironically titled "An Outpost of Progress," the best by far of the early stories and a precursor to *Heart of Darkness*, was (Conrad said) "the lightest part of the loot I carried off from Central Africa." It takes place in a lonely trading station, three hundred miles from the nearest post, on the Kasai River, a tributary of the Congo. As Conrad moved from Malaya to Africa and from romance to satire, "all the bitterness of those days, all my puzzled wonder as to the meaning of all I saw—all my indignation at masquerading philanthropy [exploitation masked by idealism]—have been with me again, while I wrote. . . . I have divested myself of everything but pity—and some scorn." In this story, the Europeans' personal weaknesses and "civilized" values cannot withstand the hostile environment, which corrupts and destroys them:

> Contact with pure unmitigated savagery, with primitive nature and primitive man, brings sudden and profound trouble into the heart. To the sentiment of being alone of one's kind, to the clear perception of the loneliness of one's thoughts, of one's sensations—to the negation of the habitual, which is safe, there is added the affirmation of the unusual, which is dangerous; a suggestion of things vague, uncontrollable, and repulsive, whose discomposing intrusion excites the imagination and tries the civilized nerves of the foolish and the wise alike.[32]

The real danger, Conrad realized, lies within these hollow men. At the end of the story, after a trivial quarrel about a bit of sugar, Kayerts shoots his unarmed companion, Carlier, and is found hanging, with his tongue sticking out, when the late company steamer finally arrives. These four tales—along with the disastrous "Return" (written in 1897), a self-conscious attempt at mere virtuosity, which no magazine editor would touch and Conrad later condemned—were published in his fourth book and weakest volume of stories, *Tales of Unrest*.

Conrad was paid £20 for the copyright of *Almayer's Folly* and an advance of £50 against a 12 percent royalty for *An Outcast of the Islands*. Unwin, who lost heavily on both books, offered the same £50 for *The Nigger of the "Narcissus,"* but Conrad, encouraged by Garnett (in a sensitive position, as Unwin's reader and employee), asked for an advance of £100. When Unwin refused, Garnett, after trying Smith Elder, introduced Conrad to Sidney Pawling, a partner of William Heinemann, who met his demands. In *The Inheritors* (also published by Heinemann), Conrad and Ford expressed their disdain for patronizing publishers and satirized Unwin as Polehampton, a shifty-eyed philistine for whom books were merely an impressive commodity:

> He was rather thin, and his peaked grey hair, though it was actually well brushed [a Conradian detail], looked as if it ought not to have been. He had even an anxious expression. . . .
>
> "I . . . eh . . . believe I published your first book. . . . I lost money by it, but I can assure you that I bear no grudge—almost a hundred pounds. I bear no grudge. . . ."
>
> The man was original. He had no idea that I might feel insulted; indeed, he really wanted to be pleasant, and condescending, and forgiving. . . .
>
> He was not a publisher by nature. He had drifted into the trade and success, but beneath a polish of acquaintance retained a fine awe for a book as such.[33]

CHAPTER TEN

Literary Friendships
and Artistic Breakthrough
1897–1898

I

On March 13, 1897, the Conrads moved from Victoria Street to Ivy Walls, a fifteenth-century farmhouse, with an annual rent of £28, just outside Stanford-le-Hope. This larger, more comfortable home had an adjoining orchard and was protected by a row of lime and elm trees. The Thames could be seen from the second-floor window. Isolated in the country with Jessie and near Hope, with whom he took Sunday sailing trips, and blocked on *The Rescuer*, which he could neither complete nor abandon, Conrad felt cut off from intellectual and literary life.

He rarely met other writers except through introductions or through their initiative. But during 1897–98 he quickly developed a rich network of friendships—a literary cross-section of the Edwardian era—as authors read and admired his work, and sent him enthusiastic letters that led to meetings. He moved from Hope and Krieger, from Galsworthy and Sanderson, and from Edward Garnett to intimacy with four of the best writers of his time: Henry James, whom he met in February of 1897, Stephen Crane in October, Robert Bontine Cunninghame Graham in November—and (as we shall see in the next chapter) Ford Madox Ford in 1898.

Conrad's friends included literary admirers who gave him practical help: Garnett and Ford; coevals: James, Wells and Kipling; experienced men of action: Casement, Crane, Graham, Hugh Clifford and Perceval Gibbon; young disciples and substitute sons: Richard Curle, Jean-Aubry and Hugh Walpole. Galsworthy, Garnett, Ford, Wells and Clifford, as well as Arthur Symons and Sidney Colvin (whom he met later on), wrote many favorable reviews of Conrad's work. Curle and Walpole published flattering books about him during his lifetime, André Gide translated his work and Jean-Aubry became his first biographer. Extremely devoted and loyal, Conrad maintained most of his friendships throughout his life, and his quarrels with Krieger and (later) with Ford distressed him deeply. When in December 1897 Krieger became angry with him when he could not repay a considerable loan, Conrad lamented to Garnett: "My soul is like a stone within me. I am going through the awful experience of losing a friend. . . . When life robs one of a man to whom one has pinned one's faith for twenty years, the wrong seems too monstrous to be lived down."

II

Conrad admired the ideas, technique and style of several older contemporary writers: Cunninghame Graham, W. H. Hudson and Thomas Hardy. But he felt that Henry James was pre-eminent. James had known Conrad's three artistic idols—Turgenev, Flaubert and Maupassant—and emulated their devotion to art and striving for perfection. Ford, who followed in this tradition and published a book on James in 1914, recalled: "James was about the only living figure writing in English that Conrad regarded as at all his equal or whose work presented to him technical problems that he could not solve. . . . He would close a book by Henry James, sigh deeply and say: 'I don't know how the Old Man does it. There's nothing he does not know; there's nothing he can't do. That's what it is when you have been privileged to go about with Turgenev.' " Like Flaubert, James "compelled admiration,—about the greatest service one artist can render to another."[1]

Though eager to meet James, Conrad was diffident about approaching him. After hesitating for seven months, Conrad, who almost never made the first overture, sent James a copy of *An Outcast of the Islands* in October 1896 with an excessively humble and flattering inscription. Referring to James' fictional creations, he scattered capital letters as liberally as the praise that filled the flyleaf: "Exquisite Shades with live hearts, and clothed in the wonderful garment of Your prose, they have stood, consoling, by my side under many skies. They have lived with me, faithful and serene—with the bright serenity of Immortals. And to You thanks are due for such glorious companionship. I want to thank You for the charm of Your words, the delight of Your sentences, the beauty of Your pages!" These compliments may have been too much for the exquisitely mannered James. He waited until February 1897 to reciprocate with an inscribed copy of *The Spoils of Poynton* and with a more subtly expressed invitation to lunch at his London flat on February 25. "He is quite playful about it," Conrad joyfully told Garnett. "Says we shall be alone—no one to separate us if we quarrel. It's the most delicate flattery I've ever been victim to." During this visit Conrad spotted the diary of Samuel Pepys, who had a notable career in the Admiralty in the seventeenth century. While browsing through the volume, he found a passage that described boarding the *Naseby* to bring King Charles II back from exile in 1660: "My Lord in his discourse discovered a great deal of love to this ship"—and used it as the epigraph of *The Nigger of the "Narcissus."*

Henry James' nephew Billy provided an amusing account of Conrad and Ford's later visits to James at Lamb House in Rye: "James would take Conrad's arm and start off with him along the road, leaving Hueffer [Ford] and Billy to bring up the rear. 'Hueffer babbled,' the frustrated nephew said, 'and I didn't listen. I wanted to hear what the great men were saying up ahead, but there I was stuck with Hueffer. Occasionally a word or two would drift back and what I always heard was—French!' " Ford's version of these visits gently satirized the strained formality of the two mandarins. They habitually spoke to each other in French, and Conrad piled on the flattery in person as he had done when writing the inscription: "The politeness of Conrad to James and of James to Conrad was of the most impressive kind. Even if they had been addressing each other from the tribune of the Académie Française their phrases could not have been more elaborate or delivered more *ore rotundo*. James always addressed Conrad as '*Mon cher confrère*,' Conrad almost bleated with the peculiar tones that the Marseillaises get into their compliments '*Mon cher maître*.' . . . Every thirty seconds!" Paul Valéry noted that Conrad had a pleasant Provençal accent and Edouard Roditi observed: "he spoke French rather slowly, though not hesitantly. He had a slight foreign accent and chose his words with great care."[2]

James was much more guarded and reserved than Conrad. Troubled by Conrad's nervousness, his peculiar temperament and his profound morbidity, James felt, when with him, a mixture of amiability and anxiety. In *The Inheritors*, Conrad and Ford portrayed James as Callan and gave an exaggerated impression of his rather theatrical mannerisms:

> He—spoke—very—slowly—and—very—authoritatively, like a great actor whose aim is to hold the stage as long as possible. The raising of his heavy eyelids at the opening door conveyed the impression of a dark, mental

weariness; and seemed somehow to give additional length to his white nose. His short, brown beard was getting very grey, I thought. With his lofty forehead and with his superior, yet propitiatory smile, I was of course familiar. . . . His face was uniformly solemn, but his eyes were disconcertingly furtive.

Four years later Conrad published in the *North American Review* an extremely vague appreciative essay on James' sophisticated novels that managed, in 2,500 words, to say almost nothing substantial or significant. The creator of the tormented Lord Jim praised James as "the historian of fine consciences" and tautologically mentioned "his own victorious achievement in that field where he is a master." When the American collector John Quinn later asked Conrad if he had underestimated James in this essay, he weakly replied: "I said he was great and incomparable—and what more could one say?" In a more sincere and revealing letter to Galsworthy of March 1899, Conrad defended the sensitively restrained James against the charge of cold-heartedness: "He is cosmopolitan, civilised, very much 'homme du monde.' . . . To me even ['The Real Thing'] seems to flow from the heart because and only because the work approaches so near perfection yet does not strike [me as] cold. . . . I argue that in H.J. there is a glow and not a dim one either. . . . His heart shows itself in the delicacy of his handling."[3]

In June 1902, when Conrad was seeking a grant from the Royal Literary Fund, James' generous support helped him to secure the vitally needed £300. James praised Conrad to Edmund Gosse, who had taken the matter up with the prime minister, and, thinking of his own failure to secure a wide audience, stated that the very merits of his work precluded popular success:

The Nigger of the "Narcissus" is in my opinion the very finest and strongest picture of the sea and sea-life that our language possesses—the masterpiece in a whole great class; and Lord Jim runs it very close. When I think moreover that such completeness, such intensity of expression has been arrived at by a man not born to our speech, but who took it up, with similar courage, from necessity and sympathy, and has laboured at it heroically and devotedly, I am equally impressed with the fine persistence and the intrinsic success. Born a Pole and cast upon the waters, he has worked out an English style that is more than correct, that has *quality* and ingenuity. The case seems to me unique and peculiarly worthy of recognition. Unhappily, to be very serious and subtle isn't one of the paths to fortune. Therefore I greatly hope the Royal Literary Fund may be able to do something for him.

Though James had immense respect for Conrad's character and achievement, and could find no technical fault in his work, he did not really like his later novels and told Ford that they conveyed a disagreeable impression. James' personal uneasiness and artistic reservations about Conrad were intensified by an encounter that took place in February 1904, when Conrad abandoned his habitual gloom as well as his customary deference toward James. Edward Garnett's sister, Olivia, was present at a gathering which included W. H. Hudson, Galsworthy, Conrad, whose books were at last beginning to sell, and Henry James. Conrad, for once gleeful, exclaimed: "I am at the top of the tree." James replied with an exaggerated self-abasement that expressed his disapproval of Conrad's impermissible boast: "I am a crushed worm; I don't even revolve now, I have ceased to turn." This incident may have affected James' criticism of *Chance*, in which Conrad employed and perhaps parodied James' convoluted narrative techniques and achieved with them a popularity greater than the Master's. James' essay on "The Younger Generation," published in the *Times Literary Supplement* of April 2, 1914, portrayed his friend as an errant disciple (Conrad by then was fifty-six), and called Conrad "absolutely alone as a votary of the way to do a thing that should make it undergo most doing." Two years later the wounded Conrad, who maintained his profound respect for the Master, told John Quinn that James had rather airily condemned his elaborate narrative methods and confessed: "I may say, with scrupulous truth, that this was the only *time* a criticism affected me painfully."[4]

In his last years, James' estimation of Conrad's work continued to fall. In a letter of February 1914 to his colleague and compatriot Edith Wharton, he was more enthusiastic about *Chance* than he would be two months later in "The Younger Generation." And he suggested (without specifying titles) that *Nostromo* and *The Secret Agent* were Conrad's last successful works and had been followed by a series of failures (*A Set of Six, Under Western Eyes* and *'Twixt Land and Sea*): "The last book [*Chance*] happens to be infinitely more practicable, more curious and readable, (in fact really rather *yieldingly* difficult and charming), than any one of the last three or four impossibilities, wastes of desolation, that succeeded the two or three final good things of his earlier time." James' final word on Conrad (in a letter of July 1915 to Edith Wharton) strangely emphasized his literary paralysis: "I haven't for instance much hope of Conrad, who produces by the sweat of his brow and tosses off, in considerable anguish, at the rate of about a word a month."

Though Conrad may not have realized, or may even have deceived himself about James' personal uneasiness and serious criticism of his work, James continued to "compel respect." As he told John Quinn in May 1916, just after James' death: "In our private relations he has always been warmly appreciative and full of invariable kindness. I had a profound affection for him. He knew of it and accepted it as if it were something worth having."[5]

III

Henry James was fourteen years older than Conrad; Stephen Crane, James' American antithesis, fourteen years younger. James, cautious and cultivated, felt at home in the drawing room. Crane, reckless and rough, belonged to the battlefield. Born in Newark, New Jersey, in 1871, the fourteenth and youngest child of a Methodist minister, Crane rebelled against his family's genteel values. He became a reporter in New York and a correspondent in the Southwest and Mexico, in Cuba and Greece; and published *Maggie: A Girl of the Streets* in 1893 and *The Red Badge of Courage* two years later. In the course of his wanderings he formed a common-law marriage with Cora Taylor, the former proprietor of the aply-named brothel, the Hotel de Dream in Jacksonville, Florida. Cora may have influenced Conrad's portrayal in *Victory* of Lena, a prostitute stranded in Java.

The Cranes pitched up in England after he had reported the brief Greco-Turkish War of 1897. They lived first in Ravensbrook, in Surrey, and then in Brede Manor, in Kent, which Ford said was very damp, hopelessly remote and full of evil influences. When the publisher Sidney Pawling asked Crane if there was anyone he would especially like to meet in England, he mentioned Conrad, whose *Nigger of the "Narcissus"* was then being serialized in William Ernest Henley's influential *New Review*. Crane—"a young man of medium stature and slender build, with very steady, penetrating blue eyes"—bore a striking resemblance to Robert Louis Stevenson. Both had an oval face, drooping mustache, long thin nose and frail tubercular body. During the luncheon in London with Conrad and Pawling, Crane provocatively declared that he was bored by Stevenson, the darling of the English literary world, who had recently died in Samoa. Conrad also thought Stevenson's reputation—based more on his charming personality and exotic life than on his romantic novels—was inflated and sympathized with Crane's criticism. By the time Pawling left at four o'clock, Conrad and Crane had established an unusual rapport. Fascinated by each other's conversation, they were reluctant to part and spent the rest of the evening walking around London and talking about everything from Greece at war to Balzac's *Comédie humaine*.

Like Conrad, Crane had been a man of action, risked danger and come close to death. He had been shipwrecked off the Florida coast in 1896 and had survived for several days in a lifeboat. This disaster, which matched Conrad's experiences on the *Palestine*, became the basis of one of Crane's best short stories, "The Open Boat" (1897). "The boat thing is immensely interesting," Conrad told Crane. "I don't use the word in its common sense. It is fundamentally interesting to me." Though Conrad complained about his relatively minor ailments while Crane was stoical about his fatal tuberculosis, they both recognized profound similarities in their temperaments. Even when Conrad felt seedy, he could, with his beloved Stevie (he never called James "Hank"), forget his worries and, for once, have a "real good time." There was in Crane, Conrad believed, "a strain of chivalry which made him safe to trust with one's life."[6] In the summer of 1899 Conrad and Crane bought a twenty-two-foot sailboat, *La Reine*, from G. F. W. Hope, moored it at Rye and used it for excursions in the Channel.

Unlike James, Crane fully reciprocated Conrad's admiration and friendship, and consistently praised him in letters, in print and in conversation. When he read Conrad's fine description of the death of the consumptive James Wait ("Something resembling a scarlet thread hung down his chin out the corner of his lips—and he had ceased to breathe"), which had for him an intensely personal meaning, he punned on the hero's name and wrote Conrad: "I felt ill over that red thread lining from the corner of the man's mouth to his chin. It was frightful with the weight of a real and present death." In an essay of March 1898, Crane agreed with James' high estimate of *The Nigger of the "Narcissus"* and praised it (with some American hyperbole) as "a marvel of fine descriptive writing. It is unquestionably the best story of the sea written by a man now alive, and as a matter of fact, one would have to make an extensive search among the tombs before he who has done better could be found." James Gibbons Huneker, another American admirer, remarked that Crane spoke as reverently of Conrad, as if he were the Blessed Virgin Mary.[7]

Crane's enthusiasm for Conrad's work prompted his suggestion that they collaborate on a play based on the theme (according to Garnett) of a ship wrecked on an island or (according to Conrad) of "a man personating his 'predecessor' (who had died) in the hope of winning a girl's heart. The scenes were to include a ranch at the foot of the Rocky Mountains, I remember, and the action, I fear, would have been frankly melodramatic." Conrad swore to Crane that he had no dramatic gift, that Crane himself possessed the requisite terseness, clear eye and easy imagination. At the same time, Conrad confessed to Graham that his "dark and secret ambition" was to write a play. But the distance between their houses, Crane's chaotic way of life and his sudden departure (with the help of an advance procured by Conrad from Heinemann) to cover the Spanish-American War, prevented the play from being written. Conrad would no doubt have profited from collaboration with Crane when he attempted to realize his dramatic ambitions toward the end of his career.

Crane, though still in his twenties, had begun to publish several years before Conrad. Impressed by Crane's fluency, which provided an astonishing contrast to his own agonized paralysis, Conrad noted: "I have seen him sit down before a blank sheet of paper, dip his pen, write the first line at once and go on without haste and without pause for a number of hours." But his reluctance to collaborate may also have been based on reservations about the all-too-easy imagination, lack of artistic perfection and absence of resonant depths in the work of his young friend. "I could not explain why he disappoints me," he told their mutual friend Edward Garnett, "why my enthusiasm withers as soon as I close the book. While one reads, of course, he is not to be questioned. He is the master of his reader to the very last line—then—apparently for no reason at all—he seems to let go his hold."[8]

Considering his genuine fondness for Crane and the sweetness of Crane's character, Conrad's first essay about him (1919) was curiously negative. Conrad wrote that Crane, who was ignorant about Balzac but honest enough to ask Conrad about him, "knew little of literature, either of his own country or of any other." Though Crane had packed an extraordinary amount of travel and experience into his short life, Conrad emphasized "his ignorance of the world at large—he had seen very little of it." Declaring that Crane was only "half aware of the exceptional quality of his achievement," he maintained that his early death was "a great loss to his friends, but perhaps not so much to literature." Conrad stressed Crane's good nature as well as the strain of weakness in his character that allowed him to be surrounded "by people who understood not the quality of his genius and were antagonistic to the deeper fineness of his nature." In an unpublished letter to an American correspondent, Conrad elaborated his condemnation of Crane's parasitic and even treacherous retinue. They did not appreciate his work, and flattered, patronized and slandered both him and his wife. Conrad strongly disapproved of this crowd, but could not persuade the good-hearted

Crane that his "friends" were not as decent as he was himself.[9] In the end, Conrad was disappointed by Crane's works as well as by his character.

In his second and much longer essay, an introduction to Thomas Beer's biography of 1923, Conrad again stressed Crane's misfortune and morbidity: "Crane had not the face of a lucky man. . . . [He had] the smile of a man who knows that his time will not be long on this earth." On his final visit to Crane in Dover on May 23, 1900, Conrad, who had seen Apollo slowly die of tuberculosis, knew that Crane was doomed: "He had been very ill and Mrs. Crane was taking him to some place in Germany, but one glance at that wasted face was enough to tell me that it was the most forlorn of all hopes. The last words he breathed out to me were: 'I am tired. Give my love to your wife and child.' "

Crane's last letter, written immediately after seeing Conrad on his last day in England, was a chivalric plea to Sanford Bennett to assist his friend. (If Conrad had known about this letter, he surely would have been more positive about and more generous to Crane in his two essays.) Crane wrote: "My condition is probably known to you. . . . I have Conrad on my mind very much just now. Garnett does not think it likely that his writing will ever be popular outside the ring of men who write. He is poor and a gentleman and proud. His wife is not strong and they have a kid. If Garnett should ask you to help pull wires for a place on the Civil List for Conrad please do me the last favor. . . . I am sure you will."[10] Two weeks later Crane died at the age of twenty-nine in Baden-weiler, in the Black Forest, where in 1904 Anton Chekhov would also die of the same disease.

Crane's death was one of a grim series that deeply disturbed Conrad at the turn of the century. In December 1899 Hope's seventeen-year-old son was sexually assaulted and murdered. His stripped and beaten body was found in a ditch in the Essex marshes less than a mile from Ivy Walls farm. Jack Hope's murder was followed, in alarming succession, by the deaths of Jessie's maid's husband from a blood clot in February 1901, of Constance Garnett's brother in a climbing accident on the Matterhorn in July 1901 and of Ford's father-in-law by suicide in February 1902.

I V

After reading Conrad's bitter satire on colonialism, "An Outpost of Progress," in *Cosmopolis* during June and July 1897, Cunninghame Graham wrote an admiring letter that led to a meeting in London in November and to a lifelong friendship. Ford described Graham as "the magnificent prose writer, rightful King of Scotland, head of the Clan Graham, Socialist Member of Parliament [and] gaolbird"—for his political protests. He was also a traveler, horseman, rancher, cattle-dealer, frontiersman, fencing-master, journalist, prospector, historian and Scottish nationalist.

Though the House of Lords had denied the claim of Graham's father to the Earldom of Monteith, which had expired in 1694, Graham continued to maintain his unrealistic claim to the crown of Scotland by descent from the medieval King Robert II. Graham's maternal grandfather, an admiral who had commanded ships in the West Indies and was a friend of the South American liberators, Bolívar and Páez, later represented Stirlingshire in the Reform Parliament of 1832. Graham's maternal grandmother was Spanish, and gave birth to his mother on the admiral's flagship off the coast of Venezuela. In 1845 Graham's father, a wealthy major in the Scots Greys, was thrown from a horse and fractured his skull. This injury caused brain damage and led to fits of violent temper; and in 1878 the family was forced to confine him in a shooting lodge.

Graham (five years older than Conrad) was born in London in 1852, and learned Spanish at the age of eight when visiting relatives in Cádiz. He went to Harrow, which he disliked, and then studied German, French and fencing at a school in Brussels. When he was seventeen his parents gave him the money to go into partnership with two Scots who had a ranch in Argentina. He arrived in Buenos Aires in 1870 and lived in the Americas for the next thirteen years. During this adventurous period he acquired physical courage and became an expert horseman. He valued energy and vitality, disliked conventional behavior, and developed a taste for violence and revolutionary politics.

In 1883 Graham's father died and he was summoned home to Scotland. In 1886 he successfully stood as an advanced Liberal and Home Ruler for Northwest Lanarkshire, which included the slums of Glasgow, and was a prominent member of parliament for six years. Frank Harris vividly described the cowboy dandy as "above middle height, of slight, nervous, strong figure, very well dressed, the waist line evenly defined, with a touch of exoticism in loose necktie or soft hat; in colouring the reddish brown of a chestnut; the rufous hair very thick and up-standing; the brown beard trimmed to a point and floating moustache; the oval of the face a little long; the nose Greek; the large blue eyes." T. E. Lawrence punctured this romantic persona by declaring: "Not much brain, you know, but a great heart and hat: and what a head of hair!"[11] Despite his class, wealth, pride and foppishness, Graham was a democratic aristocrat, a radical with Tory sympathies, an idealist and a humanitarian. He had the temperament of a soldier of fortune, and his socialism was based on a romantic conception of freedom and a profound sympathy for the underdog.

Despite their political differences, Conrad shared many of Graham's values and beliefs. Both came from a noble, feudal background and believed in the chivalric concepts of fidelity and honor. Both were men of action who had traveled widely and had extensive experience in practical affairs. Both were interested in exotic cultures, had a fondness for French and admired Mediterranean culture. Both hated tyranny and exploitation, were fiercely anti-imperialistic and believed in home rule for Scotland and for Poland. Graham had temperamental affinities with Apollo Korzeniowski as well as with Conrad, and like Apollo was a connoisseur of hopeless causes.

Conrad used Graham as a model for Don Carlos Gould in *Nostromo* and initiated the adulatory writing about him. He always insisted that Graham was a *grand seigneur* born out of his time and contrasted Graham's idealism with his own pessimism: "You with your ideals of sincerity, courage and truth are strangely out of place in this epoch of material preoccupations. . . . You seem to me tragic with your courage, with your beliefs and your hopes. . . . You are a most hopeless idealist— your aspirations are irrealisable. You want from men faith, honour, fidelity to truth in themselves and others. . . . What makes you dangerous is your unwarrantable belief that your desire may be realized. That is the only point of difference between us." Conrad also valued faith, honor and fidelity, but he had seen enough of the consequences of revolution to be convinced that Graham's idealistic radicalism was an illusion.

William Rothenstein perceived that there was also a negative, bitter and contradictory side to Graham's character: "Conrad knew that Cunninghame Graham was more cynic than idealist, that he was by nature an aristocrat, whose socialism was his symbol of his contempt for a feeble aristocracy, and a blatant plutocracy." Even staunch admirers like Edward Garnett spoke of Graham's icy disdain and sardonic contempt for the human race. After he was defeated for re-election as a Labour candidate, he angrily denounced parliament and cynically admitted: "I have been foolish enough to soil myself with the pitch of politics, and to have endured the concentrated idiocy of the Asylum for Incapables at Westminster for six years."[12]

Graham's idealism provoked some of Conrad's most serious and interesting letters. He treated Graham's socialist-republican ideas with philosophical contempt, and stated (even exaggerated for Graham's benefit) the pessimistic ideas that derived from his Polish heritage, his father's legacy, his experience at sea, the current scientific belief that the universe was tending toward inertia and his reading of Schopenhauer's *The World as Will and Idea.*

Conrad's letters to Graham, who brought out the gloomiest side of his nature, expressed the beliefs that informed his greatest works: that life is a dream and faith an illusion, that this world consists of meaningless suffering, that there are no moral absolutes and that man's tragic fate is to end in hopeless nothingness:

> Faith is a myth and beliefs shift like mists on the shore; thoughts vanish; words, once pronounced, die; and the memory of yesterday is as shadowy as the hope of to-morrow. . . .
>
> In this world—as I have known it—we are made to suffer without the shadow of a reason, of a cause or of guilt. . . .
>
> There is no morality, no knowledge and no hope; there is only the consciousness of ourselves which drives us about a world that . . . is always but a vain and floating appearance. . . .
>
> A moment, a twinkling of an eye and nothing remains—but a clot of mud, of cold mud, of dead mud cast into black space, rolling around an extinguished sun. Nothing. Neither thought, nor sound, nor soul. Nothing.

The only possible antidote, Conrad believed, was profound scepticism, which he called "the tonic of minds, the tonic of life, the agent of truth—the way of art and salvation."[13]

Graham brought out his first books, *Notes on the District of Monteith, For Tourists and Others* (1895) and *Father Archangel of Scotland and Other Essays* (1896), at the same time as Conrad began to publish. During the last forty years of his life Graham tossed off two hundred short stories and sketches, more than half of them for Frank Harris' *Saturday Review,* and eleven historical works about South America. D. H. Lawrence later exposed and condemned Graham's haste, carelessness and insincerity (a vivid contrast to Conrad's anxious perfectionism) that were the radical defects of his work: "Don Cunninghame, alas, struts feebly in the conquistadorial footsteps. . . . He writes without imagination, without imaginative insight or sympathy, without colour, and without real feeling. . . . He lifts a swash-buckling fountain pen, and off he goes. The result is a shoddy, scrappy, and not very sincere piece of work."

Conrad perceived but ignored these faults in characteristically loyal and flattering letters about the work of a man he greatly admired. He dedicated *Typhoon* to Graham in 1903 and Graham returned the compliment by dedicating *Progress* to Conrad in 1905. "I've always felt that there are certain things which I can say to you," he told Graham, "because the range of your feelings is wider and your mind more independent than that of any man I know." Graham was sufficiently intimate with Conrad to correct his pronunciation of English. Richard Curle observed that Graham, like Crane, brought out the best in his friend: "In each other's company they appeared to grow younger; they treated one another with that kind of playfulness which can only arise from a complete, unquestioning, and ancient friendship. I doubt whether the presence of any man made Conrad happier than the presence of Don Roberto."[14] Though Conrad met James, Crane and Graham infrequently, for meals and conversation, and kept in touch by correspondence, their friendship and appreciation of his work were vitally important to him.

V

In July 1897, between lunching with James and meeting Crane, Conrad—who had told Jessie he did not intend to have children—unhappily informed Ted Sanderson that she was pregnant and prepared himself for the worst: "There is no other news—unless the information that there is a prospect of some kind of descendant may be looked upon in the light of something new. I am not unduly elated. Johnson [the doctor] says it may mend Jess' health permanently—if it does not end her." Jessie felt Conrad was not pleased by the prospect of an heir; he took no responsibility for her condition and behaved as if she had "played him false." The arrival of his children, who were both dreadfully sick throughout their early childhood, always took him by surprise.

When Jessie's time came and he was sent to fetch the doctor, Conrad assumed there was no hurry and accepted the doctor's offer of a leisurely second breakfast. According to Jessie, two frantic messengers had to be sent before husband and doctor returned to Ivy Walls for the delivery. On January 15, 1898, expressing irritation, distancing himself from the event and disguising his deepest feelings, Conrad told Graham: "This letter missed this morning's post because an infant of the male persuasion arrived and made such a row that I could not hear the Postman's whistle." Describing the rather objectionable infant to his cousin in Poland, Conrad emphasized his physical unattractiveness (as he had done when describing Jessie): dark hair, enormous eyes and the appearance of a monkey. To Jessie, he exclaimed with considerable amazement: "Why, it's just like a human being."

Fearful of losing Jessie's love and attention, the forty-year-old Conrad was reluctant to accept the arrival of his son. In March 1898 he could scarcely bear the short train journey with his family to visit Stephen Crane in Surrey. Jessie, who liked to portray Conrad as a kind of superior fool, vividly recalled:

> He had taken our tickets, first class, and intended travelling in the same carriage, but—here he became most emphatic—on no account were we to give any indication that he belonged to our little party. . . . [He] seated himself in a far corner, ostentatiously concealing himself behind his newspaper and completely ignoring his family. . . . The baby whimpered and refused to be comforted. I caught a glance of warning directed at me from over the top of the paper. All my efforts to soothe the infant proved unavailing, and the whole carriage re-echoed with his lusty howls. The paper was flung aside and from all sides came murmurs of consternation and sympathy for him—the only man; the stranger in the carriage. . . . Then the whole carriage was convulsed with suppressed merriment when my young sister [Dolly] turned to Joseph Conrad and, forgetting his injunction, demanded that he should reach down the case that contained the baby's bottle.

The brooding genius was thus forced into the humiliating role of helpful father. A year later, in a letter to Helen Sanderson (who had married Ted in April 1898), Conrad suggested that he still felt distant from his son, whom he invested with adult vices: "I do not mind owning I wished for a daughter. I can't help feeling she would have resembled me more and would have been perhaps easier to understand. . . . At the age of thirteen months he is an accomplished and fascinating barbarian, full of charming wiles and of pitiless selfishness."[15] The troubled and sometimes tragic relations of father and daughter (though not father and son) were a constant theme in Conrad's works.

Wishing to pay homage to his Polish heritage, Conrad told Aniela Zagorska that the child would be baptized in the Chapel of the Cloister of the Carmelites in Southwark (though this Chapel was in North Kensington and he was not baptized there). He also explained: "I wanted to have a purely Slavonic name, but one which could not be distorted either in speech or in writing—and at the same time one which was not too difficult for foreigners (non-Slavonic). I had, therefore, to reject names such as Wladyslaw, Boguslaw, Wienczyslaw etc., I do not like

Bohdan: so I decided on Borys, remembering that my friend Stanislaw Zaleski gave this name to his eldest son, so that apparently a Pole may use it."

It is surprising that Conrad's own names (Joseph and Theodore) as well as those of his father and uncles (Apollo, Robert, Hilary, Tadeusz and Stefan), which could easily have been pronounced in English, were notably absent from this list of possibilities. Conrad's biographers have assumed that the name Borys, adapted to English and strangely spelled with a "y" instead of an "i," was typically Russian, uncommon in Poland and given "under an illusion that it is a name used in the Ukraine and by Poles living there as well." Yet it seems impossible that Conrad, who hated Russians, would ignorantly confer a Russian name on his first-born son and would spell it with a "y" for no apparent reason. In fact, Conrad chose the name carefully and was well aware that the Ukrainian-Polish Borys (as opposed to the Russian-Bulgarian Boris), the first Kievan-Slavic martyr and saint of the Ukrainian church, was and still is a prominent name in the part of the Polish Ukraine where Conrad was born.[16]

VI

Conrad had developed his methods of composition, prose style and theory of art by 1897, when he wrote his first masterpiece, *The Nigger of the "Narcissus,"* which was enthusiastically praised by his new literary friends. Though he denied (in his Author's Note to *A Set of Six*) that he made notes before writing his fiction, he did, in fact, take extensive notes from source books to refresh his memory when composing his Malayan novels, his Napoleonic novels and *Nostromo*. His "Congo Diary" as well as notebooks on the Franco-Prussian War (possibly prepared for collaboration with Stephen Crane) have survived. Conrad needed a factual basis to inspire his fiction and believed: "Imagination, not invention, is the supreme master of art as of life." His imaginative and exact rendering of authentic memories were based on reading as well as on his actual experience.

Conrad usually wrote with a common steel pen, which he sometimes saved, after it had worn out, for sentimental reasons. The manuscript of "Youth" (1898), however, was composed (atypically and in the manner of D. H. Lawrence) with pencil and in a little notebook, while lying on his stomach under a chestnut tree at Ivy Walls farm. Though Conrad always came down to breakfast at exactly nine o'clock, he was a slow and reluctant starter. In his middle and late years, he usually spent the mornings reading the newspapers and answering letters. But he often worked from half past eight in the evening until two or three in the morning and finished many novels, after a long spurt of work, in the middle of the night.

He could not face the anguished prospect of writing a long novel over a period of years. So he conceived works like *Lord Jim* as stories and claimed he was nearly finished when he still had a long way to go. When composing, he tried to visualize the movement of successive scenes. He would absorb himself in prolonged meditation about his novels until his characters and plot could be grasped, and were ready to flow through his pen and onto the paper. His ambition, as he explained in his Preface to *The Nigger of the "Narcissus,"* was to re-create and intensify reality and "by the power of the written word to make you hear, to make you feel—it is, before all, to make you *see*. That—and no more, and it is everything."[17]

A slow and painstaking writer, Conrad felt utterly exhausted after completing three hundred words—a page and a half of his script—which was his average daily achievement. While writing *An Outcast of the Islands* he agonized with pen in hand and produced only six lines in six days. Sometimes he wrote even less than this. When blocked on *The Rescuer*, for example, he produced three sentences in eight hours, but erased them before leaving his desk in despair. As Ford later told Robert Lowell: "Conrad spent a day finding the *mot juste*; then killed it."

Conrad found imaginative writing a form of exquisite torture. He converted nervous force into phrases, felt as if each page were wrenched from his very soul, and needed crisis and frenzy to complete his work. Like D. H. Lawrence, he used the metaphor of coal-mining to symbolize the exploration of the unconscious, and told Garnett: "I had to work like a coal-miner in his pit, quarrying all my English sentences out of a black night." When encouraging his friends and criticizing the manuscripts of Galsworthy, Garnett, Ford, Hugh Clifford, Norman Douglas and Warrington Dawson, he urged them to search the depths of their being and to strive for the highest standards. As he told Edward Noble—who was also born in 1857, served in the merchant marine and would publish fifteen novels of the sea between 1905 and 1929—"you must squeeze out of yourself every sensation, every thought, every image—mercilessly, without reserve and without remorse; you must search the darkest corners of your heart, the most remote recesses of your brain."[18]

Conrad had never been gratified by his creative gift, which brought many hours of unhappiness, doubt and heart-searching. Following the Romantic tradition of Nietzsche and of Rimbaud, he told Dawson, a young American disciple, that torment and agony were essential to creation: "Suffering is an attribute, almost a condition of greatness, of devotion, of an altogether self-forgetful sacrifice to that remorseless fidelity to the truth of his own sensations, at whatever cost of pain and contumely, which for me is the whole Credo of the artist." Just before completing The Nigger of the "Narcissus" he said that he could not eat, suffered from nightmares and terrified his wife. While struggling with The Rescuer he felt suicidal and thought he had suffered a mental breakdown: "The fear of this horror coming back to me makes me shiver. As it is it has destroyed already the little belief in myself I used to have." And while working on Nostromo, amidst painful attacks of gout, he exclaimed: "If I had written each page with my blood I could not feel more exhausted," and resembled the Poe-like artist of Robert Lowell's "The Severed Head," who "dripped/a red ink dribble on us, as he pressed/the little strip of plastic tubing clipped/to feed it from his heart."[19] Conditions improved slightly after 1904, when Conrad engaged Miss Lillian Hallowes as his secretary. The tall and willowy sister of a naval architect, she had (according to Borys) a vacant expression and a supercilious manner, but was able to lighten Conrad's burden.

A major cause of Conrad's artistic agony was his eternal struggle with the English language. He complained that critics who had penetrated his pseudonym considered him "a sort of freak, an amazing bloody foreigner writing in English." But even after he had published Lord Jim and Nostromo, he still felt English was a foreign tongue that demanded a fearful effort. When an acquaintance wondered "how so un-English a man in temperament, looks, and utterance as Conrad should be able to write such perfect English," Conrad replied: "Ah, if only I could write zee English, good, well! But you will see, you will see."[20]

Another difficulty was that Conrad retained many characteristics of Polish as well as of French prose style, which provided an exotic foundation and made his English seem unusual even when it was grammatically correct. Polish has longer sentences, "it is rich in adjectives, more sedate in pace, less ambiguous, and tends to the rhetorical." Conrad's overfondness for triple parallelism, especially in his early works ("all that mysterious life of the wilderness that stirs in the forest, in the jungles, in the hearts of wild men"), as well as for rhetorical abstraction ("It was the stillness of an implacable force brooding over an inscrutable intention"[21]), is more typical of Polish than English and reveals his Slavic literary legacy.

Conrad's books usually received favorable reviews. But contemporary critics, as well as James and Crane, realized that the very qualities that enhanced his reputation—his exotic style, complex narration, profound themes, pessimistic ideas—discouraged his readers and diminished the sales of his books. Reviewing *The Nigger of the "Narcissus"* in the *Spectator* of December 1897, one critic perceived: "Mr. Conrad is a writer of genius; but his choice of themes, and the uncompromising nature of his methods, debar him from attaining a wide popularity." Yet as Conrad's ideas were justified by the events of the twentieth century, he came to be admired by modern critics for beliefs that seemed more in accord with our time than with his own.

The poor sales of his books led to money troubles that persisted from 1895 until 1913, for he always spent much more than he earned. Neither a fluent nor a successful writer, with a growing family and a tendency to live above his means, Conrad found it impossible to maintain a middle-class façade or to survive on his income as a writer. Forced to borrow money from friends and editors—Adolf Krieger, Spiridion Kliszczewski (the Pole in Cardiff), Galsworthy, Garnett and Ford as well as William Blackwood, David Meldrum (Blackwood's London editor) and the American publisher S. S. McClure—he was unable to repay his debts and felt guilty about his dishonorable behavior. Alluding to his slowness as a writer, Conrad angrily told Unwin, when negotiating terms for *The Nigger of the "Narcissus"*: "I can't afford to work for less than ten pence per hour and must work in a way that will give me this magnificent income." After he had sold the American rights of the unfinished *Rescuer* to S. S. McClure for £250, he regretfully told Ted Sanderson that McClure "sends on regular cheques which is—according to his lights—right, but I pocket them serenely which—according to my lights—looks uncommonly like a swindle."[22] Despite these scruples, Conrad kept the money.

When writing became intolerably oppressive, Conrad dreamed of resuming his life in the merchant marine. Two weeks after Borys was born, he again felt the call of the sea and imagined he could take his family with him. And in August 1898, still tormented by the implacable *Rescuer*, he begged Graham to get him a Scottish ship: "To get to sea would be salvation. I am really in a deplorable state, mentally." The following month he spent three days in Glasgow, making the rounds of the shipping offices and (for the last time) searching for a command. But there were no vacant posts for masters in the vanishing Clyde clippers and Conrad was forced back to his "torture chamber."

Though Conrad tried to return to sea, he hated the reputation he had acquired as a novelist of the sea, which seemed to limit rather than to define his achievement and to discourage his readers from accepting his works on other subjects. He told friends, with considerable exasperation, that "behind the concert of flattery, I can hear something like a whisper: 'Keep to the open sea! Don't land!' They want to banish me to the middle of the ocean." He ardently wished "to get freed from that infernal tail of ships, and that obsession of my sea life."[23]

Conrad's unwelcome reputation as a sea novelist helps to explain his irrational dislike of the work of Herman Melville. Conrad called Fenimore Cooper—a lesser writer, whom he had read as a child—a constant companion, a rare artist and one of his masters. But he hated Melville's romanticism, insincerity and mysticism, and did not want to be coupled with Melville as an exotic (though less brutal) writer of the sea. "Excepting in Melville, perhaps," wrote the *Daily Chronicle* when reviewing *An Outcast of the Islands*, "we know nothing to match his scenic descriptions of tropical islands, and to say they recall *Typee* and its fellow romance [*Omoo*] is to give the highest and justest meed of praise." When Oxford University Press asked him to write an introduction to *Moby-Dick,* Conrad refused the offer and called the novel "a rather strained rhapsody with whaling for a subject and not a single sincere line of the 3 vols of it." And when the sculptor Jacob Epstein unwisely mentioned the book, Conrad burst into a furious denunciation: "He knows nothing of the sea. Fantastic, ridiculous. . . . Mystical my eye! My old boots are mystical."[24]

In an early appreciation of Melville in his pioneering *Studies in Classic American Literature* (1923), D. H. Lawrence rubbed salt in the wound by favorably contrasting Melville to Conrad: "His vision is . . . far sounder than Joseph Conrad's, because Melville doesn't sentimentalize the ocean and the sea's unfortunates. Snivel in a wet hanky like Lord Jim." Lawrence disliked the pessimism and defeatism "that pervades all Conrad and such folks—the Writers among the Ruins. I can't forgive Conrad for being so sad and giving in." In the opening lines of *Lady Chatterley's Lover* (1928), Lawrence would (by contrast) bravely declare: "The cataclysm has happened, we are among the ruins, we start to build up new little habitats, to have new little hopes." Conrad returned the compliment (before *Lady Chatterley's Lover* was published) by condemning *The Rainbow,* which had been suppressed for obscenity in 1915: "D. H. Lawrence had started well, but had gone wrong. Filth. Nothing but obscenities."[25]

VII

The Nigger of the "Narcissus" was serialized in Henley's *New Review* from August to December 1897 and published by Heinemann, in an edition of 1,500 copies, in December of that year. In this novella Conrad simplified and sharpened his style, shifted his setting from land to sea and began to establish his reputation as a nautical novelist. The mutinous crew, the violent storm and the ship on its beam-ends were based on the 136-day voyage on the *Narcissus* (June–October 1884), which left from Bombay, sailed east of Madagascar and Mauritius, round the Cape of Good Hope and west of the Azores to Dunkirk (the fictional *Narcissus* sails to London). In the story, the cook Podmore, a religious fanatic, was given the middle name of Augustine Podmore Williams, the actual model for Lord Jim. Singleton, the noble patriarch who steers through the tempest for thirty-six hours, was given the family name of Edward Garnett's mother, as a subtle tribute to her son.

The eponymous hero, James Wait, was based on Joseph Barron, a thirty-five-year-old illiterate American Negro who died at sea three weeks before the ship reached Dunkirk. His name (which sounds like "white" when pronounced by Wait, a West Indian) allows Wait to make a dramatic pun, when he first steps aboard, by simultaneously calling out his name and apparently ordering the chief mate to stop. His name suggests that the crew will wait on him while he waits for death, as a dead weight on the ship. Wait's excessive self-love and egoistic concern for his own comfort connect him to the myth of Narcissus.

Conrad's conception of the story may have been influenced by Melville's *Benito Cereno* (1856), a tale about a rebellion of Negro slaves on a Spanish ship. His use of Wait's blackness is extremely effective. It emphasizes Wait's isolation and difference; it makes him more dramatic and mysterious; it reverses his traditional social status. For he is arrogant and impudent, gives himself airs, speaks elegant English, boasts of stealing a white man's girl and persuades the crew to serve him. Wait is related to evil, the devil and black magic; and, apparently dying of tuberculosis, is associated with death, coffins and graves. A chronic malingerer, he deceives the crew into thinking he is much sicker than he actually is (so he does not have to work) and, both genuine and fraudulent, persuades himself that he is not seriously ill. Wait tests the crew's response to death, exemplifies their guilt, forces the men to identify their survival with his own and (with the help of his evil familiar, Donkin) incites rebellion and destroys the solidarity of the ship.

The two greatest moments in the novella, apart from the description of the storm that rivals "Typhoon," are the two burial scenes. In the first, Wait is buried in his narrow room by the violent tempest and the crew have to break down the walls and extract him, as in a difficult childbirth, by his "blooming short wool." In the second and final burial Wait, who had been "reborn" in the storm, dies in the calm that is superstitiously associated with his illness and that impedes the passage home. As they lift his corpse on the plank to slide it into the sea, Wait, still apparently animate, refuses to move. Finally, as his friend shrieks: "Jimmy, be a man!," they realize his shroud has been caught on a nail, and push him off the tilted board and into the sea. Through their confrontation with Wait, the complicitous crew move from innocence to experience and are forced to come to terms with the evil in themselves.

In 1897 Conrad, rarely pleased with his own work, told Crane he was dissatisfied with the conclusion of the novella: "I think however artistically the end of the book is somewhat lame. I mean after the death [which Crane had found haunting]. All that rigamarole about the burial and the ship's coming home seems to run away into a rat's tail—thin at the end." But the conclusion is actually very well done. The wind, released from Wait's malign spell once he is safely under water, suddenly rises and carries the ship to port. The paying off of the men at the end balances the mustering at the beginning. And the ironic perspective of the crew on land emphasizes the unique values of the sea. The wise old Singleton now seems "a disgusting old brute" while Donkin, who had come aboard in rags and was given a bad discharge for inciting the mutiny that was suppressed by Captain Allistoun, has found his proper element. By 1914, when Conrad had completed a number of major works and acquired considerably more self-confidence, he revised his harsh judgment in the preface to a new American edition and justly maintained: "It is the book by which, not as a novelist perhaps, but as an artist striving for the utmost sincerity of expression, I am willing to stand or fall."[26]

CHAPTER ELEVEN

Ford and Pent Farm

1898–1902

I

In early September 1898, while visiting the Garnetts at the Cearne near Limpsfield, Surrey, Conrad met Ford Madox Ford (then called Hueffer) and began the literary friendship that had the greatest impact on his work. The grandson of an eminent Pre-Raphaelite painter and son of the German-born music critic of *The Times*, Ford was closely connected to the artistic and literary establishment of Victorian England. He was a tall, thin, warmhearted twenty-five-year-old man with fair hair, pink-and-white complexion, prominent pale blue eyes, gaping mouth, rabbit teeth and ragged lemon mustache. He had published his first book while still in his teens, and later became an influential editor and a major novelist.

At the age of twenty, Ford had impulsively married the seventeen-year-old daughter of Dr. William Martindale, the author of the classic handbook *Extra Pharmacopoeia* and friend of the great physician Joseph Lister. David Garnett found Elsie Martindale attractive and exotic: "tall, high-breasted and dark, with a bold eye and a rich, high colour, like a ripe nectarine. She dressed in richly coloured garments of the William Morris style and wore earrings and a great amber necklace."

Ford—who wanted to live near the Garnetts and practice amateur agriculture—generously offered to sublet his rented house, Pent Farm in Postling, Kent; and the Conrads, pleased with the house, moved in on October 26. Though it would have seemed natural for Conrad to settle by the sea, he had seen too much of it and preferred to live inland. Like Captain Allistoun of the *Narcissus*, he "wished to end his days in a little house, with a plot of ground attached—far in the country—out of sight of the sea." Conrad tried to live like a country squire but, unlike his feudal forebears, owned neither his house nor the land around it.

Pent Farm, three miles along winding lanes from Hythe on the south coast, had a fine view of the valley of the Stour. The small, very old and charming if inconvenient house lacked water, gas and electricity. The kitchen had a wavy brick floor, and an oak beam ran across the low ceiling of the deep parlor. In a letter to his Polish cousin, Conrad described the quiet and colorful natural setting: "Behind the house are the hills (Kentish Downs) which slope in zigzag fashion down to the sea, like the battlements of a big fortress. . . . The little garden stretches out quiet, and waste land [is] intersected by hedges, and here and there stands an oak or a group of young ash trees. Three little villages are hidden among the hillocks and only the steeples of their churches can be seen. The colouring of the country presents brown and pale yellow tints—and in between, in the distance, one can see the meadows, as green as emeralds."[1]

Pent Farm also contained many Pre-Raphaelite relics that enhanced the traditional atmosphere: paintings by Ford Madox Brown and by Dante Gabriel Rossetti (as well as his death mask), a table designed by William Morris and the writing desk of the poet Christina Rossetti. The Pent was a more congenial as well as a more comfortable house than Ivy Walls. The artist Walter Crane, a former tenant, had left a couplet above the door: "Want we not for board or tent,/While overhead we keep the Pent," and while living there, Conrad maintained the hospitable traditions of his Polish ancestors. Ford lived nearby at Aldington, Wells at Sandgate, Crane at Brede Manor, James at Rye and Kipling at Rottingdean, and it was quite easy to arrange stimulating visits with them. Conrad wrote some of his best books during his decade at Pent Farm and, apart from a brief residence in Bedfordshire, spent the rest of his life in Kent.

II

Soon after meeting Ford, Conrad proposed a literary collaboration, a custom which was then very common. Kipling had collaborated with his brother-in-law Wolcott Balestier on *The Naulahka* (1891), Stevenson with his stepson Lloyd Osbourne on *The Wrecker* (1892), and the Irish novels of Somerville and Ross were also produced by a successful partnership. Ford consummated the collaboration that Conrad had planned with Marguerite Poradowska and with Stephen Crane. Conrad needed the personal stimulation if not the artistic contribution of a fellow-writer. In the course of his career he suggested joint projects with a number of younger friends: Edward Noble, Richard Curle, Perceval Gibbon, Joseph Retinger, Macdonald Hastings and J. B. Pinker.

When they first met, the forty-one-year-old Conrad was the well-established but financially unsuccessful author of *Almayer's Folly, An Outcast of the Islands, The Nigger of the "Narcissus"* and *Tales of Unrest*, all of which had earned the praise of his most distinguished contemporaries. Ford had published three fairy tales for children, a volume of poems, a novel and a biography of his artist grandfather, but did not yet have a serious literary reputation. His biographer said: "The characters in *The Shifting of the Fire* [1892] are implausible and the plot absurd. . . . The novel is written in a ludicrously elegant style." And Edward Garnett criticized his life of Ford Madox Brown as "German—cumbrous—slovenly—vague," and said that Ford tended to "generalise about things of which he knows nothing."[2]

Conrad could publish everything he wrote, but he wanted to increase his output and his income. He hoped, with Ford, to get useful ideas for his fiction, to acquire a greater familiarity with the nuances of vernacular English, to overcome his agonizing slowness, to increase his fluency and to build his self-confidence. Ford had, in the manuscript of *Seraphina* (the original title of *Romance*), an unpublishable version of a potentially popular story. Conrad thought that by polishing the work and naming himself co-author, they would be able to publish it profitably.

With this in mind, Conrad consulted various friends, and explained his motives to William Ernest Henley: "When talking with Hueffer my first thought was that the man there who couldn't find a publisher had some good stuff to use and that if we worked it up together my name, probably, would get a publisher for it. On the other hand I thought that working with him would keep under the particular devil that spoils my work for me as quick as I turn it out (that's why I work so slow and break my word to publishers), and that the material being of the kind that appeals to my imagination and the man being an honest workman we could turn out something tolerable." Buttering up Ford, Conrad said Henley had approved of the idea and had remarked: "Why don't you ask H[ueffer] to collaborate with you? He is the finest stylist in the English language of to-day." Ford knew this was untrue, for during a quarrel Henley had once screamed at him: "Who the hell are you? I never even heard your name!" Ford believed that Henley, less flattering and less enthusiastic, had casually told Conrad: "I daresay he'll do as well as anyone else."

Though Henley and Garnett encouraged him to work with Ford, James and Wells strongly disapproved. James, remarking on the dissim-

ilar traditions of the two writers, found the idea inconceivable: "To me
. . . this is like a bad dream which one relates at breakfast." Wells, also
upset by the prospect, cycled from Sandgate to beg Ford not to spoil
Conrad's style: "The wonderful Oriental style. . . . It's as delicate as
clockwork and you'll only ruin it by sticking your fingers in it." But
Wells, who had once told Conrad that he could attain artistic "dexterity"
by constant practice, later changed his mind. After Ford had anglicized
Conrad's prose, Wells decided that Conrad had been the principal bene-
ficiary: "I think Conrad owed a very great deal to their early association;
Hueffer helped greatly to 'English' him, and his idiom, threw remarkable lights on the English literary world for him, collaborated with him
on two occasions, and conversed interminably with him about the precise word and about perfection in writing."[3]

Despite their financial problems, family conflicts, prickly temperaments, physical illnesses and nervous breakdowns, Conrad and Ford
got on remarkably well together. Like James and Wells, Ford found
Conrad very strange and felt that he would never become an English
gentleman. Meeting Conrad unexpectedly in London and not recognizing him at first, Ford saw what appeared to be a shabby, "old, shrunken,
wizened man, in an unbrushed bowler, an ancient burst-seamed overcoat, one wrist wrapped in flannel, the other hand helping him to lean
on a hazel walking-stick, cut from a hedge and prepared at home. [He]
had in one tortured eye a round piece of dirty window-glass."

But they also had a good deal in common. Both had a continental
background and a European (as opposed to an insular) orientation;
since Ford was a recent convert, both were nominal Catholics. When
they were bored by a mincing comedian entertaining an appreciative
music-hall audience at the Empire Theatre, Conrad (always puzzled by
English "humor") turned to his fellow outsider and observed: "Doesn't
one in spite of everything feel a stranger in this beastly country?"—
which was just what Ford had been thinking. They admired the same
masters: Turgenev, Flaubert, Maupassant and James. They often conversed in French and followed the aesthetic conventions of the French
novel: the ironic, detached narrator, the complex revelation of plot and
the anguished striving for the *mot juste* that would exactly express the
required shade of meaning. Both writers stressed the technique of narration as much as the tale itself.

Conrad perceived Ford's potential brilliance long before it manifested
itself in his major novels: *The Good Soldier* and *Parade's End*. He affectionately called Ford, who was almost young enough to be his son,
"dear boy"—which was the way that Tadeusz and Jessie addressed

Conrad. He said Ford had become a daily habit and seemed surprised that no one else cared very much for his partner. Though conversation, which often went on until the middle of the night, was their greatest pleasure, they also shot rats together, played passionate games of dominoes, enjoyed rich meals and annual Christmas dinners (at one of them Conrad accidentally set fire to Ford's angora cat). They exchanged visits and hospitality, invited one another to meet distinguished guests, took holidays together and were drawn by the common interests of their young children, Christina and Borys, who were nearly the same age. Conrad's long, ceremonial "Protocol of the Celebration" of Borys' fifth birthday in January 1903 was a charming and unusually light-hearted parody of the strict orders he had given Jessie when she was preparing the Victoria Street "rabbit hutch" for his arrival: "you are to come right in (in overcoats) at *the front door* and walk into the parlour where there will be tea and something to eat laid out. . . . At 3.40 the Young Lady having had barely time to smooth her plumes shall proceed (attended by the Lady Regent—the Lord Regent is at liberty to swoon for fifty minutes) shall proceed—I say—to the Baronial Kitchen (where the feast is to be engulphed) to receive the guests with the young cavalier."[4]

Stephen Crane left an amusing but exaggerated description of Ford's irritating but fundamentally decent personality: "You must not be offended by Mr. Hueffer's manner. He patronizes Mr. James. He patronizes Mr. Conrad. Of course he patronizes me and he will patronize Almighty God when they meet, but God will get used to it, for Hueffer is all right." With Conrad, however, Ford restrained his habitual condescension and behaved in a perfectly correct manner. He rightly considered it an honor to collaborate with Conrad, maintained an attitude of "almost cringing respect" and—recognizing his own callowness at the turn of the century—quite simply declared: "I learned all I know of Literature from Conrad." Violet Hunt, who became Ford's mistress and supplanted Elsie Martindale, observed that Ford was even more deferential to Conrad than Conrad was to James: "[Ford] adored Conrad. I never heard him speak of Conrad without the most reverent affection. . . . In matters of literature his attitude was servile, positively. To James he posed merely as *le jeune homme modeste*, but his native arrogance appeared to be completely obliterated when Conrad was in the room. He imitated him, even to the point of cultivating in himself some one or other of Conrad's phobias."[5]

Ford learned a great deal from working with Conrad and, with his help, got his two weak novels into print (they shared the negligible royalties). But Conrad, as Wells noted, received the greatest benefits.

Throughout their friendship—which peaked for five years, slacked off for six, was severed in 1909 and warily resumed during Conrad's later years—Ford generously followed his grandfather's precept to "beggar yourself rather than refuse assistance to any one whose genius you think shows promise of being greater than your own." If Ford adored Conrad, Conrad found Ford not only useful but indispensable. He inspired Conrad's self-confidence by praising, with sincere conviction, the work that Conrad himself tended to denigrate, and provided very considerable practical assistance. Ford not only let Pent Farm cheaply, but also paid the rent when Conrad was unable to do so. In addition—though not himself wealthy and against the advice of his lawyer—he lent Conrad money and also advanced him £100 for his share of *Romance*.

Ford's literary help was even more significant. He supplied moral support, provided good working conditions, suggested words and phrases, prodded Conrad to remember forgotten incidents, took dictation, listened to Conrad reading, criticized his manuscripts and corrected his proofs. And he gave Conrad the endless pleasure of intelligent conversation about literature, their passionate mutual interest.

Ford offered Conrad several good ideas and had the uncanny ability to stimulate him to write when he would otherwise have been overcome by illness, exhaustion and despair. The incident of the foreign castaway on the English coast who could not make himself understood came from Ford's *The Cinque Ports* (1900) and helped inspire "Amy Foster" (1901). The idea for Conrad's story "Tomorrow" (1902) was, he said, Ford's suggestion and his conception. Ford helped Conrad (as we shall see) reconstruct "The End of the Tether" (1902) when the manuscript was accidentally damaged and even wrote some pages of *Nostromo* when Conrad could not keep up with the serialization. While prompting Conrad's recollections, Ford took down *The Mirror of the Sea* (1906) from dictation; and his acquaintance with anarchists (as Conrad acknowledged in the Preface) gave him the idea of *The Secret Agent* (1907). Ford also worked on *The Rescuer* and helped Conrad transform the dialogue of his story "Tomorrow" into the play *One Day More* (1905).

Jessie Conrad has described their collaboration, which often took place after the distracting wives and children had gone to sleep in the crowded cottage:

> Sometimes the two would elect to start work as we, Mrs. Hueffer and I, were retiring for the night. For hours after I had gone to bed the voices would reach me through the floor. . . . F. M. H., who was a very tall man,

would relieve his feelings by thumping the oaken beam that crossed the ceiling below. . . .

The small house seemed at times full to overflowing, and there were days when the two artists with their vagaries, temperaments and heated discussions made it seem rather a warm place. To give F. M. H. his due, he was the least peppery of the two, being a native of a less excitable nation and his drawling voice made a sharp contrast with the quick, un-English utterances of the fellow collaborator.

When their temperaments got too heated and Conrad became too caustic, even Ford would indulge in a fit of anger. The balance of power would temporarily shift as Conrad, pretending that Ford had nothing else to do, would disingenuously attempt to placate him: "Your letter distressed me a little by the signs of nervous irritation and its exasperated tone. I can quite enter into your feelings. I am sorry your wife seems to think I've induced you to waste your time. I had no idea you had any profitable work to do." When things calmed down, Conrad said that he worked better in the sympathetic ambience of Ford's house than in his own and expressed gratitude for the days spent with his partner in Winchelsea. When *Romance* was finished, he mentioned the strong bond they had formed and told Ford: "I miss collaboration in a most ridiculous manner. I hope you don't intend dropping me altogether."[6] Though Conrad did not value Ford's friendship as much as Galsworthy's, Garnett's, Crane's and Graham's, he did a great deal of work with Ford, spent much more time with him and was far more intimate with him than with his other friends.

III

The collaboration, and the visits back and forth so the men could work together, also involved the wives and children. Since Jessie did not get along with either Ford or Elsie, she added another irritant to the relationship of the two hypersensitive men. Jessie was jealous of Elsie's family background, good looks, education, intelligence, literary talent and intellectual rapport with Conrad, who had helped with Elsie's translation of *Stories from de Maupassant* (1903). And she resented the supercilious and disdainful Ford, who treated her like a servant. (Conrad could also treat her this way; when Marguerite Poradowska visited them in 1900, he suggested Jessie act as chambermaid to help her dress.)

The constant antagonism between Jessie and Ford, who made her feel socially and intellectually inferior, provided rare, if unintentional, comic relief in that hothouse atmosphere of flare-ups and break-downs. Several burlesque combats took place between the conventional house-proud wife and the slovenly bohemian guest. When Ford's panama hat got soaked in the rain, he casually put it in Jessie's oven to dry. As the grease from the hatband basted her Sunday roast, she became quite uncommonly enraged. On another occasion, Ford decided to sleep at the Conrads' house. But he found that the thin curtains let in too much light and took the blanket off his bed to cover the window. He then became cold and, while searching for another cover, discovered Conrad's frock-coat and striped trousers, which Jessie had neatly pressed and left in the drawer, and used them to warm himself. The next morning the outraged Jessie found the garments crumpled out of all recognition, and bitterly complained to Conrad about Ford's "wanton treatment" of his clothing.

Ford, on his part, mischievously related how the publisher Alston Rivers' harsh rejection of Jessie's cookbook in 1907 (he refused to buy "a collection of papers only fit for—I forget what they were fit for") was sent by mistake to the furious Conrad instead of to Ford, who had submitted the manuscript. Ford also attacked Jessie on her own territory and boasted that he was not only the best but also the most economical cook in the world. When Ford secretly substituted for his German cook and prepared *civet de lièvre à la Parisienne*, the gouty Conrad, though warned against rich foods, became ecstatic: "My dear faller. . . . The admirable Johanna has of course surpassed herself. . . . *Une telle succulence, mon cher.*"

In July 1900, after completing *Lord Jim*, Conrad took the first of four disastrous trips abroad with his family. Intending to have a working holiday, they met the Fords in Bruges, Belgium, and then moved on to Knokke, on the North Sea coast above Ostend. But Borys became dangerously ill with dysentery and the holiday was ruined. "There was a child very ill, with only Belgian doctors," Ford recalled, "abscesses in the jaw and no dentist; gout; frigid rooms into which blew the sands from Holland; intolerable winds; interminable gusts of rain." Conrad told Galsworthy that during the depressing crisis "the whole Hotel was in a commotion; Dutch, Belgians and French prowled about the corridor on the lookout for news. Women with babies of their own offered to sit up. . . . Elsie Hueffer helped a bit but poor H. did not get much collaboration out of me." Jessie (while reviving her hostility to Ford in the books she published after Conrad's death) warmly commended his behavior in the sickroom: "At this crisis I have nothing but praise for

F. M. H. He earned my [rare] gratitude and appreciation by the manner he showed his practical sympathy. He was always at hand to shift my small invalid, fetch the doctor or help with the nursing."[7]

IV

In the early years of the century Conrad and Ford collaborated on two novels: *The Inheritors* (1901), dedicated to Borys and Christina, and *Romance* (1903), dedicated to Elsie and Jessie. Inclined to minimize his share in these unsuccessful works, Conrad claimed that he did little actual writing, but engaged in many long and heated discussions with Ford. And in a letter to Garnett, he boasted of his master-slave relation with his much abused disciple: "I set myself to look upon the thing as a sort of skit upon the political (?!) novel. . . . And poor *H* was dead in earnest! O Lord. How he worked! There is not a chapter I haven't made him write twice—most of them three times over. . . . He has been as patient as no angel had ever been. I've been fiendish. I've been rude to him; if I've not called him names I've *implied* in my remarks and in the course of our discussions the most opprobrious epithets. He wouldn't recognize them. 'Pon my word it was touching. And there's no doubt that in the course of that agony I have been ready to weep more than once. Yet not for him. Not for him."

Granger, the hero of *The Inheritors*, is destroyed by falling in love with a Fourth Dimensionist, a race of people with superior powers but no emotions who will be the inheritors of the earth. The novel combines elements of science fiction, recently made popular by Wells, with contemporary political satire. It attacks King Leopold's exploitation of the Congo and Joseph Chamberlain's imperialism in the Boer War; and it has striking portraits of Casement (Soane), Garnett (Lea), Unwin (Polehampton) and Henry James (Callan). Conrad's role in the creation of this lifeless failure may have been more substantial than he suggested. For Conrad, not Ford, had been to the Congo and met Casement; and Conrad's relations with Garnett and with Unwin, rather than Ford's, are portrayed in the novel.

Conrad collaborated on *Romance* during 1901–2 when he found it impossible to work on his own more serious fiction and, as with *The Inheritors*, fatally compromised aesthetic for commercial considerations. The story, which Ford grubbed out of the British Museum, was based on the actual experience of Aaron Smith, an innocent young Englishman who was tried for piracy at the Old Bailey and narrowly escaped the gallows. The rather absurd plot takes place in about 1820 in the West Indies, which Conrad but not Ford had visited, and was meant to portray "the fiercest excitements of a romance *'de cape et d'épée,'* the romance of yard-arm and boarding pike so dear to youth," which Conrad would mock in his essay on Henry James. Though Conrad disliked Stevenson, *Romance* was a lame attempt to capitalize on and outsell the adventure genre—pirates and kidnapping, sultry and sneaky Spaniards in Jamaica and Cuba—perfected by the author of *Treasure Island* and *Kidnapped*.

Many Fordian passages, like the speech of Castro, are completely bogus: "Tell the Excellency that her orders have been obeyed. The English *caballero* has been warned. I have been sleepless in my watchfulness over the guest of the house, as the señorita has desired—for the honour of the Riegos." And in Part IV—as the good John Kemp and Seraphina escape from the evil O'Brien in Rio Medio—Conrad weighs in with a lot of technical details about ships. In opposition to their aesthetic principles, fear is declared rather than rendered: "I need not have gone to the entrance of the cave to understand all the horror of our fate." And the love interest also falls flat: "my imagination had been captured, enslaved already by the image of that young girl who had called me her English cousin, the girl with the lizard, the girl with the dagger! And with every word she uttered romance itself."[8]

But there are a few good touches in this overlong novel. Castro had "a steel blade screwed to the wooden stump of his forearm" the year before James Barrie popularized this kind of prosthesis with Captain Hook in *Peter Pan*. The strict Methodist, Mrs. Williams (the wife of the captain of the English ship *Lion*), provides an amusing contrast to the villainous pirates. And Ford created one short scene that Conrad, habitually and inexplicably, found hilarious. When an obscure peasant is questioned by a judge about his occupation, he tersely but suggestively characterizes himself by responding: "Excellency—a few goats." As soon as Ford put the words on paper, "Conrad burst into one of his roars of ecstasy. 'This,' he shouted when he was in a condition to speak, 'is genius!' And for twenty years afterwards, in every second or third letter to the writer Conrad returned to the charge. 'Excellency, a few goats . . .' he would write. 'Do you remember?' " In *The Arrow of Gold* the young Rita, a direct descendant of Seraphina, quite seriously recalls: "I used to take my goats there, a dozen or so of them, for the day."[9] In his biography, Arthur Mizener reproduces a photograph of farmer Ford, standing in a barren field with Penny, his prize goat.

As far as *The Inheritors* and *Romance* were concerned, Conrad wasted a good deal of time collaborating with Ford. Their novels exposed the weakest qualities of both writers, were worse than any novels they wrote independently, and were artistic and financial failures. But Conrad, as he had hoped, did develop a much greater fluency; and the move to Pent Farm along with Ford's tonic stimulation inspired some of his best work—*Heart of Darkness*, *Lord Jim*, "Typhoon," "Falk," "Amy Foster" and "The End of the Tether"—during their years of collaboration. Ford produced only three minor books between 1896 and 1904, but reaped the benefits after the partnership ended. Between *Nostromo* (1904) and *Under Western Eyes* (1911), Conrad published only one novel while Ford brought out eleven. In 1906 Ford dedicated *The Fifth Queen* to Conrad; and though Conrad dedicated books to an elderly lady admirer and to a sea captain he hardly knew, he never offered a book to the man who had given him the most valuable help.

V

While Conrad was intermittently engaged with Ford, he was also widening his circle of friends and writing his own books. He encouraged and helped Galsworthy to publish his first novel, *Jocelyn* (1898); and until 1914, Galsworthy continued to seek Conrad's advice about his manuscripts. Galsworthy, who was well off and would become even more so, frequently helped Conrad—as late as 1909—with loans, and payments of doctor's bills and insurance premiums. In 1910 he used his influence in official circles to get Conrad an urgently needed Civil List Pension of £100 a year. Conrad was grateful for Galsworthy's assistance, and their friendship remained close and affectionate until Conrad's death.

In 1895 Galsworthy fell in love with Ada, the wife of his first cousin. Ada was a sensitive and beautiful woman, with dark grayish hair and soft brown eyes. But they were forced to maintain a respectable façade for nine anguished years, and could meet alone only during brief holidays abroad. Not until the death of his father in December 1904 was she finally free to get a divorce and marry Galsworthy. Conrad was fond of Ada, helped with her translations of Maupassant's tales, as he had helped with Elsie Hueffer's, and wrote an introduction to her work, *Yvette and Other Stories*, in 1904.

Galsworthy was not always as strait-laced as he appeared to be, and his love for Ada did not preclude occasional seductions—even in Conrad's house. Jessie tolerantly recalled that during a weekend at Pent Farm around the turn of the century, Galsworthy suddenly developed a rare headache and retired to his room after lunch: "I had a new and desperately pretty housemaid, and all that Sunday afternoon she had been upstairs. When she appeared at last I asked where she had been. With an exasperating show of self-consciousness she hung her head and twisting her apron in her fingers in seeming embarrassment, she murmured without raising her eyes: 'Mr. Galsworthy asked me to stop and help him pack his bag.' "

Conrad and Hugh Clifford had reviewed each other's books, and met when Clifford was on home leave during the summer of 1899. The son of a major-general who had won the Victoria Cross in the Crimean War, Clifford was born into a Catholic family in 1866. He left school at seventeen, entered the colonial service in Malaya the same year, and became an expert on the Malay language, a successful diplomat and a victorious leader of military expeditions. A large, bald, rugged-looking man, forthright, energetic and impetuous, he served in North Borneo, Trinidad and Ceylon before acquiring a knighthood and becoming governor of four colonies: the Gold Coast, Nigeria, Ceylon and Malaya. In 1899 he began to publish stories in *Blackwood's* and other literary magazines. Between 1896 and 1929, simultaneously with his colonial career, he brought out sixteen books, mostly on Malaya. Though Conrad saw Clifford only during his infrequent trips home and strongly disagreed with his imperialist views, he shared Sir Hugh's Malayan background, was proud of his friendship with a literary man of action and dedicated *Chance* to the impressive "Governor," who helped the novel to achieve success in America.[10]

A very different kind of friendship, which showed the wide range of Conrad's connections, was with Miss Harriet Capes, who had written a letter praising his work as early as 1895 and met him four years later. The "charming old lady in Winchester" was born in 1849 and wrote inspirational books for children. Conrad dedicated *A Set of Six* to her in 1908 and had sufficient respect for her opinion to answer at considerable length her criticism of *Victory*. In 1915 her compilation of selections from Conrad was published by the small firm of Andrew Melrose, but because she had infringed copyright, the book was immediately suppressed. In 1922 her *Wisdom and Beauty from Conrad* was reissued with the same title and with proper acknowledgment to his publishers.

While Conrad was developing his friendships in England in 1899, an unexpected and deeply disturbing attack on his character and his honor was made by a Polish writer. In June 1897 Conrad had a brief visit from Wincenty Lutoslawski, a Polish nationalist, philosopher and author of a book on Plato, who was then studying in London and later held chairs of philosophy in Geneva, Lausanne, Paris and Vilna. Despite Conrad's elaborate directions, Lutoslawski turned up at Pent Farm six hours late and ravenously hungry. After eating heartily and stripping naked in front of Conrad, he went straight to bed, and dashed off to the station early the next morning. Conrad thought the visit was "a positive nightmare."

Kraj (The Country), a Polish journal published in St. Petersburg, "became from its founding in 1882 the center of efforts to promote conciliation between the Poles and the Russian government." (Conrad, of course, was opposed to this policy.) In an April 1899 issue, Lutoslawski gave a thoroughly misleading account of his meeting with Conrad. He claimed that Conrad had justified his writing in English by stating he was not talented enough to write in Polish and by declaring he could make more money in his adopted language.

Lutoslawski's damaging article revived the heated issue of the emigration of talent, which had begun with Mickiewicz and Chopin. Inspired by the belief that effective political action at home was impossible, emigration had been a major factor in Polish political life since the failure of the revolution of 1830. The article by Lutoslawski, a notable cultural *émigré*, provoked a vicious attack by Eliza Orzeszkowa (1841–1910), the *grande dame* of Polish literature, who was "of the suffragette type, [and] was an admired humanitarian novelist in the tradition of Auguste Comte." She equated emigration with desertion from patriotic duties, and contemptuously condemned Conrad for betraying Poland and for selling his talent to the English:

> And since we talk about books, I must say that the gentleman who in English is writing novels which are widely read and bring good profit almost caused me a nervous attack. When reading about him, I felt something slippery and unpleasant, something mounting to my throat. Really! That even creative talents should join the exodus! . . . Creative ability is the very crown of the plant, the very top of the tower, the very heart of the heart of the nation. And to take away from one's nation this flower, this top, this heart and give it to the Anglo-Saxons who are not even lacking in bird's milk, for the only reason that they pay better for it—one cannot even think of it without shame.[11]

Conrad—struggling to survive as a writer, deeply in debt and far from affluent—was tormented by these accusations of betrayal, a major theme in his fiction. There was just enough truth in the charge to be disturbing and more than sufficient distortion to enrage him. Fifteen years later, when visiting his cousin in Poland, he asked for some Polish novels, was innocently brought a work by Orzeszkowa and exploded with rage: "Bring me nothing by that hag! . . . You don't know, she wrote me such a letter once." Writing to his namesake, the historian Jozef Korzeniowski, in February 1901, Conrad justified himself by stating: "It does not seem to me that I have been unfaithful to my country by having proved to the English that a gentleman from the Ukraine can be as good a sailor as they, and has something to tell them in their own language."[12]

VI

In November 1897 the old, respectable and paternalistic Edinburgh firm of Blackwood published Conrad's "Karain" in its *Magazine* and established a fruitful connection that lasted for the next five years. Just as, at a crucial point in his career, Garnett and Henley had accepted *Almayer's Folly* and *The Nigger of the "Narcissus,"* so William Blackwood serialized "Youth" (1898), *Heart of Darkness* (1899), *Lord Jim* (1899–1900) and "The End of the Tether" (1902), published *Lord Jim* in 1900 in book form and collected the three stories—on youth, maturity and age—in *Youth* (1902).

"Youth" was based on Conrad's actual experiences on the *Palestine* during his first, promising voyage to the mysterious East in 1881. The story is narrated by Conrad's alter-ego, the forty-two-year-old Charlie Marlow, who makes his first and extremely significant appearance in Conrad's work, and returns in *Heart of Darkness, Lord Jim* and *Chance.* In the course of his narrative Marlow ironically contrasts the characteristics associated with his youth, twenty years earlier—desire to test himself, love of his decrepit ship, eagerness for exotic experience, naïve hope, the illusory conviction of strength, romantic expectations—with the reality of painfully acquired experience.

The story is structured around a dozen disasters: the October gale, the ramming by a steamer, the second gale that forces the crew to work the pumps incessantly, the return to port for the third time, the spontaneous combustion of the cargo of coal, the explosion of methane gas, the towing by a steamer, the cutting of the tow rope as the fire gets worse, the loss of the burning anchor and chain, the abandonment and sinking of the *Judea,* the request of the castaway crew of the burnt barque for passage in a steamer. The ship's motto is "Do or die," but the men are forced to do *and* die. Yet Marlow's youthful hopes enable him to maintain a cheerful attitude, and to survive all the hardships and dangers. He is proud of his performance in extreme situations and experiences a sense of omnipotence. But he realizes that such illusions can only be sustained in youth, and that he must inevitably move through experience to a more realistic awareness of man's weakness.

Like the novelists of the Great War, who took ten years to absorb, understand and interpret their traumatic experience, Conrad pondered the tragic reality of the Congo for an entire decade before transforming it into his most powerful and influential work, *Heart of Darkness*, the second story in *Youth*.[13] About ten years after Kipling began to publish, when imperialist ideas were dominant and Britain was about to fight the Boer War, Conrad contradicted the profoundest beliefs of the reading public. He revealed that Europeans and their civilization were not superior to the people and culture of Africa; that there was no moral justification for colonialism, whose basis was hypocritical and materialistic; that evil existed in the heart of all men; and that idealists would commit the most barbaric atrocities if given sufficient freedom to do so. Though Conrad's beliefs now seem absolutely convincing, his late-Victorian readers were not able to accept them. Many contemporaries misread the book, thinking that Kurtz, by his very brilliance, was a deranged aberration who should never have been sent to Africa; that if the Congo could transform an enlightened intellectual into a regressive savage, it ought to be colonized as soon as possible; and that, though Belgium's colonialism was rotten, England's was just.

Heart of Darkness is the first significant work in English literature to deny the idea of progress, which had been a dominant idea in European thought for the past four hundred years, and to question the very foundations of Western civilization. It shows the antagonistic interests of civilization and colonialism, portrays the disastrous clash of the white man and the African, and suggests the humane values that are needed to survive this conflict. Marlow, who represents the European conscience that Kurtz has abandoned in the depths of the jungle, measures colonial experience in human and moral terms. Unlike Kurtz, he is sceptical about what Western materialism can do for the Africans, and recognizes that colonialism is a completely destructive practice. He despises all the white men he meets and remains aloof from them. But he compassionately commits himself to the Africans he encounters on his journey to the interior. Their suffering reflects the white man's cruel visitation just as their honorable restraint represents a moral standard the Europeans fail to meet.

As Marlow goes up-river, the Africans—targets, slaves, skeletons, corpses and victims—mark the stages of his *via dolorosa*. Roger Casement's consular reports and Edmund Morel's crusading exposé *Red Rubber* confirmed the realistic basis of the dried human skulls that decorate

Kurtz's fence. "Twenty-one heads were brought to Stanley Falls," noted Morel, "and have been used by Captain Rom as a decoration round a flowerbed in front of his house."

In *Typee* (1846), an account of his voyage to the South Seas, Herman Melville regretted the relentless European penetration of the tropical world and the disastrous influence on traditional societies: "Alas for the poor savages when exposed to the influence of these polluting examples! Unsophisticated and confiding, they are easily led into every vice, and humanity weeps over the ruin thus remorselessly inflicted upon them by their European civilizers. Thrice happy are they who, inhabiting some yet undiscovered island in the midst of the ocean, have never been brought into contaminating contact with the white man." But, as J. A. Hobson observed in *Imperialism* (1902), the supposedly civilized Europeans sought an outlet for their instinctual aggressions in colonial conquest, and "the desire to pursue and kill either big game or other men can only be satisfied by expansion and militarism." William Cornwallis Harris' *Wild Sports of Southern Africa* (1838), the first popular African hunting book, provided, in the name of enlightenment, a brutal justification for Kurtz's injunction to "Exterminate all the brutes!": "[There is an] imperious necessity, dictated alike by reason, justice, and humanity, of exterminating from off the face of the earth, a race of [African] monsters, who, being the unprovoked destroyers, and implacable foes of Her Majesty's Christian subjects, have forfeited every claim to mercy or consideration."[14]

The only men in *Heart of Darkness* who show moral restraint, except for Marlow himself, are his cannibalistic crew. Paid with brass wire and fed on scanty rations of rotten hippo meat, these cannibals are slowly starving. The stench of the rotten hippo, which the white "pilgrims" cannot extinguish though they throw most of it overboard, is Conrad's metaphor for the corruption in the Congo. Like Montaigne's noble cannibals, these men maintain their primitive code of honor, which gives them the strength to fight hunger; and their behavior refutes any European claim to superior civilization. The only human relationship Marlow is able to establish is with his African helmsman. When the helmsman is speared by Kurtz's fanatical adorers, Marlow's shoes become filled with his blood. Though moved by the death of his companion, Marlow becomes morbidly anxious to change his shoes and socks.[15]

The antithetical roles of Marlow and Kurtz are foreshadowed by their imperialistic prototypes, mentioned at the beginning of the story when Roman Britain is compared to the Belgian Congo. And Conrad's effective echo of Kipling—"this also . . . has been one of the dark places of the earth"—suggests that Britain was once as barbaric as Africa. Like Marlow, the trireme commander is revolted by the marshes, forests and savages at the farthest reaches of the Roman world; he does not go ashore and recognizes the threat of darkness. By contrast, the citizen in a toga, like Kurtz, does go ashore, feels encircled by the savagery and is overwhelmed by "the fascination of the abomination . . . the growing regrets, the longing to escape, the powerless disgust, the surrender, the hate." In Tacitus' *Life of Agricola*, a work about the Roman conquest of Britain, a noble Caledonian chieftain, by Roman standards an "uncivilized native," observed of the invaders (as Conrad observed of the Belgians): "you cannot escape their insolence by submission and self-restraint."[16]

Kurtz's long isolation in the wilderness awakens the atavistic memory of savage passions and brutal instincts, which Henry Thoreau also experienced in the woods of Massachusetts:

> I caught a glimpse of a woodchuck stealing across my path, and felt a strange thrill of savage delight, and I was strongly tempted to seize and devour him raw; not that I was hungry then, except for that wildness which he represented. . . . I found myself ranging the woods, like a half-starved hound, with a strange abandonment, seeking some kind of venison which I might devour, and no morsel could have been too savage for me.

But Kurtz, unlike Thoreau, eventually succumbed to madness; the wilderness got into his "veins, consumed his flesh, and sealed his soul to its own by the inconceivable ceremonies of some devilish initiation."[17] Conrad thus reverses the eighteenth-century myth of isolated man's conquest of wild nature, established by *Robinson Crusoe*, and suggests instead the power of the wilderness to liberate man's evil instincts. Kurtz loses his spiritual beliefs, his moral sense and his reason—the very qualities that distinguish men from beasts.

If, as Carl Jung said, the growth of civilization and culture consists "in a progressive subjugation of the animal in man," then Kurtz's deterioration represents a "rebellion on the part of the animal nature that thirsts for freedom," and the chaos and aggression that result when civilized man gives way to his instinctual impulses. "Separation from his instinctual nature," Jung wrote, "inevitably plunges civilized man into the conflict between conscious and unconscious, spirit and nature, knowledge and faith, a split that becomes pathological the moment his consciousness is no longer able to neglect or suppress his instinctual side."[18] The dominance of Kurtz's instincts over his conscious will and his surrender to the wilderness symbolize a reversal of the idea of progress and the return of modern man to the barbarity and anarchy represented in *Heart of Darkness* by the ancient Britons. Kurtz's self-condemnation, the terse but richly ambiguous "The horror! The horror!," expresses at once a significant truth about himself and about the darkness that has eclipsed the civilized side of his character. His last words reveal that he has retained his conscience while losing control of his actions, and simultaneously refer to the dark jungle, his fascination with the abomination, his ruined reputation, his impending death and even to Marlow's misguided loyalty.

Despite Kurtz's brutality, which led him to cut off the heads of his human sacrifices, and the fact that he is the very embodiment and cause of the horrors Marlow has witnessed in the Congo, Marlow is able to call Kurtz's self-condemnation "an affirmation, a moral victory paid for by innumerable defeats, by abominable terrors, by abominable satisfactions. But it was a victory! . . . His magnificent eloquence was thrown to me from a soul as translucently pure as a cliff of crystal." He finds Kurtz's forthright evil more palatable than his colleagues' hypocrisy and villainy, and remains faithful to his "choice of nightmares." Knowing the worst about Kurtz and through Kurtz the evil in all men, Marlow admires his struggle for moral awareness and self-knowledge.

Yet by the end of the novella, Marlow is no longer able to judge Kurtz's final cry. Kurtz's moral insight does not, as Marlow believes, absolve him from the atrocities he has committed. Marlow has also become mentally unbalanced in the jungle. He has been suffering from fever and, looking into Kurtz's mad soul, experiences a moral shock, has a nervous breakdown and comes close to death.

Marlow's intense identification with Kurtz inspires his return to Brussels—the "whited sepulcher" which in Matthew 23:27 "appears beautiful outward, but [is] within full of dead men's bones, and of all uncleanness"—and his visit to Kurtz's Intended bride. Conrad told Blackwood that "in the light of the final incident, the whole story in all its descriptive detail shall fall into its place—acquire its value and its significance." Like Marlow's aunt, who got him the job in the Congo, the Intended is protected by her illusions and is out of touch with the reality of Africa. Kurtz had demanded justice on his deathbed but Marlow, the secret sharer of his guilt, remains loyal to his memory and gives him mercy. Though he ironically tells the Intended "the last word he pronounced ['horror'] was—your name," he believes that the terrible truth must be kept hidden and that men must help women to remain in their innocent world "lest ours get worse." He lies to and protects her from the truth that would destroy her life and allows her to maintain her ideal vision of her depraved fiancé. Although, as V. S. Naipaul writes in his brilliant Conradian novel, *A Bend in the River*, "The bush muffled the sound of murder, and the muddy rivers and lakes washed the blood away,"[19] the effects of evil remained in the Congo and in Brussels.

Georges Antoine Klein and Arthur Hodister, Belgian agents in the Congo, have been suggested as the originals of Kurtz. But Emin Pasha (1840–92), whom H. M. Stanley set out to rescue in 1889, was an even more important model. Four religions contributed to the making of Emin Pasha, who was born Eduard Schnitzer in Silesia. His parents were of Jewish descent, he was baptised a Protestant, attended Catholic schools and became a practicing Moslem. Educated at the University of Breslau, he earned his medical degree at Berlin. He looked professorial, had a high forehead and wore steel-rimmed spectacles. A brilliant intellectual and polymath, he was a serious chess player and a talented pianist; knew twenty languages (including Turkish, Arabic and Albanian); conducted expert scientific studies in botany, ornithology, entomology, geology, meteorology, ethnology and geography. He worked his way up from medical officer under General Charles Gordon to Governor of Equatoria Province in the Sudan and had a tremendous range of responsibilities in the bush. He was an explorer, diplomat, "administrator, commander of his troops and scientist; he was still his own doctor and a keen agricultural developer." Stanley was as impressed by Emin Pasha as the Belgians were by Kurtz. He found Emin "extremely kind and affable, accomplished in literature, an entertaining conversationalist, a devoted physician. . . . With his full sonorous voice and measured tones, [his speech] sounded very pleasantly despite the foreign accent. Upon any policy treated of in newspapers, I found him exceedingly well-informed, no matter what country was broached."[20]

Like Emin Pasha, Kurtz was a highly educated idealist, intellectual, orator, author, explorer, trader and ruler. "All Europe contributed to the making" of the cosmopolitan Kurtz, who was a "universal genius," an emissary of pity, science and progress, a representative of "higher intelligence, wide sympathies, singleness of purpose." Apart from their background and impressive personal qualities, Emin and Kurtz shared many of the same experiences in Africa. Both worked for a foreign government, were isolated from the civilized world and had disappeared for a long period of time. Both had a wife or fiancée in Europe, were reputed to have a great hoard of precious ivory, had carved out their own private kingdom and had become the ruler of cannibal tribes. Both were rescued, after a long and dangerous search, and brought out along the same route on the Congo River. Both were removed from the bush against the will of their fiercely protective followers and both left behind them great anarchy and chaos.

VII

On July 20, 1900—just before leaving on his ill-fated holiday with Ford on the coast of Belgium—Conrad (a heavy smoker, with brown-stained fingers) sent Galsworthy a vivid account of how the mild weather and the natural transitions of day and night marked the heroic completion of his first major novel:

> The end of *L. J.* had been pulled off with a steady drag of 21 hours. I sent wife and child out of the house (to London) and sat down at 9 am, with a desperate resolve to be done with it. Now and then I took a walk round the house out at one door in at the other. Ten-minute meals. A great hush. Cigarette ends growing into a mound similar to a cairn over a dead hero. Moon rose over the barn, looked in at the window and climbed out of sight. Dawn broke, brightened. I put the lamp out and went on, with the morning breeze blowing the sheets of MS all over the room. Sun rose. I wrote the last word and went into the dining room. Six o'clock. I shared a piece of cold chicken with [my dog] Escamillo. . . . Felt very well only sleepy; had a bath at seven and at 8.30 was on my way to London.

Lord Jim was based on an actual incident that Conrad had heard about while sailing in Eastern waters. On August 7, 1880, the *Jeddah* (called the *Patna* in the novel), carrying 950 Moslem pilgrims from Singapore to Arabia, had an accident that threatened to sink the ship. It was abandoned by its white officers and crew near Cape Gardafui (now Raas Caseyr), close to the Horn of Africa and the entrance to the Gulf of Aden. But the *Jeddah* did not sink, and on August 11 it was salvaged and towed into Aden by the *Antenor*. As Captain Clark of the *Jeddah* was leaving the British Consulate after reporting that his ship had been lost with all hands, Captain Bragg of the *Antenor* entered the Consulate to report the salvage. After a Court of Inquiry in Singapore, which found that the ship had never been in extreme danger, Captain Clark received a light sentence and had his certificate suspended for three years. The first mate of the *Jeddah* at the time of desertion was Augustine Podmore Williams, who was the son of a parson, later worked for a ship's chandler and became the model for Lord Jim. In a late essay on "Protection of Liners" (1914), Conrad emphasized the gravity of the crime and declared: "A charge of neglect and indifference in the matter of saving lives is the cruellest blow that can be aimed at the character of a seaman."[21]

Jim, like most of Conrad's heroes (Tom Lingard in the Malayan novels, Nostromo, Jasper Allen in "Freya of the Seven Isles"), is handsome, just as his villains (Donkin, Massy in "The End of the Tether," Heemskirk in "Freya") are ugly. Tall, powerfully built, spotlessly neat and very popular, Jim is both idealistic and paranoid. Fallible but essentially decent, he is, as Marlow keeps repeating, "one of us"—an allusion to Genesis 3:22, in which God says to the angels after Adam has eaten the forbidden fruit: "Behold, the man is become as one of us, to know good and evil." Marlow, who identifies with Jim, as he does with Kurtz, is also objective about him. He forgives both men because of their conscience, moral insight and self-knowledge.

Captain MacWhirr in "Typhoon" had "just enough imagination to carry him through each successive day, and no more." Jim, by contrast, has too much. Paralyzed during a crucial moment on his boys' training ship, he imagines he will act heroically in the future. After the *Patna* has collided with a floating derelict hulk that punches a hole below the water-line and seems to threaten the bulging rust-eaten bulkhead plates, Jim "had an unconscious conviction that the reality could not be half as bad, not half as anguishing, appalling, and vengeful as the created terror of his imagination." In a moment of panic he jumps ship, betrays his ideals and loses his self-esteem. As Hemingway perceived in his Introduction to *Men at War* (1942): "Cowardice . . . is always simply a lack of ability to suspend the functioning of the imagination. Learning to suspend your imagination and live completely in the very second of the present minute with no before and no after is the greatest gift a soldier [or sailor] can acquire."[22]

The great themes of *Lord Jim* emerge from his perfectly understandable (there was no *practical* reason for remaining on the ship if it was going to sink) but morally reprehensible act: the acute consciousness of lost honor, "the doubt of the sovereign power enthroned in a fixed standard of conduct," the quest for self-knowledge and moral identity, for absolution, self-sacrifice and redemption.

At the end of *The Nigger of the "Narcissus,"* Captain Allistoun reminds the chief mate "to wind up the chronometers tomorrow morning." In *Lord Jim* Captain Brierly, one of the court assessors at Jim's trial, who has an impeccable record at sea, carefully hangs his gold chronometer watch (an absolute measure of time) on the rail and, like Jim, jumps into the sea. Brierly's apparently unmotivated suicide casts oblique light on Jim's character. Brierly strongly identifies with the man he has judged. He believes that Jim, instead of facing a humiliating public trial, should "creep twenty feet underground and stay there! By heavens! *I* would."[23] And he too suffers from an over-developed imagination. Irrationally sharing Jim's guilt, Brierly feels that he would also reveal his fear and cowardice if confronted with a similar crisis, and prefers death to shame.

In the second half of *Lord Jim*, the hero returns to the Bornean river setting of the early Malayan novels. Stein, a wealthy and respected merchant and lepidopterist, one of the most serious and sympathetic characters in Conrad's fiction, helps Jim to escape his cycle of self-torment in Singapore and to recover his self-esteem in Patusan. The kindly Stein—an old, wise and helpful admirer, rescuer, father-figure and friend who urges Jim to come to terms with reality—is based on Conrad's Uncle Tadeusz. He even uses the Latin phrase, *usque ad finem* (steadfast "to the very end," from the Vulgate translation of Hebrews 3:14), just as Tadeusz did in a letter to Conrad of November 9, 1891.

Stein rather cryptically advises Jim "to the destructive element submit yourself, and with the exertions of your hands and feet in the water make the deep, deep sea keep you up," that is, to face rather than evade reality. Stein uses the swimming metaphor that Conrad (who could not swim) equates, in later works, with essential modes of existence: with isolation and suicide as well as with survival. In *Under Western Eyes*, Razumov "was as lonely in the world as a man swimming in the deep sea." At the end of "The Planter of Malata," Geoffrey Renouard commits suicide by setting out "calmly to swim beyond the confines of life—with a steady stroke—his eyes fixed on a star!" But in the last sentence of "The Secret Sharer," Leggatt leaves the ship "a free man, a proud swimmer striking out for a new destiny."

In a letter to Garnett of November 1900, written two weeks after *Lord Jim* was published, Conrad admitted the structural weakness of the novel: "you've put your finger on the plague spot. The division of the book into two parts [Chapters 1–20 and 21–45] which is the basis of your criticism demonstrates to me once more your amazing insight." The first half of the novel is morally ambiguous; the second half, in Patusan, shows a clear opposition between Jim and the villainous invader, Gentleman Brown. Since the second half does not have a close thematic and structural relation to the first, the impressive though flawed book breaks in two and degenerates into a romantic adventure story. Despite this weakness, Conrad was heartened by a letter from Henry James, which he sent to Garnett to counter his criticism and called "a draught from the

Fountain of Eternal Youth. Wouldn't you think a boy had written it? Such enthusiasm! Wonderful old man, with his record of wonderful work!"[24]

VIII

The composition of the "The End of the Tether" (1902), the third story in *Youth*, was interrupted by a major disaster. On the evening of June 23, 1902, a month before serialization began in *Blackwood's Magazine*, a fire broke out in Pent Farm and turned the last half of the manuscript into a mass of charred fragments. "Last night the [oil] lamp exploded here," he told Ford, "and before I could run back into the room the whole round table was in a blaze, books, cigarettes, MS—alas. The whole 2nd part of End of Tether, ready to go to E[dinbur]gh. The whole! The fire ran in streams and Jess and I threw blankets and danced around on them; the blaze in the window was remarked in Postling, then all was over but the horrid stink."

Ford as usual came to the rescue, and during the next few months helped Conrad reconstruct the manuscript. By mid-October, when *Blackwood's* was waiting for the final pages, Conrad and Ford wrote through the night till the very last minute, in the state of crisis and panic that always helped Conrad to complete his work:

> At two in the morning the mare . . . was saddled by the writer [Ford] and the stable-boy. The stable-boy was to ride to the junction with the manuscript and catch the six in the morning mail train. The soup kept hot; the writers wrote. By three the writer had done all that he could in his room. He went across the road to where Conrad was still at it. Conrad said: "For God's sake . . . another half-hour: just finishing. . . ." At four the writer looked over Conrad's shoulder. He was writing [the third from last sentence]: "The blow had come, softened by the spaces of the earth, by the years of absence." The writer said: "You must finish now. . . ." [Finally, Ford] shouted: it had come to him as an inspiration: "In the name of God, don't you know you can write those two paragraphs into the proofs when you get them back?"

"The End of the Tether" was based on Conrad's time in Singapore and on his voyages to Borneo on the *Vidar*. Though overlong, repetitive and somewhat sentimental, it provides a fascinating account of sailing in the Malay Archipelago as well as a poignant portrayal of the moral conflict of a good man who sacrifices his professional standards and personal integrity to earn money for his distant but parasitic daughter. Conrad portrays the relation between Captain Whalley's physical and moral blindness, as the idealist, defenseless against evil, is defeated by Massy, the dishonorable engineer. Conrad suggests the futility of belief in benign Providence and expresses a tragic Sophoclean theme: "that no man may count himself safe from his kind unless in the very abyss of misery."[25]

IX

Conrad's brilliant success with *Heart of Darkness* and *Lord Jim* did not solve his desperate financial problems. In January 1899, just before he finished the African novella, he was awarded his first and only literary prize: £50 from the *Academy* (where he had reviewed Hugh Clifford's book) for *Tales of Unrest*. The following month (shortly before Eliza Orzeszkowa attacked him for writing in English for mercenary motives) he told the generous David Meldrum, London editor of Blackwood's, that Adolf Krieger was pressing him for repayment of an old loan. He could not possibly repay it and the debt had destroyed their friendship:

> Either the man is nervously anxious or he wants to put pressure on me— or he is in a bad way. In any case this kind of thing will drive me crazy. I can't work after I get such letters. I did send him the £50 of the *Academy* and I owe him 130 yet. I'd rather owe it to someone else. You know the whole absurd and painful story of the broken friendship—without provocation and even any cause I could remotely guess at. Their business which he started 14 years ago with my money is very good—perfectly sound. And here I am worried with these miserable letters. . . .
>
> The man (Hope) he mentions in the letter is utterly ruined [by speculation in South African gold shares] and even if I had the heart to squeeze him I would not get any blood out of that stone.

Though Blackwood's paid well—£300 for serial rights and £200 in advance of royalties for *Lord Jim*—Conrad, working slowly and selling modestly, could not earn enough to live on. He apologized for the delays and told Blackwood: "I devote myself exclusively to *Jim*. I find I can't live with more than one story at a time. It's a kind of literary monogamism."[26] But he was, in fact, also working intermittently on *The Rescuer* and writing *The Inheritors* with Ford.

William Blackwood had been extremely patient, encouraging and generous with Conrad. He had lent Conrad money for stories not yet written and had experienced considerable trouble with the make-up of *Blackwood's Magazine* when Conrad's promised copy did not arrive in time. In late May 1902, Conrad proposed that Blackwood lend him £300 and advance him an additional £50 in return for the copyrights of "Youth" and *Lord Jim* and the security of an insurance policy worth £400. This request stretched Blackwood's tolerance to the breaking-point. He told Conrad—as Fisher Unwin had done—that he had been a loss to the firm, and refused his request.

Blackwood felt Conrad had been extremely unreliable and financially demanding. He extended short stories into novels and asked advances on serial rights for work he had not yet completed. Despite the publication of *Heart of Darkness* and *Lord Jim*, his work was not well suited to the Tory imperialism of *Blackwood's*. Conrad's break with Blackwood increased his dependence on another Scotsman, J. B. Pinker, who in September 1900 became his literary agent and, later, one of his closest friends.

CHAPTER TWELVE

J. B. Pinker and *Nostromo*

1901–1904

I

Conrad's first eleven books were brought out by six different publishers, and it was not until his twelfth work, in 1907, that he settled down for a time with Methuen—though he continued to alternate between this firm, Unwin and Dent until the end of his life. His first eight American editions were published by seven different firms, and he did not finally move to Doubleday until 1912.[1] Conrad was not good at dealing with publishers, felt wounded when they rejected his terms and was crushed when told that his books had lost money. To protect himself, he cultivated an aristocratic disdain for publishers and profits, claimed their tradesmen's behavior was discreditable and called them "strange cattle." To Garnett, who gave good advice and acted as a buffer between the mercurial artist and the sober businessmen, he both boasted and confessed that he had become expert at exploiting agents and editors. But it was a tedious and exhausting process.

When the literary agent James Brand Pinker first approached him in August 1899, Conrad frankly admitted his personal and professional faults, and warned him that he would be a risky client: "My method of writing is so unbusiness-like that I don't think you could have any use for such an unsatisfactory person. I generally sell a work before it is begun, get paid when it is half done and don't do the other half till the spirit moves me. I must add that I have no control whatever over the spirit—neither has the man who has paid the money. The above may appear fanciful to you but it is the sober truth." Ignoring these warnings, Pinker waited a year and then persuaded Conrad to let him sort out the confusion with his publishers. At this time, Pinker succeeded

Uncle Tadeusz, "Aunt" Marguerite and Edward Garnett in the role of guardian, and supported Conrad's literary career as Tadeusz had supported his career at sea. Pinker recognized Conrad's extraordinary talent, believed in his future, wanted to help him and thought he would eventually succeed.

James Pinker—a self-made man with a dash of the *arriviste*—was born in Scotland in 1863, the son of poor parents, and had very little formal education. After a brief time as a clerk at Tilbury Docks, he worked as a journalist in Constantinople, married a wealthy woman and returned to England in 1891. He became assistant editor of an illustrated weekly, *Black and White*, read for a publishing house and briefly edited the popular *Pearson's Magazine*. In 1896 he became a literary agent, with offices in Granville House, Arundel Street. He could recognize talent, and his early clients included Wilde, Wells, Crane, James and Arnold Bennett.

Pinker was a sturdy but lively man with pink cheeks and a pronounced burr—dapper, bow-tied and rather pleased with himself. Ford said that behind the benevolent spectacles was a grim gleam in his hard eyes. And Frank Swinnerton also emphasized the toughness beneath the kindly countenance: "He was short, compact, a rosy, round-faced clean-shaven grey-haired sphinx with a protrusive under-lip, who drove four-in-hand, spoke distinctly in a hoarse voice that was almost a whisper, shook hands shoulder-high, laughed without moving, knew the monetary secrets of authors and the weaknesses of publishers, terrified some of these last and was refused admittance by others, dominated editors, and of course enjoyed much power." Pinker had an expert knowledge of the trade, enjoyed close relations with publishers in Europe and America, drove a hard bargain and energetically defended the rights of his clients.

Unlike D. H. Lawrence (who later became Pinker's client), Conrad was unwilling to reduce his standard of living to match his income and cut back expenses to maintain his independence. He was, after all, an aristocrat; he had to live like a gentleman and have (even when in debt and pressed for money) maids, gardeners, secretaries, nurses, tutors, private schools, a London club, cars, holidays abroad and expensive hotels. He believed "that an artist should obtain the uttermost farthing that can be got for his work—not on the ground of material satisfaction but simply for the sake of leisure which, it seems to me, is a necessary condition of good work."[2] Conrad's anguished creation seemed to justify spending more than he earned. Almost every letter to Pinker—who must have dreaded their arrival—worried him with a demand for a favor or for cash.

In January 1901, true to his original warning, Conrad apologized to Pinker for his entanglements with several publishers, explained that he hoped to finish *The Rescuer* but had to work on other projects that would bring in money, and placed their business relations on a shaky foundation by asking payment for work that had not yet been sold:

> Would you, therefore, advance me as much as the prospect of placing the story ["Typhoon"] would justify—leaving you on the safe side. I feel I am not fair to you with all my reservations of book-rights to certain publishers and so on. However, later on, when I've cleared up my position vis-à-vis Heinemann—principally—we may be able to put our connection on a sounder basis, as far as *you* are concerned.
>
> The "knot" in the situation is the finishing of the *Rescue*. That would clear the air—but on the other side I must for the present write stuff that'll bring immediate bread and butter.

Despite the prize from the *Academy*, grants of £300 and £200 from the Royal Literary Fund in 1903 and 1908, £500 from the Royal Bounty fund in 1905, and a Civil List Pension of £100 a year in 1910, Conrad shuddered to think how much he owed Pinker, who frequently advanced him considerable sums of money. Conrad estimated that he lived on £650 a year, and by 1908 he owed Pinker as much as £1,600. The following year his total debt amounted to £2,250, for which he paid £100 annual interest. Pinker managed Conrad's finances; paid for milk, cigars, hotel rooms and a new coat for Jessie; he even replaced the money when Conrad's pocket was picked. When Conrad's bankers, Watson & Co., failed in 1904, Pinker helped cover the overdraft of £200. In 1907 Conrad hoped to settle down on a secure financial basis within three years, but in 1908 his thirteen books brought in less than £5 in royalties. In 1912 he complained to the wealthy Edith Wharton that after sixteen years of scribbling he was still living from day to day. Pinker was paying Jessie's medical bills as late as 1919.

Conrad frequently declared that he was hopeless with money matters and, addressing his benefactor as if he were Uncle Tadeusz, begged Pinker not to scold him. But this volatile situation inevitably produced explosions of temper on both sides. In January 1902, after a harsh, admonitory letter from Pinker, Conrad took offense and complained in a haughty tone that he was not being treated with proper respect: "I am not just now in the right frame of mind for the proper appreciation of a lecture. . . . Pray do not write to me as [if] I were a fool blundering in the dark. . . . Don't address me as if I were a man lost in sloth, ignorance or folly." Pinker backed down and paid up, and the quarrel blew over within a week.

With a mixture of apology and complaint, Conrad confessed: "I feel every time I write as if I were begging. I don't like it. It grows impossible," but he continued nevertheless to beg. When Jessie claimed she was entitled to an outing and insisted on coming up to London with her husband, Conrad, like a schoolboy demanding a treat, asked Pinker to meet this expense. He claimed it could not be very heavy, though it was certainly heavier for Pinker than for Conrad. The agent must have been exasperated not only by his client's poor logic, but also by the demand that he pay for Jessie's whims. It may have been on this occasion that Conrad had one of the infantile tantrums that Jessie loved to record in her memoirs:

> [He] walked rapidly into another hotel and curtly requested the waiter to "tell my wife I am here." The waiter's very natural question, "What name, sir?" had exasperated him, and he answered sharply, "Mrs. Conrad, of course." When the man returned after a short absence with the information that there was no one of that name in the hotel, Conrad called for the manager, and now, greatly irate, turned on him tensely with the command, "Produce my wife!" It was with difficulty he was persuaded that he was in the wrong hotel.[3]

In July 1904, when Conrad was forced to borrow a pound from William Heinemann for his train fare home, his literary friends got the impression that Pinker was keeping him on a very short leash. Defending himself against this charge, Pinker told Wells that some people may have "the impression that Conrad was in penury and that I was treating him with less than humanity. As a matter of fact Conrad always borrows a sovereign when he comes in. . . . In truth I have never refused Conrad any sum that he has asked for." Conrad, to disguise his humiliating situation, boasted to Galsworthy (another benefactor): "The slave obeys my behests in profound silence as a rule." But he was as grateful for Pinker's faith as for his cash, recognized that their relationship was based on friendship, not business, and said: "He has stepped gallantly into the breach left open by the collapse of my bank; and not only gallantly, but successfully as well. He has treated not only my moods but even my fancies with the greatest consideration."[4] Conrad later told his young Polish friend Joseph Retinger that if it had not been for Pinker he would have starved.

II

In the early years of the century Conrad continued to widen his circle of acquaintances. He not only met (through Wells) Major Ernest Dawson, who had served as a magistrate in the East and as an officer in the Rangoon Volunteer Rifles and had contributed stories about Burma to *Blackwood's*, but also some of his most successful contemporaries: Arnold Bennett, Bernard Shaw and Rudyard Kipling. Conrad first met Bennett in 1899 at the home of H. G. Wells. The popular Staffordshire novelist sent him *Leonora* in 1903, and for the next decade Bennett, who had impeccable taste in Conrad, consistently praised *The Nigger of the "Narcissus," Nostromo, The Secret Agent* and *Chance*.

Wells recalled that when he introduced Conrad to George Bernard Shaw in the spring of 1902, the witty but flippant Irishman "talked with his customary freedoms. 'You know, my dear fellow, your books won't *do*'—for some Shavian reason I have forgotten—and so forth. I went out of the room and suddenly found Conrad on my heels, swift and white-faced. 'Does that fellow want to *insult* me?' he demanded. The provocation to say 'Yes' and assist at the subsequent duel was very great, but I overcame it. 'It's humour,' I said, and took Conrad into the garden to cool. One could always baffle Conrad by saying 'humour.' It was one of our damned English tricks he had never learnt to tackle." The always serious Conrad, who never forgot Shaw's criticism, later told Garnett, with considerable truth: "The fellow pretends to be deep but he never gets to the bottom of things but rides off on some tricky evasion."[5] Yet he respected Shaw's good opinion and told Galsworthy that Shaw was (inexplicably) enthusiastic about Conrad's play *One Day More* and had praised him as a "real dramatist."

Conrad's relations with Kipling, his most notable rival, were much more complex. They were the only great authors who portrayed imperialism during the zenith of its power and influence. Conrad's unfamiliar subject matter and exotic settings, his themes of self-discipline and devotion to duty, led his first critics to label him a spinner of sea yarns and the "Kipling of the Malay Archipelago." Both writers employed technical expertise in their fiction, but Kipling's was acquired from books while Conrad's was learned from experience. Conrad justly thought his works were more ambitious and profound, and resented the comparison to Kipling. Comparing his own works to those of his contemporary, Conrad told a French friend: "A *national* writer like Kipling for example translates easily. His interest is *in the subject*, the interest of my work is *in the effect* that it produces. He speaks *of his compatriots*. I write *for them*."

In January 1898 Arthur Symons, reviewing a translation of Gabriele
D'Annunzio's *Il trionfo della morte* in the *Saturday Review*, contrasted *The
Nigger of the "Narcissus"* and *Captains Courageous* to continental novels
and said these two books had no idea behind them. The following
month Conrad wrote a 1,500 word defense of Kipling (and of himself)
and sent it to *Outlook*, where in 1898 he published essays on Alphonse
Daudet and on Marryat and Cooper. It was never published and has
never been found.[6]

Charles Carrington's statement that "each was an admirer of the other's work" needs some qualification. Though Conrad recommended Kipling's work to his Polish cousin, he expressed profound, if somewhat
cryptic reservations about him in two letters to Cunninghame Graham,
who was not sympathetic to Kipling's conservative views:

> Mr. Kipling has the wisdom of the passing generations—and holds it in
> perfect sincerity. Some of his work is of impeccable form and because of
> that little thing he shall sojourn in Hell only a very short while. He squints
> with the rest of his excellent sort. . . .
>
> In the chaos of printed matter Kipling's *ébauches* [rough drafts] appear
> by contrast finished and impeccable. I judge the man *in* his time—and
> space. It is a small space—and as to his time I leave it to your tender
> mercy. I wouldn't in his defence spoil the small amount of steel that goes
> to the making of a needle.

While granting Kipling's artistic polish and superiority to his rather
undistinguished contemporaries, Conrad criticized his irritating clever-
ness and the shallowness of his moral vision. By the time *Under Western
Eyes* appeared in 1911, the difference between the two writers was much
clearer and a critic could justly declare: "Mr. Conrad represents the
genius of negation as surely as Mr. Kipling represents the genius of
affirmation."[7]

Kipling's political views and justification of colonialism deeply offended the author of *Heart of Darkness* and *Nostromo*. As Conrad, whose
sympathies were always with the underdog, wrote of the Boer War:
"There is an appalling fatuity in this business. If I am to believe Kipling
this is a war undertaken for the cause of democracy. *C'est à crever de rire!*
[It's enough to make you split your sides laughing]." And the usually
patriotic Conrad used to shock Ford "by declaring that the French [who
had less racial prejudice than the English] were the only European nation who knew how to colonize; they had none of the spirit of Mr.
Kipling's 'You bloody-Niggerisms' about them." As Retinger noted,

Conrad also "had the prejudice of many of his contemporaries against what they called Kipling's reporter's style and his 'journalese.' "

Retinger was quite mistaken, however, when he claimed that "Conrad never understood the great Imperialist, and, indeed, disliked him intensely,"[8] for the difference in their political views—like Conrad's political differences with Garnett and Graham—did not interfere with their friendship. On August 30, 1904, Mrs. Kipling, impressed by Conrad, increased his stature and wrote in her diary: "Mr. Conrad, author of *Lord Jim*, comes to call. A large Pole seaman full of amusing stories." Two years later Conrad inscribed a copy of *The Mirror of the Sea* "To the memorable, for me, kindness of your reception, just over two years ago, pray add the kindly act of accepting this copy of a very small book—very small but particularly my own. Believe me, with the greatest regard, yours faithfully, J. Conrad, 4 October 1906, Pent Farm." Five days later Kipling responded with an enthusiastic note, praising "Typhoon" as well as the new book.

Conrad also visited Kipling at Burwash during the 1920s. Conrad's son John recalled that he had an enjoyable time and was in a very cheerful mood on the way home. Kipling reciprocated Conrad's admiration. A Polish diplomat and author, who met him in Madrid in 1928, recorded: "I was struck by the magnanimity with which he praised and discussed Conrad's outstanding talent that was overshadowing his own writings of recent years. . . . 'His spoken English was sometimes difficult to understand but with a pen in his hand he was first amongst us.' . . . [But] there was nothing English, according to Kipling, in Conrad's mentality. 'When I am reading him,' he continued, 'I always have the impression that I am reading an excellent translation of a foreign author.' "[9]

During 1903–4 Conrad also formed friendships with two men who belonged to the world of art and letters, had distinguished careers and were later knighted. William Rothenstein—a short, bald man with thick glasses, fifteen years younger than Conrad—was well-connected and prominent in the artistic and literary worlds of Paris and London. His friend Max Beerbohm wrote that "he wore spectacles that flashed more than any other pair ever seen. He was a wit. He was brimful of ideas. . . . He knew every one." Rothenstein was also a friend of Cunninghame Graham and had traveled with him in Morocco. In July 1903 Rothenstein came down to Pent Farm and did two portraits of Conrad, one in chalk and one in pastel (the former is now in the National Portrait Gallery, London), and their friendship developed quickly. Rothenstein lent Conrad money and helped him obtain a grant in 1905. Conrad praised his "amaz-

ing intelligence," and in 1906, while living in London, offered Rothenstein the use of Pent Farm. In *Men and Memories* Rothenstein described
Conrad's appearance with an artist's eye and ascribed to his Polish
background his nervous sensitivity and elaborate manners:

> With his piercing eyes and keen, deeply-lined bearded face, in some ways
> he looked like the sea captain, but his nervous manner, his rapid, excited
> speech, his restlessness, his high shoulders, didn't suggest the sailor. I
> accepted him at once as an artist; never, I thought, had I met anyone with
> a quicker apprehension, with such warmth of intellectual sympathy. . . .
>
> There was always an element of strain in Conrad—an excitability, which
> may have been individual, or may have been Polish. . . . While Conrad
> was extremely courteous and understanding by nature, his nerves some-
> times made him aggressive, almost violent; and like most sensitive men,
> he was strongly affected, either favourably or disagreeably, by others. . . .
> When he liked people he would admit no faults; indeed, he was inclined
> to flatter—perhaps this was a Polish trait—both in speaking and writing.

Conrad met Sidney Colvin—a thin, bald man with a white pointed
beard, a gentle scholarly face and delicate features—in February 1904.
The son of a country gentleman and East India merchant in London,
Colvin was born in 1845 and educated at Trinity College, Cambridge. An
art critic, biographer of Keats and Landor, editor and intimate of Stevenson, friend of Ruskin, Rossetti and Henry James, he had been Slade
Professor of Fine Arts at Cambridge and director of the Fitzwilliam Museum before becoming Keeper of Prints and Drawings at the British
Museum (where he had a flat) in 1884. An earnest, conservative and
rather humorless man, "in the conduct of life he was [like Conrad] all for
the traditions, perfect courtesy, an unflinching code of honour, decent
manners and a certain avoidance of the crudities [of] modern life."[10]

Frances Sitwell, an older woman who had been venerated by Stevenson and eventually became Colvin's wife, had long been separated from
her clergyman husband. But she was unable to marry Colvin, whom she
had known for thirty years, until Reverend Sitwell's death in 1903.
Though Colvin and Mrs. Sitwell had lived separately in London, she
had been the recognized hostess in his house and their liaison (curiously
like Galsworthy and Ada's) had been approved by all their many friends.
Despite Conrad's disdain for Stevenson, whom Colvin worshiped, they
soon became close friends. Colvin suggested and then produced *One
Day More* at the Court Theatre in London in June 1905, and wrote favorable reviews of *Chance*, *Victory*, *The Shadow-Line* and *The Arrow of Gold*
in the *Observer*, the *Daily Telegraph* and the *Living Age*.

III

In mid-January 1904 the Conrads rented rooms for two months in 17 Gordon Place, Kensington, close to Ford and his family, shared their household expenses and took meals with them. During this period Conrad continued to work on *Nostromo*; wrote *One Day More*; and discovered, he told the fluent Wells, that he could dictate his sea sketches to Ford at the astonishing rate of 3,000 words in four hours. In *Return to Yesterday* Ford described his dual role as prompter and recorder:

> *The Mirror of the Sea* and *A Personal Record* were mostly written by my hand from Conrad's dictation. Whilst he was dictating them, I would recall incidents to him—I mean incidents of his past life which he had told me but which did not come freely back to his mind because at the time he was mentally ill [i.e., depressed], in desperate need of money, and, above all, skeptical as to the merits of the reminiscential form which I had suggested to him. The fact is I could make Conrad write at periods when his despair and fatigue were such that in no other way would it have been possible to him. He would be lying on the sofa or pacing the room, railing at life and literature as practised in England, and I would get a writing pad and pencil and, whilst he was still raving, would interject: "Now, then, what was it you were saying about coming up the Channel and nearly running over a fishing boat that suddenly appeared under your bows?" and gradually there would come "Landfalls and Departures."

By April 15 Conrad told George Harvey, president of Harper's publishers: "I have a book which is nearly ready, a volume of Sea-sketches, something in the spirit of Turgeniev's *Sportsman's Sketches*, but concerned with ships and sea with a distinct autobiographical and anecdotal note running through what is mainly meant for a record of remembered feelings. . . . For title I thought of: *A Seaman's Sketches* or if a more general effect is desired *Mirror of the Sea*."[11] Serialized during 1904–5 and published as a book in October 1906, *The Mirror of the Sea* is a somewhat wordy, sententious and rambling memoir (not surprising, considering its mode of composition). It describes, in random, achronological order, several illuminating episodes on Conrad's ships: the *Tilkhurst*, *Loch Etive*, *Highland Forest*, *Duke of Sutherland*, *Otago* and *Mont-Blanc*. The central metaphor is that ships are alive and have their own personal qualities. The main interest of the book lies in the final chapters on Conrad's Marseilles hero, Dominic Cervoni, and the destruction of their ship, the *Tremolino*.

A few days after he arrived in London an accident occurred that affected Conrad for the rest of his life. Coming out of John Barker's department store on High Street, Kensington, Jessie "slipped the cartilage" of both knees, fell onto the pavement and badly injured the knee that had been previously dislocated and damaged by a skating accident in 1889. Partially crippled by this fall, during the next thirty years Jessie endured a dozen expensive but unsuccessful operations. Her consequent immobility led to obesity, which, in turn, further weakened her crippled knee.

In November 1904 a surgeon examined Jessie under chloroform and, according to Borys, botched the first operation. Conrad told Ford that "the mischief was not located—it was not even found. As a matter of fact Bruce Clarke (as good a man as there is, I suppose) took his patient for a pampered, silly sort of little woman who was making no end of fuss for a simple stiff joint. You may imagine to what horrible pain he put her acting on that assumption."

A year later, in October 1905, the previously imperturbable Jessie succumbed to the pressure of straitened circumstances and to the anxieties of living with a neurasthenic artist, and collapsed under the strain of Conrad's illness as well as her own. "She had a violent fit of palpitation in the morning," Conrad told Ada Galsworthy, "which alarmed me to some extent. I sent off for the doctor. His verdict is nervous breakdown of a sort; nothing dangerous in itself but with a defective heart most undesirable. . . . Fact is our life or else life in general is beginning to tell on her. The sameness of existence varied by nothing but anxiety during my fits of [asthma] and gout is I suppose proving a bit too much." By 1908 Conrad, taking the darkest view, confided to Marguerite Poradowska that Jessie's knee was much worse, that she could scarcely drag herself about and that it might all end with amputation.

Jessie compensated for her immobility and pain with quantities of rich cakes, numerous boxes of chocolates and bottles of liquor, and her heavy drinking sometimes led to embarrassing scenes. As she became increasingly heavy, her features, like raisins in a pudding, seemed to sink into her pudgy face. Conrad was probably thinking of his wife when he wrote in Nostromo of "that dull, surfeited look which can be seen in the eyes of gluttonous persons after a heavy meal."[12] Jessie occupied herself, when servants took over her household duties, by writing letters, knitting, and reading trashy novels. She played bezique and dominoes, and liked to be driven through the countryside and taken to see her mother, who scarcely seemed to appreciate these expeditions. John Conrad complained that old Mrs. George was never interested in any of the places they visited by car and, whenever they stopped in a village, expected someone to buy her a gift. Whenever Jessie's whims were not satisfied, she lapsed into tears and "stubborn dumbness."

IV

In April 1903 Conrad published *Typhoon*, his second collection of stories, which included, in addition to the title piece, the autobiographical "Amy Foster," the negligible "Tomorrow," and "Falk." The last story is set in Bangkok (with vivid descriptions of temples, town and river) and based on Conrad's experience on the *Otago*. The narrator of the story is appointed to take command after the captain has died and, because of the shortage of stores and supplies, finds it difficult to get her ready for sea. The niece who remains absolutely silent during her courtship, the disturbing mixture of ruthlessness and moral delicacy, and the theme of cannibalism made serialization impossible. Even the equable Jessie became "physically sick when [she] typed those pages. Sick with disgust at the idea of human beings having been cooked."

In the story Falk, who owns the only tugboat on the dangerous river, is led to believe that the narrator has become his rival in love for the niece of the German Captain Hermann. Falk refuses to tow the narrator's ship, which cannot leave on its own, until he pleads Falk's suit with Hermann. But Falk—like *Lord Jim* and Razumov in *Under Western Eyes*—feels compelled to clear his conscience and risk his love by confessing a reprehensible act. After his former ship had lost its propeller and drifted into Antarctic ice floes, Falk decided "the best man shall survive," killed the ship's carpenter, who tried to shoot him, and ate the unfortunate man. The merit of this overlong but interesting story lies in the humorous treatment of Falk's infatuation with the silent woman, and in the ironic contrast between his crude behavior and his fine conscience.

Conrad actually served under a Captain McWhirr on the *Highland Forest* and used his tempestuous name (with a variant spelling) for the hero of "Typhoon," a story that complements the themes of *Lord Jim*. Both works deal with human cargo: pilgrims and coolies; Jim has excessive and MacWhirr deficient imagination; Jim runs when he should have stayed, MacWhirr stays when he should have run. Faced with the unmistakable signs of a typhoon in the South China Sea, MacWhirr—whose Scots pragmatism and stubborn character cannot conceive the reality of anything he had not personally experienced—refuses to alter the course of the *Nan-Shan* [Southern Mountain]. He justifies his bizarre behavior by declaring that he cannot waste coal and must protect his sober reputation with the owners. Like the Russian in motley in *Heart of Darkness*, MacWhirr has no imagination, is unaware of the danger and, though limited, is able to survive. The description of the violent storm is a brilliant and justly famous *tour de force* during which MacWhirr exhibits his impressive faith, stoicism and courage—as well as his astonishing, dangerous and costly stupidity.

The coolies in the hold—who are returning from work in Southeast Asia and fight like beasts to recover their long accumulated wages when their sea chests are bashed open by the storm—are a human parallel to the storm. And the even distribution of the money at the end of the voyage restores the solidarity that has been threatened by the tempest. MacWhirr's belief—"a gale is a gale . . . and a full-powered steam-ship has got to face it. There's just so much dirty weather knocking about the world, and the proper thing is to go through it"—ironically, blindly and humorously reaffirms the traditional values of the merchant marine that Conrad expressed in "Well Done": "A man is a worker. If he is not that he is nothing. . . . For the great mass of mankind the only saving grace that is needed is steady fidelity to what is nearest to hand and heart in the short moment of each human effort. In other and in greater words, what is needed is a sense of immediate duty, and a feeling of impalpable constraint."[13]

Conrad worked on *Nostromo*—his longest, most complex and most ambitious novel—from December 1902 until August 1904. His previous works had been based on personal experience. But this novel (which, like many others, began as a short story) was based on imagination. While sailing to South America on the *Saint-Antoine* in 1876–77, Conrad had only the briefest experience on that continent. He had a glimpse of Cartagena, Colombia, and spent twelve hours at Puerto Cabello and three days at La Guayra on the coast of Venezuela. His creative imagination always needed the stimulus of solid facts, and he searched with a hawk-eye through personal and historical memoirs for precise details that would give authenticity to his work.[14]

In a letter to the critic Edmund Gosse, Conrad explained the composite setting of the novel: "The geographical basis is, as you have seen, mainly Venezuela; but there are bits of Mexico in it, and the aspect presented by the mountains appertains in character more to the Chilean seaboard than to any other. The curtain of clouds hangs always over Iquique [in Chile]. The rest of the meteorology belongs to the Gulf of Panama and, generally, to the Western Coast of Mexico as far as Mazatlan."

In *A Personal Record* Conrad described how he created the whole world of Costaguana: the mountains, town and *campo*: the history, geography, politics and finance; the wealth of the mine-owner Charles Gould, the idealism of his wife, Emilia, the cynicism of the journalist Decoud, the bitterness of the tortured Dr. Monygham and the pride of Nostromo, the chief of the stevedores, whose name "dominated even after death the dark gulf containing his conquests of treasure and love." When writing the novel, Conrad experienced the same loneliness, concentration, tension, responsibility and control he had felt when navigating a perilous passage on a ship:

> Neglecting the common joys of life that fall to the lot of the humblest on this earth, I had, like [Jacob] the prophet of old, "wrestled with the Lord" for my creation, for the headlands of the coast, for the darkness of the Placid Gulf, the light on the snows, the clouds on the sky, and for the breath of life that had to be blown into the shapes of men and women, of Latin and Saxon, of Jew and Gentile. These are, perhaps, strong words, but it is difficult to characterise otherwise the intimacy and the strain of a creative effort in which mind and will and conscience are engaged to the full, hour after hour, day after day, away from the world, and to the exclusion of all that makes life really lovable and gentle—something for which a material parallel can only be found in the everlasting sombre stress of the westward winter passage round Cape Horn.[15]

While he was living in London near Ford during February and March 1904, and the novel was being serialized in *T. P.'s Weekly*, Conrad could not keep up with the installments. He therefore sought the assistance of Ford, who ingeniously and effortlessly wrote sixteen manuscript pages of part II, chapter 5, imitating Conrad's style and keeping the novel going without making anything significant happen. Ford later explained to the American collector George Keating, who had bought the manuscript in Ford's hand:

> Whilst I was living in London with Conrad almost next door and coming in practically every day for meals, he was taken with so violent an attack of gout and nervous depression that he was quite unable to continue his installments of *Nostromo*. . . . I therefore simply wrote enough from time to time to keep the presses going—a job that presented no great difficulties to me. . . . I was practically under oath to Conrad not to reveal these facts owing to the misconception that might arise and nothing in the world would have induced me to reveal it now but for the extremely unfortunate sale of these pages.

The protracted composition of this vast novel of corrupt politics and futile revolution in a South American republic was more agonizing than usual. Conrad had a terror of dentists and the last thirty-six hours of solid work was interrupted by a painful extraction and concluded by an almost surrealistic incident:

> Finished on the 30th in Hope's house [where the whole family had gone for a visit] in Stanford in Essex, where I had to take off my brain that seemed to turn to water. For a solid Fortnight I've been sitting up. And all the time horrible toothache. On the 27th had to wire for dentist (couldn't leave the work) who came at 2 and dragged at the infernal thing which seemed rooted in my very soul. The horror came away at last, leaving however one root in the gum. Then he grubbed for *that* till I leapt out of the chair. Thereupon old Walton [the dentist] said: I don't think your nerves will stand any more of this. . . .
>
> At 11.30 *I* broke down just after raising my eyes to the clock. Then I don't know: two blank hours during which I must have got out and sat down—(not fallen) on the concrete outside the door. That's how I found myself; and crawling in again noted the time: considerably after one.[16]

Nostromo continued the attack on colonialism that Conrad began in *Heart of Darkness* and developed the themes of personal power, individual responsibility and social justice. In both works the country and the hero are cut off from civilization, dominated by greed, exploitation and material interests. Both portray the violent threat of nature, the sense of unreality, the moral darkness, the disintegration of humane values, the choice of nightmares, the redemptive woman and the calm yet richly suggestive conclusion in the final sentence.

Nostromo asks several important questions: What is the meaning of civilization and progress? What happens when materialism replaces humane values? How does colonialism affect traditional societies?

Conrad establishes the violent spirit of Costaguana, so different from the placidity of its somber gulf, by relating the anarchy and chaos of its history. The opening chapter, with its startling description of the enlightened Ribiera and his followers fleeing from the savage Monterist revolution, gives potent warning about the fate of progressive governments. The brutal torment of the kindly statesman Don José Avellanos and the ghastly torture of Dr. Monygham are testaments to the imbecility of political fanaticism with which another dictator, Guzman Bento, tyrannized the country. The history of Costaguana, cruelty linked with poverty and oppression, is reminiscent of the history of Poland.

The pattern formed by the characters—enslavement, corruption and betrayal—originated with Charles Gould's father and was followed by his son, by Decoud and by Nostromo, who are most directly affected by the silver. The elder Gould, who correctly predicted that he would be killed by the San Tomé mine, begged his son never to return to Costaguana. Despite these warnings, the fact that his uncle Henry had been executed during a bloody revolution and that a similar venture (the Atacama nitrate fields) had ended disastrously, Gould has fallen under the spell of the mine. He egocentrically believes that the mine, which had been the cause of moral disaster, must be made a material and moral success in order to preserve the name and honor of his family.

Gould's capitalistic ambitions, summarized in his ironic declaration early in the novel (and answered by Dr. Monygham much later, when it is apparent that Gould has failed to achieve his aims), are twofold and in opposition to each other:

> What is wanted here is law, good faith, order, security. Any one can declaim about these things, but I pin my faith to material interests. Only let the material interests once get a firm footing, and they are bound to impose the conditions on which alone they can continue to exist. That's how your money-making is justified here in the face of lawlessness and disorder. It's justified because the security which it demands must be shared with an oppressed people. A better justice will come afterwards. That's your ray of hope.

Unfortunately, the ideals that Gould wants and the country needs are incompatible with the material interests to which he pins his faith, and "law, good faith, order, security" are subordinated to the welfare and success of the mine. Ultimately, money-making is not justified by security (it is the security, not the wealth, that is to be shared with the people), and the masses continue to be oppressed in different ways. A "better justice" never comes, and nothing is ever bound to come, because the security of the mine is dependent upon the political stability of the country, and history has repeatedly proved that permanent stability is impossible to achieve.

Gould's greatest limitation is that he never fully realizes the social consequences of his actions. Though exploding the mine (which he threatens to do) might suit his own interests, it would certainly harm the lives of the workers under his protection as well as the economic future of the entire country. The tremendous power of "El Rey de Sulaco" is too personal, dynastic and irresponsible. Gould never considers what the silver is used for once it leaves Sulaco; he never fully realizes the potential evil of the mine and lacks the imaginative estimate of the silver that his wife possesses. For him, the worth of the mine is beyond doubt. He has complete faith in the financial empire of Holroyd, who has mechanized the lives of his American employees just as Gould has in Costaguana. Holroyd uses his vast profits for further imperialistic ventures and exploitation, and wants to subject the entire world to the inexorable processes that have been destroying Costaguana. When Gould agrees with Holroyd that the mining interests will dominate Costaguana along with the rest of the world, Emilia is horrified and calls it the most awful materialism, devoid of all moral principle.

Dangerously obsessed by his conception of the mine and seduced by the idea that it can redeem the country, Gould surrenders his wife's happiness. Emilia realizes that the wealth pouring out of the mine dries up her husband's feelings, and that she is being robbed of both affection and children. She believes that her mission is to save him from the effects of his obsession and from the evils of material progress. Her failure is one of the tragedies of the novel, for she can never make Charles share her vision of the mine: "It was as if the inspiration of their early years had left her heart to turn into a wall of silver-bricks, erected by the silent work of evil spirits, between her and her husband. He seemed to dwell alone within a circumvallation of precious metal, leaving her outside."[17]

Emilia sees the reflection of her own personal tragedy in the pattern of Nostromo's corruption, and in the debasement and ruination of his love for Giselle Viola. In a poignant moment she tells the mournful Giselle that she too had once been loved. When Emilia lets the silver come down the mountain to be sent north for credit, she too becomes corrupted. She redeems herself only when she tells the dying Nostromo to renounce the treasure and "Let it be lost forever."

Decoud shows that European values cannot survive in the wilds of Costaguana. He recognizes the conflict between the two worlds but cannot reconcile them: "There is a curse of futility upon our character: Don Quixote and Sancho Panza, chivalry and materialism, high-sounding sentiments and a supine morality, violent efforts for an idea and a sullen acquiescence in every form of corruption." The positive qualities are the illusions that Europe brings to Costaguana: the beliefs of Gould, the code of Nostromo, the ambitions of Decoud. The negative ones are the ghastly realities of the country that crush these ideals. The dualism is expressed in the social structure of Costaguana, in the indolence of the upper classes and the mental darkness of the lower. It is also expressed in the ambiguity of Decoud's death, for the general belief was that he died accidentally, but the truth was that he died from solitude and want of faith in himself.

Decoud's idealistic counterpart is Don José Avellanos, an ironic and pathetic figure, who suffers untold horrors under Guzman Bento, only to die fleeing from the Monterist invasion. Avellanos' naïve and passionate involvement in affairs of state is pitifully misplaced and defies the experience he recorded in his *History of Fifty Years of Misrule*. His death represents the triumph of rapacity over nobility.

In contrast to Don José, Decoud employs material interests to serve his personal ambitions. He used the wealth of the mine to bring back a well-armed General Barrios, to effect a Ribierist counter-revolution and to form an independent Occidental Republic. Though he achieves these ambitions, he betrays his love for Antonia Avellanos (a younger version of Emilia Gould) and loses his life.

The testing of Decoud's inner strength and European values, of his love for Antonia and commitment to the revolution, takes place in the greatest scene of the novel, when he finds himself threatened by the dark silence of the Golfo Placido:

> It was a new experience for Decoud, this mysteriousness of the great waters spread out strangely smooth, as if their restlessness had been crushed by the weight of that dense night. . . . The solitude could almost be felt. And when the breeze ceased, the blackness seemed to weigh upon Decoud like a stone. . . . Intellectually self-confident, he suffered from being deprived of the only weapon he could use with effect. No intelligence could penetrate the darkness of the Placid Gulf.[18]

After ten days of isolation Decoud, no longer protected by his habitual irony and scepticism, is overcome by solitude. He begins to doubt his own individuality, loses faith in the reality of his past and future actions, and sees the world as a succession of incomprehensible images. His mental agony is subtly likened to the tortured trader Hirsch, hanging from a rope that pulls his wrists above his wrenched shoulder blades, until he is shot by his interrogator, Sotillo. Decoud's "solitude appeared like a great void and the silence of the gulf like a tense, thin *cord* to which he hung *suspended* by both hands. . . . He imagined [the cord] snapping with a report as of a pistol." In the same way, "the sensation of the snatching *pull, dragging* the lighter away to destruction," which Decoud feels when the boats collide in the gulf, is similar to Linda Viola's jealousy of her sister Giselle: "A strange, *dragging* pain as if somebody were *pulling* her about brutally."[19] These parallel descriptions bind all the

European victims in a moral and physical destruction that can be delayed, but not prevented, by idealism or material interests. Hirsch's
torture recalls Monygham's, whose breakdown contrasts with Avellanos' resistance. The execution of Gould's uncle is nearly repeated
when Gould is lined up to be shot, just as Monygham is almost hanged
by Sotillo—as Hirsch was.

Overcome by the crushing sense of human futility as he struggles
against the forces of nature, Decoud shoots himself and uses the silver to
sink his body in the gulf. His death and the missing ingots seal Nostromo
to the treasure and make him its slave. Conrad's letter to Gosse illumi-
nated his conception and presentation of the main character:

> Nostromo is a man suffering intensely all the time from an exaggerated
> *amour propre*. I present him at first as complaining that, after he has brought
> the old Englishman [Sir John Holroyd] (rich enough to pay for a whole
> railway) from the mountains, he had not enough money in his pocket to
> buy himself a cigar, because his wages were not due till next week. He is
> a man with instincts for magnificence. His prestige with the great popu-
> lace is the very breath of his nostrils. The episode when he cuts (or rather
> lets the girl cut) the silver buttons off his coat in the view of the assembled
> people gives the note of his psychology. Afterwards he may be supposed
> to reflect as men of the people often do: Yes, I am a great man but what do
> I get for it.

Nostromo admires (and is measured against) the idealism of the old
Garibaldino, Giorgio Viola, in the same way that Charles admires Emilia's; and Teresa Viola's warning of betrayal and destruction echoes that
of Gould's father. Though Viola's idealism is admirable, it is ineffective
and even pitiful. Simon Bolívar's statement that those who worked for
independence have ploughed the sea is an ironic judgment of Viola's
career in South America. The noble warrior of republican principles,
who cannot live under a king, subjects his family to exile and far worse
tyranny in Costaguana. Yet Viola does follow the principle of brotherhood while Nostromo thrives solely on adulation.

Nostromo's exploits are legion. He saves Ribiera from the mob, rescues the Viola family, carries Father Corbelan's message to the wild
Hernandez, brings Holroyd over the mountains, finds a doctor for the
dying Teresa and sails into the gulf with the silver of the mine. But all
these exploits divorce action from thought. He was called upon, his
reputation demanded that he accept the challenge and he acted—
instinctively and without reflection.

The extraordinary change in Nostromo begins with his possession of the silver, and is symbolized by his Adamic awakening and rebirth into a new life at the ruined fort. His physical and mental awakening occur simultaneously, initiate his thoughtful phase and confirm his belief that he has been betrayed by the *"hombres finos."* Deprived of reputation, Nostromo seeks compensation in wealth. He has always lived amidst splendid publicity, but awakening in solitude suddenly makes him feel destitute: "on a revulsion of subjectiveness, exasperated almost to insanity, [he] beheld all his world without faith and courage. He had been betrayed!"[20]

Like Gould, Nostromo pins his faith on materialism in order to compensate for his loss of prestige. This ruins him, and his life becomes bound up with the stolen treasure. His stealthy rapacity forces him to abandon Giorgio's wife, Teresa, on her deathbed, denying her final wish, and to abandon Decoud to solitude and suicide. He betrays his love for Giselle (as Gould betrays Emilia) and agrees to marry her sister Linda so that he can continue to "mine" the buried silver on the Great Isabel.

On this island Viola protects his family with an old rifle, just as he did when Ribiera fled from Montero; but this time Nostromo returns, not to save Giorgio, but to be slain by him. The accidental murder is the final sardonic comment on Viola's violent career in South America. If idealism has killed corruption, it has also killed part of itself.

Dr. Monygham's devastating pronouncement to Mrs. Gould, prompted by his loyalty and devotion to her, carries the ideological substance of the novel. His speech evolves from the history of Costaguana and the San Tomé mine, from the terrible effects of "progress" on the traditional life of the people and from the corruption of the Europeans by the silver. His declaration is an answer not only to Gould's "material interests" speech, but also to those who, like the obtuse Captain Mitchell, continue to put their faith in the silver:

> There is no peace and no rest in the development of material interests. They have their law, and their justice. But it is founded on expediency, and is inhuman; it is without rectitude, without the continuity and the force that can be found only in a moral principle. Mrs. Gould, the time approaches when all that the Gould concession stands for shall weigh as heavily upon the people as the barbarism, cruelty and misrule of a few years back. . . . It'll weigh as heavily and provoke resentment, bloodshed, and vengeance, because the men have grown different. Do you think that now the mine would march upon the town to save their Señor Administrador?

The people of Costaguana are faced with a choice of evils, the inevitable result of unprincipled exploitation and destruction of their traditional culture.

The central tragedy of *Nostromo* is the incompatibility of material interests and moral principles. In Costaguana, as Emilia Gould realizes, "there was something inherent in the necessities of successful action which carried with it the moral degradation of the idea."[21] Gould's idealization of the silver forces him to compromise his principles, and the civilizing mission of the Europeans corrupts the mine and betrays the country.

Conrad was profoundly disappointed by the response of both critics and the reading public to his "most anxiously meditated" novel. The serialization provoked many irritated protests from readers who complained that so much space was taken up by "utterly unreadable stuff." The novel was too complex, too morally ambiguous and too critical of capitalism to be successful. Jessie remarked that *Nostromo*'s "reception was perhaps the greatest disappointment—literary disappointment— Conrad ever had. He used to say it was 'a dead frost.' " The one notable exception was Edward Garnett's perceptive review in the *Speaker*, which praised the European vision, the complex structure, the vivid characters and the ambitious themes: "This great gift of Mr. Conrad's, his special sense for the *psychology of scene*, that he shares with many of the great poets and the great artists who have developed it each on his own chosen lines, it is that which marks him out for pre-eminence among the novelists."[22]

CHAPTER THIRTEEN

Capri, Montpellier
and *The Secret Agent*

1905–1909

I

After Conrad had completed *Nostromo* and Jessie had recovered from the
first operation on her knee (at Conrad's insistence, she prepared for this
ordeal by giving an impromptu dinner for thirty people the night before
entering the hospital), they took another disastrous holiday abroad and
spent from mid-January to mid-May 1905 on the island of Capri in the
Bay of Naples. Conrad disliked trains, steamboats and hotels, worried a
great deal when he was abroad and felt travel did not suit his work,
which required the quiet and concentration he found only at home. But
he needed a change and a rest from the strain of writing and from five
attacks of gout in the last eleven months, and felt the mild Mediterranean climate would revive him and help Jessie recover.

The trip got off to a bad start in Dover when one of the men carrying
Jessie, immobile and extremely heavy, pinched his hand between her
chair and the gangway rail of the Channel ferry, and nearly dumped her
into the water between the vessel and the quay. In Rome, where they
had only fifteen minutes to change trains, the porters, in their rush and
excitement, removed Jessie's chair too soon and left her hanging from
the side of the railway car. Conrad was terrified and her nurse, Miss
Jackson, nearly fainted. Naples, bitterly cold and windy, had rough
seas, and the shipping company refused to land Jessie in Capri until the
weather changed and their boat could safely approach the Marina
Grande. After five expensive days in Naples, Conrad wrote, "the Captain took his steamer in as close in as he dared and a special big rowing
boat came off to do the transshipping. The uproar was something awful;

but I must say that for all their yelling these Italians did their work extremely well. . . . The whole affair, which had afforded the population of Capri so much innocent enjoyment, cost me 40 francs." The delays and extra tips for carrying Jessie cost considerably more than Conrad had anticipated, and he was soon sending frantic requests to Pinker for more money.

The Conrads lived at the Villa di Maria, in the center of the village, and were visited by the Galsworthys, who came over by boat from Amalfi. Miss Jackson, whom Conrad detested, got influenza and pneumonia, and had to be nursed by her patient. Conrad caught influenza and bronchitis, and suffered from nerves and insomnia. Then his face swelled up with a raging toothache. Since there was no dentist in Capri, he crossed twice to Naples to have two teeth dragged out and felt he would lose a third one as well.

By early May Conrad was thoroughly fed up and annoyed by everything on the beautiful island. The torrid climate, the hot wind from the desert and the cold wind from the hills, the steep cliffs and the azure sea—even the sea—were all "impossible." But he at least managed to pack Miss Jackson off to England, for she was impossible too. His amusing letter to Ford mentioned the homosexual ambience, complained of the mob of tourists who overran the place and prayed God to save him from another such holiday:

> The scandals of Capri—atrocious, unspeakable, amusing, scandals international, cosmopolitan and biblical. . . . All this is a sort of blue nightmare traversed by stinks and perfumes, full of flat roofs, vineyards, vaulted passages, enormous sheer rocks, pergolas, with a mad gallop of German tourists *lâchés à travers tout cela* [let loose across it all] in white Capri shoes, over the slippery Capri stones, kodaks, floating veils, strangely waving whiskers, grotesque hats, streaming, tumbling, rushing, ebbing from the top of Monte Solaro (where the clouds hang) to the amazing rocky chasms of the Arco Naturale—where the lager beer bottles go pop. It is a nightmare with the fear of the future thrown in.

Conrad formed an important friendship in Capri with Norman Douglas, who played a prominent part in the scandalous milieu that Conrad found so offensive. Borys once mentioned that his father was "disgusted" by a group of scantily clad women they had seen in a music hall. Joseph Retinger (who later became Conrad's rival in love) emphasized his conventional morality, calling him "a man of stern principles and straight lines in his private life, [who] despised weakness of character [which he had certainly exhibited in Marseilles] and the display of immorality. He disliked consequently the works of Oscar Wilde, because he had a profound contempt for his way of living." Norman Douglas declared that Conrad "was the greatest stickler for uprightness I have ever known."

Yet the adventurous and artistic side of Conrad had an interest in, a tolerance of and perhaps even a vicarious pleasure in the extremely irregular and immoral sexual lives of his intimate friends. Edward and Constance Garnett both took lovers; Galsworthy (who had sex with Conrad's maid while a guest at Pent Farm) had an affair with his cousin's wife; Sidney Colvin maintained a long-standing adulterous liaison; Ford and Wells were extremely promiscuous and lived with women who were not their wives; and Stephen Crane's companion was a former prostitute. Many of Conrad's friends were homosexuals—his French translator Vicomte Robert d'Humières, the young novelists Stephen Reynolds and Hugh Walpole, Roger Casement, André Gide and Norman Douglas—and the last three were recklessly indiscreet.[1]

The tall, handsome, leonine Douglas—a stylish and well-bred gastronome, bohemian, sexual libertine and cad—was a lover of Italy and a lover of boys. Born in Scotland in 1868, partly educated in Germany, he was a linguist and a diplomat, who had begun a promising career in St. Petersburg. A strange alloy of savage and scientist, he also wrote erudite monographs on zoology and geology. He later became a traveler and travel writer; the author of *South Wind* (1917), a hedonistic and amoral novel of Capri; and, with Pino Orioli in Florence, the successful publisher of his own works. Douglas' deepest conviction was "Do what you want to do, and be damned to everybody else," and he frankly acknowledged the pleasures of homosexual pursuit. His life was haphazardly ordered by the pragmatic necessity to "hop it" across the frontier whenever his liaisons became dangerous. "Burn your boats!" he declared. "This has ever been my system in times of stress." D. H. Lawrence portrayed the courtly but grandiose Douglas as James Argyle in *Aaron's Rod*, describing him as "decidedly shabby and a gentleman, with his wicked red face and tufted eyebrows." And Richard Aldington called him "a witty and high-spirited man, with a sane view of life, a wide range of interests and a fund of recondite knowledge."[2]

Conrad met Douglas in March 1905, was immediately impressed and described him to Pinker as a linguist and scientist, a learned, intelligent and original thinker with a fine prose style. Conrad believed in Douglas' talent (as he believed in Ford's), and gave him extremely valuable advice, encouragement and help. He placed Douglas' work in Ford's *English Review* and arranged for him to become assistant editor of that journal. In February 1908 Conrad told Douglas, who had also begun his writing career in his late thirties: "It is obvious to me that you have a distinguished future before you as a writer. And also some hard times before you get known. Think seriously of writing a novel. . . . I promise you that everything that I and two or three more can do shall be done to get the novel published with a proper flourish."

Douglas later described how Conrad had helped him revise his travel book about Tunisia, *Fountains in the Sand* (1912): "There was a story running through it: a kind of romance. I showed the thing in this form to Joseph Conrad, who read it carefully and then said: 'What is that woman doing in here? Take her out!' Out she went and all that belonged to her, and the book became what it is now." Douglas knew from personal experience "how appreciative and encouraging Conrad could be, and what infinite pains he would take with the work of other writers." In his favorable review of Richard Curle's study of Conrad, Douglas called his friend "one of the most complex and, to English minds, elusive of modern writers."[3]

When Douglas went down to stay at the Cearne in 1907, David Garnett, who was then fifteen, felt that his father, aware of Douglas' tastes, was apprehensive about the visit and "kept an eye out on them both." Conrad seemed to have no such fears about Borys, and his friendship with Douglas continued in England. Between 1905 and 1916 Douglas, who frequently visited for the day from London and spent many weekends with the Conrads, was always a welcome guest. In 1910 Conrad called him "one of my two most intimate friends."

The following August, Douglas, who had just returned to London from Italy, came down for a weekend and became seriously ill with what seemed to be heatstroke, typhoid or "brain-fever," but was actually an attack of malaria:

> He arrived in a state of high fever and hardly able to stand. We put him to bed and sent for a doctor. On Monday we sent for a nurse (after Jessie and I had been up with him for two nights and a day). To-day he does not recognize anybody, his temperature after most appalling ups and downs had reached 105°. . . .
>
> He can't be moved and indeed where could one move him? One can hear him moaning and muttering all over the house. . . . Should he die, I shall have to bury him I suppose. . . . I have seen and tended white men dying in the Congo but I have never felt so abominably helpless as in this case.[4]

Douglas' marriage had collapsed in 1903, and the following year he divorced his wife for adultery. He took care of his two small sons, Archie and Robin (the latter, born in 1902, was four years younger than Borys), in Capri for two years, and then placed them in the care of friends in England. Robin was sent to a boarding school at the age of ten, and during the next four years spent most of his holidays with the Conrads. He called Jessie "Mum" and was a close companion of the Conrads' son John. Robin later recalled that Conrad carried the tension of his writing desk to the dinner table and at the beginning of the meal "there was no conversation. Mrs. Conrad served whilst her husband made bread pills between his left thumb and forefinger. When a number of pills had been rolled and flung irritably into the fireplace, Conrad began to eat. Under the influence of his wife's cooking he gradually became more human."

Conrad was very fond of the handsome Robin, treated him like a son and worried about the future of the "manly, clever little chap." Pleased that Robin wanted to become a sailor, he paid for his clothes and school fees at Ashford Grammar School until Robin followed Borys on to the Royal Navy training ship *Worcester* in the fall of 1916. In April of that year Conrad told Richard Curle: "We couldn't sleep another wink in our lives if we chucked the kid out."

II

Douglas probably introduced Conrad to the doctor and scholar Ignazio Cerio, a member of the most esteemed family on Capri. One of the main squares on the island was named in their honor. Ignazio gave Conrad access to his collection of books on the history of Capri, and Conrad's research on Napoleon's campaigns in the Mediterranean led eventually to his late novels, *The Rover* and *Suspense*.[5]

Conrad also hoped to get some writing done on Capri, but found it more distracting than restful (Lawrence called it "a stewpot of semi-literary cats") and did as little work on the rocky island as he had done on the flat coast of Belgium. He explained to Edmund Gosse that as a foreigner he needed the stimulus of the English language and the English setting: "It's all very well for Englishmen born to their inheritance to fling verse and prose from Italy back to their native shores. I, in my state of honourable adoption, find that I need the moral support, the sustaining influence of English atmosphere even from day to day."

"Autocracy and War" (1905), which he wrote on Capri, was Conrad's response to the current Russo-Japanese war. In his longest and most important political essay, he shrewdly predicted, before Japan had defeated Russia in the naval battle of Tsushima, that this war would be won (as World War One would be won) "not from the victor obtaining a crushing advantage, but through the mortal weariness of the combatants." He even anticipated the apathetic response of the masses to reports of modern atrocities on television: "a man writhing under a cart-wheel in the street, awakens more genuine emotion, more horror, pity, and indignation than the stream of reports, appalling in their monotony, of tens of thousands of decaying bodies." But Conrad also had some blind spots. He naïvely praised the "innate gentleness" of the Japanese character. He falsely prophesied that Russia's power had finally been extinguished: "the ghost of Russia's might is laid. . . . It has vanished for ever at last, and . . . there is no new Russia to take the place of that ill-omened creation." And he endorsed Bismarck's comment: "*La Russie, c'est le néant,*" though that description applied more aptly to Poland. Conrad ended the essay by condemning Germany as the principal enemy of peace in Europe.

Conrad's essay echoed many of the themes of Apollo's vitriolic "Poland and Muscovy" (1864) and argued, as Apollo had done, that Russia was a barbaric Asiatic despotism, implacably opposed to the humane traditions of Western civilization:

> For a hundred years the ghost of Russian might, overshadowing with its fantastic bulk the councils of Central and Western Europe, sat upon the gravestone of autocracy, cutting off from air, from light, from all knowledge of themselves and of the world, the buried millions of Russian people. . . .
>
> This dreaded and strange apparition, bristling with bayonets, armed with chains, hung over with holy images; that something not of this world, partaking of a ravenous ghoul . . . still faces us with its old stupidity, with its strange mystical arrogance.[6]

"Autocracy and War," Conrad's major political statement, provided the ideological basis for the treatment of Russia in his next two novels: *The Secret Agent* and *Under Western Eyes.*

The Conrads took a tramp steamer from Naples to Marseilles on the first leg of their journey home. On that voyage Conrad, according to Jessie, lost his wallet, claimed he could not find it and behaved like a helpless infant. When he had gone to sleep, she searched his clothes, found the wallet, and invented a transparent excuse to cover his embarrassment and prevent his inevitable explosion.

In March 1905, while still on Capri, Conrad learned that William Rothenstein and Edmund Gosse had succeeded in getting him a grant of £500 from the Royal Bounty Fund. Conrad naturally expected to be given this fabulous sum in one prompt payment, and was horrified to learn, two months later, that the money would be administered by two trustees— Rothenstein and the patriotic poet Henry Newbolt—who mistrusted Conrad's extravagance and thought it wise to dole out the money more cautiously. In May, with some justice and wounded pride, Conrad complained to Gosse that the grant in recognition of his talents and services to literature had become converted into an award that he now had to beg for: "The whole affair has assumed an appearance much graver and more distressing than any stress of my material necessities: the appearance of 'Conrad having to be saved from himself'—the sort of thing that casts a doubt on a man's sense of responsibility, on his right feeling, on his sense of correct conduct." Thinking perhaps of Francis Thompson's pathetic dependence on the Meynells and Swinburne's on Watts-Dunton, the aristocratic master-mariner exclaimed: "I own to a, not I hope very peculiar, dislike of falling, even by the remotest appearance, into the class of those disorderly talents whose bohemianism, irregularity and general irresponsibility of conduct are neither in my tradition and training nor in my character." Gosse had once again cast him into the humiliating and childishly dependent role he had suffered first with Tadeusz and then with Pinker. Instead of relieving his anxieties, the grant actually intensified them.

When Conrad returned from Capri to England in mid-May, he had an interview with Henry Newbolt and followed it up with a letter asking for £250 to settle his immediate debts. These debts, which he listed in detail, included £60 toward his overdraft at Watson's Bank, £50 to his landlord toward six years' arrears in rent, taxes, and bills to four doctors and to local tradesmen. When Newbolt proposed that Conrad compound with his creditors, the equivalent of declaring bankruptcy, Conrad mentioned his extensive business experience as a commander of ships, justly said that Newbolt's suggestion would destroy his local credit and declared that "a confession of insolvency in exchange for the assistance received would *not* carry out the intention of the grant."[7] Finally, while Conrad, obsessed with the need to maintain at least the external *appearance* (to use a word he frequently employed in this affair) of wealth, alternated between outrage and humility, they agreed that Newbolt would give him checks made out to his creditors, which Conrad would then endorse and mail to them. The remainder of the grant was paid out in £15 installments until April 1906.

III

During the last half of 1905 Conrad saw one of the five London perfor-
mances of *One Day More*, worked on an early version of *Chance*, did
several more sketches for *The Mirror of the Sea*, wrote three stories that
were later collected in *A Set of Six* and tried to cope with serious family
illness. Just after he told Wells that "I stick here fighting with disease
and creeping imbecility—like a cornered rat, facing fate with a big stick
that is sure to descend and crack my skull before many days are over,"
Jessie had her "nervous breakdown of a sort" in October, and Borys
caught scarlet fever and had to enter a London nursing home in November. Two months later, as the child was about to leave the home, a
nurse burned his skin by putting too much disinfectant in his bath,
making him swell up like a balloon and break out with purple spots all
over his body. Conrad, with "death in his soul" and a gout-boot on his
foot, was becoming positively ashamed of his constant invalidism and
his persistent calamities. After learning that Jessie was pregnant, he told
Rothenstein: "I feel very shy and blushing at being let in for that thing
at my venerable age." In February 1906 the Conrads left England to
recuperate for two months in the mild climate of Montpellier, near the
south coast of France.

They stayed in the first-class Hôtel Riche et Continental on the main
square of the town, the Place de la Comédie, below the Esplanade and
the Citadel. And Conrad began to write *The Secret Agent* on the Prom-
enade du Peyrou, which was full of fountains with black swans floating on the ornamental water and which probably suggested the name
of Peyrol, the hero of *The Rover*. Henry James wrote of the Peyrou:
"nothing could be more impressive and monumental. It consists of an
'elevated platform' . . . an immense terrace laid out, in the highest
part of the town, as a garden, and commanding in all directions a view
which in clear weather must be of the finest." When Conrad arrived
in Montpellier, riots were taking place over the separation of Church
and state:

> [There is] a most extraordinary uproar reigning over the whole town, an
> amazing mixture of carnival and political riots going on at the same time.
> In the same street troops, infantry and cavalry drawn up in front of
> churches, yells, shrieks, blows—people with broken heads carried into
> chemist's shops, and through it all bands of costumed and masked rev-
> ellers pushing with songs and ribald jokes. It's extremely curious and very
> characteristic.[8]

Travel seems to have made Conrad restless. He returned to Pent Farm in mid-April 1906, and spent two weeks in mid-May in Winchelsea, collaborating with Ford on *The Nature of a Crime*, which concerned, Ford said, "the eternal subject of the undetected criminal." This novella is a first-person confession, made to his married mistress in Rome, by a wealthy, respectable man who has embezzled the money of his friend's son and who plans to kill himself to avoid shame and prison. He is reprieved at the end when the son decides not to check the accounts. He then places himself in the hands of his mistress, saying he will reform and order his affairs if she consents to marry him. This static, essentially Fordian story has no significant action. Its limited interest lies in the style and in the mode of narration, which anticipates *The Good Soldier*, and in the thinly disguised revelation of Ford's attempt to disentangle himself from his wife, Elsie. The rather thin novella was published in the *English Review* of April–May 1909 under the absurd pseudonym, Ignatz von Aschendorf (the name of a German barony that Ford imagined he might one day inherit), and (with Conrad's reluctant agreement) as a book in 1924.

During July and August 1906 Conrad borrowed Galsworthy's London house at 14 Addison Road, in Kensington, which had a garden overlooking Holland Park. His second son was born there on August 2. There was no anguish about Slavic names for John Alexander, who was named after Galsworthy. Jessie noted that Conrad, who had gradually become accustomed to fatherhood, was more pleased about the birth of John than he had been about Borys. But he felt obliged to stress John's physical unattractiveness—as he had emphasized Jessie's and Borys' when first describing them to friends—and wrote Ada Galsworthy, in the arch tone he reserved for these occasions: "I have lately made the acquaintance of a quiet, unassuming, extremely ugly but on the whole rather sympathetic young man." John was better-looking, more appealing, happier and much healthier than Borys. He got on well with his father, was a bright student and was more successful, as a child and as a young man, than his older brother, who was always something of a disappointment to Conrad.

Having escaped their usual disasters on the first visit to Montpellier, the Conrads returned (when the baby was able to travel) to the Hôtel Riche in mid-December for a six-month stay that became—so far—their worst trip abroad. The journey started promisingly, and on January 8, 1907, Conrad wrote an unusually warm and ecstatic letter to Ford, who loved southern France, once again mentioning the need for an English ambience in order to write:

I am better in this sunshine. The landscape around has magic, all bustle, all of colour alone. The villages perched on conical hills stand out against the great and sweeping line of violet ranges, as if in an enchanted country. The beauty of this land is inexpressible and the delicacy of colours at sunset and sunrise beyond the power of men to imagine. . . . And every day as I go about entranced, I miss you more and more. You ought to see this. . . . I am drunk with colour and would like dearly to have you to lean upon. I am certain that with no other man could I share my rapture. Work at a standstill. Plans simply swarming in my head but my English has all departed from me.

But Conrad's pleasure was short-lived. By the end of the month the nine-year-old Borys, extremely susceptible to illness, had trouble with his adenoids, and then caught, in terrible succession, measles, bronchitis, rheumatic fever and pleurisy, and had rheumatism in both ankles. Also suspected of having tuberculosis, which had killed both of Conrad's parents, he was seriously ill, feverish and emaciated for five dreadful months. Jessie was at her best, just as Conrad was at his worst, during a crisis. As he told Rothenstein, she "has been simply heroic in the awful Montpellier adventure, never giving a sign of anxiety, not only before the boy but even out of his sight; always calm, serene, equable, going from one to the other and apparently never tired though cruelly crippled by her leg."[9] Conrad rivaled Jessie and Borys with his own invalidism and eruptions of gouty eczema. He contributed to the crisis by having his pocket picked ("Please send me a £10 note instanter," he told Pinker, "because life without pocket money is not worth living") and by setting his mattress on fire by going to sleep with a lighted cigarette.

In mid-May, following the French doctor's advice, the Conrads moved for three months to Champel, where he had taken the water-cure after returning half-dead from the Congo in 1891, and had revisited in 1894 and in 1895, when courting Émilie Briquel. "Champel has brought me round once," he optimistically explained to Pinker when requesting more money, "and it may give me a fresh lease of mental life again now my health shows signs of general improvement." But in Geneva the baby came down with whooping cough, which required a tank of oxygen to enable him to breathe between the convulsive coughs, and reduced him (as illness had reduced Borys) to mere skin and bones. And in Champel, they had to be isolated with the contagious infant in the annex of the Hôtel de la Roseraie. Though Borys eventually recovered in Champel, Conrad was finally revolted by the town, which had once been his refuge but now had unbearably painful associations: "No more trips abroad. I am sick of them. . . . I long to get away from here. The place is odious to me; and the whole thing with its anxieties and expense sits on me like the memory of a nightmare."[10] Conrad's last, unhappy visit to Geneva influenced his negative portrayal of that city in *Under Western Eyes*.

The prolonged sickroom crisis and Borys' slow recovery from his dangerous illnesses drew father and son together for the first time. Conrad would read to Borys (and later to John) his two fantastic favorites—Edward Lear's *Book of Nonsense* and Lewis Carroll's *Alice's Adventures in Wonderland*—as well as Charles Kingsley's inspiring *The Heroes* and the books that he himself had read as a boy: Cooper's *The Last of the Mohicans*, *The Pathfinder* and *The Deerslayer*, and Captain Marryat's sea tales, *Peter Simple* and *Mr. Midshipman Easy*. But Conrad (like Tolstoy) was an exacting teacher who became short-tempered when his sons, through nervousness, seemed mentally slow. When Borys had difficulty learning to read, after their return from Capri in 1905, Conrad exclaimed: "Disgusting! I could read in two languages at his age. Am I a father to a fool?"[11]

In January 1908, five months after returning from Champel, Borys assumed the rather poignant role that Conrad had taken when Apollo was dying. As Conrad told Galsworthy: "He has not a very lively time; he plays the part of the devoted son to me, coming in several times a day to see whether he can do something for me—for I am crippled [by gout] and once anchored before the table can not budge very well." Conrad was disappointed, a few years later, when Borys failed both the examination that would have led to a university education and the entrance examination for a private school at Tonbridge. Though Borys did not show any interest in or aptitude for the nautical profession, and his poor eyesight precluded a naval career, Conrad got him a place on the training ship *Worcester*. In September 1911 he gave a moving account of leaving his son on the ship: "Poor Mons. B. looked to me a very small and lonely figure on that enormous deck, in that big crowd, where he didn't know a single soul. It is an immense change for him. Yes. He did look a small boy. Couldn't make up my mind to leave him and at last I made rather a bolt of it. I can't get him out of my eyes."

Though Conrad gave Borys a de luxe edition of his works, he never read a single one of them. Neither boy cared much about literature; they were interested only in practical things. Borys' love for cars amounted to auto-eroticism, and the series of automobiles—from a $4\frac{1}{2}$-horsepower De Dion to a Daimler that had once belonged to the Duke of Connaught—

that Conrad began to hire and then to purchase at the turn of the century became a strong common interest.

In 1913 Conrad candidly told Rothenstein that Borys, who retained a slightly simian appearance, was not "beautiful, poor boy [but] a good fellow." And he confessed to Bertrand Russell that "he found it difficult to talk to his boys or to young people, as he disliked being insincere, and at the same time he shrank from burdening them with his own experience and knowledge of life." The reasons for Conrad's constraints with his sons went deeper than he suggested, for he was often politely insincere, and he loved talking about his adventurous experiences and imparting his vast knowledge of life. Apart from his personal formality and reserve, even within his own family, he probably feared inculcating his sons, as Apollo had done to the young Conrad, with his profoundly pessimistic views.

John Conrad described a rare and moving example of intimacy with his father. Though Conrad had no hobbies, he liked to play chess and would work through the games in José Capablanca's book with John. Sometimes, when blocked in his writing in the middle of the night, he would wake up young John and ask him to "come down and give me a game of chess." After a few stimulating moves, Conrad would walk over to his desk and start writing, his pen scratching the paper while the boy dozed off in his chair. When the flow of words had revived, he would touch John's shoulder and tell him: "It's time to turn in. It's your watch below."[12]

When Conrad returned from Champel to Pent Farm in mid-August 1907, both doctors and friends advised him to leave the dampness of Kent, which seemed to harm the health of everyone in the family. By the end of the month he had found a "jolly old Farmhouse" on the estate of Sir Julius Wernher, a Transvaal mining magnate, two and a half miles from Luton in Bedfordshire and forty-five minutes from London on the Midland line. "The house is not big but roomy for its size with a walled garden in front," he told Pinker. "There is also an excellent kitchen garden with fruit trees, properly fenced and with a door to it which locks—so that one may expect some good from it. The position is excellent, 500 ft above sea level on clay and gravel. The well is 200 ft deep. . . . What seduced me most was the nearness to town combined with perfect rural isolation. I want to be in closer touch with everybody."

The Someries, as the house was called, had six bedrooms and was much bigger than Pent Farm. But it was also noisy and the locked door to the garden did not prevent the nearby farm laborers from stealing the fruit and vegetables. By January 1908 Conrad realized he had made a serious mistake (though he remained in the house for another fifteen months) and was complaining to friends: "I've not known a single moment of bodily ease since we got this new house. . . . You have no idea of the soul corroding bleakness of earth and sky here when the east wind blows."[13]

IV

Conrad began *The Secret Agent* (1907) in Montpellier in February 1906 when Jessie was in the early months of her pregnancy and completed it in Champel in June 1907 while Borys was recovering from his severe illnesses. The novel combines closely observed lower-class London interiors with the larger political theme of anarchists who threaten the stable surface of Edwardian England. Adolf Verloc, the proprietor of a squalid pornographic shop, is married to a young woman, Winnie, who has sacrificed herself to provide a home for her mother and her retarded adolescent brother, Stevie, whom she loves and treats as her child. Verloc's shop is a front for his revolutionary activities. The plot focuses on his bungled attempt to blow up the Greenwich Observatory and the destruction of the innocent Stevie, who unwittingly carries the fatal bomb. Winnie exacts revenge for Stevie's death by murdering her husband.

In the murder scene, the greatest moment in Conrad's most perfectly wrought novel, Verloc provokes Winnie beyond endurance by asserting that she is equally responsible for Stevie's death. When he says "come here" "in a peculiar tone which . . . was intimately known to Mrs. Verloc as the note of wooing," he recalls the earlier scene in which she was forced to have sexual relations with a husband she finds physically revolting. When Winnie had asked (echoing *Othello*): "Shall I put the light out?" and Verloc had snapped at her with sexual impatience, "Put it out," he foreshadowed his own death in the stabbing scene. As Winnie's knife meets no resistance and Verloc slouches on the sofa, the dripping blood merges with the ticking of the clock and suggests that time would have been stopped, and progress retarded, if Verloc had succeeded in blowing up the Observatory. At the end of the novel the political status quo is maintained. Stevie, Verloc and Winnie (who commits suicide) have died for no reason. And Mr. Vladimir, the First Secretary of the Russian Embassy, has failed in his attempt to provoke the English into deporting the anarchists who have been plotting against the Czarist regime.

Although the novel's political theme is grim enough, Verloc and Winnie's "domestic drama" expresses Conrad's considerable hostility to his wife and jealousy of his children. At the same time, it seeks to atone for Conrad's frustration and anger during the protracted period of family illness. Jessie, who assumed that Conrad was pleased by the birth of John, wrote of this novel: "As I did not know in the least what the book was about, I could not account to myself for the grimly ironic expression I used often to catch on his face, whenever he came to give me a look-in. Could it have reference to the expected baby?"

Four months after John was born, during the railway journey to Montpellier in December 1906, Conrad impulsively and irrationally opened the train window and, to Jessie's horror, threw out a package containing all the baby's clothes. Jessie bit her lip and then said calmly: "I am sure the man who finds that bundle will be looking for the baby's corpse."[14] This symbolic murder of John was a striking parallel to Verloc's destruction of his "step-son" Stevie in *The Secret Agent*. Winnie, who deceives Verloc and marries him for Stevie's sake, represents Conrad's fear of a woman who wants a father for her child more than a husband for herself.

Winnie's mother is Conrad's fictional portrayal of the placid Jessie, who was especially fat during her pregnancy, and whose crippled condition tried Conrad's patience and drained his money. Winnie's mother "was a stout, wheezy woman, with a large brown face" whose "swollen legs rendered her inactive." There was a "venerable placidity conferred upon her outward person by her triple chin, the floating ampleness of her ancient form, and the impotent condition of her legs." All the poignant themes of the novel—the poverty, cruelty, degradation and death-in-life of the Verloc household, and the sacrifice, displaced maternity and perversion of human emotions that result from it—are concentrated in the great passage when Winnie's mother is sent to the poorhouse in a funereal carriage:

> This woman, modest indeed but hardened in the fires of adversity, of an age, moreover, when blushes are not expected, had positively blushed before her daughter. In the privacy of a four-wheeler, on her way to a charity cottage (one of a row) which by the exiguity of its dimensions and the simplicity of its accommodation, might well have been devised in kindness as a place of training for the still more straitened circumstances of the grave, she was forced to hide from her own child a blush of remorse and shame.

1. Conrad's father, Apollo Korzeniowski: "A man of great sensibilities; of exalted and dreamy temperament; with a terrible gift of irony and of gloomy disposition."

2. Conrad's mother, Eva Korzeniowska: a "wide-browed, silent, protecting presence."

3. Conrad's uncle and guardian, Tadeusz Bobrowski: "The wisest, the firmest, the most indulgent of guardians, extending over me a paternal care and affection, a moral support."

4. Konrad Korzeniowski, Cracow, 1874: "He used to suffer from severe headaches and nervous attacks; the doctors thought that a stay at the seaside might cure him."

5. G. F. W. Hope: A married man with a high forehead, trimmed beard and pointed mustache, fond of cigars and of yachting.

6. Adolf Krieger: A rugged, good-looking man with thick hair and a drooping mustache.

7. Konrad Korzeniowski, Marienbad, 1883: "He had vigorous, extremely mobile features which would change very quickly from gentleness to an excitability bordering on anger."

8. Marguerite Poradowska: Jessie thought her "the most beautiful woman I had ever seen."

9. Sir Roger Casement: "He is a limpid personality. There is a touch of the Conquistador in him too."

10. Jessie George, 1896: "She is a small, not at all striking-looking person (to tell the truth alas—rather plain!) who nevertheless is very dear to me."

11. Edward Sanderson, 1896: The tall, handsome Sanderson was a prototype for Lord Jim.

12. John Galsworthy, 1906: "Tall, austere looking, with a Roman profile and tightly closed lips."

13. Edward Garnett, c. 1904: "His dark eyes and dark-grey unruly hair gave him the appearance of rugged untidiness."

14. R. B. Cunninghame Graham: "A slight, nervous, strong figure, very well dressed, with a touch of exoticism in loose necktie or soft hat."

15. Henry James, 1913, by John Singer Sargent. He had a "lofty forehead and a superior yet propitiatory smile. His face was uniformly solemn, but his eyes were disconcertingly furtive."

16. Stephen Crane, 1899: "A young man of medium stature and slender build, with very steady, penetrating blue eyes."

17. Ford Madox Ford, c. 1909: A tall, thin, warmhearted fellow with fair hair, pink-and-white complexion, and prominent pale blue eyes.

18. Hugh Clifford, 1895: A large, rugged-looking man, forthright, energetic and impetuous.

19. J. B. Pinker and Joseph Conrad, Oswalds, 1921. Pinker "was short, compact, a rosy, round-faced clean-shaven grey-haired sphinx with a protrusive under-lip."

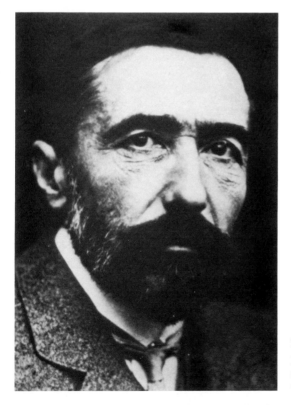

20. Joseph Conrad, 1904: "Tanned, with a peaked brown beard, almost black hair, and dark brown eyes, over which the lids were deeply folded."

21. Norman Douglas, Capri, 1912: "Decidedly shabby and a gentleman, with his wicked red face and tufted eyebrows."

22. Perceval Gibbon, 1909: A small, lively, dark, virile and sometimes brutal man, with thick blue-black hair and a sensitive mouth.

23. Jessie, her ample form draped in a shawl, serves tea in the book-lined study while Conrad, in high boots, and John, with a charming expression, stare into the camera, 1912.

24. John Quinn, 1921: A bald, thin-lipped, sharp-nosed, severe-looking lawyer, with exquisite taste in modern art and literature.

25. Richard Curle, 1923. Conrad told Curle, a tall Scotsman: "Outside my household you are the person about whom I am most concerned both in thought and feelings."

26. Joseph Retinger, 1912: "He was a narrow, green-faced young man and in the light his eyes were liver colored."

27. Jane Anderson, 1910: Wearing a long dark dress and sitting with her legs crossed at an angle to the camera, she rests her elbow on her knee and chin on her lace-gloved hand, and turns her strikingly handsome face toward the lens as her tawny hair cascades onto her shoulders from under the canopy of an enormous soft black hat.

28. Conrad, Jessie and Borys, Oswalds, 1921.

29. Gérard Jean-Aubry, 1911: He had a high forehead, small, widely spaced eyes, a sharp nose and full lips beneath a broad mustache.

30. Sir Robert Jones: A portly man with a gentle countenance, broad forehead, blue eyes, trim white mustache and jaunty bow tie.

31. Joseph Conrad, 1923: "Black eyebrows, hooked nose, hunched shoulders gave him a hawk-like look."

32. Jessie Conrad, 1926: Grotesquely obese and loaded, like a gypsy fortune-teller, with heavy beads.

Through the artistic sublimation of *The Secret Agent* Conrad revenged himself on his family by destroying the unwanted child and abandoning his ungainly and unattractive wife to the deathly existence of an almshouse. But he also expressed the tragic aspect of his antagonistic feelings.

The novel also portrayed, with grim irony, the seedy revolutionary underworld of Apollo Korzeniowski. Adolf Verloc, the reluctant *agent provocateur*, was partly based on Conrad's old friend Adolf Krieger, who, though born in an English-speaking country, had a slightly foreign air about him. Conrad had lived with Krieger, knew the details of his domestic life and was resentful that Krieger had pressed him to repay a loan when he was unable to do so. Mr. Vladimir, who forces Verloc to attempt to blow up the Greenwich Observatory, was based on the Russian General Selivertsov, shot in Paris in the 1890s. He represents Russian savagery masquerading as civilized gentility.

In his "Author's Note" of 1920, Conrad alluded to the sources that inspired the novel. The friend who told him about anarchist activities in London was Ford. The story of the actual attempt by Martial Bourdin to blow up the Observatory on February 15, 1894, was recounted in David Nicholl's pamphlet *The Greenwich Mystery* (1897). And the memoir of the Assistant Commissioner of Police was Robert Anderson's *Sidelights on the Home Rule Movement* (1906).

But Conrad does not mention the fascinating personal, biographical and literary origins of the important scene (which occurs just before Winnie's mother is sent to the charity home) when Stevie, revealing his tender feelings, begs the cabman not to whip his infirm horse by pleading: "Don't" (which is the last word Verloc utters before Winnie stabs him). Jessie wrote that during her knee operation in London in November 1904, Conrad "must have acted subconsciously part of the time he waited, and when he found himself he was standing in front of an old dray-horse with his arms literally round the animal's neck." Conrad probably knew that Nietzsche's permanent mental breakdown in Turin in 1890 occurred after he had seen a horse being whipped, had thrown his arms around the pathetic beast and had collapsed in the street. And when writing this scene Conrad certainly remembered Raskolnikov's dream, in Dostoyevsky's *Crime and Punishment* (1866), of seeing when he was a child an owner cruelly beating his old mare: "The poor little boy was quite beside himself. He pushed his way, shrieking, through the crowd to the mare, put his arms round the dead muzzle dabbled with blood and kissed the poor eyes and mouth."[15] It is worth noting that

Conrad (who disliked the morbid details) was influenced by Dostoyevsky—whom he frequently repudiated—several years before he wrote his own version of *Crime and Punishment* in *Under Western Eyes*.

Just as *Heart of Darkness* had expressed ideas that opposed the prevailing late-Victorian imperialism, so *The Secret Agent* also disturbed readers in 1907 with its prescient and prophetic political ideas. In the novel, Conrad suggested that it is foolish to believe "science is at the source of material prosperity"; that the mind and method of criminals and police were essentially the same; that assassination "has entered into the general conception of the existence of all chiefs of state. It's almost conventional—especially since so many presidents [like William McKinley in 1901] have been assassinated"; that the Professor, who perversely fingers a detonator in his trouser pocket and threatens to blow himself up, symbolizes the dangers of anarchic freedom and the absurdity of modern man who (like kamikaze pilots and Arab terrorists) carry their own death; and that the Professor's desire to exterminate the weak (which echoes Kurtz's "Exterminate all the brutes!") could lead to genocidal mania: "They are our sinister masters—the weak, the flabby, the silly, the cowardly, the faint of heart, and the slavish of mind. They have power. They are the multitude. Theirs is the kingdom of the earth. Exterminate, exterminate! That is the only way of progress."[16]

Conrad's "Author's Note," ironically enough, apologized for the very qualities of the novel that have made it most meaningful to contemporary readers: the threatening portrayal of London as the "cruel devourer of the world's light" (so different from the gas-lit security of a Sherlock Holmes novel), the depiction of the sordid surroundings and moral squalor of the inert yet menacing revolutionaries, the absurd cruelty and gratuitous outrage of the explosion that blows Stevie to bits (which inspired the concept of the *acte gratuit* in André Gide's *Lafcadio's Adventures*), and Winnie's tragic belief that "life doesn't stand much looking into" (which inspired the lines in Eliot's *Burnt Norton*: "human kind / Cannot bear very much reality.")

The Secret Agent—far from being a "Simple Tale of the XIX Century," as Conrad wrote in his dedication to H. G. Wells—created the genre of the psychological-political detective novel that had a profound influence on modern writers like Orwell, Greene, Koestler, Silone, Sartre and le Carré. He had "a considerable understanding of conspiratorial politics," Orwell observed. "He had an often-expressed horror of Anarchists and Nihilists, but he also had a species of sympathy with them, because he was a Pole—a reactionary in home politics, perhaps, but a rebel against Russia and Germany."

Conrad later attempted to minimize the power of *The Secret Agent* by insisting: "the impression of gloom, oppression, and tragedy, is too much emphasized. . . . I don't believe myself that my tales are gloomy, or even very tragic, that is, not with a pessimistic intention." Yet at the time the novel was published he admitted that his ironic treatment of a melodramatic theme, his disturbing ideas and his gloomy ideology were alien and antipathetic to the English temperament, which believed (as he said in the novel) in an "idealistic conception of legality." One reviewer described the book as "too sordid to be tragic and too repulsive to be pathetic." In January 1908 Conrad confessed to Galsworthy that the critical response and the modest sales had not lived up to his expectations: "*The Secret Agent* may be pronounced by now an honourable failure. It brought me neither love nor promise of literary success. I own that I am cast down. I suppose I am a fool to have expected anything else. I suppose there is something in me that is unsympathetic to the general public. . . . Foreignness, I suppose."[17]

V

Conrad had a genius for friendship, and his lonely occupation and intellectual isolation in the country made him especially sympathetic, responsive and hospitable. In May 1906, while collaborating with Ford in Winchelsea between his two trips to Montpellier, he met Ford's friend and neighbor Arthur Marwood. During the next few years—prior to his quarrel with Ford—Conrad also met Thomas Hardy and formed new friendships with Arthur Symons and, most importantly, Perceval Gibbon.

Born in 1868, Marwood came from an old Tory family, had attended Clifton College in Bristol and had read mathematics at Trinity College, Cambridge, though poor health had forced him to leave in his second year without taking a degree. An invalid with tuberculosis of the bladder, he lived quietly in the country with his wife, who had been his nurse. Marwood put up £2,000 to start Ford's *English Review*, which published his "Actuarial Scheme for Insuring John Doe against All the Vicissitudes of Life." He was the model for Christopher Tietjens, the idealized hero of Ford's tetralogy, and for Gerald Luscombe in his novel, *The Simple Life Limited*: "six feet tall, blond, heavy, broad-shouldered, full-chested, with a mustache, sagacious eyes, and white level teeth."

A burly Yorkshireman with a subtle and profound mind, Marwood was both physically and intellectually impressive. John Conrad called him "a big man with a happy disposition and a pleasant voice, but rather slow and methodical in his movements." Violet Hunt, noting his trouser-presses and tortoiseshell hairbrushes, considered him a bit of a dandy. And Ford, who had enormous respect for Marwood, described him as

> the heavy Yorkshire squire with his dark hair startlingly silver in places, his keen blue eyes, his florid complexion, his immense, expressive hands and his great shapelessness. He used to say of himself beside Conrad's vibrating small figure: "We're the two ends of human creation: he's like a quivering ant and I am an elephant built out of meal sacks!" . . .
>
> [He] possessed, upon the whole, the widest and most serene intelligence of any human being I have yet met. . . . [He] was a man of extraordinarily wide reading, of a memory so tenacious that he appeared to be encyclopaedic in his knowledge, and of singular wisdom.[18]

Conrad also admired Marwood's analytic mind, knowledge of literature and acute judgment, and was very intimate with him until Marwood's early death from cancer in May 1916.

In his letter to Galsworthy about the negative response to *The Secret Agent*, Conrad suggested that his work had certain affinities with the novels of Thomas Hardy, which "are generally tragic enough and gloomily written too—and yet they have sold in their time and are selling to the present day." Conrad first met Hardy through Hugh Clifford early in 1903 during lunch at the Wellington Club, and again in May 1907 at a dinner, which included Wells and Shaw, in the house of Dr. Hagberg Wright, secretary of the London Library. Yet when Hardy was asked by Jacques Rivière to contribute to the Conrad memorial issue of the *Nouvelle Revue Française* in October 1924, he either forgot their earlier meetings or ignored them in order to excuse himself from an unwelcome chore. Hardy told Rivière "that though he was an admirer of Mr. Conrad he did not know him personally."[19] No record of their conversation exists, possibly because there was no opportunity to talk at length in a large group or because the two literary giants, cautious and reserved with each other, confined themselves to pleasantries.

The poet Arthur Symons, eight years younger than Conrad, had provoked Conrad's defense of Kipling by his invidious comparison of these two English novelists to D'Annunzio. A contributor to the *Yellow Book*, editor of the *Savoy* (which published Conrad's first story, "The Idiots," in 1896) and author of the influential *The Symbolist Movement in Literature* (1899), Symons belonged to the aesthetic and decadent traditions of the 1890s. He dedicated *Figures of Several Centuries* (1916) "To Joseph Conrad, with a Friend's Admiration" and published a rather superficial pamphlet, *Notes on Joseph Conrad with Some Unpublished Letters* (1925), in which he called Conrad "a Dwarf of Genius" and inexplicably said he was about the same height as Toulouse-Lautrec. Conrad used a poem by Symons as the epigraph to *'Twixt Land and Sea*. But fearful of his friend's periodic fits of insanity, Conrad was always making excuses to avoid Symons.

Conrad was as attracted to the adventurous life of Perceval Gibbon as he had been to the lives of Stephen Crane and Cunninghame Graham. Like Crane, the son of a Congregational minister, Gibbon was born in Trelach, Wales, in 1879 and educated at the Moravian School in Königsfeld, Baden. He sailed in British, French and American merchant ships before becoming a distinguished journalist and war correspondent as well as a poet, story writer and novelist. Gibbon was captured and escaped during the Boer War, which he reported for the *Natal Witness*; he joined the *Rand Daily Mail* in 1902 and spent many years in South Africa. His first book of poems, *African Items* (1903), was followed by *Souls in Bondage* (1904), on race relations, and *Vrouw Grobelaar's Leading Cases* (1905), about the Boers. Both were strongly influenced by Conrad. His novel *Margaret Harding* (1911) was dedicated to the Conrads, and four years later Conrad dedicated *Victory* "To Perceval and Maisie Gibbon."

In November 1912 Gibbon left on twenty-four hours' notice to report for the *Daily News* the Balkan-Turkish wars in desolate Bulgaria. In mid-1915 he spent five months on the Russian front and then reported from France for the *Daily Chronicle*. When on leave in England, he confirmed Conrad's deepest hatreds by telling "the most sanguinary stories about the horrors he had seen, and spoke most critically of the Russian methods of conducting warfare and of their treatment of the civilian population." During 1918–19 Gibbon became a major in the Royal Marines and worked for British Intelligence in Italy.

Norman Douglas, who met Gibbon in Rome during the war, disliked him intensely. Douglas, who loved to expose British hypocrisy, did not know that Gibbon was (like Ford and Curle) having marriage problems with his beautiful hazel-eyed wife, nor did Gibbon know that Douglas was homosexual. In *Alone*, Douglas, put off perhaps by Gibbon's military swagger, rather unfairly portrayed him as drunken, vulgar, belligerent and lecherous:

Mr. P.G., the acme of British propriety, inhabiting a house, a mansion, on the breezy heights of north London, was on that occasion decidedly drunk

. . . and soon began pouring into my ear, after the confidential manner of
the drunkard, a flood of low talk. . . .

It was rich sport, unmasking this Philistine and thanking God, meanwhile, that I was not like unto him. . . . I listened to his outpouring of
inanity and obscenity. . . .

He finally wanted to have a fight, because I refused to accompany him
to a certain place of delights. . . . Unable to stand on his legs, what could
he hope to do there?

Gibbon was a small, lively, dark, virile and sometimes brutal man,
with thick blue-black hair and a sensitive mouth. Well known for his
forceful personality, his sharp wit and his strong views, he maintained
a filial and even reverential attitude toward Conrad. In a review of *A
Personal Record* in 1912, he praised his friend's "warm personality, radi-
ant and humane intelligence," and called the memoir "a fresh work of
the first importance, a vital and individual book, a true Conrad."[20]

Conrad met Gibbon while living near Luton in about 1908, and his
young friend soon contributed "Afrikander Memories" to the *English
Review* of May 1909 and became a client of Pinker. Gibbon's two small
daughters, Joan and Joyce, were about John's age and (like Ford's
daughters) formed a link between the two families. Speaking of Conrad's serious illness early in 1910, Jessie, who adored Gibbon, said she
was strengthened by his emotional support: "if it had not been for
Perceval Gibbon who came often and always, it seemed, in the nick of
time, I feel sure I would not have held out." During the move to Capel
House in June of that year, she sent Conrad safely away to stay with the
Gibbons, and called their friendship "perhaps the closest and, for both
Joseph Conrad and for me, the most intimate" one they had.

On this visit Conrad was as exhilarated by Gibbon, who shared his
experience of Russia and knowledge of the sea, as he had been by
Crane, for both young men had the capacity to have fun, dispel his
gloom and cheer him up. Using a striking simile, Conrad told Galsworthy: "He rushed me about on his side-car motor-bike, storming up hills
and flying down dales as if the devil were after him. I don't know
whether that is particularly good for the nerves, but on return from
these excursions I felt ventilated, as though I were a bag of muslin,
frightfully hungry and almost too sleepy to eat."[21]

The following year, when the "talented buccaneer" moved to nearby
Dymchurch, on the Kentish coast near Romney Marsh, Conrad—who
reciprocated Gibbon's admiration and took a fatherly concern in his
welfare—saw him frequently. A mutual acquaintance, Edgar Jepson,

described how excruciatingly bored he was when listening to the two old sailors endlessly discussing the marks that distinguished the passing steamers at Dymchurch. Trying to interest Pinker in Gibbon's literary career, Conrad described him as stubborn but modest, uneasy and somewhat panicky about the future. To help Gibbon as well as to provide stimulation and companionship for himself, Conrad planned in the spring of 1913 to collaborate on a play based on Gibbon's African stories. Though Gibbon knew all about actors, was direct in technique and concise in style, and seemed keen to work with Conrad, they never got very far with this project. Gibbon's marriage, which had been unhappy long before the war, apparently disintegrated. Borys, who shared Gibbon's interest in motorcycles and cars, cryptically wrote that Gibbon's life ended rather tragically. At the time of his early death in the Channel Islands at the age of forty-six, "he had deliberately abandoned, or had been abandoned by, all his other friends and was living in rather squalid loneliness."[22]

VI

In August 1908, around the time he met Gibbon, Conrad published his fourth collection of stories, *A Set of Six*, which were six but not a set. In a rather misleading letter to the publisher Algernon Methuen, Conrad exaggerated the love interest, insisted they were merely amusing and claimed they were not depressing. These supposedly light-hearted love stories include the destruction of a ship in "The Brute"; the betrayal of love and friends in a group of London anarchists in "The Informer"; a man unjustly sent to a penal settlement (which suggests the dangerous effect of politics on innocent meddlers) in "The Anarchist"; the destruction of an innocent man whose back is broken while supporting a gun carriage in "Gaspar Ruiz" (a spin-off of *Nostromo*); the terrorism of an invalid in "Il Conde"; and absurdly protracted violence in "The Duel." "All the stories are stories of incident—action—not of analysis," he told Methuen. "All are dramatic in a measure but by no means of a gloomy sort. All, but two, draw their significance from the love interest—though of course they are not love stories in the conventional meaning. They are not studies—they touch no problem. They are just stories in which I've tried my best to be *simply entertaining*." But Conrad, however hard he tried, could not possibly be "simply entertaining."

In the anecdotal "Il Conde," a Polish nobleman (based on Count

Zygmunt Szembek, whom Conrad had met in Capri, and who is mistakenly given a Spanish rather than an Italian title) is living in the Bay of Naples for his health. While the count is being robbed in a pleasant outdoor café by an Italian who belongs to the Camorra and threatens him with a long knife, "the clarionet [of the band] was finishing his solo, and [the count explains] I assure you I could hear every note. Then the band crashed *fortissimo*, and that creature rolled its eyes and gnashed its teeth hissing at me with the greatest ferocity, 'Be silent! No noise or—.' "[23] After the count has been forced to surrender his wallet and his watch, the rather leisurely robbery concludes with the sudden disappearance of the Italian, accompanied by the complicated finale of the band, which ends with a tremendous crash. In this story—influenced by the counterpoint of public platitudes and private seductions in the agricultural fair scene of *Madame Bovary*—Conrad ironically contrasts the great waves of harmony flowing from the band on that apparently peaceful evening with the life-threatening robbery, accompanied by the rolling eyes and gnashing teeth of the operatic villain who terrifies the invalid count and drives him away from the only climate that enables him to survive. In his case, the Italian proverb used as the epigraph—"*Vedi Napoli, e poi mori* [i.e., *muori*]"—is literally true.

The most interesting of these stories is "The Duel," which takes place between 1801 and 1817, and was profoundly influenced by Pushkin's "The Shot" (1831). D'Hubert combines the roles of Pushkin's Count and Silvio. Like the Count, he coolly eats some fruit before the duel (he peels and sucks an orange, while Pushkin's hero eats cherries), and begins to value his life only after he is engaged to be married. Like Silvio, he endures two shots, refuses to kill an unarmed man and proves his moral superiority by returning the forfeited life. Like Pechorin in Lermontov's *A Hero of Our Time* (1840), whose "soul is used to storms and battles, and, when cast out on the shore, feels bored and oppressed, no matter how the shady grove lures him," the two French officers fight duels to maintain martial excitement between campaigns. But their combat is an anachronistic absurdity.

Conrad's tale, based on an actual episode in dueling history, portrays with irony the naïve heroism and childlike exaltation of sentiment that reflects the romantic spirit of the Napoleonic age. Since Napoleon disapproved of dueling, officers who fought ran the risk of being broken and disgraced; but D'Hubert and Feraud neither fear the consequences nor feel remorse. After a trivial provocation—the restrained northerner D'Hubert disturbs the fiery southerner Feraud while he is talking to a lady—the former must fight to avoid ridicule.

They engage in a meaningless series of duels with swords, sabers and pistols, on foot and horseback. The duels cover sixteen years; move from France through Germany to Russia and back; parallel their promotions from lieutenant to general; coincide with the rise and fall of Napoleon; and last through the restoration of the monarchy. These duels demand a homicidal austerity of mood and represent the bloody madness of the Revolution as well as a microcosm of Napoleon's violent and destructive campaigns.

After the first four duels end with inconclusive wounds, it seems clear that the quarrel can be settled only by death. During the fifth duel, a complicated mobile combat fought with pistols in a wood, the Republican Feraud misses both shots. The Royalist D'Hubert—who had for years been exasperated by the savagery of Feraud, but had gallantly protected his enemy from political reprisals after the fall of Napoleon—refuses to kill him. But Feraud will not be reconciled, and his life loses its meaning once the combat is concluded.

D'Hubert realizes his fiancée's profound love when he learns of her grief-stricken dash to rescue him from danger. He tells her that he owes the most ecstatic moment of his life to Feraud, and subtly links his romantic passion to his absurd enmity: "But for his stupid ferocity, it would have taken me years to find you out. It's extraordinary how in one way or another this man has managed to fasten himself on my deeper feelings."

In early March 1909, seven months after *A Set of Six* was published, and after eighteen unhappy months near Luton, the Conrads moved permanently back to Kent and to the village of Aldington, between Ashford and Hythe. Ford had unaccountably rented them four small and poky rooms above a butcher's shop and near the church. Conditions were extremely primitive. Conrad's study was a windowless cubicle, the fires produced more smoke than heat, water had to be carried in from an outside well and a bucket in the garden shed served as a toilet. Borys described the noisy and smelly place that Conrad endured for the next fifteen months: "It was the upper part of a rambling house, the ground floor of which was occupied by our landlord, a pork butcher, whose shop also formed part of the building. The slaughter house and the shed where the bacon was cured, were situated at the back of the house directly under the bedroom windows. The squealing of the pigs on the weekly 'killing' days together with the smell from the old-fashioned curing shed must have been very trying."[24] The squalor of Aldington drove home to Conrad his worldly failure and his bleak prospects.

VII

Conrad's close friendship with the devoted Gibbon made it easier to sever relations with Ford when the latter's behavior became intolerable. In 1909 Ford discovered three geniuses—D. H. Lawrence, Wyndham Lewis and Ezra Pound—and published them all in the *English Review*, which he founded with Marwood and edited with the help of Conrad (who suggested the title). Ford expressed the editorial policy of the journal in a high-minded circular: "The only qualification for admission to the pages of the *Review* will be . . . either distinction of individuality or force of conviction, either literary gifts or earnestness of purpose, whatever that purpose may be—the criterion of inclusion being the clarity of diction, the force or illuminative value of the views expressed." The first issue of December 1908—which contained works by Tolstoy, Hardy, James, Conrad, Galsworthy, Hudson and Wells—immediately established it as the leading literary magazine in England.

Conrad later recalled, with fond nostalgia, the intellectual excitement of bringing out a new journal, when Ford arrived at the Someries with his assistant Douglas Goldring and his secretary Miss Thomas:

> The early *E.R.* is the only one I ever cared for. The mere fact that it was the occasion of you putting on me that gentle but persistent pressure which extracted, from the depths of my then despondency, the stuff of the *Personal Record*, would be enough to make its memory dear. . . .
>
> Do you care to be reminded that the editing of the first number was finished in that farmhouse we occupied near Luton? You arrived one evening with your amiable myrmidons and parcels of copy. I shall never forget the cold of that night, the black grates, the guttering candles, the dimmed lamps and the desperate stillness of that house, where women and children were innocently sleeping, when you sought me out at 2 a.m. in my dismal study to make me concentrate suddenly on a two-page notice of [Anatole France's] *Île des Pingouins*. A marvellously successful instance of editorial tyranny! I suppose you were justified. The Number One of the *E.R.* could not come out with two blank pages in it. It would have been too sensational. I have forgiven you long ago.

Jessie's recollections were quite different. She resented the sudden invasion of the Someries, did not consider the myrmidons (whom she had to feed) particularly amiable and declared that the women were desperately awake, not "innocently sleeping":

> Lights blazed from every room downstairs—no expense was spared. To have some four or five strangers quartered on one without more notice

than an hour or so was not exactly comfortable. Only the baby and the maids slept that night. Orders, directions, or suggestions were shouted from room to room. It was an uproar all night, and the next day the house was in a chaos. My monthly stock of provisions were soon devoured, and the great trouble was that we had to use lamps and candles. However, that nightmare came to an end at last—and there was that great amount of distinction according to my husband in the first number being edited under our roof.[25]

The instant success of the *English Review*, and Ford's new power and prestige in the literary world, improved his wardrobe but had an adverse effect on his character. As David Garnett amusingly wrote: "For a year or two Ford was to become an outstanding figure of literary London: he was arrayed in a magnificent fur coat;—wore a glossy topper; drove about in hired carriages; and his fresh features, the colour of raw veal, his prominent blue eyes and rabbit teeth smiled benevolently and patronisingly upon all gatherings of literary lions." Wells remarked that Ford, confused about his own identity, became "a great system of assumed *personas* and dramatised selves." And Richard Aldington, who satirized Ford as Shobbe in *Death of a Hero* (1929), emphasized his vanity, pomposity, selfishness, mendacity and scandalous personal life: "He repeatedly tells me that he is 'the only poet there has been during the last three hundred years' and 'the greatest intellect in England!' . . . After the comfort of his own person he really cared for nothing but his prose style and literary reputation. He was also an amazing and very amusing liar—a sort of literary Falstaff. As for his affairs with women— my God."[26]

In 1901 Ford began an affair with his wife's sister, Mary Martindale, which Elsie discovered in July 1905. Ford nevertheless continued his involvement with Mary until he left her for Violet Hunt, who had been Wells' mistress, in 1908. By 1909 he was having affairs with both Violet and with his moon-faced German "secretary," Gertrud Schlablowsky, while trying in every way to force Elsie to divorce him.

Violet, seven years older than Ford, was "a thin viperish-looking beauty with a long pointed chin and deep-set, burning brown eyes." In a witty letter of July 1910, D. H. Lawrence satirized Violet's weird dress and odd behavior: "She was tremendous in a lace gown and a hat writhed with blue feathers as if with some python. Indeed she looked very handsome. She had on her best society manners. She is very dextrous: flips a bright question, lifts her eyebrows in deep concern, glances from the man on her right to the lady on her left, smiles, bows, and suddenly,—quick curtain—she is gone, and is utterly somebody else's, she who was altogether ours a brief second before."[27]

After more than a decade of intimate friendship, Conrad and Ford quarreled in the summer of 1909 and remained completely estranged for the next two years. One provocation (Ford felt) was Conrad's failure to supply a chapter of *A Personal Record*—prompted by his desire to distance or detach himself from Ford—that was scheduled for publication in the July 1909 number of the *English Review*. In that issue, Ford printed a false explanation that Conrad found intensely irritating: "We regret that owing to the serious illness of Mr. Joseph Conrad we are compelled to postpone the publication of the next installment of his Reminiscences." Another ostensible reason for the dispute was Conrad's intense hostility to Ford's Russian brother-in-law, Dr. David Soskice, who was the head of the syndicate that owned the *English Review*. An able and industrious man, who had qualified as a lawyer in Russia, Soskice had been imprisoned for anarchist activities by the Czarist regime, fled the country, joined the Garnetts' circle of exiles in England and was helping Constance translate Conrad's *bête noire*, Dostoyevsky.

But the real reasons for the bitter quarrel, and for Conrad's refusal to give more of his work to the *English Review*, were much more complex. Just as Henry James had been afraid of Conrad's mental instability, so Conrad feared Ford's (as he feared Arthur Symons') megalomania and nervous breakdowns. He had noticed the adverse changes in Ford's character. And hating to be dragged into Ford's sexual scandals, he told Galsworthy, using the very phrase Eliza Orzeszkowa had used about Conrad: "I have been fed up in this connection of late till my gorge rises at the thought of it."

In March 1909 Elsie had called at the Conrads' house and (backed by Ford) had accused Arthur Marwood of making sexual advances. Conrad believed that Marwood was "a gallant-homme in the fullest sense—absolutely incapable of any black treachery" and was horrified at being implicated in the "beastly affair": "By such juggling with the realities of life, an atmosphere of plots and accusations and suspicions is created," he told Ford. "I can't breathe in situations that are not clear. I abhor them." Alluding to Marwood, he felt obliged to admonish Ford: "of late you have been visiting what might have been faults of tact, or even grave failures of discretion, on men who *were* your admiring friends, with an Olympian severity. . . . I have the right to warn you that you will find yourself at forty with only the wrecks of friendship at your feet."

On top of all this, after Conrad, who did not like to be disturbed by casual visitors, had declined to meet Willa Cather, Ford sent Conrad's letter (which he had written to Elsie) directly to the American writer. Naturally furious at Ford's tactlessness, deviousness and manipulation, Conrad frankly told Ford (who belatedly revealed that he had been counting on Cather's connection with McClure's to secure backing for the *English Review*): "I get your letter like a bolt from the blue throwing at my head a lot of things of which I had no previous inkling—what you never even hinted to me before—as a basis for reproaches! Telling me my attitude is *too bad!!* . . . Stop this nonsense with me Ford. It's ugly. I won't have it."[28]

The final break came in July when, provoked by Conrad's refusal to contribute more chapters, the disciple had the audacity to criticize the incomplete reminiscences of the master. Conrad haughtily replied: "If you think I have discredited you and the *Review*, why then it must be even so. And as far as the Editor of the *E.R.* is concerned, we will let it go at that, with the proviso that I don't want to hear anything more about it. But as writing to a man with a fine sense of form and a complete understanding, for years, of the way in which my literary intentions work themselves out, I wish to protest against the words—*Ragged condition.*"

The affair ended in a rather ludicrous fashion when Ford went about saying he had "called Conrad out" for a duel. "His conduct is *impossible*," Conrad complained to Pinker. "He's a megalomaniac who imagines that he is managing the Universe and that everybody treats him with the blackest ingratitude. A fierce and exasperated vanity is hidden under his calm manner which misleads people. . . . I do not hesitate to say that there are cases, not quite as bad, under medical treatment."

Ford's commitment to the highest literary standards, combined with his total lack of business ability, led inevitably to financial disaster. In December 1909, after the *English Review* had lost £2,800, the financier Sir Alfred Mond bought the magazine at a nominal price and dismissed Ford as editor. Lawrence summarized Ford's faults and virtues by saying: "Hueffer lives in a constant haze. He has talent, all kinds of it, but has everlastingly been a damn fool about his life. . . . A bit of a fool, yes, but he gave me the first push and he was a kind man."[29]

Ford retaliated for Conrad's rejection by satirizing him as Simon Bransdon in *The Simple Life Limited* (1911) and as Macmaster in *Some Do Not* (1924). In the former, Bransdon becomes a writer after ruining his health by walloping "nigger" railway crews in the Congo: "his laziness and apathy, his hairiness, his clammy hands, and his drooping eyelids give him 'the appearance of oriental and semi-blind imbecility.' " In the latter, Macmaster—who has a pointed black beard streaked with grey and wears a monocle that gives him a slightly agonized expression and the privilege of putting his face close to anybody he wants to impress—also has a dangerous weakness for large-bosomed red-cheeked shopgirls.

Despite Ford's satire, Conrad always retained a fondness for his former collaborator and warmly praised *The Good Soldier* (1915), which appeared just before Ford, though over-age and in poor health, enlisted in the army. Conrad admired Ford's extraordinary fictional women, his perfectly realized subject and the melancholy cadences of his style. Yet Conrad never re-established his close friendship with Ford. When Elsie, who had successfully sued Violet Hunt for calling herself Mrs. Hueffer, suddenly wanted to resume social relations in 1920, Conrad suspected her motives and her sincerity. Wary of becoming entangled with the embittered wife, he coldly rejected her conciliatory offer. When Ford turned up in 1924, Conrad's attitude had softened and he wanted to invite him to tea. But Jessie, still hostile, absolutely refused to entertain him. "What is the use of letting him get very friendly again," she asked Pinker's son Eric. "I dislike him profoundly."[30]

CHAPTER FOURTEEN

Breakdown and Success

1910–1913

I

Conrad's self-absorbed engagement of mind, will and conscience, and a creative effort that obliterated the external world and excluded "all that makes life lovable and gentle," had enabled him to complete *Nostromo* in 1904. He later wrote with Swiftian irony: "my sojourn on the Continent of Latin America, famed for its hospitality, lasted for about two years. On my return I found (speaking somewhat in the style of Captain Gulliver) my family all well, my wife heartily glad to learn that the fuss was all over, and our small boy considerably grown during my absence." But the creative agony of *Under Western Eyes*, begun in December 1907, was even more intense, and led to Conrad's complete nervous breakdown just after he completed it in January 1910.

During the composition of the novel Conrad suffered recurring pain from chronic gout and the ever-present anxiety about money. He often started his novels without a clear plan and had no idea where the book would end—or when. Like *Lord Jim* and *Nostromo*, *Under Western Eyes* began as a short story, but quickly absorbed Conrad and carried him onward. Though the novel kept growing and there was no prospect of completing it in the immediate future, he repeatedly told Pinker that the end was near. In the summer of 1909 Pinker, dissatisfied with Conrad's failure to deliver the long-awaited manuscript, threatened to sever their business connection. In December they reached a crisis when Pinker refused to advance any more funds and Conrad, threatening to throw the manuscript into the fire, angrily exclaimed: "In a manner which is nothing short of contemptuous you seem to be holding out a bribe—next week forsooth!—as though it were a bone to a dog to make him get up on his hind legs."

Nearing the end of the novel as well as the end of his tether, and irritated by what he considered the inordinate fees Pinker was deducting from royalties to pay off the enormous debt, Conrad exploded in a self-pitying letter to Galsworthy that described how the novel was eating up his life:

> It is outrageous. Does he think I am the sort of man who wouldn't finish the story in a week if he could? Do you? Why? For what reason? Is it my habit to lie about drunk for days instead of working? . . . I sit twelve hours at the table, sleep six, and worry the rest of the time, feeling the age creeping on and looking at those I love. For two years I haven't seen a picture, heard a note of music, hadn't a moment of ease in human intercourse—not really. And he talks of *regular supplies of manuscript.*[1]

Finally, they agreed that Pinker would stimulate productivity by advancing no more than £3 for every thousand words of manuscript that Conrad sent. Even so, Conrad feared the ambitious novel would not sell and that most of the meager proceeds would be used to pay off his massive debt to Pinker.

II

Under Western Eyes, set in about 1904, begins with a confrontation between a Russian revolutionary movement and the Czarist secret police. In January 1908, two years before completing the novel, Conrad expounded his original conception in a letter to Galsworthy:

> I am trying to capture the very soul of things Russian. . . .
>
> Listen to the theme. The Student Razumov (a natural son of a Prince K.) gives up secretly to the police his fellow student, Haldin, who seeks refuge in his rooms after committing a political crime (supposed to be the murder of de Plehve). First movement in St. Petersburg. (Haldin is hanged, of course.)
>
> 2nd in Genève. The student Razumov meeting abroad the mother and sister of Haldin falls in love with the last, marries her and, after a time, confesses to her the part he played in the arrest of her brother.
>
> The psychological developments leading to Razumov's betrayal of Haldin, to the confession of the fact to his wife and to the death of these people (brought about mainly by the resemblance of their child to the late Haldin) form the real subject of the story.

As Conrad actually wrote the novel, however, Razumov confesses to Nathalie Haldin in part IV, precluding their marriage (though she forgives him) and eliminating their child from the plot. The first part concentrates on Razumov's motivation for betraying Haldin. Resenting Haldin's assumption that he sympathizes with his cause and will help him escape, fearful of being implicated in the crime and of ruining his career, Razumov betrays Haldin but is forced by the secret police to spy for the Russian government on the revolutionaries in Geneva. The rest of the novel focuses on what happens to him after this event. When Razumov also confesses his betrayal to the revolutionaries he has met in Geneva, Nikita, who is later exposed as a police spy, expresses his "loyalty" by bursting Razumov's ear drums as punishment. Permanently deafened, Razumov is hit and crippled by a tramcar, and returns as an invalid to Russia. Razumov and the circle of revolutionaries in Geneva are meant "to capture the very soul of things Russian": the hypocrisy and mindless destruction; the compulsion to betray, to repent and to debase themselves as a way of recovering lost honor; the Dostoyevskian combination of instinctive cowardice and anguished longing for spiritual absolution.

The theme, plot and structure of *Under Western Eyes* are similar to those of *Lord Jim*. The first part of the novel focuses on the dishonorable act and the remainder of the book, set in a different place, describes the attempt to recover self-esteem after moral disgrace. Marlow's famous phrase about Jim—"one of us"—is ironically used in Conrad's Russian novel to refer to the revolutionary brotherhood. Conrad's greatest works concern the revelation of hidden guilt, the confession of a disgraceful deed. Kurtz has betrayed his colonial mission by committing the "horror" he can scarcely express; Jim admits to deserting an abandoned ship and betraying his trust as an officer; Nostromo has stolen the silver of the mine; Verloc has sacrificed Stevie; Leggatt in "The Secret Sharer" has murdered a disobedient sailor. And in *Under Western Eyes* Razumov continues this "Russian" obsession to confess, first to Nathalie and then to the revolutionaries.

Though Conrad told Galsworthy that Haldin's crime was based on the murder of the reactionary Russian official Vyacheslav de Plehve, who was blown up by a university student named Sasonov in 1904, there was probably another source of this plot—a historical event set in Geneva that suggested Razumov's betrayal of Haldin—which Conrad did not mention. In 1869 the sexually attractive nihilist Sergei Nechaev returned to Moscow from Geneva, the spiritual home of Russian revolutionaries, and "murdered a student who was a member of his [small, secret] organization, perhaps because he feared treachery, or perhaps simply to demonstrate his own power over his followers, and then fled back to

Geneva. . . . In 1872 he was arrested and extradited to Russia, where he died in prison ten years later."[2] Nechaev's murder of Ivanov, which took place on November 21, 1869, inspired the plot of Dostoyevsky's *The Possessed* (1872). Nechaev was a revolutionary colleague of Mikhail Bakunin (the model for Peter Ivanovich in Conrad's novel), and an evil influence on and would-be seducer of Natalie Herzen, whom he met in Geneva in 1870 and whose name is strikingly similar to Nathalie Haldin.

Using the English professor of languages as the narrator of the novel, Conrad cultivated an objective point of view and portrayed the Russian soul as perceived by Western eyes. In an important letter to a Polish compatriot, he stressed his dual heritage and the double focus he employed in the novel: "Both at sea and on land my point of view is English, from which the conclusion should not be drawn that I have become an Englishman. That is not the case. Homo duplex has in my case more than one meaning."

Part I (the strongest section of the novel) and the final chapter of part IV take place in St. Petersburg, and the rest of the book is set in Geneva. One city is repressive, one free; but Switzerland shelters the Communist revolutionaries who in 1917 would make Russia even more repressive than it had been under Czarist rule. Conrad not only contrasts the violent lives with the placid setting, but (provoked by memories of Borys' recent illness in Champel) satirizes the bourgeois virtues of Geneva: "there was but little of spring-like glory in the rectangular railed space of grass and trees, framed visibly by the orderly roof-slopes of that town, comely without grace, and hospitable without sympathy. . . . He saw the green slopes framing the Petit Lac in all the marvellous banality of the picturesque made of painted cardboard." In this precise and prosaic context, the professor of languages expresses the political theme of the novel (which would influence Orwell's *Animal Farm* and *Nineteen Eighty-Four*):

A violent revolution falls into the hands of narrow-minded fanatics and of tyrannical hypocrites at first. Afterwards comes the turn of all the pretentious intellectual failures of the time. Such are the chiefs and the leaders. You will notice that I have left out the mere rogues. The scrupulous and just, the noble, humane, and devoted natures; the unselfish and the intelligent may begin a movement—but it passes away from them. They are not the leaders of a revolution. They are its victims: the victims of disgust, of disenchantment—often of remorse. Hopes grotesquely betrayed, ideals caricatured—that is the definition of revolutionary success.[3]

III

Conrad's contemporary reputation had reached its height with the publication of *Lord Jim*, *Youth* and *Typhoon* in the early years of the century,
but his more mature and ambitious novels—*Nostromo*, *The Secret Agent*
and *Under Western Eyes*—were critical failures. Though Garnett wrote a
favorable review in the *Nation*, his criticism of *Under Western Eyes* in a
private letter provoked Conrad's angry defense against the charge that
he hated Russians. Alluding to the revolutionaries who gathered around
Constance and Edward, Conrad wrote: "You are so russianised my dear
that you don't know the truth when you see it—unless it smells of
cabbage-soup when it at once secures your profoundest respect. I suppose one must make allowances for your position of Russian Ambassador to the Republic of Letters." Their antithetical political views also led
to a cooling of their friendship.

Conrad's Russian novel and cast of Russian characters raise two
closely related questions: did he know Russian, and what was his attitude toward Russian novelists: Turgenev, Tolstoy and especially Dostoyevsky? Inspired by Polish pride, Conrad always denied that he knew
the Russian language, despite his five and a half years of exile in Vologda and Chernikhov during 1862–67. Though his complete ignorance
of the language and even of the alphabet seems unlikely, Conrad suggested to the Russophile Garnett that Apollo had deliberately isolated
him from the pernicious Russian influence and taught him Polish amidst
the small community of exiles: "I know extremely little of Russians.
Practically nothing. In Poland we have nothing to do with them. One
knows they are there. And that's disagreeable enough. In exile the contact is even slighter if possible, if more unavoidable. I crossed the Russian frontier [and returned to Poland] at the age of ten. Not having been
to school then I never knew Russian. I could not tell a little Russian [a
Ukrainian] from a Great Russian to save my life." But Najder, citing
Tadeusz's directions concerning Conrad's visit to Poland in 1893: "From
Brzesc telegraph for horses, but in Russian, for Oratow doesn't receive
or accept messages in an 'alien language,' " convincingly states that
"Conrad must have known some Russian. He could read the Russian
alphabet."[4]

The only Russian Conrad admired was Henry James' friend, Ivan
Turgenev, a westernized writer who lived in France. Conrad accepted
the dedication of Constance Garnett's translation of Turgenev's *A Desperate Character* in 1899, and took *A Sportsman's Sketches* as a model for
The Mirror of the Sea. The enthusiasm expressed in Conrad's late essay,

"Turgenev" (1917), provides a notable contrast to his coolness toward James and toward Crane. And his description of Turgenev's great gifts, so different from the negative Russian traits defined in "Autocracy and War," expresses an ideal standard that he himself reached in his greatest works: "absolute sanity and the deepest sensibility, the clearest vision and the quickest responsiveness, penetrating insight and unfading generosity of judgment, an exquisite perception of the visible world and an unerring instinct for the significant, for the essential in the life of men and women, the clearest mind, the warmest heart, the largest sympathy." Conrad also used this essay to contrast Turgenev's humane compassion with the grotesque pathology of the "convulsed terror-haunted Dostoievski": "All [Turgenev's] creations, fortunate and unfortunate, oppressed and oppressors are human beings, not strange beasts in a menagerie or damned souls knocking themselves to pieces in the stuffy darkness of mystical contradictions."

Conrad was also hostile to Tolstoy. He suspected Tolstoy's anti-sensualism and found his brand of Christianity distasteful. He spoke of the gratuitous atrocity of the deathbed repentance in "The Death of Ivan Ilych" and the monstrous stupidity of "The Kreutzer Sonata," in which the jealous husband who had murdered the wife he suspected of infidelity, "an obvious degenerate not worth looking at twice, totally unfitted not only for married life but for any sort of life, is presented as a sympathetic victim of some sort of sacred truth that is supposed to live within him." Jocelyn Baines notes that a "satiric allusion in a cancelled passage to Peter Ivanovich as author of 'The Resurrection of Yegor' [i.e., Tolstoy's late novel *Resurrection*] and the 'thrice famous Pfennig Cantata' ['The Kreutzer Sonata'] suggests that Conrad at least had Tolstoy in mind."[5] At the end of *Under Western Eyes* Peter Ivanovich fulfills Tolstoy's socialistic ideal by uniting himself to a peasant girl.

In contrast to his straightforward admiration of Turgenev and distaste for Tolstoy, Conrad felt both revulsion from and attraction to Dostoyevsky. Dostoyevsky's revolutionary plotting, his arrest and exile to a penal settlement, his emotional extremism, religious mysticism and desire for expiation inevitably reminded Conrad of Apollo's disastrous career and morbid temperament. In the same way, Dostoyevsky's epilepsy revived fears of Conrad's own childhood illness. He disliked Dostoyevsky's artistic characteristics and would have agreed with Vladimir Nabokov that his "lack of taste, his monotonous dealings with persons suffering with pre-Freudian complexes, the way he has of wallowing in the tragic misadventures of human dignity—all this is difficult to admire." Conrad also disliked Dostoyevsky's dominant ideas: his intense

Russian nationalism, his messianic Christian faith and his belief in Holy Russia's redemptive mission in Western Europe. Conrad disapproved in theory of Dostoyevsky, who had also been traumatized by political revolution, but shared his response to contemporary political unrest. He identified with Dostoyevsky's awareness of both the evil and the spirituality in man, with his passionate conservatism and with his deep-rooted fear of social disorder, anarchy and nihilism.

Like most Russian novelists, Dostoyevsky was extremely hostile to Poles. In *The Idiot* Aglaya marries a fraudulent Polish "count" and converts to Catholicism, whose doctrines the Orthodox Dostoyevsky detested. In *The Brothers Karamazov*, where Dostoyevsky suggests that Polish women have loose morals, an unnamed Pole who had seduced Grushenka reappears five years later as an avaricious deceiver and card-sharper. He poses as an officer, wears greasy clothes and accepts a bribe to leave Grushenka alone, but then demands even more money to complete the bargain. Criticizing its lack of clarity and its barbaric pathology, Conrad ambivalently called that novel "terrifically bad and impressive and exasperating. Moreover, I don't know what D stands for or reveals, but I do know that he is too Russian for me. It sounds to me like some fierce mouthings from prehistoric ages."[6] Just as Conrad rejected Melville because he himself had been labeled a writer of the sea, so he rejected Dostoyevsky—like Melville, a mystical novelist—because he had also been labeled and limited as a Slav.

Despite all this hostility, Borys mentioned that Dostoyevsky "was one of the authors his father read most assiduously." And *Crime and Punishment* had a more powerful influence on Conrad than the works of Flaubert, Maupassant, Turgenev or Henry James. In *Under Western Eyes*, as in Dostoyevsky's novel, the tormented conscience of a Russian soul moves from crime through agony, isolation and remorse to confession and expiation, and, cared for by a humble woman, the hero finds in the end a kind of peace. As Ralph Matlaw observed of Conrad's use of Dostoyevsky, he "was a devil who could only be exorcised by the imaginative transformation of the offensive matter."[7]

IV

Conrad's disappointment, frustration and anxiety about *Under Western Eyes* as well as his constant worry about money, dissatisfaction with his own work and physical exhaustion, were vividly recorded in Arthur Symons' letter of February 1911: "[Conrad] said: I have had £300 for the serial rights of my novel [*Under Western Eyes*]: think of those awful creatures who get thousands. I may get altogether £1,000 out of it. *Mais*, I am always under the water. (He was walking to and fro, smoking.) I am not content with my novel. It has no end. It sickens me when I have to sit down to my desk and write so many thousand words for a short story—for money. (He put his hand over his forehead! All is here!) But how can I go on?"[8]

In January 1910, after completing the novel, Conrad went up to Pinker's office in London. Resentful about Pinker's threats, innuendoes and refusal to advance money, he got into a blazing quarrel with him. In the course of the argument, Conrad either used a foreign word or became furiously incomprehensible, and the equally exasperated Pinker, striking at a weak point, declared that "he should speak English, if he could!" Five months later he icily wrote Pinker: "As it can't have escaped your recollection that the last time we met you told me I 'did not speak English to you' I have asked Robert Garnett [Edward's brother and a solicitor] to be my mouthpiece—at any rate till my speech improves sufficiently to be acceptable." After this confrontation, Conrad and Pinker were estranged for two years.

Immediately after returning to his house in Aldington Conrad had a nervous breakdown. The serious illnesses of his family and himself (every long novel since *Lord Jim* had cost him a tooth), the wrenching quarrel with Ford, the slowness of writing and long strain of creation, the intense emotional involvement with Russian material, the chronic financial problems, the fear of a negative response to his novel and the final provocation of the fight with Pinker, all contributed to his collapse. Jessie related that during the breakdown, which was accompanied by grave physical symptoms and resembled the feverish delirium he had experienced on his honeymoon, Conrad mixed imprecations against Pinker with morbid memories of his Catholic childhood and the death of his parents:

> Clearly he was very ill, and I was horrified to see his throat was swollen out level with the end of his chin, and in a moment more he rambled off in evident delirium, using his own language and muttering fiercely words of resentment against Mr. Pinker: "Speak English . . . if I can . . . what does he call all I have written." . . .
>
> Day and night I watched over him, fearful that if I turned my back he would escape from the room. I slept what little I could on the couch drawn across the only door. More than once I opened my eyes to find him tottering towards me in search of something he had dreamed of. . . .

He seemed to breathe once when he should have done at least a dozen times, a cold heavy sweat came over him, and he lay on his back, faintly murmuring the words of the burial service.

Though Conrad's creative energy had lasted until he had finished the novel, he could neither revise it nor free himself from its imaginative force. As Jessie told the *Blackwood's* editor David Meldrum: "Poor Conrad is very ill and Dr. Hackney says it will be a long time before he is fit for anything requiring mental exertion. . . . There is the M.S. complete but uncorrected and his fierce refusal to let even I touch it. It lays on a table at the foot of his bed and he lives mixed up in the scenes and holds converse with the characters."[9]

Conrad's letters to Hugh Clifford and to Norman Douglas, when he began to regain a semblance of health in mid-May, reveal that he had not recognized the gravity of his illness and still had to keep tight control of himself lest his nerves go to pieces once again:

I am somewhat shaky all over. It seems I have been very ill. At the time I did not believe it, but now I begin to think that I must have been. And what's more, I begin to see that the horrible nervous tension of the last two years (of which even my wife knows nothing) had to end in something of this sort. . . .

You may imagine what it was like to have four months taken out of one's life. I am all of a shake yet; I feel like a man returned from hell and look upon the very world of the living with dread.[10]

V

While recovering from his breakdown between February and May 1910 and as *Under Western Eyes* (his first book in three years) was going through the press, Conrad extended his range of friendships to include three Americans and a Frenchman: Agnes Tobin, Warrington Dawson, John Quinn and André Gide. Agnes Tobin, the daughter of a prosperous San Francisco lawyer and banker, was born into a large Catholic family in 1864. Linguist, translator of Petrarch and Racine, friend of Alice Meynell and of Arthur Symons (who introduced her to Conrad), she had a passion for meeting famous writers and artists. She knew George Meredith, Edmund Gosse, Francis Thompson, W. B. Yeats, André Gide, G. K. Chesterton, Ezra Pound and Augustus John—many of whom praised her character and her work.

Agnes inspired Alice Meynell's poem "The Shepherdess." Francis Meynell (Alice's son), who praised the delicacy of her head and neck, called her "beautiful, powerful, exquisite and child-attentive." Yeats first met Agnes in San Francisco during his American lecture tour in 1904 and recommended her translations to Symons: "I think them very delicate, very beautiful, with a curious poignant ecstasy, and would have written about them but for my ignorance of Italian." And to Lady Gregory he hyperbolically described Agnes as the greatest American poet since Walt Whitman. Symons described the flighty, capricious, droll and dainty Agnes as "a plump little person like her name" (which suggested a Toby jug), "bright, warm-hearted, very talkative; very amusing."[11] In August 1911 Agnes gave Conrad, whom she adored, a written introduction to John Quinn, a wealthy collector who during the next decade bought a great many of his manuscripts. And in October of that year Conrad gratefully dedicated *Under Western Eyes* "To Agnes Tobin, who brought to our door her genius for friendship from [California] the uttermost shore of the west."

Warrington Dawson, born in South Carolina in 1878, was the first of Conrad's young disciples. While hunting with Teddy Roosevelt in East Africa, he had met Ted Sanderson, who was then Town Clerk in Nairobi and who provided the introduction to Conrad. A man of reactionary social ideas and literary tastes, he was strongly influenced by the attacks on modern art in Max Nordau's *Degeneration* (1892) and opposed to what he considered the immorality of modern art. In 1913 Dawson failed to interest Conrad in the crackbrained principles of the Fresh Air Art Society; in 1924 he dedicated *Adventures in the Night* "To My Friend Joseph Conrad"; and in 1927 published his feeble novel, *The Crimson Pall*, with some letters Conrad had written to him about the art of fiction. Dawson became the model for the South Carolinian Captain J. K. Blunt, who is Monsieur George's rival for the love of Rita de Lastaola in *The Arrow of Gold*.

John Quinn (whom Conrad never met) was a successful tariff lawyer, born in Ohio in 1870 and educated at Harvard. A patron of the arts and friend of Ford, Joyce and Pound, he bought all the manuscripts Conrad offered for sale between 1911 and 1919, paying the prices Conrad asked and adding considerably to Conrad's income during those years. Conrad played the bald, thin-lipped, severe-looking Quinn like an angler with a fish, stimulating his acquisitive instinct with new prospects, and constantly discovering "lost" manuscripts in old cupboards and drawers. Their long-distance friendship was sustained not only by the acquisition of the manuscripts, but also by Quinn's admiration for Conrad and by his friendly advice and assistance to Conrad's American publisher, Frank Doubleday. During the war Conrad enhanced Quinn's collection by writing a series of long and interesting letters about world politics and the trial of Roger Casement.

In July 1911 Agnes Tobin introduced Conrad to André Gide, the greatest writer, apart from Henry James, among his friends. Gide took the epigraph to part V of *Lafcadio's Adventures* from *Lord Jim*, and adopted the concept of the *acte gratuit* in that novel from *The Secret Agent*. In 1919 Gide thought of asking Conrad to write a preface to *Straight is the Gate*, and he consistently praised Conrad's works throughout the 1920s. He felt *The Rescue*, though "encumbered," was one of Conrad's most remarkable books and "touched the most sensitive parts of my heart." Gide dedicated his *Travels in the Congo* (1927) "To the Memory of Joseph Conrad" and expressed in that book Conrad's anti-imperialist themes. He admired the art of *Typhoon* (which he had poorly translated into French) and commended Conrad for "cutting short his story just on the threshold of the horrible [second storm] and giving the reader's imagination full play, after having led him to a degree of dreadfulness that seemed unsurpassable." He also confirmed—on the spot—the greatness and impact of Conrad's African novella: "I am re-reading *Heart of Darkness* for the fourth time. It is only after having seen the country that I realize how good it is." Conrad would have been gratified to read Gide's response in his journal of February 1930 to the serious themes and complex structure of *Under Western Eyes*: "one does not know what deserves more admiration: the amazing subject, the fitting together, the boldness of so difficult an undertaking, the patience in the development of the story, the complete understanding and exhausting of the subject."[12]

In November 1919 Conrad had a sharp disagreement with Gide, who was supervising the French translation of his works, about what he considered Gide's negligent attitude toward *The Arrow of Gold* (and perhaps toward *Typhoon* as well). Deeply offended by and suffering a certain *malaise* from Gide's reply to his letter, Conrad told his French disciple Jean-Aubry that he was trying to convince Gide to abandon the difficult and troublesome translation: "I am afraid that I have quarrelled with Gide for good. The answer he sent to my request to let you have the translation of *A. of G.* is not the sort of answer you send to a man whom you take seriously. I pointed it out to him and said distinctly that this sort of thing looked as if he were taking me for a fool. At the same time he bothers me with all his scruples about the style of the translations by all three [obscure French] women! . . . I need not tell you that in all this I tried to appear more hurt than angry." A week later Conrad told Jean-Aubry that he was still bothered by the situation and was determined to wrest the translation from the women who had made him their "prey." Conrad apparently won this argument with Gide. By the following year, their anger had subsided and they resumed their cordial praise of each other's works. The disputed French translation of *The Arrow of Gold* was eventually brought out by Jean-Aubry in 1929.

In June 1910, after meeting Agnes Tobin and Warrington Dawson, and recovering from his breakdown, Conrad justified paying a higher rent of £45 a year on grounds of health and moved five miles east of Aldington to Capel House in Orlestone, near Ashford, in Kent, where he remained for the next nine years. Capel House—a seventeenth-century building, surrounded by a garden—was actually "three old cottages knocked into one—the rooms having low ceilings with oaken beams and floors that were crazily uneven." Though there was no electricity, hot water or telephone, "comfortable, old-fashioned furniture made the [small rooms] look very cosy. On the ground floor were the dining-room, living-room, the boys' room, what was called the den, full of tools, stones, in short: treasures. The first floor consisted of bedrooms and a guest-room—a large room with a low ceiling and wide windows facing the garden."[13] The more spacious quarters made it much easier for Conrad to entertain his numerous guests and admirers.

VI

Conrad told Pinker that his ambition in his random recollections, *A Personal Record*, published in January 1912, was "to make Polish life enter English literature." Andrzej Busza has pointed out the influence of Polish literature on Conrad's works: the late-nineteenth-century emigrant story on "Amy Foster," the plot of a ballad by Mickiewicz in "Karain," echoes of Stefan Zeromski's novel *The History of a Sin* in *Victory*.[14] But in *A Personal Record* Conrad defines himself in opposition to the Russian Slavic tradition while describing his life in Poland, discussing his career at sea from Marseilles to Borneo and revealing the origins of his first novel. After writing about his father and his reasons for leaving Poland, he describes his trips to the Ukraine to visit Uncle Tadeusz (whose *Memoirs* provided the material for several sections of the autobiography) and his memorable meeting with his great-uncle Nicholas Bobrowski, who, as a starving officer in Napoleon's army, had eaten Lithuanian dog. Though interesting, Conrad's fictionalized maritime memories, in *A Personal Record* as in *The Mirror of the Sea*, are often unreliable, and are most untrustworthy precisely when they appear to be frank.

In October 1909, while Conrad was working on *Under Western Eyes*, the unexpected appearance of Captain Carlos Marris—who had married a Malay princess in Penang and spent twenty-one years in the East—turned Conrad's mind back to Asia. Marris' visit inspired him to write the three stories—"A Smile of Fortune" (1911), "The Secret Sharer" (1910) and "Freya of the Seven Isles" (1912)—that comprised *'Twixt Land and Sea* (mistakenly dedicated to "Captain C. M. Harris"), a volume that equaled the stories in *Youth* and *Typhoon*. "I had a visit from a man out of the Malay Seas," Conrad told Pinker. "It was like the raising of a lot of dead—dead to me, because most of them live out there and even read my books and wonder who the devil has been around taking notes. . . . The best of it is that all these men of 22 years ago feel kindly to the Chronicler of their lives and adventures. They shall have some more of the stories they like." Conrad was especially grateful for the recognition of sailors, who could appreciate the accuracy of the setting and the evocation of atmosphere.

"A Smile of Fortune"—based on Conrad's experiences on the *Otago*—is a mixture of a fairy tale (a wild, beautiful girl confined to an exotic garden), a story of frustrated love and a social satire on the bourgeois respectability of Mauritius. While courting the strangely sulky and silent illegitimate girl, whom he actually kisses, the autobiographical captain is forced by her ship-chandler father to buy seventeen tons of potatoes. Though he sells them at the next port for a great profit, he feels corrupted by the compromise between sex and commerce, and resigns his command to avoid returning to the island.

"The Secret Sharer" portrays the theme of the double or potentially evil self that Conrad had explored with Marlow and Kurtz, Jim and Gentleman Brown, Haldin and Razumov. The story was based on an actual incident that occurred on the *Cutty Sark* in the 1880s. But Conrad's version takes place after the crime has been committed and suggests that as the young captain brings his ship dangerously close to the island of Koh-ring (off the coast of Cambodia, south of Phnom Penh), the murderer Leggatt, his secret sharer in guilt and self-knowledge, who has crept aboard in the night, lowers himself into the water to take his punishment. Basil Hall recounted the events that inspired Conrad's story:

The mate of the *Cutty Sark* was apparently a despotic character with a sinister reputation. An order which he gave to an incompetent negro named John Francis was twice disobeyed, and when he went forward to deal with Francis the insubordinate seaman attacked him with a capstan bar; after a struggle the mate got hold of the bar and brought it down on Francis' head so heavily that he never regained consciousness and died three days later. Nonetheless the captain of the *Cutty Sark*, who was by no means a hard man, is supposed to have said that it served Francis right, and he helped the mate to escape from the law. When the mate was eventually captured and tried, he was acquitted of murder and the judge, "with great pain," sentenced him to seven years for manslaughter.

Conrad confirmed the source and added that "the swimmer himself was suggested to me by a young fellow who was 2nd mate . . . of the *Cutty Sark* clipper and had the misfortune to kill a man on deck. But his skipper had the decency to let him swim ashore on the Java coast as the ship was passing through Anjer Straits [between Java and Sumatra]. The story was well remembered in the Merchant Service even in my time." Pleased, as he rarely was, by this story of sympathy, conscience and moral judgment, Conrad assured Garnett that he had achieved his artistic intention—though he modestly attributed it to luck rather than to skill: "*The Secret Sharer*, between you and me, is *it*. Eh? No damned tricks with girls there [as in the other stories in the book]. Eh? Every word fits and there's not a single uncertain note. Luck my boy. Pure luck."[15]

While defending himself against the Slavic label that Garnett misused to define him and to explain his work, Conrad told his old friend that "Freya of the Seven Isles"—his best romantic love story—was, like "The Secret Sharer," based on an actual incident: "It is the story of the *Costa Rica* which was not more than five years old when I was in Singapore. The man's name was Sutton. He died in just that way—but I don't think he died of Slav temperament. He was just about to go home to marry a girl (of whom he used to talk to everybody and anybody) and bring her out there when his ship was run on a reef by the commander of a Dutch gun-boat whom he had managed to offend in some way. He haunted the beach in Macassar for months and lies buried in the fort there." Like the trusting Captain Whalley with the treacherous Massy, Jasper Allen has his ship and his life destroyed by the villainous Heemskirk.

In this charming but tragic tale (as in "Il Conde") Conrad uses discordant music to express sexual corruption and to provide an ironic counterpoint to the action. Freya, named for the goddess of love, beauty and fecundity, the leader of the Valkyries in Teutonic mythology, likes to play Wagnerian music "in the flicker of blinding flashes." She is engaged to the handsome Jasper and plans to live on his beloved brig, the *Bonito*, as soon as they are married. In order to prevent the unwelcome advances of her loathsome Dutch suitor, Lieutenant Heemskirk, Freya rushes to the piano and fills the verandah "with an uproarious, confused resonance." When Heemskirk orders her to stop playing, she ignores his command but "could not make the sound of the piano cover his raised voice." He then repeats the order for her to stop, lifts her bodily from the piano stool and kisses her neck. Later in the story, when Freya discovers Heemskirk spying on her while she waves to Jasper aboard the *Bonito* and then trying to sneak off scot-free, she punishes him by making "the rosewood monster growl savagely in an irritated bass . . . then she pursued him with the same thing she had played the evening before—a modern, fierce, piece of love music. . . . She accentuated its rhythm with triumphant malice."[16]

But art, in this story, is no antidote to life. Heemskirk (the name of the ship of the explorer Abel Tasman), jealous of Freya's love for Jasper, vengefully grounds the *Bonito* on a reef near Macassar. Jasper, who feels his brig is a live being and extension of himself, is (like Lord Jim with Jewel) made powerless by his love for Freya. He pines away as his wreck is looted, and Freya dies of pneumonia and heartbreak in Hong Kong. In this story, which has no sacrificial, redemptive Wagnerian heroine, evil triumphs over good.

VII

During 1912 and 1913 Conrad acquired two young disciples and met two prominent aristocrats, all of whom made pilgrimages to visit him and to enjoy his conversation and hospitality at Capel House. Richard Curle, born in Melrose, Scotland, in 1883 and educated at Wellington College, worked as an assistant editor and columnist for the *Daily Mail*. His son wrote that he "travelled compulsively, driven by an inner quest he was never able to formulate, even to himself," and in the course of his restless wanderings had visited and written about many of the places that Conrad had known in the East. Like Perceval Gibbon, who also had an unhappy marriage, Curle was a moody and sometimes difficult man. "Subject to fits of profound melancholy, [he] was driven by irrational feelings of guilt, could take unreasonable exception to perfectly innocent remarks and break with people he had known for years." With Conrad, however, he always behaved perfectly.

In October 1912 Curle, through Garnett, sent Conrad copies of two critical appreciations that appeared the following month in *Everyman* and in Katherine Mansfield and Middleton Murry's little magazine, *Rhythm*. Though Conrad was a bit annoyed when Curle compared him to Dostoyevsky, stressed his Slavic qualities and emphasized his books about the sea, he was pleased by Curle's intelligence and critical insight, which (he felt) made other accounts of his work seem like "mere verbiage." Conrad wanted to meet Curle and Garnett introduced them at one of his weekly literary lunches at the Mont-Blanc restaurant on Gerrard Street in Soho. Conrad soon became quite fond of the tall, well-off Scotsman, called him a nice, sensitive fellow, and analyzed the strengths and defects of his character. Though rather immature and naïve, Curle was certainly no fool. He had an intuitive shrewdness about both life and literature, and desperately wanted to be a serious writer.

Their friendship became increasingly intimate, and by 1919 Conrad told Curle: "Outside my household you are the person about whom I am most concerned both in thought and feelings." The following year, when Curle was about to take up a newspaper job in the East, Conrad expressed his paternal feelings and sadly confessed: "I can't contemplate your possible departure for India with equanimity. . . . I can only feel that your decision is bound to affect [my life] intimately, with a sense of loss in its deeper values."[17] In 1919 Conrad dedicated *The Arrow of Gold* to Curle and the next year Curle reciprocated with the dedication of his book, *Wanderings*. Between 1912 and 1964 Curle published dozens of biographical, bibliographical and literary reviews, articles, introductions, editions, pamphlets and books—including *Joseph Conrad: A Study* (1912), *The Last Twelve Years of Joseph Conrad* (1928) and an edition of the letters Conrad wrote to him (1928)—which helped to sustain Conrad's reputation in the years following his death.

Joseph Retinger, born in 1888 and five years younger than Curle, was instrumental in reviving Conrad's interest in Poland, which had diminished since the death of Uncle Tadeusz and the attack by Eliza Orzeszkowa. The son of a prosperous lawyer, Retinger earned his law degree in Cracow and his doctorate in the humanities at the Sorbonne, and published a number of literary and political books. Though quite ugly, with sallow skin and irregular yellow teeth, Retinger had recently married a beautiful Polish wife and was also very successful with other women. Katherine Anne Porter, a former mistress, caustically portrayed him as the Polish pianist Tadeusz May in "The Leaning Tower" (1931): "He was a narrow, green-faced young man and in the light his eyes were liver colored. He looked bilious, somehow, and he continually twisted a scorched looking lock of hair on the crown of his head as he talked, a tight clever little smile in the corners of his mouth."

In November 1912 Arnold Bennett, who had met Retinger in France, introduced him to Conrad. Retinger, running the Polish Bureau in London, was trying to stimulate interest in Polish independence in the French and English press. Conrad thought the cause was hopeless, but invited Retinger down to Capel House for the day. When they spoke Polish, Retinger noticed that Conrad had the rather sing-song accent of the Ukraine. Shortly after their meeting, Conrad called Retinger an intelligent young literary man and said his wife, Otolia, was a charming Polish country girl. Otolia's mother inspired what became the ill-fated trip to Poland in July 1914 by inviting the Conrads and the Retingers to visit her country estate outside Cracow. In 1943 Retinger published his lively but sketchy and unreliable book, *Conrad and His Contemporaries*.[18]

Lady Ottoline Morrell—daughter of Lieutenant-General Arthur Cavendish-Bentinck, half-sister of the sixth Duke of Portland and generous patron of the arts—was reluctantly introduced by Henry James, who thought Conrad "the strangest of creatures." When Ottoline asked James to arrange a meeting in the summer of 1913, he at first tried to discourage her, insisting that the Polish aristocrat was a barbarian unfamiliar with polite society, and that the plebeian Jessie was not capable of entertaining the aristocracy: "Henry James held up his hands in horror, and was so perturbed that he paced up and down the grey drawing-room. . . . 'But, dear lady . . . but, dear lady. . . . He has lived his life at sea—dear lady, he has never met "civilised" women. Yes, he is interesting, but he would not understand you. His wife, she is a good cook. She is a Catholic as he is, but . . . No, dear lady, he has lived a rough life, and is not used to talk to—.' "

Ottoline was born in 1873 and married Philip Morrell, an old Etonian, lawyer and liberal MP, in 1902. During her marriage she had affairs with the painters Augustus John and Henry Lamb, the art critic Roger Fry and the philosopher Bertrand Russell. Ottoline was described by Osbert Sitwell as an "over-size Infanta of Spain." Extremely tall and striking, with dyed red hair and jutting jaw, nasal voice and neighing laugh, she wore extravagant costumes that resembled the plumage of an exotic bird. A baroque, flamboyant, eccentric and even grotesque personality, she had a malicious sense of humor and an exalted though indiscriminate devotion to the arts. Though not herself a good conversationalist, she was an encouraging and generous hostess. Her salons were characterized by high spirits and high-mindedness, pacifism, poetry and all that was ultra-modern in the arts.

Ottoline's vivid description of Conrad's looks, character, behavior and speech belied James' horrific forebodings:

> Conrad's appearance was really that of a Polish nobleman. His manner was perfect, almost too elaborate; so nervous and sympathetic that every fibre of him seemed electric, which gave him the air of a highly-polished and well-bred man.
>
> He talked English with a strong accent, as if he tasted his words in his mouth before pronouncing them; but he talked extremely well, though he always had the talk and manner of a foreigner. It seemed difficult to believe that this charming gentleman with high square shoulders, which he shrugged now and again so lightly, and the unmistakably foreign look, had been a captain in the English Merchant Service, and was, too, such a master of English prose. He was dressed very carefully in a blue double-breasted jacket. He talked on apparently with great freedom about his life—more ease and freedom indeed than an Englishman would have allowed himself. He spoke of the horrors of the Congo, from the moral and physical shock of which he said he had never recovered.[19]

Conrad had no interest in joining Ottoline's impressive social circle—which included D. H. Lawrence and eminent members of what came to be known as the Bloomsbury group—at her house in Garsington, near Oxford. But he did allow her to introduce him to Bertrand Russell in September 1913. Grandson of a prime minister, brother of an earl, author with A. N. Whitehead of *Principia Mathematica* and lecturer at Trinity College, Cambridge (where he invited Conrad for a weekend), Russell was one of the leading intellects in England. An immediate sympathy sprang up between the two men, who became good friends though they rarely saw each other. Russell's enthusiastic report to Ottoline was surprisingly emotional, for Conrad evoked a deep response in him by revealing his intimate thoughts about his Polish background, his experiences in Africa, his rootlessness and (an increasingly common subject) his exhaustion as a writer:

> It was *wonderful*. I *loved* him & I think he liked me. He talked a great deal about his work & life & aims, & about other writers. At first we were both shy & awkward—he praised Wells & Rothenstein & Zangwill & I began to despair. Then I asked him what he thought of Arnold Bennett, & found he despised him. Timidly I stood up for him, & he seemed interested. . . . Then we went [for] a little walk, & somehow grew very intimate. I plucked up courage to tell him what I find in his work—the boring down into things to get to the very bottom below the apparent facts. He seemed to

feel I had understood him; then he stopped & we just looked into each other's eyes for some time, & then he said he had grown to wish he could live on the surface & write differently, that he had grown frightened. His eyes at the moment expressed the inward pain & terror that one feels him always fighting. Then he said he was weary of writing & felt he had done enough, but had to go on & say it again. Then he talked a lot about Poland, & showed me an album of family photographs of the 60's—spoke about how dreamlike all that seems, & how he sometimes feels he ought not to have had children, because they have no roots or traditions or relations. He told me a great deal about his sea-faring time & about the Congo & Poland & all sorts of things. At first he was reserved even when he seemed frank but when we were out walking his reserve vanished & he spoke his inmost thoughts. It is impossible to say how much I loved him.

In November 1921 Russell linked Conrad to tradition and honored him (as G. F. W. Hope had done) by naming his son after the novelist. Deeply moved by Russell's tribute, which connected him to an illustrious English family, Conrad wrote: "Of all the incredible things that come to pass—that there should be one day a Russell bearing mine for one of his names is surely the most marvellous. . . . I am profoundly touched—more than I can express—that I should have been present to your mind in that way and at such a time."[20]

VIII

The great irony of Conrad's artistic career was that he had poor sales for his greatest books and popular acclaim for his late, inferior work, which he himself called "secondhand Conradese." During a chance meeting in Ceylon in 1909, Hugh Clifford had persuaded Gordon Bennett, the owner of the *New York Herald*, to serialize Conrad's latest novel in his newspaper and to buy the book in advance. Conrad had started and abandoned *Chance* (then called "Dynamite") as early as 1898, but inspired by the lucrative payment, he wrote the novel, with relative ease, between June 1911 and March 1912. In March Conrad gave Pinker his familiar, precise but less agonizing account of completing the book in the dark shadows of the night: "the last words were written at 3:10 a.m. just as my working lamp began to burn dimly and the fire in the grate to turn black. It's my *quickest* piece of work. About 140 thousand words in 9 months and 23 days. I went out and walked in the drive for half an hour. It was raining and the night was still very black." The epigraph from Sir Thomas

Browne on fortune was found by Arthur Marwood and the novel was gratefully dedicated to "Sir Hugh Clifford, K.C.M.G., whose steadfast friendship is responsible for the existence of these pages."

Because of its multiple narrators and frequent shifts in time, *Chance* (1913), of all Conrad's books, was the most difficult to read and the most unlikely to become a popular success. Henry James, in his essay of 1914 on "The Younger Generation," which caused Conrad considerable pain, spoke harshly of the narrative clutter: of its "eccentricities of recital" and "that baffled relation between the subject-matter and its emergence which we find constituted by the circumvallations of *Chance*." Yet the novel sold ten thousand copies in the first few months and—in contrast to *Under Western Eyes*, which had sold only four thousand—reached a record, for Conrad, of 13,200 in two years.

What factors, despite very considerable narrative obscurity and the characteristic Conradian theme of emotional isolation, accounted for the astonishing success of *Chance*? Apart from the serialization in the *New York Herald*, which exposed Conrad to his widest readership, there was a very successful publicity campaign organized by the young, energetic Alfred Knopf, who was then working for Doubleday, a long and favorable review by Sidney Colvin in the *Observer*, a catchy title, chapter headings for the first and only time in Conrad's fiction, the drawing of an attractive lady on the dust jacket,[21] a romantic and sentimental heroine who is cruelly victimized and then rescued by love, and, rare for Conrad, an affirmative (despite two sudden deaths at the end) as opposed to a tragic conclusion.

In *Chance*, Flora de Barral, the daughter of a confidence man and financial swindler who has been sent to prison, is harshly treated by her embittered governess and then rescued by her neighbors, Mr. and Mrs. Fyne. Flora contemplates suicide but is stopped by Mrs. Fyne's brother, Captain Roderick Anthony, the son of a famous but unpleasant poet (based on Coventry Patmore). Flora elopes with Anthony, who takes her on his ship, the *Ferndale*, but scrupulously refrains from consummating the marriage. When de Barral is released, he joins them but is bitterly jealous of Anthony. Powell, the second mate of the *Ferndale*, sees de Barral putting poison in Anthony's brandy and warns him of the danger. Wrongly thinking that Flora has tried to poison him, Anthony says he will let her off the ship at the next port. Flora replies that she does not want to leave, and they embrace. De Barral, his plot foiled, takes the fatal drink and dies. Later, a ship collides with the *Ferndale* and Anthony goes down with his vessel. Flora is saved and marries young Powell.

Like the heroine of James' *What Maisie Knew* (1897), Flora is an innocent victim who is contaminated by adult corruption. There are many obstacles impeding Flora's redemptive love for Anthony: her father's crime and then his jealousy, her cruel treatment by the evil governess (the best chapter in the novel), her own sense of unworthiness, her morbid sensitivity, her suicidal despair and her dubious desire to marry Anthony in order to provide a refuge for her father. But she eventually manages to overcome all these impediments.

The notorious Frédéric Humbert and Whitaker Wright financial frauds were the actual basis for de Barral's swindles. But there were also other intriguing biographical sources: Wells was the model for Mr. Fyne, Coventry Patmore for Carleon Anthony and Conrad himself—the son of a poet, who became a sea captain—for Roderick Anthony. Most importantly, as Thomas Moser notes, Conrad gave some of Ford's objectionable traits to the "cold, vain, self-deluded charlatan" de Barral, who "looks, talks, and acts like Ford." And (to extend Moser's argument) Ford's young daughters, Christina and Katherine—who were victimized by the anger and scandal when Ford left his wife, and by the ruin and disgrace when he was sent to prison in 1910 for failure to pay alimony—must have influenced Conrad's portrayal of the innocent Flora. Moreover, Conrad had told Galsworthy: "My view of M[arwood] is that he is a gallant-homme in the fullest sense," and in *Chance* he connects Captain Anthony to Arthur Marwood by using the identical phrase and writing that Anthony "is what the French call *un galant homme.*"[22] In *Chance*, the jealous Ford's figurative attempt to poison Marwood's reputation by accusing him of trying to seduce Elsie is transformed into de Barral's literal attempt to poison Anthony for loving his daughter. Thus, another aspect of Flora's complex character may have been based on Elsie Hueffer, the subject of a vicious sexual struggle, so painful to Conrad, between Marwood and Ford.

CHAPTER FIFTEEN

Return to Poland
and *Victory*

1914–1915

I

The astonishing success and unprecedented royalties of *Chance* combined with the enthusiastic invitation of the Retingers propelled the Conrads into a dangerous and disastrous journey to Austrian Poland that surpassed all the horrors of their previous expeditions to Belgium, Capri and Montpellier. On May 29, 1914, Conrad finished *Victory*, which had begun as the short story "Dollars" in April 1912. He was now eager for travel and for a change of routine.

He had predicted Austria and Germany's conflict with Russia in "Autocracy and War" when he wrote: "War is with us now; and, whether this one ends soon or late, war will be with us again." But in July 1914, when the lights were going out all over Europe, Conrad failed to notice the *Götterdämmerung*, refused to pay attention to what he called "alarmist rumours," and took his wife and children to Poland after an absence of twenty-one years. When the Austrian heir to the throne, Archduke Ferdinand, and his wife were assassinated in Sarajevo on June 28, Conrad thought he would simply be replaced by one of the numerous shadowy archdukes who populated central Europe, and casually told Richard Curle: "That's of no importance. . . . He wasn't anybody in particular. It won't lead to anything."

Why did Conrad, who was congenitally pessimistic, and Retinger, who was professionally concerned with international affairs, blindly walk into the midst of the conflagration only two days after Austria-Hungary delivered its ultimatum to Serbia? Conrad later explained his lack of awareness by stating that he had been entirely absorbed in his work and his plans, had not looked at a newspaper for a month, had failed to notice the ominous signs or to interpret them correctly and simply had not thought about the danger. When caught behind enemy lines in a Polish mountain resort, he excused himself by telling Pinker: "I have not found myself in this position through any fault of mine. No one believed in the war till the last moment when the mobilization order caught us in Cracow."[1]

Deceived perhaps by the fact that there had not been a major European war since Napoleon's defeat in 1815, Conrad allowed himself to be carried away by the enthusiasm of his family. The man who had seemed so strange and rootless in England desperately wanted to return to his past, to show his sons his origins and traditions, and to revisit his homeland as a successful author with an international reputation—though in Poland he was still better known as the son of Apollo Korzeniowski than as an English novelist. Retinger, eager to awaken Conrad's patriotic memories and to enlist him in the nationalist cause, took him to Cracow. But they never reached the house of Otolia's parents, which was only sixteen miles from the town, just across the frontier in Russian territory.

At Jessie's request, the Conrads and Retingers left Harwich for Hamburg on July 25 and took the long route to Europe across the North Sea. Conrad tried as usual to impress his traveling companions by establishing nautical intimacy with the captain of the ship. But, Retinger reported, the captain took Conrad for an author and a tourist, and looked down upon him "as only a sailor can look down on a landlubber. And the more Conrad fussed, the more the captain looked askance at him and finally he gave him clearly to understand that he thought him to be a liar. . . . Really the scene was painful, and there was some pathos in it."

After touring the port and the zoo in Hamburg, they continued their journey by train to Berlin and, having lost two trunks along the way, arrived at the Grand Hotel in Cracow late in the evening of July 28—when Austria declared war on Serbia. On his first night in Cracow (where he had lived during the last three months of Apollo's life), still restless despite the long journey, Conrad took a nostalgic moonlit walk with Borys into the immense and solitary Market Square in the center of the old town. He saw there the landmarks of his boyhood: the Cloth Hall, the Town Hall Tower and St. Florian's Gate (through which his father's funeral had passed in 1869), and heard the traditional bugle call sound the hour from the spire of the Gothic Church of the Holy Virgin. In "Poland Revisited" (1915) Conrad recorded the chiaroscuro of this solemn moment in exalted prose: "To our right the unequal massive towers of St. Mary's Church soared aloft into the ethereal radiance of the air, very black on their shaded sides, glowing with a soft phosphorescent sheen on the others. In the distance [three streets to the north] the Florian Gate, thick and squat under its pointed roof, barred the street with the square shoulders of the old city wall."

Jessie—more down to earth, struck by the strangeness of it all, immobilized by her crippled knee and confused by her inability to speak any foreign language—recalled, on first entering Cracow, that "the road paving seemed extremely primitive, and the odour of stables and bad draining was somewhat sickening." Noticing her disgusted expression, Conrad sharply remarked: "This is not England, my dear; don't expect too much." When they finally left the Cracow railway station, which sheltered many wounded soldiers, on their way out of the country in October, Jessie caught sight of a huge pail of human limbs—which might have appealed to Conrad's cannibalistic character, Falk. Though the two months among foreigners were a severe trial for Jessie's nerves, she said she understood her husband better after visiting his country: "So many characteristics that had been strange and unfathomable to me before, took, as it were, their right proportions." A friend who met the Conrads in Corsica in 1921 observed, more bluntly, that "Jessie hated the Poles, found them [as she often found Conrad] hysterical and unbalanced, slovenly and helpless, and, as for morals—they simply hadn't any!"[2]

On their first day in Cracow—where Conrad had attended an Austrian school from 1868 to 1874 and from where he had taken his leap into another life at the age of sixteen—he took Borys to visit the university and the Jagiellonian Library. The librarian, coincidentally called Jozef Korzeniowski, showed them Apollo's manuscripts and letters, which Conrad thought had been lost. Conrad was deeply moved by the letters, which expressed a touching concern for Apollo's young son. As they left the main quadrangle, they heard the news of the German ultimatum to Russia. Father and son also visited Apollo's grave in Radowice Cemetery, which bore the inscription "Victim of Muscovite Tyranny." Here, for the first and only time in his adult life, Conrad kneeled down in prayer.

The next day Conrad took his family to the Wawel, the historic hill with fine views of the old town and the Vistula River, on which stood the ancient castle of the Polish kings and the sacred cathedral where they had been crowned and buried. That evening in the Grand Hotel he suddenly recognized and embraced a white-haired man, Konstantyn Buszczynski, the son of his first guardian and his old schoolmate, who invited the Conrads to visit, the following day, his prosperous sugar beet estate ten miles outside the city. As they drove back through the flat farmland to the hotel on July 31, they saw all the horses, requisitioned by the Austrian soldiers, taken out of their plows and carts.

As soon as Britain declared war on Austria, Conrad, a naturalized British citizen, would risk internment for the duration of hostilities. On August 2, fearful of being imprisoned or caught in a battle, he took his family to stay in the Villa Konstantnowska, owned by Aniela Zagorska (the niece of Conrad's distant cousin Alexander Poradowski), in Zakopane, a resort in the Tatra Mountains, about sixty-five miles south of Cracow. As he explained to Galsworthy in a letter of August 1, he decided to retreat to this remote but pleasant place where he had friends rather than try to escape during the confusion and chaos of the first days of the war. They boarded the last civilian train that was allowed to leave Cracow for the next three weeks:

> This mobilization has caught us here. The trains will run for the civil population for three days more: but with Jessie as crippled as she is and Jack not at all well (temperature) I simply dare not venture on the horrors of a war-exodus. So urged and advised, and after long meditation (24 hours), I have decided to take myself and all the unlucky tribe to Zakopane (in the mountains, about 4 hours [by] rail from here) out of the way of all possible military operations. I had rather be stranded here, where I have friends, than try to get away and be caught perhaps in some small German town in the midst of the armies.

In the hotel on his fifth and last night in Cracow, Conrad met with a group of Polish intellectuals to discuss the fate of their country. Conrad was sympathetic to Austria, before it entered the war against Britain, and moved by his compatriots' faith in Jozef Pilsudski's Polish Legion, which was fighting for Austria against Russia. He listened to their expressions of hope that a major conflict between the powers that had divided Poland might eventually lead to some sort of independence, guaranteed by the Western powers, if the Russian territory were recaptured and placed under loose Austrian sovereignty. But he was, as usual, extremely pessimistic. In a letter of February 1918 to John Quinn, he recalled his words to the Poles on that sad evening and indirectly explained why he had originally left Poland: " 'If anybody has got to be sacrificed in this war it will be you. If there is any salvation to be found it is only in your own breasts, it is only by the force of your inner life that you will be able to resist the rottenness of Russia and the soullessness of

Germany. And this will be your fate for ever and ever. For nothing in the world can alter the force of facts.' "

And in his essay "First News" (August 1918), he explained how ugly and dangerous the situation looked to the friendless and hopeless country that was no longer able to take refuge in the stoic acceptance of its tragic fate: "I saw in those faces the awful desolation of men whose country, torn in three, found itself engaged in the contest with no will of its own and not even the power to assert itself at the cost of life. All the past was gone, and there was no future, whatever happened; no road which did not seem to lead to moral annihilation."

During his two stimulating but nerve-racking months in Zakopane, a mountain village surrounded by pastures, clear streams and waterfalls, Conrad sat for a crayon portrait by Kazimierz Gorski and read a great deal of modern Polish literature. He endlessly analyzed news of the volatile political situation that, filtered through Austrian propaganda, gradually reached them. He endured the strain of living amidst compatriots who dismally watched the ruin of all their hopes. And through Walter Hines Page, a founder of Doubleday and now American ambassador to England, he got in touch with Frederick Courtland Penfield, who during 1913–17 was the American ambassador to Austria-Hungary. A Catholic, born in New Haven in 1855 and educated at Princeton, Penfield began his career as a journalist on the *Hartford Courant*. He had served in diplomatic posts in London and Cairo, and was married to one of the wealthiest women in the world.[3]

On October 8, after a two-month wait, the Conrads finally, with the help of Polish friends in Zakopane, obtained permission to travel by train from Cracow to Vienna. Setting out after midnight during a heavy snowstorm, they traveled to the nearest railway station in an open carriage drawn by a pair of wild and shaggy horses, which must have reminded Conrad of the open sleigh ride to Uncle Tadeusz's estate in the early 1890s.

They spent five days in Vienna, where Jessie, with stubborn persistence and the help of an interpreter, tracked down and recovered in the main railroad station the two trunks that had been lost en route to Berlin in late July. With the help of Ambassador Penfield, whom Conrad met in Vienna, they were permitted to leave the enemy capital on October 18 and reached Milan, in still-neutral Italy, on the 20th. A week later, Conrad reported, orders were issued to have them detained until the conclusion of hostilities. He described their narrow escape, during a lull in the war, in an exciting letter to Galsworthy:

The great rush of German and Austrian re-inforcing troops was over for a time and the Russians were falling back after their first advance. So we started suddenly, at one in the morning, on 7th [i.e., 8th] Oct. in a snow-storm in an open conveyance of sorts to drive 30 miles to a small railway station where there was a chance of finding something better than a horse-truck to travel in with *ma petite famille*. From there to Cracow, some fifty miles, we sat *18* hours in a train smelling of disinfectants and resounding with groans. . . . Our journey to Vienna was at comparatively lightning speed; 26 hours for a distance which in normal conditions is done in five hours and a half. But in Vienna I had to go to bed for five days. Directly I could put foot on the ground again we made a fresh start, making for Italy.

The Conrads made their way from Milan to Genoa and visited the old port, which he was to describe in the opening chapters of his last novel, *Suspense*, before boarding the *Vondel*, a Dutch mail boat en route from Java, on October 25. They reached England on November 3 and Conrad once again took to his bed with a severe attack of gout. In 1920 he dedicated *The Rescue* to Frederick Penfield: "in memory of the rescue of certain distressed travellers effected by him in the world's great storm of the year 1914."

In 1914 Richard Curle introduced Conrad to new friends, Ralph Wedg-wood, a railway magnate from the illustrious family of pottery manu-facturers, and his wife, Iris. Born in 1874 and educated at Clifton and Trinity College, Cambridge, Ralph became a brigadier-general and di-rector of docks in France from 1916 to 1919. Conrad dedicated *Within the Tides* (1915) to the Wedgwoods "in gratitude for their charming hospi-tality in the last month of peace," and Ralph became an executor of Conrad's will. Conrad's letters to the Wedgwoods, written in the months following his return to England, show that he was profoundly disturbed by the war and unable to concentrate on his own work: "However reasonably optimistic one can be, the thoughts of this war sit on one's chest like a nightmare. I am painfully aware of being crippled, of being idle, of being useless with a sort of absurd anxiety. . . . It seems almost criminal levity to talk at this time of books, stories, publication. This war attends my uneasy pillow like a nightmare. I feel oppressed even in my sleep and the moment of waking brings no relief."

Dame Veronica Wedgwood, the distinguished historian, who was four years old when Conrad first met her parents, explained the basis of his friendship with Ralph and provided a rare glimpse of Conrad from a child's point of view:

My father admired Conrad's writing and unusual personality and history, and Conrad probably admired my father's intelligence and cultural and intellectual interests. (He had been an "Apostle" at Cambridge.) Richard Curle was a mutual friend.

As a young child I was impressed by what seemed an exotic personality with beautiful if overelaborate manners and a funny accent. I "approved" of him because he took great notice of me as a child. I have a recollection of a good looking, not very tall man coming occasionally to see me in the nursery.[4]

II

In *Victory* (published in 1915), the last major novel he completed before the Great War and (apart from *The Shadow-Line* in 1917) his last great work, Conrad returned to the setting of his earliest novels, the Malay Archipelago. Most of the action takes place on the remote island of Samburan, near Sourabaya, on the north coast of Java in the Dutch East Indies. There Axel Heyst, following his father's pessimistic philosophy, has attempted to isolate himself from human entanglements.

While briefly staying in Sourabaya at a hotel run by the malicious Schomberg, Heyst, prompted by a kindly instinct, rescues Lena, an itinerant prostitute in a musical whorehouse run by the cruel Zangiacomos, and brings her back to the island.[5] Like Heyst with Lena, Conrad rescued the young Jessie from a commonplace existence, took her to an island (the Île-Grande in Brittany) for their honeymoon and found he had nothing to say to her.

Enraged that Heyst has "stolen" Lena from him, Schomberg sends an evil trio—Mr. Jones, Martin Ricardo and Pedro, who have been gambling in his hotel and intimidating his guests—to steal Heyst's treasure (which does not actually exist) and to destroy his enemy. *Victory* portrays, in that violent confrontation, Heyst's conflicting desires for solitude and emotional commitment, and Lena's self-sacrificial wish to protect him, which merely intensifies his lack of feeling and inability to respond to her.

The main characters in *Victory*—also the title of a story by Cunninghame Graham in *Thirteen Stories* (1900)—are closely connected to those of Conrad's earlier works. Lena and Captain Whalley in "The End of the Tether" share the same misguided optimism, Heyst and Decoud in *Nostromo* the same cynical pessimism. The powerful and influential fathers of both Heyst and Charles Gould in *Nostromo* forcefully indicated the paths for their sons to follow and both sons, to their fathers' great sorrow, define their lives in opposition to their parents' predestined plans.

Victory has many similarities in plot and character to the second half of *Lord Jim*. Stein, a good German, is balanced by Schomberg, an evil German who appears in both novels. Captain Davidson, a narrator of the novel, is like Captain Marlow; Heyst's servant Wang resembles Jim's servant Tamb Itam. Jim is morally crippled by his cowardly behavior on the *Patna*; Heyst, who believes: "I only know that he who forms a tie is lost. The germ of corruption has entered into his soul," is emotionally crippled by his father's negative philosophy. Both are unable to live up to their own ideals and take refuge in a remote tropical island. Jim rescues Jewel, Heyst rescues Lena; both men rather archly say: "command me." Both women adore their men and try in vain to protect them. Though Gentleman Brown is supposed to be the son of a baronet and Heyst is a Swedish baron, the closest link is between Gentleman Brown and Gentleman Jones. Both arrive on the island by boat, unexpectedly and in decrepit condition. Both villains menacingly suggest that the heroes have had the same experiences, motives and guilt as they themselves, and fiercely condemn what they consider to be a guise of moral superiority. In *Victory*, as in *Lord Jim*, there was "an assumption of common experience; a sickening suggestion of common guilt, of secret knowledge that was like a bond of their minds and of their hearts."[6] Both heroes are unarmed and unable to defend themselves because of their involvement with a woman. Jim lacks the will to kill Gentleman Brown, Heyst lacks the spirit to kill Gentleman Jones, and both willingly die for idealistic reasons.

Victory is Conrad's most misunderstood, underrated and controversial novel. Critics invariably quote the ostensible theme—"woe to the man whose heart has not learned while young to hope, to love—and to put its trust in life!"—as a life-affirming exhortation that exemplifies the weaknesses of the book: its obvious idea, wooden characters and melodramatic plot. But the theme is actually more complex than this. Since Heyst had not learned the lessons of the heart *while young*, he can never learn them later in life and is doomed to emotional sterility. The novel does not reveal Conrad's failure to depict a mature love relationship; it portrays, with great subtlety and daring, the failure of love in an idyllic setting.

Heyst's emotional and sexual failure negates Lena's responsiveness, capacity to love and trust in life. And the idea that a woman's sacrificial devotion can redeem a man who is incapable of love is undermined by a concurrent and even more powerful theme: that men who withdraw from normal human relations and deny life are doomed and damned beyond redemption. Conrad's discreet sexual allusions reveal the subtle tension between the overt and covert themes, and the complex motivation of the characters. They also suggest that the extravagant emotions and violent actions are inspired by the perverse sexual passions that surge beneath the surface of the novel.

Conrad's portrayal of the misogynist Jones, an evil homosexual who nevertheless has the most forceful and impressive speeches in the novel, reveals that he was fascinated and frightened by what was then considered sexual perversion. But the literary and social conventions of the time (which made characters like Ricardo call his enemies "ill-conditioned skunks" and "animated cucumbers") precluded any direct discussion of this theme. When Macdonald Hastings, who was dramatizing the novel, asked Conrad to explain the character of Jones, he evasively replied: "There is a strain of peculiar craziness about the gentleman. The novel only faintly suggests it."[7] *Victory* is a deliberate compromise between Conrad's desire to write openly about homosexuality and his need to suppress the theme and to surround the sexual core of the novel with reticence and evasion. This conventional restriction exaggerated Conrad's characteristic tendency toward ambiguity, allusiveness and abstraction.

Conrad's extremely complex narration, in which the action shifts back and forth in time and is usually related indirectly, makes it impossible to know exactly what is going on between Morrison (a sea captain whom Heyst rescues) and Heyst, Heyst and Lena, Lena and Ricardo, or Ricardo and Jones: the sexual relationships of all the characters remain ambiguous. Their story is related partly by a representative white man in Java and partly by Captain Davidson, who could not possibly be aware of the dialogue of Heyst and Lena when they are alone on Samburan. Davidson is a kindly, *normal* figure who is incapable of understanding the strange sexuality of Jones and Ricardo and dismisses them as grotesque rascals. His lack of insight ironically underlines the contrast between the conventional and the subterranean themes.

Conrad also accentuates the ambiguity of the characters by emphasizing their extreme isolation and the unreality of the exotic setting. And all the characters deceive each other, for base or noble motives. Heyst, Lena and Mrs. Schomberg deceive Schomberg, Schomberg deceives Jones and Ricardo, Ricardo twice deceives Jones, Lena deceives Ricardo, Wang deceives Heyst, and both Heyst and Lena fear they have been deceived by each other. At the violent climax of the novel Heyst, Lena,

Jones and Ricardo meet their death in a chaos of misapprehension. Finally, even the minor characters are not what they seem to be. Zangiacomo is really a German with a dyed beard; the oppressed and terrified Mrs. Schomberg hides behind a mask and is quite capable of resolute action; the manly, military, bearded and broad-chested Schomberg is actually a coward; and "plain Mr. Jones" is neither plain, nor a gentleman, nor Jones.[8]

Victory's structure is based on a recurrent pattern of human relationships. Heyst's rescue of Lena is like his rescue of Morrison, Ricardo's assault on Lena is like Schomberg's, Lena's dependence on Heyst is like Ricardo's dependence on Jones, and Ricardo's tenuous control of the violent Pedro is like Jones' control of Ricardo. Even Wang's relations with his wife, whom he persuades to run away with him and then keeps safely hidden in the jungle, parodies Heyst's inability to protect Lena. The effect of this intricate pattern is to bind all the characters in a common tragic destiny and to emphasize the irony of Heyst's desire to remain detached and isolated—invulnerable because elusive.

Heyst's relationship with Morrison is introduced as a subject of speculation and gossip: "Heyst became associated with Morrison on terms about which people were in doubt." No one knew the real reason why they became partners because each wanted to keep it hidden: Morrison out of embarrassment, Heyst out of delicacy. A rumor soon sprang up that Heyst, "having obtained some mysterious hold on Morrison, had fastened himself on him and was sucking him dry," and Schomberg warned people not to get caught in Heyst's web. But the narrator makes it clear that when Heyst rescued Morrison from the Portuguese authorities on Timor, he soothed him and shared his distress. Unlike the traders who had a wife in every port, Morrison was "rather ascetic than otherwise." He begged Heyst, like a lover, not to "spurn and ruin him," and urged Heyst to become a partner and retrieve his money, though Morrison's foolish generosity had ruined his trading ventures. So Heyst, the temperamental opposite of Morrison, became the victim of Morrison's emotional demands.

Morrison's pathetic belief that Heyst was his divine savior, and Heyst's feeling that he had rescued Morrison from one fate only to deliver him to a worse one, made Heyst "deem himself guilty of Morrison's death." Thus Schomberg's venomous slanders that their homosexual friendship suddenly ended when Heyst discarded Morrison and sent him to die in England, which Lena repeats to Heyst, exacerbate his sensitivity and guilt, and make him more vulnerable to the evil designs of Jones.

When Heyst first tells Lena about Morrison he is unaware that she has already heard Schomberg's version of the story. He mentions "some hidden weakness" in his character and emphasizes the similarity of his relationship to Morrison and to Lena: "I use the word [cornered] because it expresses the man's situation exactly, and because you just used it yourself." Lena's response to this casual allusion is extremely emotional:

> "What do you say?" she whispered, astounded. "A man!"
> Heyst laughed at her wondering eyes.
> "No! No! I mean in his own way."
> "I knew very well that it couldn't be anything like that," she observed under her breath.[9]

Heyst's forced laughter disguises his uneasiness about Lena's violent reaction. His reassurance that Morrison was cornered by financial trouble is met by her *sotto voce* relief that Morrison was not, as she had feared, a cornered homosexual.

When Heyst actually mentions the name of Morrison, Lena repeats it in an appalled tone, suddenly realizes that her rescuer was involved with Morrison and is profoundly upset. She then astounds him by repeating Schomberg's accusation that "there never were such loving friends to look at as you two; then, when you got all you wanted out of him and got thoroughly tired of him, too, you kicked him out to go home and die." And this, of course, is what the insecure Lena fears will happen if Heyst also grows weary of her clinging emotional demands and awkward attempts to express her gratitude. Despite Heyst's strenuous denials, there is something about his character and behavior that makes Lena retain her suspicions about his dubious relations with Morrison. Her doubts about his rectitude have the moral effect of a stab in the back and help to undermine his resistance to Jones and Ricardo.

Lena is the focus of passion in the novel and inspires powerful emotions in Schomberg, Heyst and Ricardo, though none of them is sexually successful with her. Both Schomberg and Heyst offer to liberate Lena from Zangiacomo's bondage and to provide her with protection and security. The difference between them, of course, is that the ludicrous Schomberg, the victim of a belated passion, revolts Lena with his crude sexual demands while the more passive and gentlemanly Heyst (who shrinks from the idea of competition with Schomberg) merely says, "Pray command me." Lena runs away with Heyst not because she is attracted to his bald head and long mustaches, but because she is desperate to escape from both Zangiacomo and Schomberg. And Mrs.

Schomberg, who knows that her husband wants to get rid of her, helps Lena not out of sympathy and charity, but out of a desire to protect her own marriage and security.

Though Schomberg disliked Heyst before the arrival of Lena (because of his involvement with Morrison, his aloofness and even his temperate drinking habits), the thwarted passion, the wounded vanity and especially the humiliation of being deceived and defeated by someone he considered far less virile than himself are responsible for his violent hatred. Schomberg also feels that, like Heyst, Jones and Ricardo use his hotel as a base for their secret plots against him. And when he concocts the story of Heyst's treasure and sends the avenging furies to Samburan, he hopes to free himself from their dangerous presence at the same time that he destroys Heyst and Lena. Ricardo represents Schomberg's lust for Lena just as Jones manifests his hatred of Heyst.

Heyst's ambivalent rescue of Lena, which is prompted by a generous feeling that his father would have defined as a form of contempt called pity, is both a repetition of his sympathetic response to Morrison and an unusually impulsive act. Heyst is known as a "queer chap," completely detached from "feminine associations" and even earthly passions. And when Davidson hears that his friend has run off with Lena he can hardly believe it and exclaims: "He's not the man for it . . . being a gentleman only makes it worse." Davidson's statement is ambiguous, but like Schomberg, Ricardo and Jones, he seems to question Heyst's manliness. By calling Heyst a gentleman he not only stresses the social differences between Heyst and Lena, but also uses the term that is constantly applied to Jones and that Jones derisively applies to Heyst in order to link the Swede with himself. When Heyst first looks at Lena (whose face is not described) he has "the sensation of a new experience." They immediately reverse their male and female roles as Lena challenges him to do something to save her and Heyst, hiding his ineffectuality behind a cavalier statement, says "What would you wish me to do?"

Heyst and Lena have nothing to say to each other, either in Sourabaya or Samburan, and their basic lack of communication is symbolized by the profound silence of the island. Heyst's emotions are severely repressed and Lena cannot eliminate the fear and distrust of women that he inherited from his father. Heyst defensively insists that he is sceptical and has no illusions, and even when his heart becomes "infected" he never forgets how easily women betray men.

Like Lena, Heyst never knew his mother and was devoted to his father, who also had failed to learn *while young* to put his trust in life. His father's portrait and library dominate Heyst's small house on Samburan and emphasize his permanent influence, and Lena's tenderness, love and self-sacrifice cannot overcome Heyst's spiritual and emotional starvation. The passive Nordic gloom of the Heysts is characterized by a melancholy atmosphere, mutual unhappiness, lack of understanding, failure to communicate and silent despair.

Lena tells Heyst that she will stand by him as she once stood by her father; and after she has helped Ricardo to escape from her room, Heyst (who has failed to protect her against Ricardo) assumes his fatherly role and puts the exhausted Amazon to bed as if she were a child. Though Heyst feels more comfortable in the role of a father than a lover, Lena refuses to be filial, transposes her repressed feelings from Ricardo to Heyst and experiences a kind of vicarious orgasm: "She felt the woman's need to give way, the sweetness of surrender. . . . She was surprised by a wave of languid weakness that came over her, embracing and enveloping her like warm water, with a noise in her ears as of a breaking sea."[10]

Lena quite naturally complained of her solitude in Schomberg's hotel, and seemed white and spectral when Heyst first embraced her. But on the island, when she falls in love with Heyst, Lena is still intensely lonely and feels that her very existence depends on a man who is unable to respond to her love and to satisfy her desperate need for emotional reassurance. Lena's fears are intensified by Wang, who seems to vanish out of existence rather than out of sight; and she tells Heyst: "if you were to stop thinking of me I shouldn't be in the world at all. . . . I can only be what you think I am."

Lena's ontological fears and sense of unreality are presumably caused by her lack of sexual relations with Heyst, who once tried to sleep with her but was unable to do so. They are in the archetypal romantic situation of lovers alone (for three months) on a desert island, and though Heyst's vanity is flattered by the (nominal) possession of a woman and Lena's by a belief that she can provide the absolute sacrifice that will satisfy Heyst's obscure needs, they are both deluded and unhappy. Heyst attempts to defend his emotional sterility and sexual impotence by alluding to his "hidden weakness," suggesting that love *prevents* sex and stating that "when one's heart has been broken into the way you have broken into mine, all sorts of weaknesses are free to enter." Heyst's complaint makes Lena feel guilty about *his* sexual inadequacies as well as her sexual desires. She rather fearfully asks, "What more do you want from me?"; he seems to want companionship without emotional responsibility and answers, "The impossible, I suppose." And her pathetic apology: "I only wish I could give you something more, or better, or whatever it is you want,"[11] suggests she is both frightened and desperate.

Their mutual misunderstanding is so complete that when Heyst hides Lena from Jones and Ricardo for her safety, she thinks he is ashamed of her. Lena's almost suicidal desire for self-sacrifice is at once an attempt to punish herself for living "unlawfully" with Heyst, to compensate for Heyst's impotence by elevating their relationship to a higher plane, and to make herself worthy of his love. The abject Lena realizes that she can never hope to understand or to satisfy Heyst, and feels ashamed of her emotions, "as if her passion were of a hopelessly lower quality, unable to appease some exalted and delicate desire of his superior soul." This is Lena's rationalization of the superiority of Heyst's coldness to her all-too-human passion.

Heyst's sexual doubts and fears are intensified by Lena's guilty confession: "I am not what they call a good girl." This allusion to her extensive sexual experience—the inevitable result of an abandoned childhood and the hopeless grip of poverty—confirms Schomberg's accusation (euphemistically expressed in the novel) that Lena is a whore: "He shot out an infamous word which made Davidson start. That's what the girl was." Lena's admission also lends substance to Ricardo's claim (which parallels Jones' claim about Heyst) that he and Lena have a great deal in common. Most important, it worries and intimidates Heyst (though not, as Lena thinks, for moral reasons) by forcing him to compare his own lack of "feminine associations" with Lena's extensive experience.

Heyst reveals that he has neither conscious nor subconscious desires for women and tells her directly: "I've never killed a man or loved a woman—not even in my thoughts, not even in my dreams. . . . To slay, to love—the greatest enterprises of life upon a man! And I have no experience of either."[12] Just after this assertion Heyst and Lena have an apparently unsatisfactory sexual encounter. "With her hand she signed imperiously to him to leave her alone—a command which Heyst did not obey." The next chapter begins, according to novelistic convention, as they get up from the ground and Lena arranges her hair while Heyst retrieves her sun helmet. It is significant that Heyst makes his unusual overture at the very moment he "detests" Lena for believing Schomberg's slanders and is "disgusted" with himself for being contaminated by the evil in the world. His sexual approach to her is inspired not by love or passion, but by a resolute desire to overcome his feelings of inadequacy and to experience one of the two "greatest enterprises of life."

It is clear from their subsequent dialogue that Heyst's sexual advance has failed to satisfy Lena and merely heightened her belief that he does not love her. They also intensify Heyst's feeling of incompleteness and of "the *physical* and moral sense of the *imperfections* of their relations." When they return home he goes straight to his books and tries to sanction (or rationalize) his dissatisfaction with one of his father's philosophical epigrams: "Of the stratagems of life the most cruel is the consolation of love—the most subtle, too; for the desire is the bed of dreams." Lena seems to challenge this high-minded cynicism with the frank accusation: "You should try to love me!" Heyst replies in confusion, "Try . . . but it seems to me—," and then falls silent. Though his sexual attempt has been unsuccessful, he comforts himself with his favorite belief that "he who forms a tie is lost. The germ of corruption has entered into his soul."[13]

The difference between Lena's and Heyst's view of reality is reflected in her desire for a victorious self-sacrifice and his belief that she has corrupted their Eden. As Lena recklessly plans to disarm Ricardo and save Heyst, even at the cost of her own life, Heyst (especially at the moment he watches Ricardo kissing Lena's feet) sees Lena as the disobedient Eve who awakens the original Adam in him and introduces evil into their paradise. He quite unjustly blames her for the intrusion of Jones and Ricardo and for the treachery and desertion of Wang.

Heyst realizes that his inability to love is related to his inability to kill, but he is unable to assert himself when Jones and Ricardo invade the island and when Wang steals his revolver. While Ricardo strokes his knife and Jones fondles his gun, Heyst is profoundly aware that he is disarmed, without a weapon, "not sufficiently equipped," that is, unmanned and impotent in the physical as well as the sexual sense. Whereas Schomberg felt that he lost his courage when he lost Lena and would be a much stronger man if she were at his side, Heyst feels that Lena weakens him, makes him vulnerable, and forces him to lie, to cringe and to humiliate himself for her sake: "All his defences were broken now. Life had him fairly by the throat." By contrast, Lena is inspired by Heyst's affection and seems to grow in physical as well as moral stature. In Schomberg's hotel she seemed small, weak and frightened, but when Ricardo first spies her "she loomed up strangely big and shadowy at the other end of the long, narrow room."

Though Heyst never desires Lena, she attracts Ricardo as she had attracted Schomberg. Ricardo's instinctive violence is barely suppressed and only held in subjection by the rational influence of Jones; his passion contrasts with Jones' passivity and apathy just as Lena's contrasts with Heyst's. Ricardo recognizes their similarities, for both have their origins in the dregs of mankind and both are precariously dependent upon gentlemen with strange sexual habits.

The sexual relationship of Lena and Ricardo reveals aspects of their characters that are repressed in their liaisons with Heyst and Jones. When Ricardo emphasizes their common background, attacks their gentlemen and undermines Lena's fragile security, he is trying to convince her that he can give her what Heyst has failed to provide. He wants to display, not hide Lena, and naïvely asks her to call him "husband." Though Ricardo increases Lena's doubts about Heyst, he also intensifies her guilt and her craving for sacrifice and redemption.

Since the passionate Lena is a "bad girl" with considerable sexual experience and Heyst is clearly unable to satisfy her emotional or physical needs, she subconsciously responds to Ricardo's sexual assault. Yet it is obvious that if Lena is to remain the redemptive heroine and achieve the ironic victory, she cannot actually be raped by Ricardo. Just as we realize that Davidson could not possibly know what he is narrating and that Ricardo would not really speak as he does in the novel, so we are also aware that the rape scene would not actually take place as Conrad describes it. Though he overtly portrays a conventional scene in which the heroine defeats the villain, he also covertly yet unmistakably suggests an alternative—and more convincing—reality.

There is considerable evidence to suggest that Ricardo's attempted rape has upon Lena the psychological and emotional effect of an actual rape, and that he thinks she derives a certain satisfaction from his violent attack. Despite Conrad's explanations, it is impossible to believe that Lena could successfully resist the surprise attack of the armed Ricardo; her "fingers like steel" and "muscles like a giant" are a startling contrast to the frail and frightened Lena of Sourabaya, with her "slender white bust" and prettily crossed feet. Ricardo's assault and her complicity in his escape lead to an unusual bond of intimacy between them. He believes "A woman that does not make a noise after an attempt of that kind has tacitly condoned the offence," and he talks to her tenderly, as if they had slept together. He has, in fact, torn open her sarong and seen her naked body, and his "sudden relaxation of the terrific hug" leaves him "crestfallen."

Finally, Ricardo's knife is an obvious symbol of his penis. He boasts "I carry a pretty deadly thing about me" and Lena remarks that he could rape her only "with that thing stuck in my side." When Lena disobeys Heyst and secretly meets Ricardo in the evening, the phallic connotations of the bone-handled weapon become glaring: "a tremor of impatience to clutch the frightful thing, glimpsed once and unforgettable, agitated her hands." Lena symbolically consummates her sexual combat with Ricardo when she seductively steals his knife: "she let it slip into the fold of her dress, and laid her forearms with clasped fingers over her knees, which she pressed desperately together. The dreaded thing was out of sight at last. She felt a dampness break out all over her."[14]

Though Ricardo is sick of crawling on his belly for Jones and wants to free himself from his master's sexual domination, he gets perverse pleasure from debasing himself before Lena and makes the paradoxical but revealing statement about his own fantasies: "What you want is a man, a master that will let you put the heel of your shoe on his neck." Ricardo's mastery consists of persuading Lena to satisfy his masochistic urges. He substitutes foot-fetishism for sexual intercourse and tells Lena that he is "as tired as if I had been pouring my life-blood here on these planks for you to dabble your white feet in." When Ricardo surrenders his knife he demands her foot, and as she slowly brings it out from under her dress he throws himself on it greedily and "clasping her ankle, pressed his lips time after time to the instep, muttering gasping words that were like sobs, making little noises that resembled the sounds of grief and distress."[15]

Ricardo's assault on Lena illuminates her unhappy relationship with Heyst as well as Ricardo's connection with Jones. Though Ricardo's violent lust for Lena is an ironic reflection of Heyst's sexual failure, he achieves orgasm with Lena in a fashion that is as bizarre as his relations with Jones. All three men (as well as Schomberg and Wang) share a common misogyny, which is manifested in Heyst's impotence, Jones' homosexuality and Ricardo's exhibitionism, voyeurism and fetishism.

Ricardo's relationship with Jones, as everyone notices, is scarcely secretarial. Ricardo admits that Jones "seemed to touch me inside somewhere," and at the first opportunity he attaches himself to his Governor and becomes, as Jones salaciously boasts to Heyst, "absolutely identified with all my ideas, wishes, and even whims." Ricardo is Jones' paid lover and has the "morals of a cat," and the marks on his face suggest the great as well as the small pox. Ricardo enjoys deceiving Jones, having furtive little flings (which never amount to anything and are therefore tolerated by Jones), and attempting to excite himself and confirm his masculinity by making sexual overtures to women, like Lena, whom he threatens with violence but is actually afraid to sleep with.

Conrad is most explicit about the sexual anomalies of the handsome and shrill-voiced Jones, an invalid who dies in his gorgeous blue silk dressing-gown. Jones has a violent and passionate hatred of women, and his obviously feminine eyelashes and waspish penciled eyebrows make him appear "unnatural," "vicious," "depraved" and "disgusting." In Mexico, Jones had picked up ragged and bare-legged street urchins for his pleasure, and the brazen girls asked Ricardo "if the English *caballero* in the *posada* was a monk in disguise, or if he has taken a vow to the *sanctissima [sic] madre* not to speak to a woman, or whether— You can imagine what fairly free-spoken girls will ask."[16]

During Heyst's confrontations with Jones—which parallel the previous encounters of Heyst with Lena, and of Lena with Ricardo, and which lead directly to the tragic climax of the novel—Jones confirms Schomberg's accusations and Lena's suspicions by recognizing the homosexual element in Heyst that has led to his fear of women, his guilt and his impotence. Though Jones never directly accuses Heyst of homosexuality, he enjoys implicating his victim in his own corruption and stresses the similarities between himself and his secret sharer.

Jones complains bitterly to Heyst that he was hounded out of society by a lot of highly moral souls and states that his presence on the island is not more morally reprehensible than Heyst's: "Something has driven you out [too]—the originality of your ideas, perhaps. Or your *tastes*." And in their final meeting Jones insists that he has remained closer to his origins, breeding and traditions than Heyst: "Not everyone can divest himself of the prejudices of a gentleman as easily as you have done." Though Jones knows nothing of Heyst except the malicious gossip he has heard indirectly from Schomberg via Ricardo, he is able to wound Heyst with insinuations that awaken his guilt about Morrison. Jones considers himself more open and honest than Heyst because he admits his homosexuality instead of trying to repress and deny it, and preys on the world instead of evading it. Jones carries the philosophy of Heyst's father (who also wore "an ample blue dressing-gown") to the logical extreme of negation. For just as Heyst (like his father) believes that men are evil and the earth is "the appointed hatching planet of calumny enough to furnish the whole universe," so Jones believes he is justified in exacting retribution through ferocity and violence.

While Ricardo is pursuing his masochistic gratifications, Heyst awakens Jones' doubts about his faithful secretary just as Ricardo had stirred Lena's suspicions of Heyst, and Jones discovers that the well-groomed Ricardo (who has recently become concerned with his appearance) has been deceiving him with Lena. In a rage of jealousy and disgust Jones rushes out to murder Ricardo and finds him kissing Lena's feet. At that fatal moment, when Jones aims at his lover and shoots Lena, Heyst becomes painfully aware of his sexual failures and is convinced that Lena has deceived him.

When the dying Lena insists "I would never, never have let him . . . get it back," even if she had to stab Ricardo, she reiterates the thematic connection between loving and killing. Heyst repeats that though women have their own weapon (guile), he has been a "disarmed" (impotent) man all his life. Then, in a moment of sudden fury, Heyst seems to recognize Lena's corporality for the first time and to re-enact Ricardo's assault: he "started tearing open the front of the girl's dress" and stared at the "little black hole," made by the bullet, beneath her swelling breast. Lena's sexual excitement during her morbid consummation with Heyst accounts for her swelling breast as the blood flows from her wound, and she clasps Ricardo's knife "like a child reaching eagerly for a toy." Despite his final "thematic" pronouncement, Heyst never abandons the idea that "he who forms a tie is lost"; and his inability to grant Lena's dying wish to take her in his arms—even as a formal gesture of consolation—confirms the emptiness of her thoroughly ironic victory.[17] As the villains kill each other, Heyst is agonized by his impotence and his guilt about Lena's meaningless sacrifice. He "couldn't stand his thoughts before her dead body" and attempts to punish and purify himself by a fiery death.

Homosexuality, though rarely made explicit, has an important function in *Victory*. The clever, witty, depraved Jones is a classic villain who is guilty of murder and theft as well as sexual corruption. But Heyst's repressed homosexuality and impotence symbolize in sexual terms the conflict between his desire for isolation and his need for love. His relationship with Lena (who is also called Alma) represents a spiritual as well as a sexual struggle, for she is trying to save him not from death, but from a kind of death-in-life that is the tragic legacy of his father's philosophy. Conrad uses the homosexual theme to portray Heyst's emotional sterility and denial of life. Heyst's failure to respond to Lena's love after his first generous impulse leads to the victory of pessimism and negation over devotion and sacrifice.

Victory, published in America in March 1915 and in England in September, was even more successful than *Chance*. It also had a much more provocative dust wrapper on which Lena, with long hair streaming on to the breast of her sarong, straight-arms the pajama-clad Ricardo, who cowers on a chest after attempting to assault her. Conrad soon earned his enormous advances—£1,000 for serial rights and £850 for book rights—for the first and second printings were exhausted on the date of publication, and his most exciting and poignant novel sold an unprecedented 11,000 copies in the first three days. Until the success of *Chance*, all Conrad's English editions were printed in runs of between 1,500 and 3,500 copies. After *Chance*, *Victory* had a first English printing of 10,000, *The Arrow of Gold* (1919) of 20,000 and *The Rescue* (1920) of 25,000. But Conrad was unable to capitalize on his long-awaited success as an author during the war years. And he could not shake off his depression until 1916, when he met and fell in love with the beautiful and bohemian American journalist Jane Anderson.

CHAPTER SIXTEEN

Jane Anderson

1916–1917

I

The vivacious and reckless Jane Anderson, ignored or neglected by Conrad's biographers, had a significant influence on his life.[1] He fell in love with her, met her secretly and—seizing the last chance for sexual romance—wrote her passionate love letters. She became his mistress in the summer of 1916 and was the only woman, apart from Jessie, whom we know he slept with. She distracted and rejuvenated him when he was depressed by the war, and inspired him to engage in the propaganda effort by going on sorties in planes and ships, and by writing of his experiences. (Rebecca West wrote that Jane "was always going up in planes and down in submarines.") Jane flirted with Borys, who fell for her in Paris during his leave from military service. She also became Joseph Retinger's mistress, broke up his marriage and, by arousing Conrad's jealousy, damaged their friendship. Jane stimulated Conrad's interest in journalism, in films and in America. And she was the principal model for the seductive Rita de Lastaola in *The Arrow of Gold*, the first novel he published after the war.[2]

An only child, Jane was born Foster Anderson in Atlanta, Georgia, on January 6 in about 1888.[3] Her mother, Ellen Luckie, a wealthy and beautiful socialite, was the daughter of Foster Luckie, who owned and developed a great deal of property in Atlanta, and for whom Luckie Street was named. Soon after Jane's birth her apparently ill-matched parents separated, and her rough, likable father, Robert "Red" Anderson, took off for the Southwest. Kitty Crawford, Jane's college friend, described him as "a tall, handsome, reckless-looking man with a humorous quirk to his mouth and blue-steel sharpness in his eyes." Retinger gave a more colorful and no doubt exaggerated account of Jane's father:

When I first met him he was seventy-eight. His breakfast consisted of a bottle of whiskey and a 2 lb. steak. Anderson had been an associate of Buffalo Bill. He was the head of the police while the Panama Canal was being constructed under General Goethals [c. 1909–14], and later was Marshal of Arizona, when Arizona was still a territory. He once showed me his revolver, which had twenty-eight notches, and told me they represented the criminals he had killed, not including Mexicans. At seventy-eight he had a mistress, a woman of not more than thirty-five, who was in love with him.

The future law officer revealed his short temper and punctilious conscience during an incident that took place on May 8, 1891, in Globe, Arizona. He appeared in court, charged himself with assault and battery, and confessed that he and another man "had some words this morning and I struck him with my fist. I don't know how many times. I want to make this complaint [sic] and pay my fine" of eight dollars.[4]

In 1903, when Jane's mother was being tried in a murder case, Jane was sent away to Demorest, Georgia, to live with her grandmother. Though Ellen "was acquitted of the accessory charge, the word went round that the jury was soft-hearted because she was an attractive woman. Her brother, Dan Luckie, assumed the blame and confessed to the murder on the eve of departing for South America." Jane attended Piedmont College in Demorest from 1903 to 1904, "although it is not certain she completed a full year's work, since she was expelled according to the records on May 13, 1904 . . . for unauthorized departure from the campus, about which there were very severe rules at that time."

Ellen Luckie died soon after the scandalous trial. And Jane was sent to stay with her father, who was almost a complete stranger to her. He was living with an elderly Mexican housekeeper in the wild frontier town of Yuma, Arizona, near the borders of California and Mexico, and was town marshal from 1904 to 1908.[5] Though isolated and lonely in Arizona, Jane learned to ride horses, to love the desert and to observe the ways of the Indians. She called her father "Daddy Bob"; he called her "Baby," adored her and spoiled her outrageously. In about 1906 "Red" Anderson, deciding that Jane needed an education that was unobtainable in Yuma, enrolled her in Kidd-Key College, north of Dallas, in Sherman, Texas.

Mrs. Lucy Kidd-Key, the founder of the very proper women's college (which closed before World War One), was an aristocratic, conservative, elderly southern lady, married to a retired Methodist bishop. While at Kidd-Key College Jane, who loved music, diligently practiced the piano.

After hearing the Polish pianist Ignacy Paderewski perform at a concert in Dallas, she made Chopin her favorite composer, constantly played his works and was awarded a special certificate in music.

The autobiographical stories, poems and editorials in the *Kidd-Key Journal* of December 1, 1908, which listed "Jane Foss Anderson" (her original name now abbreviated and placed second) as Editor-in Chief, reveal how the twenty-year-old displaced Southern college girl saw herself and was seen by her contemporaries. In her short story "With Long Distance From 7 to 9 p.m.," a beautiful, elegantly dressed young woman meets a varied group of people who are making long-distance calls in the phone company office. And she shocks them by putting a call through to the Crown and Anchor Saloon (which sounds more like an English pub than a western bar): "She was all silk and lace from head to heel. She had hair like the sunbeams, a skin like a roseleaf, and big eyes, blue as a June sky." In her romantic and formulaic work called "Story," a cowboy-economics professor in the West courts a modern girl with Southern manners who will not express her feelings for any man. But when he risks serious injury and is thrown from a horse while breaking broncos, she rushes to his side and declares her love.

A doggerel poem about Jane, with a drawing of her in an enormous hat and long flowing dress, reinforces the image of a Southern belle who defied convention and was determined to make a striking impression:

> If you wish to see a funny sight
> Just look at Janie Foss—
> (We really hate to state the fact,
> But she's our Journal Boss.)
> She wears a hat so very large
> Her face you cannot see,
> The shape of which said head-piece
> Doth vex the Facul—ty.

Jane's first political pronouncement was an editorial called "Enterprise," written during the jingoistic presidency of Teddy Roosevelt, which patriotically asserted: "America is a nation to be admired and respected by other countries."

According to the information on her passport Jane was five feet seven inches (slightly taller than Conrad), with red hair, blue eyes, fair complexion, high forehead, oval face, small nose and mouth, and round chin. Kitty Crawford, who adored Jane and thought her the most beautiful girl she had ever seen, wrote that "her face, framed with curly hair, was

rather broad, with widely-spaced violet-blue eyes, a pert upturned nose
and the flawless complexion of her southern heritage. Tall and slender,
graceful and assured, with large eyes looking directly at one, she dominated a scene the moment she entered the room . . . queenly, trium-
phantly beautiful, and with a veneer of international sophistication."

In the spring of 1909 Jane suffered a disaster at Kidd-Key that must
have reminded her of the expulsion from Piedmont in the spring of
1904. During her senior year, "Red" Anderson's letters suddenly
stopped. Oscillating between adoration and neglect, he disappeared
without paying her tuition and deserted her for the second time in her
life. Kitty observed that though friends helped Jane with money, "the
foundations of her life were shaken cruelly by this experience." She did
not have enough credits to graduate from college, or enough money to
continue, but distinguished herself that year in French and in English
literature.

After college, Jane went to New York, where she intended to become
a fiction writer, and Kitty became a reporter in San Antonio. In the
course of her work Kitty met the distinguished composer and music
critic Deems Taylor, who was born in 1885, and asked him to help Jane
find a job. He did so, they fell in love—Taylor said "she has a face like
a flower!"—and were married on September 26, 1910. In a photograph
taken at the time of her wedding, Jane looks like a woman in her early
twenties. Wearing a long dark dress and sitting with her legs crossed at
an angle to the camera, she rests her elbow on her knee and chin on her
lace-gloved hand, and turns her strikingly handsome face toward the
lens as her tawny hair cascades onto her shoulders from under the
canopy of an enormous soft black hat.

Kitty wrote that Buffalo Bill Cody, "one time Indian scout and proprietor of a Wild West show, was a poker-playing friend of Daddy Bob,
and an affectionate admirer of Jane." Colonel Cody gave Jane a letter of
introduction to one of his New York friends, George Harvey, editor of
Harper's Weekly, where Jane published eight western stories between
April 1910 and February 1913. Jane's competently written but sentimental and melodramatic stories—which also appeared before the war in
Munsey's, Collier's and *Harper's* monthly—frequently concern an obstacle
to love that is overcome through a sudden twist in plot, and conclude in
romance as bad guys are redeemed by good women or prostitutes rescued by good men. Many of the stories are set in Arizona, concern
Mexicans and Indians, test men's courage, criticize injustice, and show
strong sympathy for the maimed and wounded underdog.

During 1914–15 Jane also earned money by writing articles for the

naturalist and popular science author William Beebe, curator of ornithology at the Bronx Zoo. At this time Jane expressed doubts to Kitty
about her competence to write on unfamiliar subjects and resentment
about publishing her own work under someone else's name: "I am to do
a whole book for Will, now. . . . This is to be a book about all the
countries I have never seen—the Lord only knows what I would write if
I had been there. . . . I'm going to try and get the book out before
spring. I mean the book which is to be published at the same time as his
monograph. . . . I know I'm getting a rotten deal—what with everybody
believing that I've flunked in my work, and Beebe getting all manner of
credit for the stuff."[6]

II

On September 24, 1915, possibly financed by a Denver man who was
infatuated with her, Jane sailed to Europe on the *Baltic* and became a war
correspondent in London. She rushed to the scene when a German
Zeppelin was shot down in a village near London, borrowed a nurse's
uniform to get close to the carnage, "saw a lot of Germans frying in
somebody's pasture" and wrote the story. She got a job on the *Daily
Mail* and was commissioned by the *Daily Express* to write a series of
articles about the effect of the war on people in villages and farms.

Jane was also permitted to inspect a damaged submarine and to interview the officers who had brought it safely home. And she was "the
first woman to make a flight across London in one of His Majesty's war
machines." On May 18, 1916, the London *Times* stated: "The following
article by Mrs. Jane Anderson, a well-known American writer, describes
a remarkable feat of courage and seamanship on the part of the officers
and crew of a British submarine." Two weeks later *The Times* said of her
effective (though not blatant) war propaganda, "A Woman's Flight Over
London": "The following account of a trip over London in a military
aeroplane was contributed to the *New York Tribune* by Miss [no longer
"Mrs."] Jane Anderson, who recently described the return to port of a
British submarine which had been badly damaged in a collision with a
mine."[7] These articles show Jane's considerable courage, enterprise and
ability to persuade political and military officials to let her go wherever
she wanted and do whatever she wished. Even more extraordinary for
a woman during World War One were Jane's fearless and frequent visits
to the trenches and the battlefronts of France.

While in London Jane became friendly with Conrad's friends Arnold

Bennett and H. G. Wells, and with Wells' mistress, Rebecca West. The brilliant Miss West, herself an accomplished journalist, was far more impressed by Jane's beauty than by her mind. She suggested that Jane was an inordinately ambitious, not very talented and politically naïve woman, who slept her way into journalistic success with influential men like Sir Leo Money and Lord Northcliffe, the owner of the *Daily Mail* and *The Times*:

> She was very beautiful with orange hair that I am sure was of nature, a slender figure, a ravishing complexion, and great charm of manner. . . . I associate her in my mind with Sir Leo Money who, I think, introduced me to her. . . .
>
> She was a goodnatured, silly, melodramatic ass, and I don't know whether she was a pro-German enthusiast of the *Bund* variety or just an adventuress with a taste for the exceptional. . . . I can't really think that she would be a useful observer. The paucity of her journalistic equipment was universally remarked, so I don't think she could have got by without raising some suspicions. . . .
>
> We [Wells and West] rather liked her, and I do not think she knew one belligerent side from another. . . . She was far too simple-minded to be taken as a serious interviewer in the war.

Jane's limitations, behavior and success were similar to those of Mary Welsh, Irwin Shaw's mistress during World War Two, whom he portrayed as Louise M'Kimber in *The Young Lions*: "she seemed to know every big-wig in the British Isles. She had a deft, tricky way with men, and was always being invited to weekends at famous country houses where garrulous military men of high rank seemed to spill a great many dangerous secrets to her."[8]

Lord Northcliffe, born in 1865, the son of a Dublin barrister, was one of the most powerful men in England. Conrad and Ford had portrayed him as Mr. Fox, "full-faced, with a persuasive, peremptory manner . . . very successful in launching papers." He also owned the *Evening News*, the *Daily Mirror* and the *Observer*, and was created a viscount in 1917. Northcliffe was clearly attracted to Jane and probably became her lover. As she wrote to Kitty in July 1917: "Some two or three times a week I went down for tea with him at his office. . . . A curious, antagonistic intimacy sprang up and lived between us for some time. It terminated, of course, in a quite unnecessary quarrel. . . . My chief regret was the breaking of the somewhat innocuous bond between Northcliffe and me."

In 1915 Jane had asked both Wells and Northcliffe to secure her an invitation to visit Conrad. When Jane herself finally wrote, enclosing an introduction from Northcliffe, who had not yet met Conrad but "presumed upon his prestige to dictate the letter," Jessie replied that he was ill with an attack of gout and could see no one. Though this was the truth, Jane took it as "a chilly bit of fiction which left me singularly cold on the reading of it." She eventually managed to secure her own invitation and, after meeting Conrad, had the pleasure of introducing Northcliffe to him. On July 1, 1916 (Conrad told Pinker), Northcliffe visited Capel House during his first wartime holiday, arriving from Broadstairs, on the Kentish coast, at noon and staying until five. He looked very tired, spoke devotedly of his mother, and became very friendly with John Conrad and Robin Douglas, who dragged him away to look at birds' nests. Conrad later told Cunninghame Graham that Northcliffe "himself was absolutely genuine. He had given me one or two glimpses of his inner man which impressed me."[9]

Jane also told Kitty of "the loyal welcome unfailingly extended to me by Sir Leo Money and Lady Money," who had introduced her to Rebecca West. Sir Leo Chiozza Money was born in Genoa in 1870. A noted economist and journalist, and former Fabian on the radical wing of the Liberal Party, he was the author of *Riches and Poverty* (1905). He had been an MP for East Northamptonshire since 1910, was knighted in 1915 and, as private secretary to Lloyd George (whom he introduced to Jane), was a member of the wartime government from 1916 to 1918.

In view of the scandals Sir Leo was later involved in, it seems clear that he had a sexual interest in Jane and may also have been her lover. In April 1928 Sir Leo and Miss Irene Savage, a twenty-two-year-old factory worker, were charged (in the euphemistic language of that time) "with being concerned together with behaving in a manner reasonably likely to offend against public decency at Hyde Park." In other words, while sitting under a tree, they were probably kissing and fondling each other. The police claimed that when he was arrested Sir Leo desperately exclaimed, "I am not the usual riff-raff. I am a man of substance. For God's sake let me go." The defendants were remanded on bail with Lady Money as surety for both. But a parliamentary debate and three leading articles in *The Times* the following month criticized the police for their improper questioning of Miss Savage and for their insistence that she have a medical examination, and Sir Leo was awarded ten guineas costs against the police.

This incident would have been forgotten if the hot-blooded Sir Leo had not become involved five years later in a similar event with another working-class woman. In September 1933 the sixty-three-year-old Sir Leo was accused of assaulting a girl in a railway compartment by pas-

sionately kissing her on the lips. He admitted kissing her hands but
denied the graver charge, claiming the girl's motive in accusing him was
that she had recently been jilted and was hostile to men. In this case,
however, the judge thought Sir Leo's admission suggested misconduct.
He was convicted and fined two pounds—yielding a net profit in the
two cases of £8.10.0—and decided for financial reasons not to appeal the
case.[10]

III

In April 1916 chance events enabled Jane to achieve "the greatest ambition of [her] life" and to meet "the greatest writer in the world." When
Conrad was ill at home with gout, Jessie attended the London exhibition
of Jo Davidson's bust of her husband, where she met the charming
American journalist Gordon Bruce of the *New York Herald*. He told Jessie
that he would soon be flying to France and offered to take her message
to Borys, then serving with the Mechanical Transport Corps. The Conrads invited Bruce to lunch on April 16 and he immediately accepted,
asking if he could bring a young lady with him.

Jessie recorded that the young lady, Jane Anderson, made a "very
great impression" on Conrad and, it seems, on everyone else as well.
When Jane sat before the fire and a married French Red Cross officer
with whom she was flirting placed two tall vases full of flowers in front
of her and made a deep bow, Conrad gave a "rather vexed laugh," held
out his hand to help his guest to rise and upset both vases while doing
so. John Conrad, who was nine years old at the time, vividly remembered this party. He thought Jane was extremely attractive, had a good
figure and was elegantly dressed, and mentioned that Jessie later became jealous of her: "She was vivacious and not against having a mild
scrap with me, rolling me on the floor while my father looked on with
amusement [and, perhaps, a desire to join in the rolling]. All the other
women who came were married, some rather staid and practically every
one of them nervous and on their best behaviour." But Jane won their
hearts with her charming Georgia accent and her free and easy American manners.

Conrad and the French officer were not the only ones to be sexually
attracted to Jane. As they were cycling down a hill, the wind caught
Jane's long skirt and blew it well above her knees. Jane properly told
young John: "You should not look round when that happens!" but he
candidly replied: "Oh, why not? I think your legs are very beautiful!"

Jane played music for Conrad even more effectively than Émilie Briquel had done in Geneva. As Robin Douglas noted: "Having captivated us, [Mrs.] Taylor then made two more easy conquests in Mr. and Mrs. Conrad. After tea we went into the drawing-room, where the 'American flying girl' played and sang negro songs of the cotton fields and plantations. Conrad listened, spellbound by the plaintive melodies of the South."[11] The Georgia peach did not try out her Chopin polonaises on Conrad, who always associated music with sensuality, but moved him nevertheless with her lively and unconstrained performance.

Jane, also moved by this visit, carefully described Conrad's speech, accent and appearance as well as his house, wife and children in long letters to Deems Taylor and to Kitty Crawford:

[Conrad was] talking very fast and making tremendous motions with his hands and his shoulders. His voice is very clear and fine in tone, but there is an accent which I never heard before. It is an accent which affects every word, and gives the most extraordinary rhythm to phrases. And his verbs are never right. If they are in the place they should be—which is seldom— they are without tense. . . .

His head is extraordinarily fine in the modelling, although the forehead is not high. There are certain planes above the eyes, however. It is the pose of his head, which is a little shrunken into his shoulders, which gives the impression of strength. His mouth, although not clearly defined under the gray moustache, is full but sensitive. But it is his eyes which are the eyes of genius. They are dark, and the lids droop except in moments of intense excitement. They are dark brown, in which the pupil does not show. And there is in them a curious hypnotic quality. . . .

"I would show you," he said, "ze spire of ze cathedral as you would see it from ze hills—but my car is broken, and we do not go. Zis will be for anuzzer time."

One early afternoon—it was Sunday, I drove up to Capel House. What shall I say of that Kentish farmhouse, set within the confines of an old moat, with a garden bright with flowers, and above all the intense shadow of towering pines. Oh, there are no words for the love and beauty I found there!

Jessie Conrad is one of the great women of this earth. She came walking across the little living room to meet me, leaning heavily on her cane. She has walked with this cane for eighteen [i.e., twelve] years. She was smiling. Jessie is always smiling. I loved her then. The spell of Conrad's genius lives in that house but the soul of Jessie Conrad lies behind that genius.

And there was my Brother John. He has the magnificent age of ten [i.e.,

nine]. We went that day for a long walk together—down the old lane
through the woods back of Capel to gather primroses. We brought them
back in the late afternoon to give to Jessie.

Thus it came about that Capel House became my home. . . . Each weekend I went down, giving whatever I could, for with the older son at the
front, there is always another shadow over Capel deeper than the shadow
of the pines.

Jane also sent Kitty's daughter, Jane Anderson Jenkins, a doll that had
been dressed by "Lady Conrad."

Two revealing photographs were taken (perhaps by Gordon Bruce)
during Jane's visit. In the first, a tall, thin, elegant Jane, her eyes mo-
mentarily closed during the long exposure, leans over and embraces
(though her hands cannot meet) the stolid bulk of an impassive, double-
chinned Jessie, who appears to be holding a dishrag. In the second,
Conrad wears a dashing bowler hat, monocle, highly polished boots and
leather gaiters. With his arm resting negligently on the door of the high
open car and his right leg raised on the running board, he beams
fondly—and uncharacteristically—at Jane. She, holding a white fur-
piece and wearing smart pointed boots and a high plumed hat, returns,
with an engagingly tilted head, his more than affectionate regard.[12]

Joan Givner observed that Jane could be "entertaining, even brilliantly
amusing, but at other times she was morbid, oversensitive, and easily
upset." In the summer of 1916, when Jane collapsed from exhaustion,
pneumonia and a nervous breakdown, the Conrads saw the darker side
of her character. Jessie heard of her illness, visited her in a London
hospital and, when she was better, had her moved (with Conrad's encouragement) to Capel House for a five-week convalescence. "There
was so much she had seen of the horrors of the war," Jessie wrote, "and
under circumstances few women, other than those engaged as nurses,
could have dreamt of. She had made a passage across the Channel in a
hospital ship, been present at least once very close to where a German
machine had come down in flames. . . . When she came to us after a
spell of these adventures she spent a month practically in bed. Her
nerves were decidedly ragged, and she made an interesting invalid."[13]
Jane's mental breakdown (which may have reminded Conrad of his own
in 1910) had been caused by her difficult and unstable childhood as well
as by the war. It is scarcely surprising that Conrad felt solicitous and
Jessie maternal, and that Jane found in their domestic life at Capel House
a secure refuge from the wounded, mutilated and dead men she had
seen at the front.

Conrad's letters to his friends and to his wife suggest that he fell in love with Jane as desire mingled with pity during her convalescence. In August 1916, as Jane was recovering, he aroused Pinker's interest by inviting him to meet an amusing and pretty young woman. And that month—complimenting Jane, expressing his feelings in a paternal guise and concluding with an uncharacteristic expression that alluded to the charming heroine of *The Mikado*—he told Curle: "We made the acquaintance of a new young woman. She comes from Arizona and (strange to say!) she has an European mind. She is seeking to get herself adopted as our big daughter and is succeeding fairly. To put it shortly she's quite yum-yum."

On September 14, when Jane had recovered and returned to London, Conrad went to her flat for tea, stayed for dinner and possibly consummated their affair. In a letter to Jessie—the ostensible subject of their conversation—Conrad described how they both put on elaborate dress for this momentous occasion, and how he supposedly remained passive while she revealed intimate details of her personal life, which had become rather precarious because of her quarrel with her lover and employer, Lord Northcliffe:

> I changed into my yachting suit and then went on to Jane's where after 3 cups of tea I recovered somewhat. She kept me to dinner, put on a charming frock for me and behaved generally in a charming manner. She talked of you and the boys a good deal. Rather a lot of herself. Very curious. Very nebulous of course. No facts but a lot about sensations, intelligence and so on. You know what I mean—I fancy she feels her position to be not without danger (of a shake up) and would be perhaps glad to know (or to feel) that you, I mean *you* personally as a woman (as distinct from *us*) would be likely to stand by her—I was very reserved on these matters generally.

Two weeks later Conrad, who had been corresponding with Jane, told Jessie about her current relations with Northcliffe, maintained the convenient fiction that Jessie and Jane were devoted to each other, and took up the equine metaphor he was fond of using to describe the two women: "Had a letter from your pair-mate about N'cliffe. N. obviously cooled down a lot. Letter curiously indefinite but I seem to see that N. has found some new American wonder. Just what I expected. But this is strictly between us. The dear Chestnut filly is obviously put out. Am trusting the dearest dark-brown mare to steady that youngster in her traces." He also told Jessie to be circumspect about showing Jane the presents he had sent her, lest Jane become jealous. And in late September, anticipating vicarious pleasure, he instructed Jessie to embrace Jane on his behalf: "Give my love to Jane and if the signs are propitious you may even go so far as a hug, or something of the kind. I wish I was there to see it. I never cared to see you kissing other women as you know. But this one is different."[14]

At the beginning of her first book on Conrad, which does not mention Jane, Jessie claimed that she generously gave him complete freedom to do as he wished in their marriage: "I determined that his bonds should rest lightly on him; that to all intents and purposes he should feel as free as if he had remained a bachelor." But when her intention was tested by his sexual passion for Jane, the groom (to adopt Conrad's imagery) jerked the bridle and brought the restive stallion to a halt. As Conrad noted in "Because of the Dollars": "A stupid woman with a sense of grievance is worse than an unchained devil."

The affair came to a crisis on September 18, 1916, when Conrad (who had taken a flight in a warplane) met Jessie in Folkestone, where she had been staying with John and Jane. In Jessie's account, the first thing Conrad asked when his train arrived was: "Where is your stable-companion?" And he was disappointed when told she had not come. Perhaps during a quarrel with Jessie, Jane had boasted of Conrad's love letters and made Jessie suspect his fidelity. Furious at his "little back-sliding," Jessie had greeted his pretense of innocence with a frigid hauteur. The "fair American" had also intercepted the letters that Conrad always wrote to Jessie with great regularity and, as his wife remarked of Jane's selfishness and malice, she "had been amusing herself at my expense. The seriousness of that deliberate attempt to spoil our long understanding affection had probably never struck her and more than likely would not have troubled her if it had."

When they returned to the hotel Conrad had a stormy interview with Jane and must have reproached her for her reckless indiscretion. According to Jessie, she later discovered while sorting his books Conrad's love letter to Jane: "The letter would have proved all she had said. It was a very high flown epistle, without signature or superscription, but there was no mistake who had written it." When confronted with the incriminating evidence, Conrad angrily "flung it into the fire, and turning to me suggested a way of procuring something I had expressed a wish for. A usual form of any penitence, that followed no accusation and no apology."[15] Conrad, significantly, did not deny Jessie's accusation of betrayal and bought her off rather cheaply with a long-coveted present. Jessie knew his affair did not seriously threaten their marriage, and Conrad apparently became more devoted than ever.

Conrad tried to live up to the gallant role Jane offered him, but knew he had no future with her. He had no wish to become involved, as Ford and Elsie had, in a squalid and embarrassing public scandal. He felt a need to preserve appearances, and believed that passion, especially between an older man and a young woman, was essentially ludicrous and potentially destructive. As he wrote in "A Smile of Fortune": "Jacobus became suddenly infatuated with one of the lady-riders [in the traveling circus]. What made it worse was that he was married. He had not even the grace to conceal his passion."

Though Jessie did not want Jane to stay with them any longer, she remained with the Conrads, to maintain appearances, until they left Folkestone two days later, and continued to see them at least until the end of 1916. In mid-December Conrad sent her pre-war Western stories to Pinker, discussed her complex character, analyzed her personal weaknesses and enthusiastically recommended her work:

> The best point about her is that though very earnest about her production she has not the slightest conceit about her. . . . The novel she has planned being essentially autobiographical may make a success by a sort of wild sincerity that will be the distinctive mark of it I guess: for that is her great characteristic. She has gifts but her personality is inwardly in such a tangle that one can't tell what all these gifts will amount to in the end. Personally she lacks judgment and determination in the conduct of her life. But she is as frank and open as a woman can be, I believe, and all her instincts are rather generous than otherwise. With all her airs of independence and her consciousness of her own intellect you will find her a most amenable creature and by no means naturally ungrateful.[16]

Conrad's affair with Jane illuminates the most obscure aspect of his character: his sexual attitudes and sexual life. Halverson and Watt observe that "it must have been a great experience for Conrad to get to know intimately someone so open, so gifted, so lovely, and so unlike anyone else he had ever known." And, they might have added, so different from the very proper French girls who had rejected and humiliated him, and from his boring "lump of a wife."

When Conrad met Jane in 1916 he was fifty-eight and she was about twenty-eight. His sexual relations with the crippled Jessie (about fifteen years older than Jane) must have been, for most of their marriage, very limited. Unless Conrad had discreet affairs—which his obsessive work habits, lack of money, neurasthenia and agonizing guilt made unlikely—he probably led a nearly celibate life. A photograph in John's book, taken in the garden of Capel House, shows Jane bending over to hug the boy while looking toward the camera. Jessie—who was only five feet two inches tall, weighed two hundred pounds and looked old enough to be Jane's mother—props herself up with a cane and glances suspiciously at her while Conrad—with sporty waistcoat, gold chain and cigarette—beams at her with jaunty delight. Jane was Conrad's last (and perhaps first) chance to sleep with a beautiful, well-born woman. He knew this and seized the opportunity.

Curle remembered Conrad telling him, "in that final way of his, how much safer it was for a woman to be married to a *roué* than to an idealist"—though Conrad of course was an idealist. Cunninghame Graham called him *"un homme à femmes,"* and in 1915 Conrad confessed that he was still capable of losing his old but still impressionable heart. Two years later, speaking of a model for an imaginary portrait of Alice Jacobus, the heroine of "The Planter of Malata," and thinking of Jane, Conrad wrote that the search for "Titian-red hair" would be amusing.[17]

Many of Conrad's friends commented on his attraction to women, and believed that Jane had been his mistress. In *Some Do Not,* Ford, who knew him intimately, wrote of Macmaster (based on Conrad): "He had passages when a sort of blind unreason had attracted him almost to speechlessness towards girls of the most giggling, behind-the-counter order, big-bosomed, scarlet-cheeked." And in Ford's *The Simple Life Limited,* Bransdon, though not particularly interested in women, sometimes takes them for sordid weekends in Brighton.

Rebecca West remarked that Conrad thought Jane "was so marvellous." Joseph Retinger thought Conrad had had extramarital ventures and described them as *"de louches passes"* (sordid engagements). Richard Curle, like Ford an intimate friend, said Conrad "always had an eye for a pretty face and a pretty ankle," and believed "there may have been a *tendresse* with the American journalist." And Graham Greene, who was passionately interested in Conrad and may have been privy to inside information, maintained in his review of Jessie's second book that Conrad had been "unfaithful to her in his old age."[18]

The most convincing evidence, however, came from George Seldes, a professional journalist who interviewed Conrad and knew Jane, and whose brother Gilbert was, between 1918 and 1919 (during her separation from Retinger), Jane's lover. In 1916 the London office of the United Press asked George Seldes to interview Conrad about the fighting capacity of British submarines. Jane, whom George Seldes called a redhead of "spectacular beauty," was living in Conrad's house. He politely referred to her as "my ward," but George Seldes suspected she was actually his mistress. Unlike Rebecca West, George Seldes agreed with

Conrad that Jane was an extraordinary woman with a bright mind. She was known as "a good newspaperman," which in those days was a great compliment for a woman journalist. George Seldes also saw a love letter to Jane in which Conrad wrote, with his wittiest man-of-the-world manner: "I don't see why my last mistress should not be Borys' first."[19]

Jane's adoration of Conrad, unconventional sexual attitudes and willingness to sleep with great men; Conrad's powerful attraction to Jane, quasi-celibate life with Jessie and desire to grasp the final opportunity for sexual adventure; the evidence of the photographs taken during Jane's visits; the invitation to Jane to convalesce in his household and enliven his domestic life; their meetings in London; the stilted tone he adopted when discussing Jane in his letters and describing her in *The Arrow of Gold*; Jane's revelation of Conrad's love for her; his quarrel with Jessie about his "back-sliding"; his tacit admission of guilt when she discovered his love letter; Jessie's jealousy of Jane; and Conrad's serious quarrel with Retinger after he had become Jane's lover, all seem to indicate that Jane was Conrad's mistress.

IV

Having conquered the hearts of Conrad, the French officer, young John, Robin and, for a time, of Jessie, Jane bewitched both Borys and Retinger. Between her convalescence and the showdown in Folkestone, Jane said that she intended to look up Borys in Paris; but Conrad, thinking she might try to seduce him, sharply replied: "None of that, you let the boy alone." In July 1917, however, after he had been forced to sever his own liaison with Jane, he stimulated Borys' interest by writing to him that Jane (whose French was excellent) had a suite at the luxurious Hôtel Crillon. He summarized her attractions, mentioned that she was involved with Retinger, then living in Paris, and bluntly advised Borys to "take care not to make a damned fool of yourself"—as Conrad may have felt he had done. He also told Pinker, with stoic resignation: "If he must meet a 'Jane' it's better he should meet her at nineteen than at twenty-four."[20]

The five days Borys (who was about ten years younger than Jane) spent with "the glamorous lady from Arizona" in hotels, restaurants and nightclubs during his first leave in Paris were among the happiest of his life, for the awkward and inexperienced youth immediately fell in love with her. When he told Retinger that he was having dinner with Jane, her Polish lover said he was disappointed that Borys had "abandoned" him. While Borys was dining with the *femme fatale* they were summoned by Retinger's landlady, who "said that [he] had been working far too hard and had developed some sort of nervous disorder." This illness was undoubtedly connected with his unhappy relations with Jane, who, with Borys, "spent the remainder of the night holding him down in the bed during fits of hysteria."

As Borys was about to return to his unit, Jane got him into trouble and then out of it. She was late in returning to the hotel to say goodbye, he missed his military train and was arrested for overstaying his leave. Jane then promised: " 'I'll have you out of that in no time at all.' She did just that—within an hour I was back in her sitting room—she certainly had friends in the right places." And Borys had another day of leave. When, Borys said, he finally returned to the front, Conrad "expressed the hope that the enemy would keep me sufficiently pre-occupied to enable me 'to get Jane out of my system.' "

Retinger's much more serious love affair with Jane began in Paris and continued in America. He followed her there after the war, and Jane and her friend Katherine Anne Porter became rivals for his love. Porter thought Retinger was a well-informed and brilliant conversationalist and—despite his gaunt physique and simian features—"the most attractive man she had ever met." Retinger's description of Jane's attractiveness, ability and sympathetic personality echoes Conrad's letter about Jane to Pinker and explains why both Poles fell in love with her:

> Brilliant and beautiful, she turned the heads of many conspicuous and famous men in Europe and in her own country. Exceptionally gifted, a good newspaperwoman and short-story writer of more than average talent, she had a marvellous capacity for listening and understanding. After she arrived in London in 1916, and until she left a year or so later, Conrad saw a lot of her. She became part-heroine in one of his last novels *The Arrow of Gold*. She was one of the very rare persons whom Jessie could not stand. . . . She also, after the War, caused a certain estrangement between Conrad and myself.[21]

The similarities between Jane and Rita de Lastaola, the mistress of the autobiographical hero of *The Arrow of Gold* (1919), are even closer than Retinger suggested. The novel expresses Conrad's passion of the war years more than the passion of his youth in Marseilles. Jane, the Southern model for the heroine, matches Warrington Dawson, the Southern model for the South Carolinian character, J. K. Blunt. The "four magic letters" of Rita's name have the same number of letters as Jane's, and the Royalist friend who acts as George's second in his duel with Blunt has a married sister called Jane. Both Jane and Rita have blue eyes and rust-colored hair. And even Conrad's generalized description of Rita suggests his strong attraction to her model: "All that appertained to her haunted me with the same awful intimacy, her whole form in the familiar pose, her very substance in its colour and texture, her eyes, her lips, the gleam of her teeth, the tawny mist of her hair, the smoothness of her forehead, the faint scent that she used." And Jane's "familiar pose" is, in fact, repeated in Rita's. Jessie wrote: "Miss A—— seated herself before the fire like an idol"; in *The Arrow of Gold*, Rita is seen "sitting cross-legged on the divan in the attitude of a very old idol."

Jane's "airs of independence," her flirtation with Borys (a partial compensation for the loss of Conrad), her liaisons with Lord Northcliffe and Sir Leo Money, her connections "in the right places" and political influence with high-ranking officials are all clearly reflected in *The Arrow of Gold*, which ends as Rita abandons Monsieur George. Conrad describes the magnetic Rita as "a woman formed in mind and body, mistress of herself, free in her choice, independent in her thoughts." Her sister Therese asks: "Did she tell you about a boy, the son of pious and rich parents, whom she tried to lead astray into the wildness of thoughts like her own." And Captain Blunt remarks that "every bald head in this Republican Government gets pink at the top whenever her dress rustles outside the door."

Conrad heard from Jane for the last time in April and May 1919, just after *The Arrow of Gold* had been published in America, when she sent him two telegrams about buying the film rights to his novels. After Jane's first business-like telegram Conrad placed the matter in Pinker's hands and did not respond to the warmer tone of the second one, which asked him to extend the option and sent her tender salutation: "Dearest love, Jane Anderson."[22]

CHAPTER SEVENTEEN

The War Years

1916–1918

I

Apart from the interlude with Jane Anderson, the war years for Conrad, as for most people, were rather grim. Borys, like Ford, was at the front and provided a constant source of anxiety. Roger Casement's trial for treason and Norman Douglas's trial for homosexuality forced Conrad to dissociate himself from these two old friends. Though exhilarated by his brief foray into war service, he did not produce effective propaganda for the British war effort. He got into an imbroglio with John Quinn about the sale of his manuscripts. He acquired two new disciples, Hugh Walpole and Gérard Jean-Aubry, and became very friendly with Jessie's new doctor, Sir Robert Jones. But he was deeply troubled by the incurable condition of Jessie's knee. He published and wrote several works, including *Within the Tides* and *The Arrow of Gold*, but only *The Shadow-Line* matched the standard of his finest books. He was forced to answer an anti-Semitic attack; and was deeply involved, through Retinger, in Polish affairs. But his gloomy prognostications were often inaccurate and he was surprised when Poland finally became independent in 1918.

After failing his entrance examination to Sheffield University, Borys (who was only seventeen and a half) had volunteered for military service. He obtained a commission with the help of Cunninghame Graham and in September 1915 joined the Mechanical Transport Corps, where he could utilize his expert knowledge of car engines. In mid-February 1916 Borys was attached to the heavy artillery of the 34th Brigade near Armentières. The following month Conrad proudly sent Galsworthy an account of Borys' military duties and noted the strange similarity to his boyhood years on the naval training ship:

He is in command of the advanced detachment and sees his captain only once or twice a week. Apart from being always at the call of the gunners for anything unexpected that may have to be done, his work is regular. It consists in running munitions convoys at night while a certain proportion of the day he spends in overalls, grubbing under the cars, as the advanced detachment must be in a state of absolute efficiency at any instant of night or day. He writes cheerful boyish letters in the same tone as his *Worcester* correspondence. We send him a tuck-box now and again. It's as if he were still at school.

Ford had volunteered for service at the age of forty-two in order to dissociate himself from his embarrassing pre-war German chauvinism and to confirm his English patriotism. He sent Conrad several moving letters, alluding to their old joke: "Excellency, a few goats!" and describing his precise aesthetic perceptions of the horrors of the trenches. In September 1916 Ford said he had spent six continuous weeks within reach of German missiles; in December, gassed and shell-shocked in a Rouen hospital, he reported: "As for me, *c'est fini de moi,* I believe, at least as far as fighting is concerned—my lungs are all charred up & gone."[1]

Conrad had once affirmed an outmoded belief in the divine right of kings and had seriously doubted whether contemporary representative governments could guarantee liberty. But he was a fervent English patriot during the democratic war against absolute monarchies. As he wrote of the hero's father, Sir Charles Latham, in *Suspense*: "He loved his country, believed in its greatness, in its superior virtue, in its irresistible power. Nothing could shake his fidelity to national prejudices of every sort."

Conrad's patriotism eclipsed personal loyalty when his old friend Sir Roger Casement was convicted of treason in 1916. Conrad did not see Casement from the time they met at dinner in London in 1896 until Casement visited him to press for assistance in the Congo Reform Association Movement. On January 3, 1903, Casement recorded in his diary: "Went to Conrad at Pent Farm, Stanford, near Hythe, and spent a delightful day with him. Back by last 8.20 train." In about 1905 the Conrads again invited Casement to spend the night in their home. Jessie revealed that the conversation inevitably focused on their common experiences in the Congo:

Sir Roger Casement, a fanatical Irish Protestant, came to see us, remaining some two days as our guest. He was a very handsome man with a thick dark beard and piercing, restless eyes. His personality impressed me greatly. It was about the time when he was interested in bringing to light certain atrocities which were taking place in the Belgian Congo. Who could foresee his own terrible fate during the war as he stood in our drawing-room passionately denouncing the cruelties he had seen.[2]

In 1910 Casement repeated his success in the Congo with another thorough, human and influential report about atrocities committed on the Indians who worked on rubber plantations in the Putumayo region of the Peruvian Amazon. In 1911 Casement was knighted for his work in Africa and the Amazon, and while on leave that year from his post as British consul in Rio de Janeiro, met Conrad by chance and for the last time in the Strand.

Jessie's reference to Casement's "terrible fate" alluded to the last phase of his extraordinary career. He retired from the Colonial Service in 1913 on the grounds of poor health, and became active in the Irish nationalist movement. He then went to America to gather support for that cause, and traveled from there to Germany in November 1914. At the time of the abortive Easter rebellion in 1916, Casement was landed on the Irish coast from a German submarine. The British, who had broken the German code, knew of his movements and he was captured immediately. In June 1916 he was convicted of treason and sentenced to hang. His appeal was rejected, despite his distinguished service, and he was executed in August. During the last months of Casement's life, Conrad once again came into conjunction with him.

John Quinn, an Irish nationalist, was active in gathering American support for Casement. Between Casement's arrest and trial, Conrad sent Quinn a substantial letter, expressing his disenchanted recollections of Casement's volatile politics and commenting caustically on the futility of his irrational behavior:

> One only wonders, in one's grief, what it was all for? With Britain smashed and the German fleet riding the seas, the very shadow of Irish independence would have passed away. The Island Republic (if that is what they wanted) would have become merely a strongly held German outpost—a despised stepping-stone towards the final aim of the Welt-Politik. . . .
>
> We never talked politics. I didn't think he had really any. A Home-ruler accepting Lord Salisbury's patronage couldn't be taken very seriously. He was a good companion; but already in Africa I judged that he was a man, properly speaking, of no mind at all. I don't mean stupid. I mean that he was all emotion. By emotional force (Congo report, Putumayo, etc.) he made his way, and sheer temperament—a truly tragic personality: all but

the greatness of which he had not a trace. Only vanity. But in the Congo it was not visible yet.

Conrad's description of Casement's emotional and self-sacrificial nationalism was uncomfortably close to his accounts of his father's suicidal Polish patriotism; and the consequences of Apollo's role in preparing the rebellion of 1863 were, like Casement's in 1916, both personally and politically disastrous. The anguished memories aroused by this striking similarity must have influenced Conrad's hostile attitude toward Casement.

Retinger, who was intimate with Conrad at the time of Casement's trial, described his unusually harsh judgment of the fanatical Irishman: "Roger Casement . . . he despised. In fact, I remember when after his trial and his condemnation during the War somebody, I believe it was Fisher Unwin, the publisher, circulated an appeal for pardon and asked Conrad's signature, he refused it with vehemence, telling me at the time that he once shared a hut in the Congo with Casement, and that he ended by utterly disliking the man."[3] At the time of his complete alienation from Casement in 1916, Conrad retrospectively revised his original opinion of his Congo companion, for his "utter dislike" was diametrically opposed to the warm and enthusiastic feelings he had first felt about the "intelligent and very sympathetic" man.

It is disappointing to discover that Conrad did not wish to save the life of a former friend, however despicable he considered his actions and character. There were two principal reasons for Conrad's violent change of attitude, apart from the war hysteria which carried away even the sober British Cabinet. The first reason was political. Apart from the uneasiness he felt about the similarity between Apollo and Casement, Conrad embraced the overzealous nationalism of the foreigner who had adopted an alien country as his own. This alone would have ensured his condemnation of any treasonable activity against England. As he explained to John Quinn, his Polish sympathy for oppressed peoples did not extend to the Irish: "I, who have seen England ever since the early eighties putting on the penitent's shirt in her desire for conciliation, and throwing millions of her money with both hands to Ireland in her remorse for all the old wrongs, and getting nothing in exchange but undying hostility, don't wonder at her weariness." He did not believe Casement would hang, and justified England's harsh suppression of the Easter rebellion on the grounds that she was fighting for her life against Germany and had to defend herself against a stab in the back. In other countries, Conrad thought, the suppression would have been infinitely more severe. In a later conversation with his relative Karola Zagorska, Conrad justified his behavior by stating that Casement got exactly what he deserved: "Casement did not hesitate to accept honours, decorations and distinctions from the English Government while surreptitiously arranging various affairs that he was embroiled in. In short: he was plotting against those who trusted him."[4] Though Conrad may not have known it, this statement was inaccurate. Casement first accepted his well-earned honors, but did not plot against those who trusted him until *after* he had left the consular service in 1913.

There was also a second reason for Conrad's behavior: Casement's sexual inversion. At the time of his arrest Casement's astonishingly frank homosexual diaries were discovered by Scotland Yard, and copies of the diaries were privately shown to influential people (ambassadors, bishops, members of Parliament, even King George V) in order to discredit Casement's character and extinguish all sympathy for him. After his conviction, the newspapers publicized these private diaries and one of them exclaimed: "It is common knowledge that Sir Roger Casement is a man with no sense of honour or decency. His written diaries are the monuments of a foul private life. He is a moral degenerate." Like most men in 1916 Conrad (the creator of Mr. Jones in *Victory*) was revolted by homosexuality. Just as Captain Hermann said of Falk (in Conrad's story of that name): "He hoped I would say nothing of all this ashore, though. He wouldn't like it to get about that he had been intimate with an eater of men—a common cannibal,"[5] so Conrad did not like it to get about that he had shared a hut in the Congo with a notorious homosexual. In his reaction to Casement, Conrad too "was all emotion," and the public revelation of Casement's inversion destroyed the last of Conrad's compassion.

II

Just before Conrad met Jane Anderson in April 1916 (the month Casement was arrested) she had been intensely engaged as a war correspondent, reporting on Zeppelin crashes, damaged submarines, flights over London and the horrors of combat in France. Her exciting and dangerous life intensified Conrad's attraction. And it must have made the former sailor, who had risked danger in his youth, feel—with Ford and Borys fighting at the front—like a useless old man. Violet Hunt said Conrad could not rest until he obtained a dangerous war job of his own.

Jane, more than anyone else, inspired him to match her achievements, test his courage and prove himself to her. In February 1916 Conrad told Quinn that some sort of war service, despite his decrepit condition, would compensate for his inability to write, pull him out of his depression and provide a sense of purpose: "Fact is I am hard up simply because I haven't been able to write of late to any serious amount. I have been affected mentally and physically more profoundly than I thought it possible. Perhaps if I had been able to 'lend a hand' in some way I would have found this war easier to bear. But I can't. I'm slowly getting more and more of a cripple—and this too preys on my mind not a little."

After falling in love with Jane during her convalescence at his house in the summer of 1916, Conrad, rejuvenated and no longer a "cripple," was ready to serve. In September he was contacted by Admiral Sir Douglas Brownrigg, who "came to the conclusion that it was time the doings of the wonderful merchant navy should be written up. . . . I therefore approached Mr. Joseph Conrad. . . . He travelled all over the country and had access to every ship and the free entry into every port in which the Royal and Mercantile Navies were cooperating." Though Conrad doubted his ability to write persuasive propaganda, as Jane had done, he seized the opportunity to participate in the war.

On September 14 Conrad visited the naval station on the east coast at Lowestoft, where he had first landed in England in 1878. He inspected the port, watched firing practice and was made to feel at home by the men. On September 16 he took a two-day voyage on the minesweeper *Brigadier*. And on September 18 (the day of the crisis with Jessie and Jane in Folkestone), wearing a flying coat complete with cap and goggles, he took an eighty-minute flight from the Royal Naval Air Station, up the coast at Yarmouth, in a Short biplane that bucked a sixty-mile-an-hour gale. Describing his experiences in "Flight" (1917), he said that though he had some trouble scrambling into the little plane, the first feeling to emerge after take-off "was the sense of security so much more perfect than in any small boat I've ever been in; the, as it were, material stillness and immobility." After landing on the water of the North Sea, the sometime invalid morbidly reflected: "when next time I leave the surface of this globe, it won't be to soar bodily above it in the air. Quite the contrary."[6]

In early November Conrad sailed into stormy seas from Granton, near Edinburgh, on a ship repairing the nets that defended the port from enemy submarines:

Before long the ship was fairly washed away and blown off from her station [Conrad wrote Jessie]. Her captain, a lieut., said to me, "I don't think we can do any good work to-day." I said: "For God's sake, let's get out of this." And we got out accordingly. I was never so pleased in my sea-life to get into shelter. . . .

On Saturday I went out with the Commodore inspecting and gun testing in the Firth of Forth. While we were at it 3 divisions of our newest destroyers came in from the sea. It was an exceedingly fine sight.

On November 6 Conrad set out on a twelve-day cruise on the HMS *Ready*, a "Q-boat" sailing under a Norwegian flag and disguised as a merchant vessel to entice German submarines into a deadly trap. Two days later, entering into the belligerent spirit and adopting the prevailing schoolboy slang, he told Pinker: "Hopes of bagging Fritz high." But no hostile ships were sighted and the voyage was fortunately uneventful. He told Jessie that on November 17, when the commander landed Conrad on the Yorkshire coast at Bridlington, the strange-looking foreigner "hadn't gone a dozen yards before [he] was stopped, arrested in fact, and taken to the police station."

Apart from "Flight," Conrad wrote only commonplace tributes to the merchant navy, "Well Done!" and "Tradition" (Northcliffe's *Daily Mail* paid a princely 250 guineas for the latter in March 1918), and "The Unlighted Coast," about shooting at a low-flying Zeppelin from a fog-bound ship, which was not published until after his death. The one story that emerged from this experience was "The Tale" (1917), which appeared in his posthumous collection *Tales of Hearsay*. This story takes place during the submarine warfare of World War One and describes how an English captain finds a neutral vessel that claims to be lost but, he believes, is actually aiding the enemy. To discover the truth, he sends it on a suicidal course in heavy fog. The honest neutral follows it and the ship is destroyed on the rocks. Though the captain has done his duty, he nevertheless feels acute uneasiness, moral doubt and guilt: "At the time I was certain. They all went down; and I don't know whether I have done stern retribution—or murder; whether I have added to the corpses that litter the bed of the unreadable sea the bodies of men completely innocent or basely guilty."

Despite the physical strain, Conrad's two months of war service had—like his motorcycle rides with Perceval Gibbon—an exhilarating effect. Even after the war, John Conrad noted, his father "changed from the gouty invalid I knew to an able and energetic seaman almost as soon as his feet touched the deck."[7]

III

The witty and cynical Norman Douglas had been Conrad's frequent guest since 1905 and his fourteen-year-old son, Robin, who had noted Jane Anderson's conquest of Conrad, continued to spend his school holidays at Capel House. Though Douglas, like Oscar Wilde, had been married and had two sons, Conrad was well aware of his sexual tastes, which on several occasions had got him into serious trouble in Italy. On November 27, 1916—only three months after Roger Casement was hanged for his sexual as well as his political crimes—another good friend was involved in a homosexual scandal. *The Times* reported:

> At Westminster Police Court yesterday, before Mr. Francis, NORMAN DOUGLAS, a well-dressed, middle-aged man, described as an author . . . was charged by the police as a suspected person. There was a further charge against the prisoner of assault on a boy of 16, whose schoolmaster signed the charge-sheet.

The boy testified that on November 18 Douglas had spoken to him in the Natural History Museum, treated him to some cakes in a tea shop and brought him back to his flat:

> On getting into the flat the prisoner lit a gas fire, sat on a chair, and then committed the offense complained of. Witness did not say anything, but tried several times to get away, but prisoner pulled him back. Prisoner kissed him and gave him a shilling.

Conrad desperately wanted to protect Robin, and to dissociate himself from the scandal. Borys remembered that "his father's instant reaction on seeing *The Times* report was 'We must have the boy to stay, at once.' . . . There was no rupture [with Douglas]. He is sure of that. And it would not have been like his father. Also, it would not have been concealed from Borys [at war in France at the time]—everything was talked about openly." But Compton Mackenzie reported that Conrad cautiously refused to post bail for Douglas.

Robin remained at school and did not return to Capel House until the Christmas holidays. In early December Conrad told Pinker that he dreaded having to lie to poor Robin about the reason for his father's disappearance, and angrily exclaimed about Douglas: "I wish to goodness the fellow had blown his brains out. He has been going downhill for the last 2 years and I did once or twice ask him most seriously to consider his position. But it was impossible to do anything for him. Lately he has been avoiding us all."[8] In January 1917, after the fourth hearing of his case, Douglas solved his immediate problems and avoided jail by jumping bail and leaving England.

Conrad had difficulties of quite another sort with John Quinn, who had been buying his manuscripts ever since Agnes Tobin first introduced them in 1911. Conrad had promised Quinn that he would never sell his manuscripts to anyone else as long as Quinn kept his collection intact. Quinn maintained his side of the agreement. But in the fall of 1918 Richard Curle introduced Conrad to the wealthy collector, bibliographer and (it was later discovered) notorious forger, Thomas Wise, who persuaded Conrad to part with the first draft of *The Arrow of Gold* and the incomplete manuscript of *The Rescue* (which was complete in typescript). Conrad, who had been writing relatively little and needed money immediately, clearly broke his promise to Quinn.

Part of the new attraction was that Wise, who held Conrad "spellbound by the flow of his utterance," offered in conjunction with Clement Shorter a publishing as well as a purchasing scheme. Shorter, as editor of the *Illustrated London News*, had wanted to serialize *The Rescue* in 1898. (In the *Sphere* of October 1915 he had published a damaging review that led to the suppression of D. H. Lawrence's *The Rainbow*, which had been published by Methuen the same year as, and advertised in the back pages of, Conrad's *Victory*.) Beginning in February 1917 with Conrad's one-act play *One Day More* (based on "Tomorrow"), Shorter brought out five privately printed pamphlets of Conrad's works (including "Well Done!," "First News," "The Tale" and "The Polish Question") in editions of twenty-five copies on hand-made paper. In 1919 Wise took control of this project and that year published ten more finely printed essays, which earned Conrad £200 and were later included in *Notes on Life and Letters* (1921). During 1919–20 Conrad, on to a good deal, took over this enterprise from Wise and printed eight of his essays and two stories ("Prince Roman" and "The Warrior's Soul") in these expensive limited editions.

Conrad could thus realize the maximum profit from his work by selling not only the serial and book rights but also the manuscripts and his copies of the valuable pamphlets. Wise had already forged a 1902 printing of *The Nigger of the "Narcissus."* In return for their current lucrative arrangement, Wise had persuaded the obliging Conrad to lend his authority to a fake edition of *Chance*, with a pasted-in 1913 title page, and to write: "The title-page of this book is a genuine copy of the original title dated 1913, at first removed, and subsequently restored to the volume."[9] This bogus edition was given scholarly authority in Wise's Conrad bibliography of 1920, which also advertised the privately printed editions and enhanced the value of his own extensive collection of Conrad's books and manuscripts.

In September 1919 Shorter, who may have resented being ousted by Wise, put Conrad in an extremely awkward position by telling Quinn, during a visit to America, that Conrad had been selling the bespoke manuscripts to Wise. Though Quinn's appetite for Conrad's works was unsated and he continued to buy them whenever he could, he angrily challenged Conrad about this breach of faith. Conrad could offer only the most feeble excuses, and his embarrassment was compounded by the fact that he had promised the dedication of *The Arrow of Gold* to Quinn but actually gave it to Curle. In several letters to Quinn, Conrad assured his baffled and infuriated patron that he would offer him instead the novel he planned to write about Napoleon. Conrad died before completing *Suspense*, which was seen through the press by Curle, who disliked Quinn and made sure that Quinn did not get the dedication.

IV

Conrad compensated for Borys' lack of interest in literature, his academic and nautical failures, and his absence from home during the war by adopting a series of substitute sons. They were all a generation younger than Conrad, and helped his career by writing about and translating his works. He met Warrington Dawson in 1910, Richard Curle in 1912, Hugh Walpole and Gérard Jean-Aubry in 1918. Born in Auckland in 1884, the son of a clergyman who became Bishop of Edinburgh, Walpole was educated at King's School, Canterbury, where he was cruelly bullied, and at Cambridge. Ingenuous, handsome and rather pathetic, he had been a schoolmaster and a book reviewer for the *Standard*, brought out his first novel in 1910 and served with the Red Cross in Russia during the war. The mediocre but prolific novelist was an ardent worshiper of Henry James and had published a short study of Conrad in 1916. Though he had not learned much from his masters, James in "The Younger Generation" had indulgently praised Walpole while criticizing Conrad's *Chance*. Like Casement and Douglas, Walpole was a homosexual and later maintained that "he had offered himself to the Master and that James had said, 'I can't, I can't.' "

Walpole met Conrad through Sidney Colvin, and on January 23, 1918, recorded that Conrad began the friendship by speaking of his romantic adventures and his early works, as if to establish his credentials and avoid all talk of contemporary issues:

Conrad even better than I had expected—looking older, very nervous, rather fantastic and dramatic somehow—his eyes I think—"an intellectual Corsair." He talked eagerly, telling me all kinds of things about his early life. Delighted when I said I liked *Nostromo* best, although he said *The Nigger* was *the* book! Cursed the public for not distinguishing between creation and photography.

By September 1919 Conrad referred to Walpole, who had supplemented Curle (now in South Africa), as the most intimate of his younger friends. Apparently ignorant of Walpole's homosexuality, Conrad said that he would try to hold out until Walpole returned, perhaps with a new wife, from his American lecture tour. Walpole dedicated *The Cathedral* to Conrad in 1922. But in February 1928, four years after Conrad's death, his attitude changed from adulation to retrospective mockery: "Conrad never said anything very interesting in his last years; he was too preoccupied with money and gout. He was only thrilling when [in great pain] he lost his temper and chattered and screamed like a monkey."[10]

Gérard Jean-Aubry, two years older than Walpole, was a musicologist and literary critic from Normandy who had been living in London since 1916. He had a high forehead, small, widely spaced eyes, a sharp nose and full lips beneath a broad mustache. A friend of Gide and translator, editor and biographer of Conrad, he helped enormously, during the two decades after Conrad's death, to sustain his reputation in England and in France. They first met when Jean-Aubry came to Capel House in May 1918, and he soon became a frequent visitor and stimulating companion. Conrad respected his erudition, hard work and intellectual integrity, and Jean-Aubry proudly told a friend: "he is kind enough to show interest in and even affection for me, which count a lot in my life here." In 1919 Conrad begged off a dinner invitation from Sir Robert Jones in order to attend Jean-Aubry's lecture on French poets at the Royal Institution in Liverpool; and he would accompany the Conrads on their drive through France in 1921. In 1923 Conrad dedicated *The Rover* to him "in friendship, this tale of the last days of a French brother of the coast";[11] and in 1924 Jean-Aubry helped place John, who wished to learn French, in a pastor's home in Le Havre.

Despite his usefulness and good works, Jean-Aubry (like Gibbon and Curle) had a touchy side to his character, and could be impatient and humorless. He once startled a woman whose infant had disturbed him by exclaiming: "I hate children!" John Conrad described him as "so serious, always on his dignity and prone to take umbrage at the least provocation and always impeccably attired, seemingly for ever flicking invisible specks of dust or hairs from his clothes." His rival Curle, who criticized Retinger for his endless loans from Conrad, also spoke cuttingly against Jean-Aubry, "explaining that the reason for the [very] small amount of his own writing in the second volume of the *Life and Letters* was that the publisher refused to give him further advances" and he was desperate to finish the book somehow and get paid.

Borys kept up a brave front when he had his first home leave in January 1917. When writing to Quinn, Conrad seemed proud of the "good-tempered, imperturbable serenity in his manner, speech and thoughts—as if nothing in the world could startle or annoy him anymore. . . . He looks wonderfully robust and had developed a respectable moustache. . . . We got on extremely well together. We talked not only of war but of the other two 'W'—women and wine."[12] But the Conrads were terribly worried about Borys throughout the war (as well as during his leave in Paris with Jane Anderson). On October 10, 1918, a month before Armistice Day, they finally received the dreaded news. Borys had been gassed and shell-shocked during the advance of the Second Army on the Menin-Cambrai road in northeast France. He was partly buried, with several other men, by a German salvo of high explosive and gas shells. But he sent a reassuring word, from the hospital in Rouen where Ford had been in December 1916, that he was only slightly shaken up. The trauma, in fact, had serious psychological effects and made it extremely difficult for Borys to settle into civilian life when the war was over.

Jessie's problems with her crippled knee (as well as with her longstanding valvular heart defect) were as serious as Borys' condition, and another constant source of worry. Despite her disastrous series of operations, Conrad continued to maintain a naïve and ill-founded faith in doctors and hoped that the distinguished orthopedic surgeon Sir Robert Jones would finally be able to cure her.

The son of a journalist and editor, Jones was born in Rhyl, Wales, the same year as Conrad, grew up in London, was educated at Sydenham College and attended medical school in Liverpool. After qualifying in 1878, he concentrated on treating crippled children and performed as many as twenty-five operations a day at the Royal Southern Hospital in Liverpool. He published several standard books on orthopedic surgery and established an international reputation as the most accomplished surgeon of his time. In 1896, a year after Roentgen's discovery, Jones took the first X-ray in England. He became a major-general in the Royal Army Medical Corps during the war and was knighted in 1917. Kindly, sympathetic, exuberant, old-fashioned and over-optimistic, Jones was a portly man with a gentle countenance, broad forehead, blue eyes, trim white mustache and jaunty bow tie. He was an excellent shot, boxer, cricketer and horseman.

In December 1917, when it looked as if Jessie's leg would have to be amputated, the Conrads moved for three months to a flat in Hyde Park Mansions on Marylebone Road in London, so that Jones could treat her knee joint. The following June, when Jones finally decided to operate (for the first time since her accident in 1904) on the stiff and septic knee, which had first become infected during the journey to Poland, they moved up to London for another two months. Jones took away the knee-cap, excised the cartilage and made a new socket. In December 1919 the Conrads traveled north to his headquarters in Liverpool for Jessie's third operation. But in February 1920 Conrad confessed to Gide that "after three years of suffering, three major operations, and three incisions, she still walks with crutches." The following month, after Jessie's fourth operation—a four-inch cut to the bone, followed by three days of intense pain—Conrad told Galsworthy that there remained a suspicious spot on the leg that would require yet another operation. Jessie's persistent periostitis (inflammation of the bone), which originated in the septic knee of 1918, required a fifth operation in July 1920 and, though Conrad observed that she could not be carved indefinitely, a sixth took place in June 1924. Jessie, a model patient (though impatient with the suffering of others), bore her hopeless condition with fortitude and forbearance. The great difficulty, as Borys explained, was though Jones had made Jessie's condition more bearable, "he arrived on the scene too late to fully repair the damage done by his predecessors." Though Jessie tried to exercise, she was unable to do so and continued to gain weight. As Conrad exclaimed in Corsica in 1921: " 'She has grown huge . . . ever since I knew her she was plump—but now she is enormous—enormous' and he threw up his hands and eyes."

In late September 1922 the Conrads and John traveled to Liverpool to visit Jones, who took them on a disappointing three-day tour of North Wales and of Mount Snowdon, where Gelert, the trusty hound of Prince Llewelyn, was buried. Jones' biographer, Frederick Watson, wrote:

Joseph Conrad was taken by car on a most forbidding day to see the famous Beddgelert Pass. Unfortunately, to him it was not even a name once heard. And the whole valley was shrouded in a cold and drenching mist. Conrad—who had an attack of gout—shivered and peered and finally relapsed into what I presumed was a Polish resignation. But Robert

Jones was unconquerable. He had a great and intense patriotism for the traditions of Welsh history. As we passed through the swirling mist up the pass he spoke not without emotion of Gelert, and Conrad glowered and shivered and maintained a silence which seemed to descend into depths unplumbed by the English temperament. At last when we stopped at the summit where, in happier circumstances, a view could be obtained, he broke his silence.

"Who was this Gelert?" he asked rather sharply.[13]

Conrad, though sick and cold, was dragged into the mountains where he could not see anything. He was naturally miserable, as anyone would be, but Watson attributed his gloomy behavior to his unfathomable Polishness rather than to the uncomfortable circumstances of the journey. This incident reveals that Conrad, the indelible foreigner, was frequently misunderstood by the English.

Conrad soon recovered from his petulant mood, but Jessie never fully recovered her ability to walk. Despite the recurrent pattern of apparent success and optimistic prognosis, followed by acute disappointment and another excruciating operation, Conrad sent Jones an unusually warm and appreciative Christmas greeting in 1922.

I send you all the best wishes which gratitude, affection, and the greatest possible regard can inspire. There is no man to whom I owe more than I owe to you, and what your humanity and skill has given to us has been given with a generosity and warmth of heart which nothing in this world can repay.

May all that is good attend you, and all who are dear to you, is the prayer of, Most affectionately yours, JOSEPH CONRAD.

V

In February 1915, a month before *Victory* appeared, Conrad had published *Within the Tides*, his weakest collection of stories. "The Inn of the Two Witches" is an awkwardly narrated Spanish-Gothic tale in the manner of Edgar Poe and Stevenson's "Olalla" (1885). During the Peninsular War an English naval officer, searching on land for a trusty seaman, discovers that he has been murdered for his money and crushed to death by a heavy four-poster bed at the inn of the two witches ("There was something grotesque in their decrepitude"). "The Partner," an equally melodramatic but more ironic tale of pointless evil, is related in breathless phrases and recalls the plot of the earlier and much finer

"The End of the Tether." In the later story the unscrupulous partner of the good captain's brother bribes the mate to wreck the ship so he can collect the insurance money and start a patent medicine business. The partner then comes aboard the wrecked ship and locks the mate, who has tried to blackmail him, in the cabin so he will drown. When the captain enters the cabin to get the money he has left there, he is shot by the mate, who escapes from the ship but cannot collect his bribe from the partner.

"Because of the Dollars" was adapted by Conrad into a weak two-act play, *Laughing Anne*, in 1923. In this story Captain Davidson, who had appeared as Axel Heyst's friend in *Victory*, warned by the sympathetic Laughing Anne, foils a plot to steal the government dollars he is transporting in his ship. After she is murdered for betraying the thieves, Davidson rescues her son. But his wife resents the child and leaves him. Ruined (like Heyst) by his altruistic deed, "he will have to go downhill without a single human affection near him because of those old dollars."

The theme of a man paralyzed by love—which Conrad had portrayed in *Lord Jim*, "Freya of the Seven Isles" and *Victory*—recurs in the most interesting and substantial of the four stories, "The Planter of Malata." In a great colonial city in the East, the lonely planter Geoffrey Renouard falls in love with Felicia Moorsom. She is searching for her former fiancé, who had disappeared when under a cloud of suspicion and was subsequently found to be innocent. Renouard knows that the suspect fiancé, whom she now wishes to rescue and marry, had been the assistant on his island and had died there. Reluctant to tell her the truth and unable to give her up, Renouard takes Felicia and her father to his island to meet the man. After revealing the truth to her and declaring his love, he is rejected by the deceived and angry woman, and drowns himself—setting out "calmly to swim beyond the confines of life." Despite the absurd plot and operatic declaration of love, there is real pathos in Renouard's loneliness and suffering, which transcend the money-grubbing schemes described in the other stories in *Within the Tides*. Toward the end of 1915 Conrad, aware that his later work was inferior, complained to Galsworthy: " 'The Planter of Malata' alone earned eight times as much as 'Youth,' six times as much as 'Heart of Darkness.' It makes one sick"[14]—though he would surely have been even more unhappy if he had earned *less* money as his career developed and his reputation increased.

The Shadow-Line (1917), Conrad's last great work, written in a purer prose style and from the depths of his own experience, is infinitely superior in its revelation of a troubled state of mind to the stories in *Within the Tides*. Originally called "First Command," it was (as we have seen) based on his experiences while sailing the *Otago* from Bangkok to Singapore early in 1888. The chief steward of the Officers' Home in Singapore, who wants to get rid of the ne'er-do-well Hamilton because he will not pay his bills, encourages him to try for the dead captain's job and hides the letter offering that position to the autobiographical narrator-hero. The steward was actually based, Conrad wrote, on "a meagre wizened creature, always bemoaning his fate, [who] did try to do me an unfriendly turn for some reason or other." And Captain Giles, who also lives in the Officers' Home and whose guiles secure the berth for the narrator, was based on a well-known "man called Patterson, a dear, thick, dreary creature with an enormous reputation for knowledge of the Sulu Sea," northeast of Borneo. The title of the story refers not only to that twilight region between the naïve self-confidence of youth and the more introspective wisdom of maturity, but also to the entrance to the Gulf of Siam, where the former captain was buried and where the ship is mysteriously becalmed off the island of Koh-ring (which also appeared in "The Secret Sharer").

The redemptive figure of Ransome, a seaman with a bad heart who signs on as a mere cook, provides a moral and physical contrast to the deranged chief mate Burns, who had hoped to take command of the ship by bringing it to Bangkok, where (he thought) there would be no qualified masters. The contrast between Ransome and Burns recalls that of Singleton and Donkin in *The Nigger of the "Narcissus,"* in which the burial of the dead man breaks a calm spell instead of creating one. The obstacles that confront the narrator hero who becomes the new captain are formidable: they are becalmed, the reproachful men are feverish and enfeebled by cholera and malaria, the medicine has been stolen, the chief mate is superstitious and unreliable, the second mate is inexperienced, the captain must remain constantly awake and Ransome might die at any moment. But as in "Youth," the young captain narrowly escapes death, survives the crucial ordeal and believes "a man should stand up to his bad luck, to his mistakes, to his conscience, and all that sort of thing. Why—what else would you have to fight against?"[15]

The Arrow of Gold, written fairly rapidly between late July 1917 and June 14, 1918, conflates Conrad's youthful experiences in Marseilles and his love affair with Jane Anderson. On December 31, 1917, half-way through the novel and dissatisfied with his work, he lamented to Ted Sanderson (who had returned from Africa), as he had to Galsworthy: "with groans and imprecations, I have been working every morning. You can imagine what sort of stuff that is. No colour, no relief, no tonality; the thinnest possible squeaky bubble. And when I've finished with it, I shall go out and sell it in a market place for 20 times the money I had for the *Nigger*."[16] Conrad later justified his operatic plot by explaining that Rita's renunciation of Monsieur George after their love idyll (like Violetta's sacrifice for Alfredo in Verdi's *La Traviata*) was a noble and redemptive act: "By going away beyond his reach she gives him the supreme proof of her love, stronger than mere passion, stronger than the fear of her own and of his suffering."

VI

Conrad was always sensitive about his incongruous role as a foreigner writing in English. In August 1918, during the intense xenophobia that prevailed in the final phase of the war, he felt obliged, in the liberal *New Republic*, to answer Frank Harris, who had attempted to insult him by calling him a Jew in print. In this letter Conrad clarified the issue by providing elaborate documentary evidence to prove that he was not Jewish. He also publicly expressed his honest and humane feelings about this sensitive subject: "I don't feel annoyed in the least. Had I been an Israelite I would never have denied being a member of a race occupying such a unique place in the religious history of mankind."[17]

Since Conrad has repeatedly been accused of anti-Semitism, the complex question of his attitude toward the Jews deserves thorough investigation.[18] Conrad enjoyed warm personal relations with a number of Jewish friends: William Rothenstein, who frequently lent him money and was instrumental in getting him government grants; Alfred Knopf, whose initiative had helped Conrad achieve his first commercial success with *Chance* in 1913; Jacob Epstein, to whom he sat and whose work he greatly admired; and Bruno Winawer, whose play he praised and translated into English in 1921.

Conrad's allusions to and portrayal of Jewish characters in his fiction is entirely sympathetic. In *Nostromo*, he describes Hirsch, the hide merchant from Esmeralda, as a fearful Jew. He is captured and tortured by the savage Sotillo, who wants to find out where the silver treasure is hidden. His captors tie a rope to Hirsch's wrists and throw it over a wooden beam; and, with a yell of agony and despair, he is jerked off his feet and left hanging. Despite protracted torment and whipping, Hirsch remains silent. Finally, driven beyond endurance, and "with the sudden flash of a grin and a straining forward of the wrenched shoulders, he spat violently into [Sotillo's] face"—and was immediately shot dead. Hirsch's brave but self-destructive act, which Conrad treated compassionately, was the only form of defiance left to him.

Yankel, the Jewish innkeeper in "Prince Roman," is based on Jankiel the Jew in Mickiewicz's national epic, *Pan Tadeusz*. In that poem Jankiel treats his Polish hosts to an impromptu dulcimer concert to celebrate their common liberation from Russian rule. "The honest Jew," Mickiewicz wrote, "loved his country like a Pole." In Conrad's tale of exemplary, sacrificial patriotism Yankel, "a portly, dignified Jew, clad in a black satin coat reaching down to his heels and girt with a red sash," is a Polish patriot. He remembers the noble role of the Polish divisions during Napoleon's march on Moscow, tells Prince Roman that the popular rising has begun and hopes "Perhaps this time [a common Judeo-Christian] God will help."[19] Conrad's characterization of Yankel, who plays a minor but significant role in the story, was undoubtedly his tribute to the part played by the Jews in the revolution in 1863.

In October 1911 Conrad had been deeply distressed by a favorable review of *Under Western Eyes* in the *Morning Post*. Speaking of the English teacher of languages who narrates the story of Russian revolutionaries in Geneva, the anonymous critic speculated: "The professor, we cannot help fancying, must have been a Jew, holding the balance between the West and the East." As soon as he read the review, Conrad sent a furious, hypersensitive letter to Galsworthy claiming that this passage, which clearly concerned a character in the novel, was

> incomprehensible, unless meant as a hint that I, being a Jew, am especially fit to hold the balance between East and West! I believe that some time ago that preposterous Papist Belloc has been connecting me with Father Abraham, whether to hurt me or to serve me, or simply because he's an idiot—I don't know. . . . It's an absurd position to be in, for I trust I have no contemptible prejudices against any kind of human beings and yet it isn't pleasant to be taken out of one's own skin, as it were, by an irresponsible chatterer.[20]

Conrad begins the letter with an irrational misreading, connects this criticism to an earlier one by the notorious anti-Semite Hilaire Belloc—who admired Conrad, had written a favorable article on *Almayer's Folly* and had been sent an inscribed copy of *Nostromo*—and concludes by dissociating himself from odious bigotry.

During the war years Conrad was closely involved with the affairs of Poland (the supposed source of his Jewish origins and his anti-Semitic feelings), from his entrapment behind enemy lines in Austrian Galicia in

August 1914, to his pronouncements on Polish independence in 1918. Characteristically pessimistic about Polish prospects while in Cracow and Zakopane, he later told Cunninghame Graham that "the sheer despair of these people seeing nothing but ruin and ultimate extinction whatever would happen was very hard to bear." In August 1914 he set forth his views in a memorandum, written in Polish but intended for the British Foreign Office, which revealed his orientation toward the Catholic and relatively liberal Austria:

> Germany (Prussia), though it cannot be defeated, nevertheless can be subdued to a certain degree and the only way to this end is to support the demands of Austria as far as they concern Polish territories—precisely to increase the anti-German elements in the setup of this empire [and] to create an equilibrium against Prussian preponderance in Europe. In this respect England cannot count on Russia—first, because Russia will be defeated—and secondly (and chiefly) because Prussia and Russia may come to an understanding in the near future.

In "A Note on the Polish Problem" (1916) Conrad advocated an Anglo-French protectorate as the ideal form of moral and material support for the new Polish commonwealth. After the revolution of October 1917 Russia, which had suffered disastrous defeats, came to an understanding with Germany in the Treaty of Brest-Litovsk and withdrew from the war.

Conrad's attitude toward Russia was consistently negative. When Curle, at the beginning of the war, expressed faith in their Russian ally, Conrad contemptuously repeated that Russia was bound to let England down. He was not pleased by the February revolution in Russia and did not see that it might possibly benefit Poland. In May 1917 he told Quinn that Russia was still the same untrustworthy ally that it always had been, and in February 1918 was prescient about the danger of revolution spreading in Western Europe: "Whatever happens Russia is out of the war now. The great thing is to keep the Russian infection, its decomposing power, from the social organism of the rest of the world." In May 1924, soon after Lenin's death, Conrad condemned the horror and stupidity of the Russian Revolution. And Ford recorded that Conrad anticipated both Trotsky's and Orwell's idea of the "revolution betrayed": "he was accustomed to declare *all* revolutions always have been, always must be, nothing more in the end than palace intrigues: intrigues either for power within, or for the occupancy of, a palace."[21]

In March 1916 Conrad emphatically told his American editor that the United States should *not* enter the war. After the war, he admitted that

American intervention had been a great piece of luck for the Allies; but he mistrusted Woodrow Wilson's windy rhetoric and naïve idealism, and felt Poland would be sacrificed by "some pretty ugly compromise." On Armistice Day, November 11, 1918, Lloyd George expressed the banal and mindless sentiments that seemed appropriate to the occasion and had no more basis in reality than the rabid patriotism that since 1914 had been used to justify the war: "I hope we may say that thus, this fateful morning, came an end to all wars." Conrad, by contrast, had grave doubts about the future and prophetically warned Hugh Walpole, who had recently returned from Russia: "The great sacrifice is consummated—and what will come of it to the nations of the earth the future will show. I cannot confess to an easy mind. Great and very blind forces are set catastrophically over all the world."[22]

In 1918 Poland was finally freed after 123 years of foreign oppression and recognized as an independent state. Poland was not brought back to life by the realization of its traditional hopes—by a Polish revolt, by Russia's foreign wars or by the intervention of the Western powers—but by an unexpected Bolshevik revolution *within* Czarist Russia and by a four-year cataclysm that had destroyed the vast empires of Turkey, Austria, Germany and Russia. Conrad's reaction, conveyed to his political correspondent John Quinn, once again warned against the threat of Russia and repeated the emotional sentiments that Apollo had first expressed in "Poland and Muscovy": the cause of independence "enables the three times devastated and impoverished country to put forth its physical strength, and on the very morrow of rising from [the grave to take up] its old historical part of the defender of civilization against the dangers of barbarism, once Tartar and Turkish, and now even worse, because arising no longer from the mere savagery of nomad races, but from an enormous seething mass of sheer moral corruption—generating violence of a more purposeful sort." Conrad's deep-rooted personal and historical pessimism—which linked him to Polish and European contemporaries and distinguished him from positivistic coevals like Kipling, Wells and Galsworthy—was his most important intellectual contribution to English literature and to English thought.[23]

CHAPTER EIGHTEEN

Fame and America

1919–1924

I

Conrad's energy and powers declined after *The Shadow-Line*, when he started dictating rather than writing his work, and during the last five years of his life he began to spend his recently acquired wealth and rest on his previous achievements. He brought out a collected and a de luxe edition of his works, continued to sell his manuscripts, and took an active interest in his French and Polish translations. He indulged his taste for music and finally finished *The Rescue*. He wrote literary and political essays and gathered them in *Notes on Life and Letters*, composed a silent film scenario based on "Gaspar Ruiz," translated Bruno Winawer's Polish play *The Book of Job*, adapted *The Secret Agent* for the stage, and wrote two historical novels: *The Rover* and *Suspense*. He traveled in grand style to Corsica and to America, met T. E. Lawrence and received disciples, was offered and declined honorary degrees and a knighthood, was painted and sculpted, and played the public figure.

Yet it was difficult for Conrad to enjoy his late success. He had had a miserably unhappy childhood, an arduous life at sea and in the Congo, and a difficult time as a writer. He now lived on a grand scale, could not put a brake on expenditures and was frequently short of money. He suffered from the effects of the war, from attacks of gout and from heart disease; he constantly worried about Jessie's knees and about Borys' postwar problems with money. He still found it difficult to write and recognized the radical decline in his work. In his early sixties, exhausted and prematurely aged, he often had to fight off fits of depression. The demons of anguish and doubt tormented his old age.

The landlord of Capel House died in early 1919 and his son, who wished to live there himself, gave the Conrads notice. They had never owned a home and had lived in Capel House for a decade. In March they had to move and lived for six months at Spring Grove in Wye, eight miles northeast in the direction of Canterbury. Spring Grove was a furnished seventeenth-century manor, with lovely Adam fireplaces, but it was too large for the family and Conrad instinctively disliked it. In the fall they found Oswalds in nearby Bishopsbourne, five miles southeast of Canterbury, and moved there on October 6.

Conrad's last house cost £250 a year and was the finest one of all. Nearly a century old, it was surrounded by tall trees and three gardens whose ivy-covered walls had communicating doors. The elegant façade of the two-story house had nine high sash-windows and a small portico supported by two columns. Equipped with electricity and central heating, it also had two cottages and a bowling green. But there was one drawback: situated in a hollow and surrounded by woods, it lacked a good view. Conrad and Jessie, who took separate bedrooms, hired a staff of seven to look after their needs: a butler, two gardeners, two housemaids, a cook and a nurse. The servants and spaciousness of Oswalds allowed Conrad to indulge in traditional Polish hospitality and he frequently had guests on the weekends as well as for longer stays. He had come a long way in the last decade from the four rooms in Aldington next to a slaughterhouse.

Conrad's popularity and literary reputation continued to rise after *Chance, Victory* and *The Shadow-Line*. The critical studies by Richard Curle (1914), Wilson Follett (1915) and Hugh Walpole (1916) were followed by Thomas Wise's *Bibliography* (1920), Commander Sutherland's *At Sea with Joseph Conrad* (1922), appreciations by Ruth Stauffer (1922) and Ernst Bendz (1923), and Christopher Morley's memoir of the American visit, *Conrad and the Reporters* (1923).

At the beginning of the war Frank Doubleday had approached Conrad with the idea of a collected edition of his works, modeled on those of Hardy and James, but the plan had been postponed at the author's request until the end of hostilities. In July 1919 Conrad told Quinn, who was assisting in and sometimes disturbing the negotiations, that by 1914 he had established a substantial and unquestionable reputation, based on the admiration of distinguished minds in America, England and Europe. In addition to his regular income of about £2,000 a year, Conrad received an advance of $12,000 for the 780 sets of the American collected edition of 1921, and another £10,000 for the English de luxe edition of 1922. Conrad, who received six sets of the latter, kept one for himself and gave the others to Borys (who never read them) and to John, to Garnett and Gide, who had significantly helped his career in England

and in France, and to the much-admired surgeon Sir Robert Jones. Conrad's late works were also lucrative. *The Rescue* earned £3,000 in serial rights and *The Rover* sold 26,000 copies in England

II

Conrad associated music with dramatic moments, heightened emotions and passionate love. He was particularly fond of opera—especially of Meyerbeer, Verdi and Bizet—and used operatic gestures, language, themes and plots throughout his career. These characteristics culminate in his late work, *The Rescue*, which is deliberately—though not always successfully—melodramatic and operatic. Toward the end of his life, after a hiatus of twenty years, the techniques of opera helped Conrad complete this underrated novel. His extensive knowledge of music and his attempt to achieve intensity through operatic strategies suggest the spirit and mode of the work.

Music played a surprisingly pervasive role in Conrad's life and art. The courtship and marriage of Conrad's parents were like an operatic plot. Apollo courted Eva unsuccessfully during the lifetime of her father, who disapproved of her feckless suitor; she waited six years after her father's death before she finally defied his wishes to marry the man she loved. During Apollo's confinement for revolutionary activities in the Warsaw Citadel in 1861, he translated Victor Hugo's play, *Le roi s'amuse* (1832), the source of Verdi's *Rigoletto* (1851). Eva and little Conrad, in operatic fashion, stood outside the father's cell, followed him into exile and begged for medical aid on the long road to Vologda. And Conrad's first childhood recollection concerned his mother and music. During his early years in Marseilles, he first heard Italian and French operas.

Giacomo Meyerbeer—who was born Jakob Beer in Berlin and, like Conrad, changed his name and made his career in a foreign country— was the cosmopolitan pupil of Abt Vogler (the subject of Browning's poem). His *Huguenots* (1836) had been praised by Théophile Gautier and admired by Conrad's hero, Ivan Turgenev, who heard his mistress Pauline Viardot sing the role of Valentine in this opera and of Fidès in the premiere of *Le Prophète* (1849). Meyerbeer's astonishing reputation declined, after vicious attacks by Richard Wagner, in the late nineteenth century; and in June 1910 the conservative Conrad told Galsworthy: "I suppose that I am now the only human being in these Isles who thinks Meyerbeer a great composer."[1]

Conrad had scant opportunity to attend the opera during his long years in Asian waters, though in a rare conversation with a cultured English gentleman, Mr. Senior, when the *Duke of Sutherland* was docked in Sydney harbor in October 1879, he "touched in our discourse, upon science, politics, natural history, and operatic singers." When he was marooned on his last ship, the *Adowa*, in 1893, awaiting French immigrants to Canada who never materialized, Conrad (who as a boy had devoured the novels of Walter Scott) recalled that he was berthed near the Opera café in Rouen where Emma Bovary "had some refreshment after the memorable performance of [Donizetti's] opera which was the tragic story of [Scott's] Lucia di Lammermoor in a setting of light music."

Conrad's account of his hapless courtship of and proposal to the already engaged Eugénie Renouf in Mauritius in 1888 "suggests soap opera or Puccini." And his equally unsuccessful wooing of Émilie Briquel in Champel in 1895 was also accompanied by musical motifs. Émilie recorded in her diary that Conrad liked to listen to her play the piano and was particularly fond of pieces by Schubert, Massenet and Chopin. Before parting from Émilie forever, Conrad gave her the score of *Carmen* and attentively turned the pages while she played.

Borys claimed that Conrad's personal "repertoire was limited to the music of the two operas, *Carmen* and *Cavalleria Rusticana*; the Toreador song from the former being his favourite. . . . During our stay in Montpellier [in 1906] a performance of the opera *Carmen* was given by a touring company and, as soon as my Father heard of this, he became very excited and insisted that we should all go to the Theatre."[2] Jessie confirmed that during relatively rare moments of contentment he would whistle passages from *Carmen* or sing them in his leisurely bath. And he named his dog (a present from Stephen Crane) Escamillo, after the matador in the opera.

Though he was most deeply moved by *Carmen*, Conrad's interest and taste in music (which he pronounced "moozik") were actually more extensive than Borys suggests. Robin Douglas noted that "he loved music, and would sit back with his eyes closed when his wife played the piano"—which may have reminded him of happy hours with his mother and with Émilie Briquel. He was even more entranced when Jane Anderson "played and sang negro songs of cotton fields and plantations."

A number of Conrad's friends were serious musicians, and he met some of the finest pianists and composers of his time. Galsworthy's wife Ada had studied piano in Dresden and wrote songs; Conrad's favorite cousin Karola Zagorska, was a singer; his friend and future biographer,

Gérard Jean-Aubry, was a musicologist. His distinguished compatriot Artur Rubinstein, introduced by Norman Douglas, visited Conrad in May 1914. In September 1898 Conrad heard Ignacy Paderewski (whose father, like Conrad's, had been exiled for revolutionary activities and who, in 1919, became the first prime minister of an independent Poland) playing the piano on the recently invented phonograph. And in America in May 1923 he was introduced to Paderewski by Woodrow Wilson's adviser Colonel House. He also met Maurice Ravel at the London salon of Lady Colefax in April and again in October 1923, when they discussed the tone and music value of poetry.

Conrad was quite naturally an admirer of the music of Chopin, who had also, as a teenager, left Poland permanently. He sometimes whistled motifs from the mazurkas or nocturnes, and considered Polishness the distinctive feature of Chopin's music. In his review of *The Secret Agent*, the Slavophile Edward Garnett compared Conrad to the most famous Pole of the nineteenth century: "It has the profound and ruthless sincerity of the great Slav writers mingled with the haunting charm that reminds us so often of his compatriot Chopin." When in 1920 the American pianist and composer John Powell expressed a wish to play Chopin for Conrad, the novelist arranged a recital in his home. He also heard Powell perform at public concerts.

Conrad's novel, praised by Garnett, also appealed to his distinguished contemporary Claude Debussy. In a letter of July 8, 1910, Debussy, noting Conrad's cool irony, wrote: "Have you been reading J. Conrad's novel *The Secret Agent* in *Le Temps*? It contains an absolutely delightful set of scoundrels, and the ending is really sublime. It is described in the most calm and detached way and it is only after thinking about it that you say to yourself: 'But these people are monsters!' "[3] Conrad had an extensive knowledge of music, which was associated with sensuality and with some of the most significant moments of his life: the first memory of his mother, his first months in France, his courtship of Émilie Briquel and his love for Jane Anderson.

Conrad's operatic novel, *The Rescue*, his most representative work, links the beginning to the end of his career. As he told Thomas Wise in October 1918, the novel shows "the modifications of my judgment, of my taste, and also of my style during the 20 years covering almost the whole writing period of my life." Conrad began the novel on his honeymoon in March 1896, but did not complete it until 1919.[4] Thomas Moser suggests that Conrad abandoned the novel "because the subject was uncongenial, because he could not write the love story of Lingard and Edith." But there was also a more practical reason. S. S. McClure had paid him for American rights and, always pressed for money, he had to complete other projects to bring in more cash.

Conrad's intentions, early and late, may be discerned from letters to his editors. In September 1897 he told William Blackwood that the novel portrayed an overwhelming and irrational passion as well as the familiar elements of an adventure story: "I want to convey in the action of the story the stress and exaltation of the man under the influence of a sentiment which he hardly understands and yet which is real enough to make him as he goes on reckless of consequences. . . . Of course the paraphernalia of the story are hackneyed. The yacht, the shipwreck, the pirates, the coast—all this has been used times out of number"—and would be used yet again when he collaborated with Ford on *Romance*. Two years later, still absorbed in his struggle with the novel, he told Blackwood's London editor, David Meldrum: "Everything is there: descriptions, dialogue, reflexion—everything—everything but the belief, the conviction, the only thing needed to make me put pen to paper."

In his memoir of Conrad, the publisher Frank Doubleday recalled that the long-delayed novel appealed to a great number of readers: "After twenty years . . . I received a letter from Conrad saying he had now found a way to complete *The Rescue*. . . . Nobody can tell where the old part ended and the new began. . . . Fifty thousand copies were sold—an unheard of sale for Conrad." And in his "Author's Note" Conrad explained: "I saw the action plainly enough. What I had lost for the moment was the sense of the proper formula of expression, the only formula that would suit." That formula, which Conrad finally found, after many experiments and frustrations, in 1918, was the operatic mode of intense emotions and the operatic theme of the insoluble conflict between honor and passion. Captain Lingard "rescued the white people but seemed to have lost his own soul in the attempt."[5]

In *Suspense*, his last, unfinished novel, Conrad wrote of "oriental courts full of splendours and crimes, tyrannies and treacheries and dark dramas of ambition, or love." Like Verdi in *Aida* and Puccini in *Turandot*, Conrad thought the operatic mode—romantic, rhetorical and histrionic —particularly well-suited to an exotic and primitive eastern setting.

There are many good things in *The Rescue: A Romance of the Shallows*,[6] in which the rescuer of a victim is himself the victim of the woman he rescues. Tom Lingard is torn between his promise to restore a young Malay prince as ruler of his country and his emotional involvement with Edith Travers, whose yacht, with her husband and their friend d'Alcacer, has foundered on a remote island of the Archipelago. The four ships in the novel each represent a separate world and system of values; and Travers' *Hermit*, Jörgenson's *Wild Rose* and the floating fortress and powder-keg *Emma* are a contrast, an echo and a parody of Tom Lingard's *Lightning*. (Unlike Jasper Allen in "Freya of the Seven Isles," who remains tragically faithful to his ship, Lingard transfers his passion from the beloved brig to Edith Travers.) The scene in which Travers and Edith express their hatred of each other (part V, chapter 1) equals the brilliant social satire in *The Secret Agent* and *Chance*. Unlike *Almayer's Folly* and *An Outcast of the Islands*, which deal with the later phases of Lingard's career, *The Rescue* does not portray the corruption of the white man by the tropics, but describes corrupt whites stranded in and contaminating the tropics. D'Alcacer, like Decoud in *Nostromo*, is a fascinating, sarcastic, world-weary European intellectual who, when faced with unaccustomed violence and the threat of death, expresses his all-too-human weakness by telling Edith: "I should like to get a warning, just something that would give me time to pull myself together, to compose myself as it were. I want you to promise me that if the balance tips against us you will give me a sign."

André Gide, a talented pianist, admired *The Rescue*, recognized its musical structure and wrote Conrad: "The subject itself, the secret song, only appears later, but so soon as one begins to perceive the extraordinary melody—the duet by Mrs. Travers and Lingard—it becomes clear that its full significance could not be brought out earlier and we are able to be congratulated on our delay."

The most significant and revealing scene in the novel is the intimate conversation between Lingard and Edith (a positive contrast to the bitter conversation with her husband) in which they discuss opera, emphasize the theatrical aspect of the novel, and introduce the themes of illusion and reality. Edith's Malay costume, which she has exchanged for European clothes and to which her husband objects, is part of this illusion. It strips her of her past and makes her part of Lingard's strange and unfamiliar world. Edith explains that when she walked out of the stockade on Lingard's arm,

> "It seemed to me that I was walking on a splendid stage in a scene from an opera, in a gorgeous show fit to make an audience hold its breath. You can't possibly guess how unreal all this seemed, and how artificial I felt myself. An opera, you know. . . ."
>
> "I know. I was a gold digger at one time. Some of us used to come down to Melbourne with our pockets full of money. I daresay it was poor enough to what you must have seen, but once I went to a show like that. It was a

story acted to music. All the people went singing through it right to the very end."

"How it must have jarred on your sense of reality," said Mrs. Travers, still not looking at him. "You don't remember the name of the opera?"

"No. I never troubled my head about it. We—our lot never did."

"I won't ask you what the story was like. It must have appeared to you like the very defiance of all truth." . . .

"I assure you that of the few shows I have seen that one was the most real to me. More real than anything in life."

Mrs. Travers, remembering the fatal inanity of most opera librettos, was touched by these words.

Edith, emphasizing the theme of illusion, and the unreality of their existence, tells Lingard that her whole life has seemed like a show and that she has not been taken in (as he has) by the action on the stage. Lingard's speech reminds her of a great actor's voice and she also looks on the Malay Settlement "as on the face of a painting on a curtain." Later on, d'Alcacer reinforces the theme of unreality by warning Lingard that women like Edith lead men in an illusory ritual dance, which men take seriously though it has nothing to do with sincerity, good faith or honor: "Woe to him or her who breaks it. Directly they leave the pageant they get lost."[7] Lingard's great tragedy is that he mistakes illusion for reality. Enchanted by Edith, he loses his will and (like Lord Jim and Axel Heyst) can no longer respond to the actual world.

The origins of *The Rescue* go back not only to the manuscript of 1896, but also to Conrad's first exposure, in Marseilles in 1874, to Bizet and Meyerbeer. In a positive and extremely perceptive contemporary review of the novel, Katherine Mansfield described Edith Travers as the very embodiment of the *femme fatale*: "She is the flower of corruption, the poisonous vine that can only feed upon the life of another. And Lingard is her perfect, willing prey." Edith, in fact, plays Carmen to Lingard's Don José and leads him directly to his dishonor and doom. At the end of the novel, when Lingard discovers that Jörgenson has blown up the *Emma* and killed Hassim and Immada, whose kingdom Lingard had promised to restore, he alludes to the love-philter in *Tristan and Isolde* and asks himself: "Who could tell what was real in this world? He looked about him, dazedly; he was still drunk with the deep draught of oblivion he had conquered for himself. Yes—but it was she who had let him snatch the cup."

Conrad thought Meyerbeer a great composer; and the explosion of the

Emma that provides the tragic climax of the novel ("All the guns and powder I have got together so far are stored in her") is modeled directly on the explosion that takes place at the end of Meyerbeer's *Le Prophète*. As early as 1899, while working on *The Rescue*, Conrad planned to collaborate with Ford on "a great novel about the Ana Baptists."[8] In the opera, the cellar-dungeon of the Palace of Münster has been turned into a powder-magazine. In the final scene (Act 5, Scene 2) Jean, the false prophet, decides—like Jörgenson in *The Rescue*—to kill himself with all the wicked Anabaptists. He lights a fire in the Banquet Hall and, when all his enemies are present, the powder explodes and the palace collapses.

When completing *The Rescue* Conrad once again sought the advice of his first literary mentor, Edward Garnett. Hurt by Garnett's severe but just criticism of the second part of *Lord Jim*, Conrad had not shown his work to Garnett for eighteen years. In June 1919 Garnett, with characteristic insight, saw the disparity between the operatic emotion and the rather static action of the novel. Using a musical metaphor, he told Conrad: "The *tone* of the expression perhaps does not harmonize with the drama." The following year, when the novel was published to popular acclaim, Conrad justified Lingard's final renunciation, emphasized his artistic integrity, explained the emotional impact of the explosion and conceded the truth of Garnett's criticism:

> If I had hung Mrs. Travers for five minutes on Lingard's neck (at the last meeting) [the critics] would have been perfectly satisfied. To her I would only advance in palliation that one must take account of facts. The blowing up of the *Emma* was a fact. It destroyed suddenly the whole emotional situation not only for them but also for me. To go on after that was no joke. And yet something had to be done at once! I cared too much for Mrs. Travers to play pranks with her on the line of [operatic] heroics or tenderness; and being afraid of striking a false note I failed to do her justice—not so much *in action*, I think, as in expression.[9]

III

Stimulated by the excitement and financial rewards of the theater, by Galsworthy's success as a dramatist, by Macdonald Hastings' stage adaptation of *Victory*, which opened at the Globe Theatre in London on March 26, 1919, and had an unexpectedly successful run into June, and by Pinker's sale of the film rights of his works for an astonishing £3,000, Conrad became interested during his late years in the movies and the theater. Sceptical of enterprises that destroyed all suggestiveness, he told Curle: "The Movie is just a silly stunt for silly people—but the theatre is [even] more compromising since it is capable of falsifying the very soul of one's work both on the imaginative and on the intellectual side."

Nevertheless, commissioned by the Famous Players–Lasky Corporation of America in the fall of 1920, he wrote in collaboration with Pinker an unpublished eighty-one-page typed scenario for a silent film. It was based on his story of revolution in South America, "Gaspar Ruiz," and called "The Strong Man." In November 1920 Conrad provided an aesthetic justification of the project and told Wise how he had tried to visualize the scenes of the story: "It is in no sense a collection of notes, but a consecutive development of the story in a series of descriptions, just as the whole thing presented itself to me when I first began to think the subject out in its purely visual aspect. Such a line of composition being perfectly novel to me, I found it necessary to write it all down so as to have the whole thing embodied in a definite shape, before I could attempt to elaborate it into a detailed presentation for the reading of the Film's Literary Editor."

Though Najder unequivocally states that Conrad's film scenario "has not survived," the manuscript is at Yale and the typescript at Colgate, whose catalogue notes: "The script was composed before the advent of the sound track. Hence dialogue is reduced to the skeletal subtitle, and visual narration accordingly exploited: effects of body movement, physical tableaux, and symbolic gestures like the raising of the cross, and its converse, the fall of a tree."[10] The scenario, told in a retrospective frame story, describes six aspects of the hero's life: at home, as soldier, as outlaw, as officer, as guerrilla chief and as sacrifice in war. "The Strong Man," more descriptive than dramatic, is filled with stale phrases, windy rhetoric and operatic melodrama reminiscent of *Romance* and *The Rescue*. The theme, announced on the title page, is Gaspar's devotion to a woman and his unjust fate.

Conrad conveys the theme in a series of short descriptive scenes that roughly follow the plot of his original story. Gaspar saves his master's daughter Dona Erminia from a falling tree, he is forcibly conscripted into the revolutionary army, Erminia's family is dispossessed by the rebels. Gaspar is captured by the Royalists, is retaken by the revolutionaries and is condemned to death. The preternaturally strong man bends the prison bars to allow the water bucket to pass through; he pretends to be dead after the fusillade and, though badly wounded, survives the execution. He crawls back to Erminia, recovers from the sword slash on his neck and, as the Royalists search for him, saves Erminia from an earthquake in which her aged parents perish. He then approaches the revolutionary authorities with a plan of heroic action that would redeem him and prove his loyalty. Erminia encourages him to declare his love, they marry and she bears a child. Now the wife of a rebel, she is betrayed and captured by the Royalists. Gaspar besieges the fort, the heavy guns arrive but their carriage falls into a precipice. The guns are then lashed to Gaspar's stout frame and, as the Royalist troops arrive to relieve the garrison, he dies, after firing three salvoes, from a broken back. Deranged by the tragedy, Erminia hands her infant to a friend and (like Tosca) flings herself into the abyss.

An example of Conrad's dialogue (on cards on the screen) and of his descriptive passages give some idea of the heightened but bogus emotions of the proud Spanish types:

> "You are a rebel. I will have you shot."
> "I care not. I was forced to serve."

> Dona Erminia walks down the path with a dish of boiled maize, in which there is a wooden spoon, in her hand. She hands it to him with perfect aloofness and he receives it with grateful humility.

It is scarcely surprising that this amateurish work was, as Conrad feared it would be, rejected by Famous Players–Lasky early in 1921.[11]

Conrad worked on the dramatic adaptation of *The Secret Agent* from about November 1919 until March 1920. His letters to Pinker and Galsworthy reveal the weakness of conception, the inevitable artistic loss in the transformation from novel to stage, the mistaken attempt to include all the incidents and his doubts about the futility of the project:

> As I go on in my adaptation, stripping off the garment of artistic expression and consistent irony which clothes the story in the book, I perceive more clearly how it is bound to appear to the collective mind of the audience a merely horrible and sordid tale, giving a most unfavourable impression of both the writer himself and of his attitude to the moral aspect of the subject. . . .
>
> I've managed to ram everything in there except the actual cab-drive [of Winnie's mother to the charity home]. It was very interesting to do—and perfectly useless.

The play was not produced until two and a half years after Conrad finished it. On June 30, 1922, four months before opening night, Conrad, thinking of Hastings' success with *Victory*, naïvely hoped for a two-month run, accompanied by critical recognition and praise. He could not bear to attend the opening night on November 2, but spent the evening at the nearby Curzon Hotel with a young writer, R. L. Mégroz, who recorded: Conrad's "state of mind would have been, in most men, one of intense excitement. The contrast between his gentle speaking voice and his restless manner was remarkable. From time to time he would leave the smoke-room where we sat and inquire at the office for a message, presumably a message from the Ambassadors Theatre. He at any rate confessed to a splitting headache when excusing himself from eating anything with me about eight o'clock. He confined himself to coffee, and numerous French cigarettes."[12]

If Conrad (perhaps remembering Henry James' humiliation in 1895 at the opening of his play *Guy Domville*) was too shy and nervous to attend the first night, Jessie, who liked the theater, was glad to "represent the firm." Though she modestly claimed "the wife must be content with reflected glory if married to a famous man," she prepared herself that night for her later role as great writer's *grande dame*. As Conrad told a friend five days later, Jessie, flattered by the compliments and courtly respects of the crowd around her box, and by the respectful speeches from the stage after the final curtain, had the time of her life.

Despite popular acclaim on the first night, Conrad's friends felt the actors had performed badly and the play had failed to grip the audience. The critics responded unfavorably to the defective stagecraft and the absence of dramatic power. Conrad confessed: "If it had been a criminal act it could not have been more severely condemned," and the play closed after only a week. Yet Arnold Bennett, who had always admired Conrad's work, disagreed with the negative verdict on *The Secret Agent*, praised the play as Bernard Shaw had praised *One Day More* in 1905 and told Pinker's son: "I think that Act I and the first two scenes of Act II are superb. To my mind the third [i.e., the second, with the Assistant Commissioner and Inspector Heat] scene of Act II is comparatively weak, and the author has not been well served by his interpreters here. Act III is not equal to Act I, but it is very good, except that the last scene is a great deal too long. The scene between husband and wife before she kills him is simply magnificent. The play is extremely interesting, dramatically, as well as in all the details of psychology."[13]

I V

On July 28, 1920—between completing the stage version of *The Secret Agent* and writing the film scenario of "The Strong Man"—Cunninghame Graham brought T. E. Lawrence down to Oswalds to meet Conrad. Hugh Walpole, who was also there for the weekend, described Lawrence as "mild, small, modest, with fine eyes. Said the [Arabian war] legend about him all untrue. Talked of [fine] printing and the Crusades." As they sat in the walled garden Conrad, identifying an actual person with the villain of his play, stepped across the grass and said: "Verloc's just left." Walpole turned just in time to see "a fat, humped figure going out of the gate—some journalist from Canterbury."

In January 1935, four months before his death, Lawrence vividly recalled this meeting and described to the printer Bruce Rogers (who had carved a wooden figurehead of Conrad, based on Walter Tittle's portraits) Conrad's pointed beard and mustache, his gouty walk and his drooping eyes: "How fortunate that Conrad had that streamlined face . . . or hair on his face, anyhow. What I shall always remember is his lame walk, with the stick to help him, and that sudden upturning of the lined face, with its eager eyes under their membrane of eyelid. They drooped over the eye-socket and the sun shone red through them, as we walked up and down the garden."

While composing his masterpiece, *Seven Pillars of Wisdom*, and fascinated by the writer's craft, Lawrence had praised Conrad's rhythmical, suggestive, incantatory style in a letter to Frank Doubleday, who later brought out the trade edition of Lawrence's account of the Arabian campaign:

> You know, publishing Conrad must be a rare pleasure. He's absolutely the most haunting thing in prose that ever was: I wish I knew how every paragraph he writes (do you notice how they are all paragraphs: he seldom writes a single sentence?) goes on sounding in waves, like the note of a tenor bell, after it stops. It's not built in the rhythm of ordinary prose, but on something existing only in his head, and as he can never say what it is he wants to say, all his things end in a kind of hunger, a suggestion of something he can't say or do or think. So his books always look bigger than they are. He's as much a giant of the subjective as Kipling is of the objective. Do they hate one another?

And in December 1923 Lawrence observed in a letter to another mutual friend, Sydney Cockerell, that though Conrad had already completed his greatest works, there were still powerful passages in his weary but poignant valedictory novel, *The Rover*: "What a fine effort for a man who has written all he wants and is carried only by the momentum of old effort. Magnificent. He could write in his sleep."[14]

After meeting T. E. Lawrence and completing his film scenario, Conrad sought the Mediterranean sun and the Napoleonic ambience that would inspire his final novels, *The Rover* and *Suspense*. On January 23, 1921, he and Jessie left by car, with a nurse and chauffeur, for Corsica. The oval-shaped French island, where Napoleon was born in 1769 and which still maintained a wild tradition of blood feuds and banditry, has some of the most spectacular scenery in Europe. The east coast is flat, the center steeply mountainous and the west coast made up of rugged capes and cliffs.

John was at school in Tonbridge; and Borys accompanied them as far as Armentières, where his too vivid descriptions of the battles upset Conrad. When Borys returned to work in England, he was replaced by Jean-Aubry, who accompanied them as far as Lyons. They then traveled down the Rhône valley to Marseilles, where Conrad had begun his nautical career in 1874. They crossed by boat to Ajaccio in early February and stayed at the elegant but stiffly formal Grand Hôtel, where they met the Pinkers.

Conrad's first trip abroad since the disastrous expedition to Poland was, like his previous journeys, rather miserable. As he complained to Jean-Aubry, he could neither relax nor work: "I am nervous, exasperated, bored. . . . We haven't made any excursions. It is cold in the afternoon. The hotel is detestable. The Corsicans are charming (I mean the people) but the mountains get on my nerves with their roads which turn, turn in indefinite corniches. One wishes to roar." In Ajaccio he also met the young French writer H. R. Lenormand, who noted that "the spectres of fatigue and of creative inertia were haunting him." Conrad frequently confessed: "I can no longer work! . . . I can't find the words to match my thought. I'm never sure what it is I'm affirming. I am out of my mind."[15]

Despite doubts and despair, Conrad disciplined himself to work until the very end. He returned to Oswalds on April 10 and translated Bruno Winawer's satiric play, *The Book of Job*, in June. He had read extensively for the background of his Napoleonic novels both in England and in Corsica, began *The Rover* on October 9, finished it on June 27, 1922, and published it in November 1923.

The eponymous Rover is old Peyrol, another fictional embodiment of Dominic Cervoni, the heroic sailor and smuggler of Conrad's youthful

days in Marseilles. After a lifetime of adventure, Peyrol retires to a farm
near Toulon (on the south coast of France, east of Marseilles) where he
boasts of his past exploits, but longs for a period of rest on shore. The
farm is owned by the beautiful young Arlette, whose parents have been
murdered in the French Revolution and who arouses Peyrol's more than
paternal feelings. But when she falls in love with young Lieutenant Réal,
who arrives at the farm on a secret mission against the English Mediterranean fleet, Peyrol volunteers for a dangerous attempt to deceive the
English about the disposition of the French fleet and sacrifices himself in
order to save Réal for Arlette. The ending of this novel resembles the
conclusion of *Chance*, where the older Captain Anthony goes down with
his ship, leaving Flora free to marry young Powell. There is also a hint
of Jane Anderson in *The Rover*. Arlette has witnessed the bloody orgies
of the French Revolution as Jane had witnessed the horrors of World
War One; and Peyrol, the old sailor, gives up Arlette to young Réal as
Conrad gave up Jane (in effect) to his young rival Retinger. Though
quite readable, *The Rover* is a geriatric adventure story that recalls *Romance* just as *The Rescue* recalled the Bornean setting and themes of
Almayer's Folly and *An Outcast of the Islands*.

Conrad's brilliant description of the Mediterranean landscape—which
resembles a long cinematic panning-shot that moves from the sky and
the mountains to the trees on the plain and the red-tiled roofs of the
farmhouses—had a direct impact on Ernest Hemingway, who read the
novel as soon as it appeared and imitated it three years later in *The Sun
Also Rises*:

> There were leaning pines on the skyline, and in the pass itself dull silvery
> green patches of olive orchards below a long yellow wall backed by dark
> cypresses, and the red roofs of buildings which seemed to belong to a
> farm. (Conrad)

> [The mountains] were wooded and there were clouds coming down from
> them. The green plain stretched off. It was cut by fences and the white of
> the road showed through the trunks of a double line of trees that crossed
> the plain toward the north. As we came to the edge of the rise we saw the
> red roofs and the white houses of Burguete ahead strung out on the plain.
> (Hemingway)

At the end of *The Rover* Conrad introduces an actual historical character when the English Captain Vincent, who has captured old Peyrol's
ship, is interviewed by Lord Nelson aboard his flagship, *Victory*. Physically exhausted, anxious about his blockade of the Toulon fleet and

concerned with Napoleon's plans for an expedition to Egypt, Nelson foreshadows his own death: "His empty sleeve had not yet been pinned on his breast and swung slightly every time he turned in his walk. His thin locks fell lank against the pale cheeks, and the whole face in repose had an expression of suffering with which the fire of his one eye presented a startling contrast. . . . 'I will stick to my task till perhaps some shot from the enemy puts an end to everything.'" Captain Vincent, enormously impressed by Nelson's courage and wisdom, "left the *Victory*, feeling, like all officers who approached Lord Nelson, that he had been speaking with a personal friend; and with a renewed devotion for the great sea-officer's soul dwelling in the frail body of the Commander-in-Chief."[16]

On February 8, 1922, while working on *The Rover*, Conrad suddenly lost a close friend. J. B. Pinker, though ill with influenza, had sailed to America on business aboard the *Aquitania*. He had come down with pneumonia by the time he reached New York and died at the Biltmore Hotel, at the age of fifty-eight. Deeply shocked by the loss of the man who had for so long provided financial and emotional support, Conrad wrote Pinker's son Eric, who took over the business: "Twenty years' friendship and for most of that time in the constant interchange of the most intimate thoughts and feelings created a bond as strong as the nearest relationship. But you know enough to understand the depth of our grief here and our sense of irreparable loss."[17]

Conrad had conceived the germ of his last novel, *Suspense*, as early as January 1912, when he told Pinker that he had thought of the story but could not decide whether to set the novel during the occupation of Toulon by the British fleet in 1793, the siege of Genoa in 1796 or Napoleon's escape from Elba in 1815. A major source for the plot was the *Mémoires* of the Comtesse de Boigne. In that book, as in Conrad's novel, the heroine (like Winnie Verloc in *The Secret Agent*) agrees to marry an older man in order to provide security for her family. As in *The Nature of a Crime*, *Suspense* foreshadows but does not resolve the incestuous love of the main characters and does not explain how Adèle d'Armand will free herself from old Count de Montevesso so she can marry her handsome young half-brother and childhood friend, Cosmo Latham. (Ford finally developed the theme of innocently incestuous passion in *his* Napoleonic novel, *A Little Less Than Gods*, 1928.)

Like *The Rover*, *Suspense* is sympathetic to the Royalists and extremely critical of the bloodthirsty revolutionaries. It opens in Genoa during Napoleon's confinement on Elba, prior to the Hundred Days and his defeat at Waterloo, as the Italians plot to free him in order to gain independence from Austria. The novel notably lacks the quality promised by the title, the supposed "state of suspense in which all classes live here from the highest to the lowest, as to what may happen next. All their thoughts are concentrated on Bonaparte." The novel ends inconclusively as Cosmo becomes involved with Attilio (the last Cervoni-figure) and a group of Italian conspirators. Conrad had little to say at the end of his life, but kept writing out of mere habit, and almost achieved, in this negligible work, the ideal described in James Thurber's parody of Henry James: "to write a novel in which not only nothing happened but in which there were no characters."[18]

V

In March 1916 (before America entered the war) John Quinn suggested that Conrad—like Dickens and Wilde—make a triumphant lecture tour in America, but the idea did not appeal to him and he replied with a somewhat superficial excuse: "There's nothing I would have liked more than to give readings from my novels—but it's impossible. About 5 years ago after an attack of gouty throat I lost my voice completely. It fails me even in ordinary conversation if it is at all prolonged. A sustained effort such as a lecture or reading is out of the question."[19] Conrad also told another American correspondent, more frankly, that he was sensitive about his foreign pronunciation, which became stronger as he grew older (Paul Valéry was astonished by his "horrible" accent in English), and was unwilling to make an embarrassing and disadvantageous impression in public.

But the post-war success of his collected edition and late novels made Conrad more receptive to the importunate invitation of Frank Doubleday, who did not suggest a lecture tour, promised to take good care of him and persuasively argued that the good publicity would greatly increase the sales of his books. In order to test his powers of public speech and gauge the effect on his audience, Conrad gave his maiden address at a banquet in honor of the merchant marine at the University Club in Liverpool (then a great port) in December 1919. Four years later in April 1923, on the eve of his departure, he gave a brief congratulatory speech at the annual meeting of the Lifeboat Institution in Aeolian Hall in London. Confident of his voice and speaking ability, Conrad accepted Doubleday's invitation. In the spring of 1923 he finally made the transatlantic voyage that he had planned to take from Rouen to Canada on the *Adowa* in December 1893.

Several American critics have followed the mistaken assertions of Joseph Retinger and Hugh Walpole, who claimed that Conrad's "attitude towards Americans was pronouncedly cool, and he rarely invited them to his house," that "in selling his books in America he felt exactly like a merchant selling glass beads to African natives."[20] Conrad was angry that the Americans had rejected his film scenario in 1921 and apprehensive that Pinker (six years younger) had died on a recent voyage to the United States. But he certainly did not dislike Americans. In fact, Conrad had frequently benefited from the kindness and generosity of American authors, diplomats, patrons and publishers; and he had a great number of American acquaintances and friends, who often enjoyed his warm hospitality.

Edwin Markham admired his work; Theodore Dreiser and Jack London (with whom he corresponded) praised *Chance* in a publicity pamphlet of 1913; H. L. Mencken and James Gibbons Huneker (whom he met in October 1912) repeatedly admired his works in print; and Christopher Morley would publish a favorable pamphlet about his American visit. John Powell had performed for Conrad in his home and dedicated the *Negro Rhapsody* to him; and he would be painted by Walter Tittle and sculpted by Jacob Epstein. Conrad had met Owen Wister through Henry James, contributed to Edith Wharton's wartime charity book and entertained Ellen Glasgow at Oswalds. Gordon Bennett had helped to establish his American reputation by serializing *Chance* in the *New York Tribune*; Alfred Knopf and Frank Doubleday had been responsible for his first publishing success. He dedicated *Under Western Eyes* to Agnes Tobin, who introduced him to André Gide (his French translator) and to John Quinn (the source of a decade of enrichment); and dedicated *The Rescue* to Frederick Courtland Penfield, who, with Ambassador Walter Hines Page, rescued him from Poland after the outbreak of the war and saved him from years of internment in Austria. He greatly admired Henry James, became an intimate friend of Stephen Crane, was fond of Warrington Dawson, frequently saw Grace and Catherine Willard, and fell in love with Jane Anderson. Conrad was closely and happily involved with Americans during the last twenty-seven years of his life and it was only natural, if not inevitable, that on April 21, 1923, he should sail to America, where he was treated like visiting royalty and rapturously received.

Conrad left from Glasgow on the 26,000-ton *Tuscania*, which could carry 1,300 passengers, sharing a communicating cabin with the artist Muirhead Bone, whose brother David was captain of the ship. Captain Bone, extremely attentive and eager to please his passenger, instructed his officers to address him as "Captain Conrad." The company was good and the voyage smooth, and (with only forty-eight first-class passengers) the accommodations were spacious. But Conrad disliked the massive steamship and the numerous mechanical gadgets that almost turned the officers' job into an indoor occupation—no more difficult than running a tramway in bad weather. In an uncharacteristically witty essay "Ocean Travel" (May 1923), the austere old salt condemned the luxurious and idle life:

> [A man] finds in his ship the usual sort of hotel, with its attempts at all kinds of sham comforts, all the disadvantages of a gregarious life, with the added worry of not being able to get away from it. . . .
>
> The modern passenger may be able to walk a good many miles in his ship in the course of the day, but this is the only thing which differentiates him from the bales of goods carried in the hold.

Though Conrad had kept his name off the passenger list and tried to avoid publicity, pandemonium broke out when he docked in New York on May 1. "I will not attempt to describe to you my landing, because it is indescribable," he told Jessie. "To be aimed at by forty cameras held by forty men [that look as if they came out of the slums] is a nerve-shattering experience. Even Doubleday looked exhausted after we had escaped from that mob—and the other mob of journalists. Then a Polish deputation—men and women (some of these quite pretty)—rushed me on the wharf and thrust enormous nosegays into my hands. . . . I went along like a man in a dream and took refuge in D's car." Conrad was suffering from asthma, felt quite ill and, Walter Tittle observed: "looked very tired and weak, and walked slowly. His voice was quite hoarse."[21]

Conrad stayed at Doubleday's estate in Oyster Bay on Long Island. He gave innocuous interviews during a press conference and, his host reported, "went so far as to try to make a speech to some of the heads of our departments, but practically broke down. . . . He spoke [English] in such a way that it was extremely difficult to understand. Two stenographers tried to take down his speech at Garden City, but they could only understand a few words." During Conrad's visit, Scott Fitzgerald came over from nearby Great Neck and, in a typically childish episode, got drunk with Ring Lardner and danced on Doubleday's lawn in order to pay homage to the novelist. But Fitzgerald was apprehended by the caretaker and thrown off the grounds for trespassing before he could gate-crash the house and attract Conrad's attention.

The highlight of the trip was Conrad's lecture and reading to an audience of two hundred people on May 10. This appearance took place in the lavish mansion at the corner of Park Avenue and 69th Street that belonged to the enormously wealthy and prominent railroad magnate Arthur Curtiss James. The reports of this grand occasion vary considerably. Stressing the elegance and effectiveness of the event, Conrad claimed that "the evening at Mrs. Curtiss James' was a most fashionable affair—and what is more a real success. I gave a talk and readings from *Victory*. One hour and a quarter with an ovation at the end. They were most attentive. Laughs at the proper places and snuffles at the last when I read the whole chapter of Lena's death."

Christopher Morley, in an enthusiastic pamphlet published by Doubleday, seemed to confirm that the talk (clearly related to the famous Preface to *The Nigger of the "Narcissus"*) was quite brilliant:

> [Conrad offered] the most astonishing recreation of the actual process of an artist's mind . . . [showing] how observation, intuition, surmise, are never for an instant idle; how, throughout life, he gleans matter and suggestion here and there, in the most surprising and unlikely places; and how isolated perceptions, kindled years apart and oceans asunder, are evidently knitted together by synthesizing art.

But Morley made the rather dull and diffuse talk sound more interesting and coherent than it really was. In "Author and Cinematograph," partly based on his experience with "The Strong Man" scenario, Conrad had declared, more prosaically:

> The general fundamental condition of visuality, of animation, applies to all the masters of creative art—and also to some that are not masters. . . .
>
> Fundamentally the creator in letters aims at a moving picture—moving to the eye, to the mind, and to our complex emotions which I will express with one word—heart. . . .
>
> I don't mind confessing that many of my ambitions have been concentrated on the visuality and precision of images.[22]

Frank Doubleday, who had obviously been preparing his panic-stricken guest for the public ordeal, vividly recalled: "He was in a state of nervous collapse, and I was not far behind. I remember that I was almost in a trance when I got up to make the introduction, and I was surprised to hear myself say [not quite accurately], 'This is the first time that Mr. Conrad has ever spoken in public, and please God, if I have anything to do with it, it will be his last.' It was the last. It nearly killed him, because of his extreme nervousness."

The liveliest and probably most accurate account (though it places the mansion on Fifth Avenue and says that Conrad spoke for double the actual time of his talk) was written by Countess Palffy, whose caustic eye captured the atmosphere of rich philistines in search of but disappointed by a lion of high culture:

> Three different powerful ladies—noted for three separate, "interesting" lines—had combined to invite the guests. A banker's wife of international renown, a lovely intellectual [Mrs. Doubleday], and the richest patroness [Mrs. Curtiss James] of the organised charities and Community Chest Drives. . . . There was a distinct sprinkling of white heads and dull blue evening dresses.
>
> The ballroom was very large even for a Fifth Avenue palace. The very beautiful, very old Spanish tapestries—it was a "Peninsular" house, and a patio with a fountain had been let in to the middle of a steel structure— were dry cleaned and duly disinfected; the primitifs were varnished. . . .
>
> Under the glare of electric lights hanging from the chandelier . . . a man with a beard stood on a raised dais. He had the hunted look of a hare caught and about to be strangled by a poacher. His breath came in gasps, his voice shook. . . .
>
> What a pity, though, that his pronunciation was so bad. . . . [He] spoke English with a guttural Polish twist. Good came out ringingly as "gut," and blood as "blut," which fitted in curiously with the complex beauties of his phrases. . . .
>
> He had been talking now for nearly two hours and a half. . . . [At the end, when the heroine Lena dies], "capturing the very sting of death in the service of love," Conrad's voice broke. . . . [He] was moved to sudden tears. Conrad, and all who had followed him there, drunk on Conrad.

After a few days of rest, the Doubledays took Conrad on a ten-day motor trip through New England, visiting New Haven, Boston, Cambridge and Concord, and staying at a country house. He returned to Oyster Bay on May 24, sailed with the solicitous Doubledays on the *Majestic* on June 2 and reached Southampton in a week. Three months later, in a letter to Bruno Winawer, he compared the journey, which had begun as a dream and had nearly killed him with kindness, to his dreamlike flight in a seaplane in September 1916: "I felt all the time like a man *dans un avion*, in a mist, in a cloud, in a vapour of idealistic phraseology; I was lost, bewildered, amused—but frightened as well. . . . Obviously some power is hidden behind it—great power undoubtedly—and certainly talkative. Its chatter reminds one of a well-trained parrot. It makes me shiver! . . . I have feelings of great friendship towards many people there. . . . Indeed, one month is not enough to comprehend such a complicated machinery. Perhaps a whole life would not be sufficient."[23]

During his month in America Conrad had met a great number of people, but had studiously avoided his former benefactor, John Quinn. In a letter of November 1923 to the Irish playwright Lady Gregory, the prominent and powerful Quinn, a notorious anti-Semite, expressed rage at being rejected by the author he had idolized but never met: "During the time Conrad was here he saw every second rate newspaperman and attended a reception arranged by Mrs. Doubleday and a tuft-hunter named Mrs. James, to which Jew dealers were invited but they did not invite me." Quinn had perforce accepted the sale of the manuscripts to Wise and continued to buy from Conrad while patiently awaiting the dedication of *Suspense*. But Conrad, in poor health and anxious to avoid an unpleasant confrontation, feared the long-nurtured explosion of anger (which Quinn expressed in his letter). As Ford explained: "Conrad was afraid to see him. . . . He was a sick man himself. . . . And he was told [by Doubleday] that Mr. Quinn had a violent temper. . . . The publishers advised him not to see him. . . . The last time I had seen Conrad he told me he had refused to see Quinn. But he had felt bad about it."[24]

In November 1923, the month he wrote to Lady Gregory and six months after Conrad left America, Quinn sold all his inscribed books and manuscripts at a spectacular auction at the Anderson Galleries in New York. Quinn did not need the money and had complex motives for selling. The public explanation was that he was moving to smaller quarters and no longer had room for his magnificent collection of literature and art. But he was also very ill and close to death, and wanted to settle his affairs. Moreover, the publicity connected with Conrad's American visit had increased the price of his manuscripts and Quinn wanted to sell at the height of Conrad's fame. Most important, he was furious about the way he had been treated by Conrad and the Doubledays—he had phoned Oyster Bay several times and never received a reply—no longer valued Conrad's works so highly and wanted to retaliate for their rudeness.

The 231 works by Conrad, for which Quinn had paid $10,000, achieved astonishing prices and sold for $111,000. A. S. W. Rosenbach of Philadelphia bought about three-quarters of them for $72,000. The manuscript of "Youth," which Quinn had bought for $75, was sold to the composer Jerome Kern for $2,000. Doubleday accused Quinn of profiteering and said that he ought to pay part of the proceeds to Conrad. Quinn, who had had some rows with Doubleday about Conrad's collected edition, retaliated by calling the gentile publisher a Jew.

Though Conrad told at least one acquaintance that "he was deeply hurt at his MSS being sold" by Quinn, he remained stoically indifferent in letters to close friends. Writing to Edward Garnett and to Sydney Cockerell on November 21, Conrad seemed to feel that Quinn had the right to break his promise after Conrad had broken his, and rightly felt that the sale had actually enhanced his reputation: "Yes, Quinn promised to keep the MSS. together—but the mood passes and the promise goes with it. . . . I have nothing to complain of. Quinn paid me the prices I asked—altogether about £2,000 since 1912 [i.e., 1911], or a little more, and the money came very conveniently then. Truly I have never had such a success. People who had never heard of me before are now aware of my name and others quite incapable of reading a page of mine to the end have become convinced that I am a great writer."[25]

Conrad returned from America on June 9 to receive shocking news. Borys had been invalided out of the army in April 1919 and (Curle said) "returned from the war morose and silent and obviously a changed man mentally." After the war, expecting to inherit a great deal of money from Conrad, he became recklessly extravagant. Borys had several unsuccessful jobs in the motor trade, went deeply into debt and, when pressed, told his creditors that his father had invested £1,000 for him in the United States. When Conrad, who had often been in debt but was punctilious about repayment, discovered that he was implicated in Borys' lie, he felt heartbroken.

Just before Conrad left for America, Borys told Jessie that he had secretly married a lady he had met during the war in an officers' canteen in France. Jessie wisely kept the disturbing news from Conrad until he returned from his journey and then, as tactfully as possible, broke it to him in their London hotel room. Predictably enough (Jessie related) Conrad exploded, refused to accept the truth and was enraged that he had not been informed:

> I had the habit of calling him "boy" when I wished to be extra friendly. "Boy dear . . . Borys is married." . . . Joseph Conrad started up in bed, gripping my arm with cruel force. "Why do you tell me that, why don't you keep such news to yourself?" . . .
>
> "I suppose you are certain of what you have told me?" Somewhat surprised, I answered at once, "Quite," and proceeded to explain the means I had taken to verify the news directly he had started for [the ship

in] Glasgow. He interrupted me with scant ceremony. "I don't want to
know anything more about it. It is done, and I have been treated like a
blamed fool, damn. . . .

"What has he got to keep a wife on? And let me tell you I don't like the
way this has been done in secret. I wasn't to know then, why should I
now?"[26]

Though Jessie never explained why Borys married secretly, it is possible
to guess his reasons. Chronic money troubles and an erratic post-war
career made Borys fear that his parents felt he could not support a wife
and would disapprove of his choice. He wanted to act as an independent young man rather than as an obedient child, and made his decision
without seeking their approval.

Conrad soon accepted his new daughter-in-law, but Borys' problems
with money continued. In July 1927, three years after Conrad's death,
when Borys was running a garage and deeply in debt to men who had
financed his business, his extravagance led to disaster. He perpetuated
a fraud and swindled a friend by telling a Mrs. Dorothy Bevan that he
had £2,900 and that if she would give him £1,100 more he could buy his
father's manuscripts for £4,000 and resell them for an immediate profit
of £1,000. Mrs. Bevan gave him the money. But Borys had neither the
£2,900 nor the seller and buyer of the manuscripts. He had paid off his
urgent debts with her money, was publicly exposed and sentenced to
prison for a year.

VI

In May 1912 Conrad had enthusiastically written to Quinn: "I see in my
paper that Henry James is going to be made a Litt. D. of Oxford. *Hono-
ris Causa*. Well done, Oxford!" Yet when Conrad was offered the same
honor in 1923 from the universities of Oxford, Cambridge, Edinburgh,
Liverpool and Durham, he declined. His letter of February 18 to the
Vice-Chancellor of Cambridge University, though elegantly phrased,
does not explain his "obscure" reasons for refusal: "I am very much
indebted to you for the friendly thought of conveying to me privately
the intention of the Senate-Committee of your University. An obscure
feeling taking its origin, perhaps, in acute consciousness of the inward
consistency of a life which at this day may, with truth, be said to have
been lived already, compels me to decline an academic degree." Nor,
since Conrad was like James a foreigner, does Curle's explanation—"he

always declined because he felt that they ought to be reserved for men of British birth"[27]—seem convincing. Though he had enjoyed his weekend at Cambridge with Bertrand Russell and had welcomed recognition from academic critics, the old sailor, unlike James, had not completed high school or attended a university. He modestly felt, therefore, that it would be inwardly consistent to remain outside the university tradition.

The following year, in May 1924, Conrad received a long official envelope that he thought was a demand for taxes, but was actually the offer of a knighthood from the Socialist prime minister, Ramsay MacDonald. The lower-class Jessie, who proudly included Lady Northcote and Lady Millais among her local friends, must have put considerable pressure on Conrad to accept the knighthood. And it is rather surprising that the staunch patriot refused the offer that King George V was willing to confer upon him. Five of his close friends had already accepted knighthoods: Hugh Clifford in 1909, Roger Casement and Sidney Colvin in 1911, Robert Jones in 1917, Ralph Wedgwood in 1924; and six others would accept them in the future: Edmund Gosse in 1925, William Rothenstein in 1931, Sydney Cockerell in 1934, Hugh Walpole in 1937, David Bone in 1946 and Jacob Epstein in 1954. Influenced perhaps by Kipling's and Galsworthy's refusal of knighthoods a few years earlier, Conrad wanted to remain independent. He may not have wished to accept the honor from a Socialist government and aimed for bigger game: the Order of Merit and the Nobel Prize.

In November 1923, before he refused the knighthood, he was buoyed by hopes that the French and the Swedes favored him for the Nobel Prize. He naïvely imagined that *The Rover* would increase his chances and told Jean-Aubry: "Yeats has had the Nobel Prize. My opinion about that is that it is a literary recognition of the new Irish Free State (that's what it seems to me), but that does not destroy my chances of getting it in one or two years." Two inferior Polish writers—Henryk Sienkiewicz and Wladyslaw Reymont—won the Prize in 1905 and (when Conrad hoped to get it) in 1924; among his friends, Kipling had won it in 1907, Galsworthy would do so in 1932 and Gide in 1947. But the Prize usually went to safe mediocrities and Conrad, like most of his great contemporaries—Tolstoy and Chekhov, Ibsen and Strindberg, Zola and Twain, Meredith and Swinburne, Hardy and James as well as Ford, Forster, Joyce, Wyndham Lewis, Woolf, Lawrence, Frost, Stevens, Pound, Proust and Valéry—did not win it.[28]

In March 1924 an honor of a different sort came to Conrad when Muirhead Bone persuaded him to sit several hours each morning, for twenty-one days, for the sculptor Jacob Epstein. John Conrad wrote of the disciplined sea captain: "My father had very definite ideas about sitting for a portrait. . . . He maintained that once he had taken up his pose he should not make any movement whatsoever." Conrad had previously been sculpted, drawn, painted, etched, carved and caricatured by Jo Davidson, Muirhead Bone, William Rothenstein, Walter Tittle and many lesser artists, but Epstein's tragic bust is the greatest of the twenty-six images of Conrad.

Epstein (like T. E. Lawrence and H. R. Lenormand) noticed Conrad's hooded eyelids and deep-rooted sense of despair about his work:

> Conrad had a demon expression in the left eye, while his right eye was smothered by a drooping lid, but the eye glowed with a great intensity of feeling. The drooping, weary lids intensified the expression of brooding thought. The whole head revealed the man who had suffered much. . . .
>
> Conrad gave me a feeling of defeat; but defeat met with courage. He was crippled with rheumatism, crotchety, nervous, and ill. He said to me, "I am finished." There was pathos in his pulling out of a drawer his last manuscript to show me that he was still at work. There was no triumph in his manner, however, and he said that he did not know whether he would ever finish it. "I am played out," he said, "played out." . . . He appeared a lonely, brooding man, with none too pleasant thoughts.

But Conrad, well pleased with Epstein's powerful icon of "defeat met with courage," told Curle: "The bust of Ep. has grown truly monumental. It is a marvellously effective piece of sculpture, with even something more than a masterly interpretation in it. . . . It is wonderful to go down to posterity like that."[29]

Epstein mentioned that Conrad, who suffered from hypertension related to gout, had had a mild heart attack while he was posing. And complaints about ill health, which made him savage, misanthropical and pessimistic, as well as expressions of longing for death, became frequent during the last years of his life. On November 12, 1923 (the month of the distressing Quinn sale), Dr. Fox of nearby Ashford told him, "in his horrid way," that he had (like Ransome in *The Shadow-Line*) a "flabby heart." Though Conrad feared a breakdown in health and a lingering end, he also believed that gouty people went out suddenly. A week later he described himself to Hugh Walpole as a tottering, staggering, shuddering, shivering, crocky, seedy, gouty wretch. Jessie noted that in 1924 he suffered such severe fits of depression that he could scarcely rouse himself to speak. And he told Curle that he was conscious of his approaching death and was not very sorry to die. On July 3, 1924, he repeated an expression he had used in a desperate letter to H. G. Wells in October 1905 and told Major Ernest Dawson: "I feel (and probably look) horribly limp and my spirits stand at about zero. Here you have the horrid truth. But I haven't been well for a long time and *strictly entre nous* I begin to feel like a cornered rat."

Richard Curle, Borys, his wife, Joan, and their six-month-old son arrived at Oswalds for the Bank Holiday weekend on August 1 and found Conrad apparently well. The next day Conrad took Curle out in his car to see the new house he was thinking of renting. Though he suffered a sudden pain in his chest—it was another slight heart attack— he insisted they continue the journey. But when they got within a mile and a half of the house, he felt worse and agreed to turn back.

Dr. Fox diagnosed the heart attack as acute indigestion. And a second doctor, who ordered a cylinder of oxygen and said Conrad should have his teeth removed as soon as possible, agreed that there was no cause for alarm. That evening, sensing the worst, Conrad told Borys: "You know I am *really* ill this time." At 8:30 on the morning of Sunday August 3 Conrad and Jessie (immobile in her bed after another operation) were alone in their adjoining rooms. He gasped the command: "Here . . . you" and she heard a heavy shuffling sound, a dull thump and then silence. His heart had stopped beating, he had slipped from his chair to the floor and, at the age of sixty-six, was suddenly dead.

Though Conrad had no religious belief, he was given a Catholic funeral by Jessie, who could not walk and did not attend the ceremony. It incongruously took place on August 7 amidst the crowded and flag-festooned Canterbury Cricket Festival. Conrad's sons, Edward Garnett, Cunninghame Graham, Sir Hugh and Lady Clifford, Alice Rothenstein, Richard Curle, Jean-Aubry, Sir Ralph and Lady Wedgwood, Alec and Ernest Dawson, James and Muirhead Bone, W. W. Jacobs and Count Edward Raczynski, who represented the Polish minister, attended the Mass at St. Thomas' Catholic Church. At the graveside in Canterbury cemetery Father Shepherd read the Catholic burial service. "So we left him," Graham wrote, "with his sails all duly furled, ropes flemished down, and with the anchor holding truly in the kind Kentish earth." The moving epigraph from Spenser's *The Faerie Queene*, which Conrad had used on the title page of *The Rover*, was cut into the grey granite:

Sleep after toyle, port after stormie seas,
Ease after warre, death after life, does greatly please.[30]

The Later Life
of Jane Anderson

1918–1947

I

During the first thirty years of her life Jane Anderson—whose bizarre childhood in Georgia and Arizona included her genteel mother's involvement in a murder trial and her wild father's two desertions—became a stunning beauty, an enterprising journalist and the mistress of great men. The last thirty years included espionage, the break-up of her nominal marriage, alcoholism, drug addiction, physical degeneration, abject poverty, imprisonment, torture, propaganda for the Spanish Fascists, treason for the Nazis and arrest in Austria—followed by her second release from prison and her mysterious disappearance.

Jane's sexual contacts with influential politicians and with senior British and French officers were invaluable for espionage as well as for journalism. Rebecca West heard that Jane had been a German agent during World War One. And that rumor is partly substantiated by her FBI and Army Intelligence files, which note: "On December 23, 1917, our Embassy reported that Mrs. Jane Anderson Taylor was on the suspect list of the Inter-Allied command in Paris and was on terms of intimacy with the staff of the Japanese Embassy in Paris. . . . In 1917 she had a suite at the Hotel Crillon and was playing an amazingly important role for a very young and pretty woman. She was in very close relations with both the Italian and Japanese Ambassadors"—both of whom were allies.

Deems Taylor, troubled by their long separation, visited Jane in Paris in the winter of 1917, but she must have felt constrained by his presence and their relations did not improve. In the spring of 1918 she returned to America to rest from her three years as a war correspondent. On the *Rochambeau* she met the Harvard graduate and writer Gilbert Seldes, who was going back to America to enlist in the army. He fell in love with her and they had an engagement party when the ship reached New York. Deems Taylor's daughter later heard that Jane had "returned from overseas, arrived at [Taylor's] house, was told by a janitor that he was married to someone else (untrue), and immediately left and sued for divorce [in 1918] without seeing him." Jane fell victim to the post-war influenza epidemic, began to drink heavily and take barbiturates and, according to William Beebe, "was back in New York, living in most reprehensible circumstances. She needed someone to pull her out."[1]

In the summer of 1918 Jane got in touch with her college room-mate at Kidd-Key, Kitty Crawford Jenkins, who was recovering from tuberculosis in Colorado. They agreed to share Watson Lodge, a summer cottage on Cheyenne Mountain, near Colorado Springs, and were soon joined by Gilbert Seldes and by Kitty's Texas friend Katherine Anne Porter. But things went badly in Colorado Springs. Jane, who praised everything European and disparaged America, considered Porter uneducated and provincial. Unable to rest, Jane lived in a constant frenzy of activity, wanted to become an actress and made frequent trips to Hollywood, where she tried to sell film rights to Conrad's works. She appropriated Kitty's medicinal whiskey and refused to pay her share of the household expenses. In a letter to Kitty of 1918, she admitted her faults, her inordinate ambition and her reliance on the favors of men: "I am arrogant, vain, selfish. I am outcast—voluntarily in some measure. The scope of my ambition conforms in no possible measure to the confines of normal life. . . . I've learned by long and various experience that no woman is going to help me when there is a man ever so slightly, or ever so deeply, involved in the matter."

Jane's mental state was as poor as her physical condition. In Colorado Springs she broke her foot. She also became addicted to drugs, which had been prescribed by a London doctor for nervous tension and insomnia, and which led to irresponsible and irrational behavior. Joan Givner writes that Jane spent the first hours in Gilbert Seldes' "bed each night and afterward returned to her own bed, took barbiturates [five grains of veronal] for her 'war nerves,' and remained sedated until noon the next day."

In *Ship of Fools* (1962), Porter alluded to Jane's later marriage to a Spanish nobleman and used her as the model for the predatory Condesa, a political exile who is being deported from Cuba to Tenerife. The Condesa is extremely beautiful, highly nervous, takes drugs, caresses her own body, has a powerful effect on men, is said to sleep with the Cuban medical students, seduces and corrupts Dr. Schumann, and convinces him to supply her with narcotics. The captain of the ship analyzes her self-destructive character: "I was told she is a dangerous revolutionist, an international spy, that she carries incendiary messages from one hotbed of sedition and rebellion to another, that she incites to riot. . . . My own opinion is, she is one of these idle rich great ladies who like excitement, who get into mischief and make more mischief without in the least understanding what they do . . . and she has got her fingers badly burnt."[2]

After Gilbert Seldes told friends that something had gone wrong and his relations with Jane were finished, Retinger came from Mexico to America to continue his own unhappy affair with Jane. She introduced him to her father at the Lafayette Hotel in Washington. Retinger's friend wrote that he "fell passionately in love, but this did not give him any joy. Instead it caused him extreme distress, landed him in considerable trouble and affected his health." Joan Givner notes that Retinger was "described by his daughter as a person of weak sexual drives, [and] seems to have been a less than passionate lover. In this area as in others, he preferred intrigue and complicated situations. . . . His tragedy was centered in his belief that he had betrayed his country and ideals by falling in love with the beautiful unattainable Jane Anderson."[3] During the war Lord Northcliffe, jealous of Retinger's success with Jane and eager for revenge, had withdrawn his support for a project that was vital to Polish interests. Retinger took pills for his heart condition, and once tried to kill himself with an overdose. In the early 1920s he and Jane concocted several wildly impractical political schemes: assisting the Balkans at the Peace Conference, settling Jews in the Dominican Republic, creating a Polish navy, plotting what Jane called a "simple and workable" plan to kill Lenin. After Retinger faded out of her life, Jane had affairs with Woodrow Wilson's former campaign manager, William McCombs, and with the Texas politician Stephen Austin.

In 1921, while attempting to become an actress, Jane was arrested in Los Angeles for failure to pay her hotel bill. In mid-1922 she borrowed money and returned to Europe. W. N. Ewer, the foreign editor of the *Daily Herald*, said he "first met Jane in the early twenties through my friend Dai Ballusek, then a young newspaper correspondent; later Netherlands Delegate to the U.N. and Netherlands Ambassador in Moscow. They were engaged. But it was a brief engagement. She was tall, copper-haired, very handsome, intelligent, attractive. With always a touch of mystery about her. . . . She had been a protégée of Northcliffe's. Some said more than a protégée. I just do not know. . . . Soon after we first met, she was associated with a Canadian named Boyer." In the early 1930s, before her second marriage, Ewer "received a letter from Jane, written from a convent in France. She had, she said, been right down in the Paris underworld, drugs, crime and all. The nuns had rescued her. Now she was herself again." Jane was then "a raddled, blowsy woman, very very drunk."[4]

II

Partially rehabilitated by the Catholic nuns, Jane met the Marqués de Cienfuegos at a reception at the American Embassy in Paris. In a letter to H. G. Wells of April 1933, she praised Cienfuegos' sensitivity, wealth, practicality and good looks: "you'll like the Marqués. He has an infallible perception of the beauty of the written word and stands in awe of your work. . . . He smokes his cigars, makes millions of francs, and doesn't much trouble about abstractions. Nevertheless, his handsome sur-faces match up very well with his soul, and he's anchored me down to reality."

A contemporary photograph of the Marqués shows a dapper-looking Spaniard with fedora, gloves, cane and a double-breasted suit. Jane, who wears a fur-piece and clasps his arm, has completely lost her beauty and become a dumpy matron.[5] According to the FBI file, she married Marqués Eduardo Alvarez de Cienfuegos in the Cathedral of Seville on October 23, 1934.

The FBI also provided biographical information about Jane's second husband. He was born on April 13, 1896, in Miajadas, province of Bada-joz, Spain, and was for more than twenty years Master of the Guards in the household of King Alfonso XIII. He is described as a well-to-do Spaniard who owned and operated cork plantations, but in 1940 resided in and managed the Hotel Lincoln in Havana, where he also owned a professional gambling house. His wealth must have fluctuated wildly, for Jane told H. G. Wells that he "makes millions of francs," but (ac-cording to Rebecca West) she had also written to an unnamed friend in Paris "saying that she was staying at a hotel there with her Spanish husband, and would be glad if he would lend her some money."

Reliable information from reference books in Spain reveals (if the FBI files are correct) that the Eduardo Alvarez who married Jane Anderson was *not* the Marqués de Cienfuegos. The real 3rd Marqués de Cienfue-gos, José María de Pertierra y González-Alegre, was born in Oviedo in the first years of the century. He succeeded to the title in 1915, married Carolina Fernández de Henestrosa y Chávarri on July 12, 1942, and died without issue on September 19, 1944.[6] There is no mention of Jane in connection with the real Marqués, whose place and date of birth, Christian names, wife's name, date of marriage and date of death are entirely different from those of Jane's husband. This new evidence substantiates the FBI's final conclusions: it "did not believe that he was a bona fide Count. . . . He did not have any obvious means of support, or any known occupation. . . . In short, this individual appears to be a gigolo or a parasite."

When the Spanish Civil War broke out in July 1936 Jane's husband, a right-wing Royalist who had had several relatives executed by the left-wing Loyalists, inevitably sided with Franco's Fascists. Jane adopted his political views. She returned to Spain as a reporter for her old newspaper the *Daily Mail*, was arrested in Madrid by the Loyalists on September 23 and accused of espionage. There is some doubt (since she is the only source of information) about what happened to Jane in prison. Civilians on both sides were treated with exceptional severity and stories of atrocities were common. But it is certain that her experience in prison—combined with her unstable childhood, breakdown during the war, drug addiction after the war and collapse in Paris in the early 1930s—crippled her emotionally, wrecked her physically and transformed her into a fanatical anti-Communist.

Jane, who had apparently converted from Protestantism at the time of her marriage, ignored the charge that she was a spy and claimed (according to the FBI) that she "was tortured and twice condemned to death for being a Catholic." In a propaganda piece, the Irish Fascist leader Eoin O'Duffy, who fought on Franco's side in Spain, quoted Jane as saying: "When arrested I demanded to be taken before the Spanish Government. The twenty-three-year-old female Red commandant replied: 'Government! This pistol is Government. Who do you think you are talking to anyhow? Do you know who I am? Do you know how many people I have already killed? I killed one hundred and eighty-nine.'" Another writer maintained that Jane had "escaped a firing squad by a hair." Victor Woerheide of the U.S. Justice Department (who probably heard the story from Jane) told Kitty Crawford that "when the Loyalists captured her they stripped her and cast her, the only woman, and completely nude, into a bullpen with one hundred and fifty men." Since Jane never mentioned being raped, this story seems doubtful. William Schofield wrote, with some exaggeration, that Jane "had entered prison as one of the beautiful women of Spain. When she came out she was haggard from scurvy and badly scarred by rat-bite. Her face was deeply lined. Her eyes carried a gleam that was near insanity and near terror, and that stayed with her for weeks."[7] After the intervention of the United States government on behalf of its citizen, Jane was released, after three weeks in prison, on about October 13, 1936, on condition that she immediately leave Spain.

In September 1937 (two months after Ernest Hemingway spoke for the Loyalist cause in New York and Los Angeles) Jane—accompanied by her husband, sponsored by the National Council of Catholic Women and organized by the Lecture League of New York—gave a series of speeches in America that combined commerce and politics. She spoke in places like the Church of the Holy Child in Philadelphia, sold tours to Spain in order to show the horrors the Communists were committing during the Civil War and passionately supported the Axis powers in their struggle against Russia. The *Catholic Digest* said she was "the world's greatest woman orator in the fight against Communism," and the popular and influential Monsignor Fulton Sheen called her "one of the living martyrs." A college friend who saw Jane in New York in 1938 and evidently disliked her political views told Kitty Crawford that she "was big and fat and pop-eyed. . . . She had degenerated into a cold, soulless creature completely without feeling or consideration for others. It was very evident that she used drugs. How supremely awful!"[8]

III

In the fall of 1938 Jane was recommended to the Fascist Ministry of Propaganda by Merwin Hart, a New York lawyer and president of the National Economic Council, which opposed the social legislation of Roosevelt's New Deal. She returned to Spain early in 1939 and accepted their offer to become an agent for Franco. She then sailed for New York via South America on the Puerto Rico Line on February 8, 1940, apparently returned to Spain in the fall of 1940 and remained there until the spring of 1941, when she went to Berlin and lived in the Pension Continental on the Kurfürstendamm. In his diary of October 21, 1939, Joseph Goebbels, the Nazi Minister of Propaganda (who must have heard about Jane from his Spanish colleagues and realized how useful she could be), recorded: "Anderson's statements in New York are still the big sensation." On May 10, Jane charmed and impressed Goebbels, who noted their meeting: "Discussed new propaganda for the USA on the short-wave service with an American woman, Jane Anderson, and Herr von Bülow. I intend to take a greater personal interest in this area from now on."[9]

Jane started by writing for *News from Germany*, a Nazi propaganda magazine in English, which E. U. von Bülow sent at her request to the Philippine Consul in Madrid. On April 14, 1941, nine months before America entered the war, she began to broadcast Nazi propaganda to the United States. She spoke every Sunday and Thursday at 9 p.m. from the studio of the German *Reichrundfunk* on the outskirts of Berlin, and was presented as "the world-famous Catholic, twice condemned to death by the firing squad in Spain, whose lectures in the United States were endorsed by the Archbishop of Washington." Wearing the uniform of the Spanish Red Cross, with its dark-blue cape and Basque beret, Jane emphasized in overheated prose the Communist atrocities during the war and accused the Red Anti-Christ of beating little children black and blue because they believed in God: "The smell and sight of the corpses in Spain, like the bouquet of a pagan wine served in the chalice of Utopia by the jeweled hand of the Kremlin, was to inebriate the savage lusts and passions of superimposed vengeance." Jane attempted to persuade her listeners that the American people were being duped by Jewish, war-mongering, plutocratic leaders, that "Hitler is an immortal crusader, a great lover of God, who has struck back against the universal enemies of mankind" and that Germany "gives the Church the strength of her sword, the weight of her wealth, and the protection of her law."[10]

Jane's charming southern accent had disappeared from her propaganda speeches and been replaced by a harsh, nasal, hysterical, rabble-rousing voice. The FBI agent monitoring the broadcasts noted her astonishing vocabulary, her long, complex sentences and the crescendo of her diatribes: "As she reaches the climax of her presentations she gradually works herself into a white heat, her words now tumbling over one another like logs shooting over a waterfall." The mixed metaphors and hyperbolic rhetoric of one characteristic passage suggest that her arguments were not very persuasive:

> The American brain trust, alien to and superimposed upon the land of Old Glory, is but a branch of the International Secret Superstate which holds equally Soviet Russia, plutocratic England, and Roosevelt's America in the hollow of its hybrid hand. . . . Roosevelt has pulled a brass band out of his hip pocket, and a concentration camp from under the coattails of the brain trust. . . . Roosevelt consolidated with Churchill in the simultaneous declaration of war upon Japan . . . so the American people have gone to war to save Stalin and the international banker which are one and the

same. . . . [Roosevelt] supported the hand of Communist China, the wealth of the American nation he offered as a footstool to Stalin, the mightiest murderer of modern history.

In a story of April 6, 1942, that sounds rather like American war propaganda, *Time* explained the abrupt termination of Jane's broadcasts by quoting her description of a meal she ate in a luxurious cocktail bar: "On silver platters were sweets and cookies. I ate Turkish cookies, a delicacy I am very fond of. My friend ordered great goblets full of champagne, into which he put shots of cognac to make it more lively. Sweets and cookies, not bad!" *Time* then claimed that when the American Office of War Information translated her speech and rebroadcast it to Germany, it had a demoralizing effect on the masses were who starving during the war: "Jane went off the air, has not been heard from since."[11] The FBI reported that Jane did not speak between March 17, 1942 (on April 26 the Germans announced: "Mrs. Anderson is not yet able to continue her talks"), and June 12 and 19, 1944, when she broke her silence. One of her talks referred to Joseph Conrad and enabled an informant to identify her as Jane Anderson.

On June 12, 1941, an article in the liberal New York newspaper *PM* alerted the United States government to Jane's broadcasts. After America entered the war in December 1941 the authorities began to gather evidence against her. In July 1943 Jane, Ezra Pound and six others were indicted for treason for broadcasting propaganda from Germany and Italy against the United States and its wartime allies. Jane disappeared from Berlin after her last broadcast on June 19, 1944. She lived first in Baden-Baden (a health resort west of Stuttgart) and in southern Germany, then crossed with her husband into the Austrian Tyrol and hid in Ehrwald (northwest of Innsbruck) until the war ended in May 1945. She tried at least twice to enter Switzerland. And she gave herself away to the American military authorities by asking the Spanish Red Cross to repatriate her to Spain from the village of Egg, in the Bregenz Forest, in the northwest corner of Austria.

In April 1947, after evading the military police for two years, Jane was arrested and imprisoned in Salzburg, awaiting return to the United States for prosecution. But six months later on October 27 Jane, who had been freed from a Loyalist prison through the intervention of the American government, was freed from an American prison. The treason charge was dismissed by the Federal District Court in Washington because of insufficient evidence to convict her. Two years later, in 1949, Katherine Anne Porter—convincingly guessing that Jane had returned to Spain in 1948 (as she had tried to do just after the war) and to the protection of Franco—angrily protested that Jane, despite treasonable broadcasts, had been set free:

> Just a year or two ago there was exonerated in an American court another, a woman, who had no talents except for political intrigue of a low kind. She did for Hitler, by radio from Berlin, exactly the same work that Pound did for Mussolini in Italy. . . . She is living no doubt comfortably in Spain, and the judge in freeing her in absentia remarked in effect that even if she was working for Nazism, the great point was that she was defending religion and morality. I have heard no complaints about this case, and though she seemed to suffer a debased form of religious mania, I have never heard her called insane.

Deems Taylor's daughter had "a vague recollection of someone writing to him in the 1950s and saying that Jane was in a boarding house somewhere in Europe."[12] Ironically, her life exemplified the Conradian themes of divided loyalties, imprisonment, degradation, treachery and betrayal. No one has ever discovered when and where Jane died.

The Quest
for Jane Anderson

It is common when writing a biography to become fascinated, even obsessed, by certain figures in the subject's life who take on an independent existence and seem worthy of a full-length study. The attempt to find out about the various phases of Jane's life, to understand her intriguing character and to gather evidence to prove she was Conrad's mistress was the most interesting and complicated part of my research. It led to several fortunate breakthroughs and to the discovery of some primary sources of information: the papers of Kitty Crawford, the papers of Deems Taylor and the 446-page FBI file on Jane.

While spending the summer of 1989 in Berkeley, re-reading Conrad's works and the biographical books about him while seated on a balcony overlooking San Francisco Bay, I interviewed Ian Watt, a former teacher and leading Conrad scholar. Professor Watt gave me several valuable leads. He told me that during the war Jane had been involved with Sir Leo Money, who "had something odd about him"; that she had been the mistress of Gilbert Seldes; that she had been a friend of Katherine Anne Porter and had been discussed in Joan Givner's biography. Ian Watt also said that he and another former student John Halverson had written a long-contemplated essay on Jane and that as soon as it was accepted for publication, he would send me the typescript. The Halverson-Watt essay cited John Edwards' important article; it also quoted a letter from Deems Taylor, Jane's long description of her first meeting with Conrad, Rebecca West's perceptive analysis of Jane's character and W. N. Ewer's recollections of Jane in the 1930s.

Lord Desmond Harmsworth, whom I had known when writing about Wyndham Lewis, could not enlighten me about Jane's relation with his uncle Lord Northcliffe. But while searching through my books on modern English history I came across a reference to Sir Leo Money's scandals in A. J. P. Taylor's *English History, 1914–1945*, which led me to the accounts of the two incidents in *The Times*. While looking through the index, I also found two war reports by Jane published in *The Times*.

Gilbert Seldes' son Timothy, a literary agent, knew nothing about Jane. But John Edwards sent a memoir by Gilbert. I had interviewed Gilbert's brother George Seldes when writing my life of Hemingway. I phoned the sprightly ninety-nine-year-old George Seldes in Vermont, he gave me his clear recollections of Jane and I read more about her in his autobiography, *Witness to a Century*. Simon & Schuster did not forward my letter to Joan Givner, but when I phoned her in Regina, Saskatchewan, she was extremely helpful. She sent me many pages of biographical material and the beautiful photograph of Jane that is reproduced in this book, and gave me the address of Kitty Crawford's daughter, Jane Anderson Jenkins. After several phone conversations with Mrs. Jenkins and her daughter, they generously agreed to send me copies of Kitty's papers, which contained photographs, newspaper clippings, the *Kidd-Key Journal*, letters from Jane to Kitty and Kitty's memoirs of Jane.

I had once sat next to the lively nonagenarian composer Virgil Thomson during the first performance of his early work in Berkeley and questioned him about Hemingway's relations with Gertrude Stein. I now hoped that Thomson might be able to put me in touch with Deems Taylor's daughter, and in one of his last letters he suggested I write to the American Society of Composers, Authors and Publishers, of which Taylor had been president. They forwarded my letter to Joan Kennedy Taylor, who answered my questions about her father and Jane, and traveled from New York to her summer house in western Massachusetts to show me his papers.

I requested Jane's FBI file (as I had requested Hemingway's) through the Freedom of Information Act in August 1989, but had still not received it in January 1990. After I wrote to Senator Timothy Wirth about the long delay, the FBI files as well as the Department of the Army reports were sent immediately. They described the Marqués, traced Jane's propaganda career in America, Spain and Germany, and threw considerable light on her personality.

The greatest potential discovery would be Conrad's letters to Jane. In order to find them and learn when and where she died, I made strenuous efforts to get in touch with her husband's descendants. A friend in Málaga and the Spanish Embassy in Washington both said that the woman who had inherited the title was the Marquesa Doña Isabel Pertierra y González, who lived in the Hotel España in Oviedo, Spain. I wrote two letters to the hotel in Oviedo, received no answer and then tried to telephone. But the operator who gave telephone information for Spain did not answer for an entire week—and seemed as if she never would. I finally obtained the number of the Gran Hotel España (there was no Hotel España) from a travel agent. But when I called the hotel I was told that they had never heard of the Marquesa and that she certainly did not live there. When I asked the desk clerk to look up her address in the local telephone book, she replied: "There are too many Cienfuegos in Oviedo!" By the time I learned that the Marquesa had moved to the Hotel Principal in Oviedo, it was too late: the spinster had died without issue in 1989.

Hugh Thomas, author of *The Spanish Civil War*, had helped with my research on Hemingway. He suggested I write to the ministry in Madrid that was responsible for titles. But the Jefe del Area of the Subsecretaria of the Asuntos de Gracia of the Ministerio de Justicia said that the *Guía Oficial de Grandezas y Títulos* merely listed the address of the Marquesa as "Hotel España, Oviedo." Back where I started but still desperate to find the Marquesa's descendants, I wrote to Dr. Ian Gibson, who lived in Madrid and whose biography of García Lorca I had just reviewed for the *American Scholar*. Intrigued by my quest, Ian Gibson sent information that proved, when compared to the facts in the FBI file, that Jane's husband was a bogus marqués.

Though I had achieved most of my major goals, there were still several other trails to follow. The Georgia Department of Vital Records said they had no birth records before 1919, so Jane's birthdate could not be verified. The Arizona Historical Society told me when "Red" Anderson had been Town Marshal, but the Yuma Historical Society, the Yuma Sheriff's Department and the Yuma County Law Enforcement historian did not answer my letters. There were no references to "Red" Anderson in books on George Goethals and Buffalo Bill Cody, and, apart from a reference in a book on Arizona history, I could not find out any more about him. No references to Jane appeared in Rebecca West's papers at Yale; Retinger's daughter Marya (born in 1927) did not answer my letter and was no longer listed in the London telephone directory; and his editor, John Pomian, who did not know where his daughters Malina and Stasia were, closed another circle by suggesting I contact Ian Watt "as he knows far more than I do." But the New York Public Library sent copies of Jane's telegrams to Conrad. And the archivist Mary Lane provided fascinating new material about Jane's family background, the murder trial and her year at Piedmont College. Finally, I tried to track down

Notes

Chapter One: The Polish Heritage

1. Norman Davies, *Heart of Europe: A Short History of Poland* (Oxford, 1984), pp. 308, 174.

2. Joseph Conrad, "Autocracy and War" in *Notes on Life and Letters*, and *A Personal Record*, Kent Edition, 26 volumes (Garden City, New York, 1926), 3.86 and 6.46. All subsequent citations of volume and page will be to this edition.

3. Piotr Wandycz, *The Lands of Partitioned Poland, 1795–1918* (Seattle, 1974), pp. 180–181; "Prince Roman," *Tales of Hearsay*, 26.48, 29; Zdzislaw Najder, "Conrad's Polish Background," *Conradiana*, 18 (1986), 4. For a discussion of Mickiewicz and his contemporaries, see Czeslaw Milosz, "Romanticism," *The History of Polish Literature*, 2nd ed. (Berkeley, 1983), pp. 195–280.

4. Quoted in G. Jean-Aubry, *Joseph Conrad: Life and Letters* (Garden City, New York, 1927), 2.194; "Author's Note" (1919) to *A Personal Record*, 6.ix; Davies, *Heart of Europe*, p. 331.

5. *Conrad Under Familial Eyes*, ed. Zdzislaw Najder, trans. Halina Carroll-Najder (Cambridge, England, 1983), p. 16; *A Personal Record*, 6.ix.

6. Zdzislaw Najder, *Joseph Conrad: A Chronicle*, trans. Halina Carroll-Najder (Cambridge, England, 1983), p. 5, and Introduction to *Familial Eyes*, p. xiii. There is some uncertainty about Eva's birthdate. Gérard Jean-Aubry, *The Sea Dreamer*, trans. Helen Sebba (Garden City, New York, 1957), p. 19, and Najder, *Familial Eyes*, p. xiii, state she was born in 1831. Jocelyn Baines, *Joseph Conrad: A Critical Biography* (London, 1959), p. 6; Frederick Karl, *Joseph Conrad: The Three Lives* (London, 1979), p. 36; and *The Collected Letters of Joseph Conrad*, ed. Frederick Karl and Laurence Davies (Cambridge, England, 1983–88), 2.245—hereafter cited as *Letters*—give her birthdate as 1833. I

believe 1833 is more accurate. Eva married at the age of twenty-three and died at thirty-two.

In quoting Conrad's letters up to 1908, I have used this excellent Cambridge edition of Conrad's *Letters*.

7. Quoted in Gustav Morf, *The Polish Shades and Ghosts of Joseph Conrad* (New York, 1976), pp. 11, 41, 7.

8. Czeslaw Milosz, "Joseph Conrad in Polish Eyes," *The Art of Joseph Conrad*, ed. Robert Stallman (1960; Athens, Ohio, 1982), p. 38; Quoted in Andrzej Busza, "Conrad's Polish Literary Background and Some Illustrations of the Influence of Polish Literature on His Work," *Antemurale* (Rome), 10 (1966), 119.

Chapter Two: A Polish Childhood

1. The population figures vary according to different sources. The *Encyclopedia of Ukraine*, ed. Volodymyr Kubijovyc (Toronto, 1984), 1.204, gives the total population of Berdichev in 1860 as 51,500, which would make the number of Jews (if 85%) about 43,775. The *Encyclopedia Judaica* (Jerusalem, 1971), 4.590, lists the Jewish population in 1861 as 46,683. The *Entsiklopedicheskii Slovar*, ed. F. A. Brokgauz and I. A. Efron (Petersburg, 1891), 3a.490–492, states the Jewish population in 1864 was 62,000, or 80% of the total of 77,000. (This entry was translated for me by Eugene Petriwsky.) If all these figures are correct, then the number of Jews in Berdichev grew very rapidly in the early 1860s.

For Rabbi Isaac ben Levi, see H. M. Rabinowicz, "The Great Defender," *The World of Hasidism* (New York, 1970), pp. 49–54.

2. *Familial Eyes*, pp. 32–33; Busza, "Conrad's Polish Literary Background," p. 191; Joseph Conrad, "The First Thing I Remember" (1921), *Congo Diary and Other Uncollected Pieces*, ed. Zdzislaw Najder (Garden City, New York, 1978), p. 98.

3. Quoted in Andrzej Walicki, *Philosophy and Romantic Nationalism: The Case of Poland* (Oxford, 1982), p. 338; A. P. Coleman, "Poland Under Alexander II: The Insurrection of 1863," in *The Cambridge History of Poland*, ed. W. F. Reddaway (Cambridge, England, 1950), p. 369.

4. *A Personal Record*, 6.ix; R. F. Leslie, *Reform and Insurrection in Russian Poland, 1856–1865* (London, 1963), p. 122; Quoted in Baines, *Joseph Conrad*, p. 10.

5. *A Personal Record*, 6.24; *Familial Eyes*, pp. 81, 63; Najder, *Joseph Conrad*, p. 21.

6. Ford Madox Ford, *Joseph Conrad: A Personal Reminiscence* (London, 1924), p. 74; *Familial Eyes*, p. 66; *Under Western Eyes*, 22.33.

7. *Entsiklopedicheskii Slovar*, 7.59–60; *Familial Eyes*, pp. 66–68.

8. *Familial Eyes*, p. 70; Edward Crankshaw, "Conrad and Russia," in *Joseph Conrad: A Commemoration*, ed. Norman Sherry (London, 1974), p. 98.

9. Quoted in Jean-Aubry, *Life and Letters*, 1.8; *The Arrow of Gold*, 1.18; *Suspense*, 25.23, 105.

10. Coleman, "Poland Under Alexander II," p. 384; Honoré de Balzac, *Cousin Bette*, trans. Anthony Bonner (New York, 1961), p. 197. For Balzac's other comments on Poles and Poland, see pp. 35, 55, 97, 195 and 197; *Letters*, 3.492.

11. D. H. Lawrence, *The Rainbow* (New York, 1964), p. 45; Norman Davies, *God's Playground: A History of Poland* (New York, 1982), 2.352, 356; Quoted in Leonard Schapiro, *Turgenev: His Life and Times* (Cambridge, Mass., 1982), p. 203.

12. R. F. Leslie, *History of Poland since 1863* (Cambridge, England, 1980), p. 38; Peter Brock, "Polish Nationalism," in *Nationalism in Eastern Europe*, ed. Peter Sugar and Ivo Lederer (Seattle, 1969), p. 329.

13. Quoted in Czeslaw Milosz, "Joseph Conrad's Father," *Emperor of the Air* (Berkeley, 1977), p. 176; Najder, *Joseph Conrad*, p. 18; See H. Sutherland Edwards, *The Private History of a Polish Insurrection* (London, 1865), 1.199–202.

14. *Familial Eyes*, pp. 77–78, 84, 79; Thomas Mann, *The Magic Mountain*, trans. H. T. Lowe-Porter (1924; London, 1957), p. 241.

15. *A Personal Record*, 6.24; *Familial Eyes*, pp. 91–92.

16. *Familial Eyes*, pp. 98, 100, 102, 105.

17. Milosz, "Joseph Conrad's Father," p. 181; Quoted in Jean-Aubry, *Life and Letters*, 2.289; *Letters from Joseph Conrad, 1895–1924*, ed. Edward Garnett (Indianapolis, 1928), p. 245.

18. *Familial Eyes*, p. 120; "Poland Revisited," *Notes on Life and Letters*, 3.168–169; *Letters*, 2.247; Søren Kierkegaard, *Journals*, ed. and trans. Alexander Dru (London, 1938), p. 132; Zdzislaw Najder, Introduction to *Conrad's Polish Background: Letters to and From Polish Friends* (London, 1964), p. 11.

19. Quoted in Baines, *Joseph Conrad*, p. 109; *A Personal Record*, 6.45.

20. Quoted in Baines, *Joseph Conrad*, pp. 22–23; Quoted in Najder, *Joseph Conrad*, p. 35.

21. *Lord Jim*, 21.6; *The Letters and Journals of James Fenimore Cooper*, ed. James Franklin Beard (Cambridge, Mass., 1960), 2.124–125.

22. Quoted in B. L. Reid, *The Man from New York: John Quinn and His Friends* (New York, 1968), p. 360; *Familial Eyes*, p. 201; Quoted in Jean-Aubry, *Life and Letters*, 2.289.
23. *'Twixt Land and Sea*, 19.183.

Chapter Three: Marseilles and the Carlists

1. *A Personal Record*, 6.xvi.
2. *A Personal Record*, 6.124–125; Najder, *Joseph Conrad*, p. 41.
3. *A Personal Record*, 6.122–123; 137.
4. *The Mirror of the Sea*, 4.152–153; Quoted in Karl, *Joseph Conrad*, p. 143; *The Mirror of the Sea*, 4.162–163.
5. Quoted in Karl, *Joseph Conrad*, p. 145; *Victory*, 15.xii.
6. Quoted in Jean-Aubry, *Life and Letters*, 1.39n.
7. *Polish Background*, pp. 59; 37–38. According to the *Entsiklopedicheskii Slovar* (1893), 10a.932, one Russian ruble was then worth US $1.33, French franc 3.3 and British 27 pence. Five francs were worth one dollar and 25 francs equaled one pound.
8. *Polish Background*, pp. 39–40, 42.
9. J. H. Retinger, *Conrad and His Contemporaries* (New York, 1943), p. 30.
10. Raymond Carr, *Spain, 1808–1975*, 2nd ed. (Oxford, 1982), pp. 184–185, 188. See also Edgar Holt, *The Carlist Wars in Spain* (London, 1967), and Martin Blinkhorn, *Carlism and Crisis in Spain* (New York, 1975).
11. *The Arrow of Gold*, 1.4–5; See Robert Bernard Martin, "The Valley of the Cauteretz, 1830," *Tennyson: The Unquiet Heart* (London, 1980), pp. 114–122.
12. *The Mirror of the Sea*, 4.157; Busza, "Conrad's Polish Literary Background," p. 179; Ford, *Joseph Conrad*, p. 83.
13. *The Mirror of the Sea*, 4.158–159; 164; 172, 179–180.
14. G. F. W. Hope, "My Life at Sea and Yachting" (unpublished typescript), pp. 200–201, quoted in Norman Sherry, *Conrad's Western World* (Cambridge, England, 1971), p. 124; Quoted in Jean-Aubry, *Life and Letters*, 2.228.
15. *Polish Background*, pp. 176, 41, 177.
16. *Chance*, 4.183; *Letters*, 1.191; John Conrad, *Joseph Conrad: Times Remembered* (Cambridge, England, 1981), p. 181.
17. *Polish Background*, pp. 54, 177.
18. *A Personal Record*, 6.122.

Chapter Four: English Sailor

1. *Letters*, 2.35; *Notes on Life and Letters*, 3.155.

2. *Notes on Life and Letters*, 3.150, 152–153; Quoted in Dale Randall, "Conrad Interviews, No. 2: James Walter Smith," *Conradiana*, 2 (1969–70), 88. He repeated this anecdote in "Conrad for 'Movies' But Can't Sell One," *New York Times*, May 8, 1923, p. 16.

3. *Polish Background*, pp. 60, 62.

4. Robert Foulke, "Life in the Dying World of Sail: 1870–1910," *Journal of British Studies*, 3 (1963), 118; *A Personal Record*, 6.35; *Polish Background*, p. 179.

5. Foulke, "Dying World of Sail," p. 110; Retinger, *Conrad and His Contemporaries*, p. 50; *Lord Jim*, 21.10.

6. Quoted in Norman Sherry, *Conrad's Eastern World* (Cambridge, England, 1966), pp. 238n, 317; Jessie Conrad, *Joseph Conrad as I Knew Him* (New York, 1926), p. 45.

7. Conrad spent seven months on land (January–August 1880) between the *Europa* and the *Loch Etive*; five months (April–September 1881) between the *Loch Etive* and the *Palestine*; six months (March–September 1883) between the *Palestine* and the *Riversdale*; six months (October 1884–April 1885) between the *Narcissus* and the *Tilkhurst*; eight months (June 1886–February 1887) between the *Tilkhurst* and the *Highland Forest*; seventeen months (March 1889–August 1890) between the *Otago* and the *Roi des Belges*; and fourteen months (September 1890–November 1891) between the *Roi des Belges* and the *Torrens*. This amounts to five out of twelve years on land, excluding time in foreign ports between voyages.

8. *Polish Background*, p. 63; *Letters*, 1.15; See Andrew De Ternant, "An Unknown Episode in Conrad's Life," *New Statesman and Nation*, 31 (July 28, 1928), 511.

9. Quoted in Najder, *Joseph Conrad*, p. 64; Richard Curle, *Caravansery and Conversation* (London, 1937), p. 160.

10. *The Mirror of the Sea*, 4.139, 45, 139; See Joseph Conrad, "Christmas Day at Sea" (1923), *Almayer's Folly and Last Essays* (London, [1957]), p. 252.

11. *Polish Background*, pp. 73–74, 71–72.

12. *Youth*, 16.5, 14, 16, 23, 40–41.

13. Quoted in Baines, *Joseph Conrad*, p. 74; Jean-Aubry, *Life and Letters*, 2.183.

14. Quoted in Sherry, *Conrad's Eastern World*, pp. 297–298; Quoted in Najder, *Joseph Conrad*, p. 78.

15. *Polish Background*, p. 93; *Letters*, 1.7–8.

16. R. L. Cornewall-Jones, *The British Merchant Service* (London, 1898), p. 292; Geoffrey Ursell, "Conrad and the *Riversdale*," *TLS*, July 11, 1968, pp. 733–734; Rupert Hart-Davis, *Hugh Walpole* (1952; London, 1985), p. 179. In "Mr. Conrad Is Not a Jew," *New Republic*, 16 (August 24, 1918), 109, Conrad ignored the *Riversdale* certificate and wrote that his personal history "is carried on documentarily by a series of my discharges (V.G. as to 'character' and V.G. as to abilities) as seaman and officer in the British Merchant Service up to the year '94."

17. Jean-Aubry, *Life and Letters*, 1.76–77; Quoted in Paul Kirschner, "Conrad: An Uncollected Article," *Notes & Queries*, 25 (August 1968), 294; Jean-Aubry, *Life and Letters*, 1.77–78.

18. Najder, *Joseph Conrad*, p. 85; *Letters*, 1.17.

19. Quoted in Muirhead Bone, "Joseph Conrad—A Modern Ulysses," *Living Age*, 322 (September 13, 1924), 553; *The Mirror of the Sea*, 4.10.

20. Quoted in Baines, *Joseph Conrad*, p. 85; Quoted in Najder, *Joseph Conrad*, p. 91; *Polish Background*, pp. 113–114.

Chapter Five: From Second Mate to Master

1. *A Personal Record*, 6.116–117, 112–114.

2. *Chance*, 2.4–6.

3. *A Personal Record*, 6.114–116.

4. Conrad, "Outside Literature," *Last Essays*, pp. 260–261.

5. *A Personal Record*, 6.117; Hans van Marle, "Plucked and Passed on Tower Hill: Conrad's Examination Ordeals," *Conradiana*, 8 (1976), 105, my italics; John Georgeson Sutherland, *At Sea with Joseph Conrad*, Foreword by Joseph Conrad (London, 1922), p. 127.

6. *Typhoon*, 20.20; *Notes on Life and Letters*, 3.219–220.

7. Najder, *Joseph Conrad*, p. 66, gives the address as Dock Street. Frederick Karl and Laurence Davies, the editors of the *Letters*, I.214n, say the school was in the Well Street Sailors' Home.

8. Najder, *Joseph Conrad*, pp. 65–66; *A Personal Record*, 6.112; *Notice of Examinations* (London: HMSO, 1870), p. 4.

9. Conrad, "Memorandum . . . ," *Last Essays*, p. 298. The standard work on this subject was Robert Stevens, *On the Stowage of Ships and Their Cargoes* (Plymouth, 1858).

10. *The Mirror of the Sea*, 4.52–54. Sterne's cry: "Captain Whalley! Leap! . . . pull up a little . . . leap! You can swim." (*Youth*, 16.333) recalls Lord Jim's leap from the *Patna* just as Whalley's drowning with iron in his pockets echoes Captain Brierly's suicide.

   Conrad was fascinated by the sensual sound and suggestion of Whalley's ship, the *Sofala* (the old name of Beira, on the northeast coast of Mozambique), and used variants of the name three times in the next decade. The heroine of *Romance* (1903) is *Seraphina* (little angel), Bunter's ship in "The Black Mate" (1908) is the *Sapphire* and Leggatt's ship in "The Secret Sharer" (1910) is the *Sephora* (zephyr). Perhaps, to Conrad, these names suggested *sophia* (Greek: wisdom)—the name of the principal cathedral in Kiev (only one hundred miles from his birthplace) and a popular name among the nobility of the Ukraine.

11. *Notice of Examinations*, p. 7; Edward Blackmore, *The British Mercantile Marine* (London, 1897), pp. 186, 243.

12. Conrad could not have written novels in Polish on nautical subjects that demanded a technical vocabulary.

13. Alfred Henry Alstoun, *Seamanship* (London, 1860), p. 8.

14. *Lord Jim*, 21.136.

15. Jean-Aubry, *Life and Letters*, 1.156.

16. *Letters*, 2.323.

Chapter Six: Eastern Voyages

1. See Gerald Morgan, "Conrad's Unknown Ship [the *Falconhurst*]," *Conradiana*, 12 (1980), 187–195; Quoted in Gene Moore, "Conrad in Amsterdam," *Conradiana*, 21 (1989), 85.

2. *The Mirror of the Sea*, 4.49, 51, 54.

3. *Lord Jim*, 21.12; *The Mirror of the Sea*, 4.55.

4. Jean-Aubry, *Life and Letters*, 1.94; *The Shadow-Line*, 17.4; Unpublished letter to R. H. Fitzherbert, October 15, 1922.

5. Jean-Aubry, *Life and Letters*, 2.186; *A Personal Record*, 6.74; Quoted in Sherry, *Conrad's Eastern World*, p. 115.

6. David Steinberg, ed., *In Search of Southeast Asia: A Modern History* (New York, 1971), p. 74; Graham Irwin, *Nineteenth-Century Borneo: A Study in Diplomatic Rivalry* ('s-Gravenhage, 1955), pp. 174, 153, v. The old partition marks the present border between Malaysian and Indonesian Borneo.

7. J. S. Furnivall, *Netherlands India* (Cambridge, England, 1934), p. 223; Amry Vandenbosch, *The Dutch East Indies: Its Government, Problems and Politics* (Berkeley, 1942), p. 154.

   For other aspects of Dutch colonial rule, see: Frank Marryat, *Borneo and the Indian Archipelago* (London, 1848), which Conrad used as a source for his Malayan novels; E. S. de Klerck, *History of the Netherlands East Indies*, 2 vols. (Rotterdam, 1938); Bernard Vlekke, *Nusantara: A History of the East Indian Archipelago* (Cambridge, Mass., 1943); J. S. Furnivall, *Colonial Policy and Practice: A Comparative Study of Burma and Netherlands India* (Cambridge, England, 1948); Nicholas Tarling, *Anglo-Dutch Rivalry in the Malay World, 1780–1824* (London, 1962); and Nicholas Tarling, *Piracy and Politics in the Malay World* (Melbourne, 1963).

8. *Letters*, 2.230; *'Twixt Land and Sea*, 19.148. For a passionate condemnation of Dutch colonialism, see E. D. Dekker's *Max Havelaar* (1860), which was reviewed by D. H. Lawrence in 1927. See D. H. Lawrence, *Phoenix*, ed. Edward McDonald (London, 1936), pp. 236–239.

9. *The Shadow-Line*, 17.4; *Lord Jim*, 21.13; Quoted in Jean-Aubry, *Life and Letters*, 1.101n, 2.103.

10. *The Shadow-Line*, 17.47–48; "Falk" in *Typhoon*, 20.188.

11. Quoted in Sherry, *Conrad's Eastern World*, p. 216; Cornewall-Jones, *The British Merchant Service*, p. 289.

12. "Falk" in *Typhoon*, 20.155; John Conrad, *Joseph Conrad*, p. 189; Bertrand Russell, *Autobiography, 1914–1944* (1968; New York, 1969), p. 226.

13. Conrad, "Geography and Some Explorers" (1924), *Last Essays*, pp. 236–237; Quoted in Karl, *Joseph Conrad*, p. 256.

14. *'Twixt Land and Sea*, 19.34–35, 56.

15. Quoted in Baines, *Joseph Conrad*, p. 98; *'Twixt Land and Sea*, 19.81.

16. Jean-Aubry, *Life and Letters*, 1.116; *Polish Background*, p. 126.

17. *A Personal Record*, 6.68; Quoted in Busza, "Conrad's Polish Literary Background," p. 188. Jean-Aubry corrected numerous mistakes in his edition of Conrad's *Lettres françaises* (Paris, 1930). See René Rapin, "Le Français de Joseph Conrad," *Lettres de Joseph Conrad à Marguerite Poradowska* (Genève, 1966), pp. 15–53.

18. Thomas Mann, "Joseph Conrad's *The Secret Agent*," *Past Masters and Other Papers*, trans. H. T. Lowe-Porter, (New York, 1933), p. 233; Ottoline Morrell, *Memoirs, 1873–1915*, ed. Robert Gathorne-Hardy (New York, 1964), p. 237; Jean-Aubry, *Life and Letters*, 2.206 (see also 2.296).

Chapter Seven: Into the Congo

1. *A Personal Record*, 6.13 (Conrad, extremely fond of this anecdote, also mentioned it in *Heart of Darkness* [1899], in *Youth*, 16.52, and in "Geography and Some Explorers," 1923, *Last Essays*, p. 235); *Youth*, 16.xi, 51–52.

2. Quoted in Albert Lubin, *Stranger on the Earth: The Life of Vincent Van Gogh* (1972; London, 1975), pp. 260, 251; *Letters*, 1.84.

3. Jessie Conrad, *Joseph Conrad and His Circle* (New York, 1935), p. 70. Photographs of Aniela and Marguerite appear opposite each other in Najder, *Joseph Conrad*.

4. *Youth*, 16.53; *Letters*, 1.55, 70.

5. *A Personal Record*, 6.26, 22; Quoted in Najder, *Joseph Conrad*, pp. 119–120.

6. Quoted in G. Jean-Aubry, *Joseph Conrad in the Congo* (London, 1926), p. 41; *Letters*, 1.52.

7. Conrad, "Geography and Some Explorers," *Last Essays*, p. 236; *The Inheritors*, 5.31–32. In *Letters*, 1.49 (May 1890), Conrad sends regards to his Polish acquaintances, Mr. and Mrs. Meresch, whose name is almost the same as the Duc de Mersch.

8. *Letters*, 1.52. In *Heart of Darkness*, 16.61, Conrad writes: we passed "trading places—with names like Gran' Bassam, Little Popo." Grand Popo, which he changes to Little Popo to balance Grand Bassam, is a port in Dahomey (now Benin).

9. Conrad, *Congo Diary*, p. 7; *The Inheritors*, 5.181.

10. Quoted in Sherry, *Conrad's Western World*, p. 34; *Letters*, 3.101–102; Conrad, *Congo Diary*, p. 7.

11. Quoted in Giovanni Costigan, "The Treason of Roger Casement," *American Historical Review*, 60 (1955), 288; Roger Casement, "The 1903 Diary," in Peter Singleton-Gates and Maurice Girodias, *The Black Diaries of Roger Casement* (New York, 1959), p. 164.

12. *Black Diaries*, pp. 190, 100, 104, 152, 118.

13. *Black Diaries*, pp. 104, 188, 193; Quoted in H. Montgomery Hyde, *The Trial of Sir Roger Casement* (London, 1960), p. cxxx.

14. Conrad, *Congo Diary*, p. 7; Albert Thys, *Au Congo et au Kassai* (Bruxelles, 1888), quoted in Jean-Aubry, *Life and Letters*, 1.128.

15. Conrad, *Congo Diary*, pp. 9, 15; *Youth*, 16.71.

16. *Youth*, 16.73; *Polish Background*, p. 128; W. Holman Bentley, *Pioneering in the Congo* (London, 1900), 1.210, quoted in Sherry, *Conrad's Western World*, p. 60.

17. E. D. Morel, *King Leopold's Rule in Africa* (London, 1904), quoted in

Najder, *Joseph Conrad*, pp. 134–135; Conrad, "Geography and Some Explorers," *Last Essays*, p. 235. Otto Lütken, "Joseph Conrad in the Congo," *London Mercury*, 22 (May 1930), 42, mentions that Tipoo-Tib, the most notorious Arab slaver and paid official of the Congo Free State, was then in control of the Congo above Stanley Falls. In *Heart of Darkness*, the Company Station, the Central Station and the Inner Station correspond to Matadi, Kinshasa and Stanley Falls.

18. Quoted in Sherry, *Conrad's Western World*, p. 110; Quoted in Enid Starkie, *Rimbaud in Abyssinia* (Oxford, 1937), p. 132.

19. *Letters*, 1.62–63; *Youth*, 16.49–50.

20. *Polish Background*, p. 133; Quoted in Jean-Aubry, *Conrad in the Congo*, p. 71.

21. Quoted in Lütken, "Conrad in the Congo," p. 41; *A Personal Record*, 6.14.

22. G. F. W. Hope, "My Life at Sea and Yachting," quoted in Sherry, *Conrad's Western World*, p. 90.

23. Garnett, Introduction to *Letters from Conrad*, p. 8; *Letters*, 1.75.

Chapter Eight: Sailor to Writer

1. *The Mirror of the Sea*, 4.133; *Polish Background*, pp. 147–148; *Letters*, 1.189.

2. Basil Lubbock, *The Colonial Clippers*, new ed. (Glasgow, 1948), pp. 133–134; Conrad, "The *Torrens*: A Personal Tribute," *Last Essays*, p. 242; *A Personal Record*, 6.17–18.

3. William Rothenstein, *Men and Memories* (1931; New York, 1934), 2.164; Quoted in James Gindin, *John Galsworthy's Life and Art* (Ann Arbor, 1987), pp. 65–66.

4. John Galsworthy, "The Doldrums," *From the Four Winds* (1897), reprinted in *Forsytes, Pendyces and Others* (London, 1935), pp. 188–190, 193–194; John Galsworthy, *Castles in Spain* (London, 1927), pp. 74, 87, 75.

5. *Polish Background*, p. 169; *Letters*, 1.130.

6. *A Personal Record*, 6.11, 5.

7. Frank Bullen, *The Men of the Merchant Service* (London, 1900), pp. 26, 91; Blackmore, *The British Mercantile Marine*, p. 169; David Bone, Introduction to *The Nigger of the "Narcissus" and Other Tales* (London, 1959), p. viii.

8. Sutherland, *At Sea with Conrad*, p. 134; Ford, *Joseph Conrad*, p. 237;

Ford Madox Ford, "Conrad and the Sea," *Portraits from Memory* (1936; Chicago, 1960), p. 76; *Notes on Life and Letters*, 3.55.

9. *A Personal Record*, 6.68, 98–99; *Notes on Life and Letters*, 3.13; Henry James, *Letters*, *1895–1916*, ed. Leon Edel (Cambridge, Mass., 1984), 4.419.

10. *Letters*, 1.148; *A Personal Record*, 6.31.

11. *Letters*, 1.86; *Polish Background*, pp. 165, 148; *Letters*, 1.129.

12. *Letters*, 1.111, 151; Marcel Proust, *Swann's Way*, trans. C. K. Scott Moncrieff (New York, 1956), p. 66.

13. *Letters*, 1.163–164; Mabel Edith Reynolds, *Memories of John Galsworthy* (London, 1936), p. 26; *Letters*, 1.153.

14. *Letters*, 1.165, 173, 180.

15. *The Letters of D. H. Lawrence*, *1901–1913*, ed. James Boulton (Cambridge, England, 1979), 1.362; John Conrad, *Joseph Conrad*, p. 58; David Garnett, *The Flowers of the Forest* (New York, 1955), p. 155.

16. Garnett, Introduction to *Letters from Conrad*, pp. 2–3n, 12, 9.

17. *Letters*, 2.198; *The Inheritors*, 5.46.

18. Quoted in *Letters*, 2.130 n2; Sir Hugh Clifford, *A Talk on Mr. Joseph Conrad and His Work* (Colombo, 1927), p. 4. Though Clifford set up as an authority on the Malay language, the first volume of his Malay dictionary was so badly received that he abandoned the three-volume project. See Harry Gailey, *Clifford: Imperial Proconsul* (London, 1982), p. 32.

19. The main source books were: Captain Edward Belcher, *Voyage of the H.M.S. Semarang* (1848); Alfred Russel Wallace, *The Malay Archipelago* (1869); and Major Fred McNair, *Perak and the Malays* (1878). Conrad places the novel in its historical context by referring to the unsuccessful war against the Acheen (i.e., Atjeh), whom the Dutch fought in Sumatra between 1873 and 1904. See *Almayer's Folly*, 11.48.

20. *Letters*, 2.130, 180.

21. *Almayer's Folly*, 11.179, 195, 88–89.

Chapter Nine: Courtship and Marriage

1. Desmond MacCarthy, "Conrad," *Portraits* (London, 1931), p. 68; Henry-Durand Davray, "Joseph Conrad," *Mercure de France*, 175 (octobre 1, 1924), 33–34.

2. Ford, *Joseph Conrad*, p. 57; Jo Davidson, *Between Sittings* (New York, 1951), p. 118.

3. Vio Allen, "Memories of Joseph Conrad," *Review of English Litera-*

ture, (April 1967), 79, 82; Letter from Adam Curle to Jeffrey Meyers, October 26, 1989; H. G. Wells, *Experiment in Autobiography* (New York, 1934), p. 525; Jessie Conrad, *Conrad as I Knew Him,* p. 103.

4. *Lord Jim,* 21.238; *Typhoon,* 20.187; *The Rescue,* 12.95; Jean-Aubry, *Life and Letters,* 2.125.

5. John Conrad, *Joseph Conrad,* pp. 78–79.

6. Wells, *Experiment in Autobiography,* p. 525. See also: Arnold Bennett, *Letters,* ed. James Hepburn (London, 1970), 3.315; Ford, *Joseph Conrad,* p. 18, and Ford, "The Other House" [review of Jean-Aubry's biography], *New York Herald Tribune Books,* October 2, 1927, VII.2; Richard Curle, *The Last Twelve Years of Joseph Conrad* (London, 1928), p. 10; Henry Newbolt, *My World as in My Time* (London, 1932), p. 300.

7. *Letters,* 2.44; 1.211; 284, 287.

8. Quoted in Baines, *Joseph Conrad,* p. 288; Quoted in Rupert Hart-Davis, *Hugh Walpole,* p. 286; *Typhoon,* 20.169; *Tales of Unrest,* 8.136.

9. "Freya of the Seven Isles," *'Twixt Land and Sea,* 19.156; *Joseph Conrad and Warrington Dawson,* ed. Dale Randall (Durham, N.C., 1968), p. 198; *Lord Jim,* 21.272.

10. *Letters,* 1.223; Quoted in Najder, *Joseph Conrad,* p. 178; *Letters,* 1.236–237. Najder reproduces a photograph of Émilie.

11. Quoted in Najder, *Joseph Conrad,* pp. 179, 185; *Letters,* 1.244; Najder, *Joseph Conrad,* p. 189.

12. *Lord Jim,* 21.156; Borys Conrad, *My Father, Joseph Conrad* (London, 1970), p. 13; *Letters,* 2.29.

13. Violet Hunt, *I Have This to Say* (New York, 1926), p. 195; Borys Conrad, *My Father,* p. 18; Quoted in George Jefferson, *Edward Garnett: A Life in Literature* (London, 1982), p. 268.

14. Jocelyn Baines, *Joseph Conrad,* p. 171; Jessie Conrad, *Conrad as I Knew Him,* p. 3; Jessie Conrad, *Conrad and His Circle,* p. 12; Jessie Conrad, *Conrad as I Knew Him,* p. 105; Joseph Conrad, "Marriage," in George Keating, *A Conrad Memorial Library* (Garden City, New York, 1929), p. 448.

15. *Within the Tides,* 10.209; *Letters,* 1.265–266; Jessie Conrad, *Conrad and His Circle,* p. 271; *Youth,* 16.287.

16. *Letters,* 1.274, 272; 271.

17. *The Oxford Textbook of Medicine,* ed. D. J. Wetherall *et al.,* 2nd ed. (Oxford, 1987), 9.127; Jessie Conrad, *Conrad as I Knew Him,* p. 35.

18. *The Mirror of the Sea,* 4.101; *Letters,* 1.305; Jessie Conrad, *Conrad and His Circle,* pp. 43–44; Garnett, Introduction to *Letters from Conrad,* p. 24.

19. Richard Curle, *Last Twelve Years of Conrad,* p. 145; John Conrad, *Joseph Conrad,* pp. 157–158.

20. *Letters*, 2.240–241; Jessie Conrad, *Conrad as I Knew Him*, p. 130.

21. Jessie Conrad, *Conrad as I Knew Him*, p. 44; David Garnett, "Joseph Conrad," *Great Friends* (New York, 1980), p. 16.

22. Quoted in John Halverson and Ian Watt, "Notes on Jane Anderson, 1955–1989," *Conradiana* (forthcoming); Virginia Woolf, *A Writer's Diary*, ed. Leonard Woolf (New York, 1953), p. 25; Morrell, *Memoirs*, p. 233; Letter from Dame Veronica Wedgwood to Jeffrey Meyers, September 23, 1989.

23. *Letters*, 1.370; *Chance*, 2.159.

24. Jessie Conrad, *Conrad as I Knew Him*, p. 118; *Typhoon*, 20.113, 107, 135; Jessie Conrad, *Conrad and His Circle*, p. 26; *Typhoon*, 20.139, 142.

25. Norman Sherry, ed., *Conrad: The Critical Heritage* (London, 1973), pp. 47, 6, 53.

26. *An Outcast of the Islands*, 14.xi–xii; *Letters*, 1.171; 185; 245. See also *Letters*, 1.330 and Jessie Conrad, *Conrad as I Knew Him*, p. 144.

27. *An Outcast of the Islands*, 14.250; 360 (the spaced periods are Conrad's); *Critical Heritage*, pp. 8, 79, 74–76.

28. *Letters*, 1.279; 281; G. Jean-Aubry, ed., *Twenty Letters to Joseph Conrad* (London, 1926), n.p.

29. Lawrence, *Letters*, 1.144; Conrad, *Letters*, 2.138; *Chance*, 2.37; Wells, *Experiment in Autobiography*, p. 527.

30. Quoted in Hart-Davis, *Hugh Walpole*, p. 168; Wells, *Experiment in Autobiography*, pp. 528, 530; H. G. Wells, *Boon* (New York, 1915), pp. 136, 147; Siegfried Sassoon, *Diaries, 1923–1925*, ed. Rupert Hart-Davis (London, 1985), p. 236.

31. *Letters*, 1.288, 296; 301; Max Beerbohm, "The Feast," *A Christmas Garland* (1912; New York, 1960), p. 242.

32. *Tales of Unrest*, 8.ix; *Letters*, 1.294; *Tales of Unrest*, 8.89.

33. *The Inheritors*, 5.51, 88.

Chapter Ten: Literary Friendships and Artistic Breakthrough

1. *Letters*, 1.416–417; Ford, *New York Herald Tribune Books*, VII.2; Ford Madox Ford, *Return to Yesterday* (1932; New York, 1972), p. 34; Jean-Aubry, *Life and Letters*, 2.206.

2. *Letters*, 1.307; 342; Quoted in Leon Edel, *Henry James: The Master, 1901–1916* (Philadelphia, 1972), p. 48; Ford, *Return to Yesterday*, p. 31; Edouard Roditi, *Meetings with Conrad* (Los Angeles, 1977), p. 16.

3. *The Inheritors*, 5.17–18; *Notes on Life and Letters*, 3.17, 11; Quoted in Reid, *The Man from New York*, p. 244; *Letters*, 2.174.

4. James, *Letters*, 4.232; Quoted in Simon Nowell-Smith, *The Legend of the Master* (London, 1947), p. 135; Quoted in Reid, *The Man from New York*, p. 245.

5. James, *Letters*, 4.703; *Henry James and Edith Wharton: Letters, 1900–1915*, ed. Lyall Powers (New York, 1990), p. 345; Quoted in Reid, *The Man from New York*, p. 245.

6. "Stephen Crane: A Note Without Dates" (1919), *Notes on Life and Letters*, 3.50; *Letters*, 1.415; "Stephen Crane" (1923), *Last Essays*, p. 321.

7. *The Nigger of the "Narcissus,"* 23.155; *Twenty Letters to Joseph Conrad*, n.p.; Stephen Crane, "Concerning the English 'Academy,' " *Bookman*, 7 (March 1898), 23; John Berryman, *Stephen Crane: A Critical Biography*, revised ed. (1962; New York, 1977), p. 201.

8. "Stephen Crane," *Last Essays*, pp. 337, 319; *Letters*, 1.416.

9. *Notes on Life and Letters*, 3.50–51; Conrad's unpublished letter, with no date or addressee, is in the Library of Congress.

10. "Stephen Crane," *Last Essays*, pp. 322, 317; *Notes on Life and Letters*, 3.52; *The Correspondence of Stephen Crane*, ed. Stanley Wertheim and Paul Sorrentino (New York, 1988), p. 651.

11. Ford, *Return to Yesterday*, p. 45; Frank Harris, "Cunninghame Graham," *Contemporary Portraits*, 3rd series (New York, 1920), p. 45; T. E. Lawrence, *Letters*, ed. David Garnett (London, 1939), p. 750.

12. *Letters*, 2.25, 1.424–425; Rothenstein, *Men and Memories*, 2.44; Quoted in A. F. Tschiffely, *Don Roberto* (London, 1937), p. 263.

13. *Letters*, 2.17, 427, 30, 70; 359.

14. D. H. Lawrence, "*Pedro de Valdivia* by R. B. Cunninghame Graham," *Phoenix*, p. 356; *Joseph Conrad's Letters to Cunninghame Graham*, ed. C. T. Watts (Cambridge, England, 1969), p. 180; Quoted in Herbert West, *A Modern Conquistador: Robert Bontine Cunninghame Graham* (London, 1932), p. 114.

15. *Letters*, 1.367; 2.17; Jessie Conrad, *Conrad and His Circle*, pp. 57–58; *Letters*, 2.173.

16. *Letters*, 2.24; See Karl, *Joseph Conrad*, pp. 416–417; Najder, *Joseph Conrad*, p. 225; and Najder, Introduction to "The Sisters," *Congo Diary*, p. 45. For the history and meaning of the name Borys, see *Ukraine: A Concise Encyclopedia*, ed. Volodymyr Kubijovyc, 2 vols. (Toronto, 1963, 1971), 1.978–979, 2.120, 137; *A Thousand Years of Christianity in Ukraine*, ed. Osip Zinkewych and Andrew Sorokowski (New York, 1988), pp. 24, 31, 51; *The Millennium of Ukrainian Chris-*

tianity, ed. Nicholas Chirovsky (New York, 1988), pp. 92, 229, 337. I am grateful to Eugene Petriwsky for this information.

17. *A Personal Record,* 6.25; *The Nigger of the "Narcissus,"* 23.xiv.

18. Robert Lowell, "Ford Madox Ford," *Notebook,* revised ed. (New York, 1970), p. 120; *Letters to Garnett,* p. 214; *Letters,* 1.252. Lawrence also believed: "Coal is the symbol of something in the soul, old and dark and silky and natural" (*Collected Letters,* ed. Harry Moore, New York, 1962, p. 852).

19. Warrington Dawson, *The Crimson Pall: A Novel, with Letters Exchanged on "Critical Novelists" by Joseph Conrad and the Author* (Chicago, 1927), p. 24; *Letters,* 2.85, 3.100; Robert Lowell, "The Severed Head," *For the Union Dead* (1964; New York, 1967), p. 53.

20. *Letters,* 3.488; C. Lewis Hind, *Naphtali* (London, 1926), p. 73.

21. Najder, *Joseph Conrad,* p. 116; *Heart of Darkness,* in *Youth,* 16.50; 93. For discussions of Polonisms in Conrad's style, see Gustav Morf, *The Polish Heritage of Joseph Conrad* (London, 1930); A. P. Coleman, "Polonisms in the English of Conrad's *Chance,*" *Modern Language Notes,* 46 (1931), 463–468; Busza, "Conrad's Polish Literary Background" (1966); Adam Gillon, "Polish and Russian Literary Elements in Joseph Conrad," *Proceedings of the Vth Congress of the International Comparative Literature Association* (Amsterdam, 1969), pp. 685–694; and I. P. Pulc, "The Imprint of Polish on Conrad's Prose," *Joseph Conrad: Theory and World Fiction,* ed. Wolodymyr Zyla and Wendell Aycock (Lubbock, Texas, 1974), pp. 117–139.

22. *Critical Heritage,* p. 93; *Letters,* 1.308; 2.71.

23. *Letters,* 2.88; Conrad, *Lettres françaises,* p. 78; *Conrad to a Friend: 150 Selected Letters from Joseph Conrad to Richard Curle* (Garden City, New York, 1928), p. 147.

24. *Critical Heritage,* p. 63; *Letters,* 3.408; Jacob Epstein, *An Autobiography,* 2nd ed. (New York, 1963), p. 76.

25. D. H. Lawrence, *Studies in Classic American Literature* (London, 1924), p. 132; Lawrence, *Letters,* 1.465; Epstein, *Autobiography,* p. 76.

26. *Letters,* 1.410; *The Nigger of the "Narcissus,"* 23.ix.

Chapter Eleven: Ford and Pent Farm

1. David Garnett, *The Golden Echo* (New York, 1954), p. 36; *The Nigger of the "Narcissus,"* 23.31; *Letters,* 2.131–132.

2. Arthur Mizener, *The Saddest Story: A Biography of Ford Madox Ford*

(New York, 1971), p. 18; Quoted in Thomas Moser, *The Life in the Fiction of Ford Madox Ford* (Princeton, 1980), p. 39.

3. *Letters*, 2.107; Ford, *Joseph Conrad*, p. 37; Quoted in Edel, *The Master*, p. 47; Ford, *Joseph Conrad*, p. 51; Wells, *Experiment in Autobiography*, p. 531.

4. Ford, *Joseph Conrad*, p. 238; Ford, *Return to Yesterday*, p. 290; *Letters*, 3.9.

5. Ford, "Stephen Crane," *Portraits from Memory*, p. 45; Ford Madox Ford, *Letters*, ed. Richard Ludwig (Princeton, 1965), p. 127; Hunt, *I Have This to Say*, p. 38.

6. Ford Madox Ford, *Memories and Impressions* (1911; New York, 1985), p. 219; Jessie Conrad, *Conrad and His Circle*, p. 66; *Letters*, 2.219; 408.

7. Ford, *Return to Yesterday*, pp. 240, 280; Ford, *Joseph Conrad*, p. 118; *Letters*, 2.287; Jessie Conrad, *Conrad and His Circle*, p. 71.

8. *Letters*, 2.257; *Notes on Life and Letters*, 3.15; *Romance*, 7.169; 383; 105.

9. Ford, *Joseph Conrad*, pp. 147–148; *The Arrow of Gold*, 1.109.

10. Jessie Conrad, *Conrad and His Circle*, p. 74. For Conrad's friendships with Galsworthy and with Clifford, see Gindin, *John Galsworthy's Life and Art*, and Gailey, *Clifford: Imperial Proconsul*.

11. Brock, "Polish Nationalism," p. 333; Milosz, "Joseph Conrad in Polish Eyes," p. 42; Eliza Orzeszkowa, "The Emigration of Talent," *Kraj*, 16 (April 23, 1899), quoted in Ludwik Krzyzanowski, "Joseph Conrad: Some Polish Documents," *Joseph Conrad: Centennial Essays*, ed. Ludwik Krzyzanowski (New York, 1960), p. 114. In Cracow in 1869, Apollo had helped start a newspaper, also called *Kraj*, which had no connection with the St. Petersburg journal.

12. Quoted in Jerzy Illg, " 'Polish Soul Living in Darkness': Letters from Joseph Conrad-Korzeniowski to Wincenty Lutoslawski," *Conradiana*, 14 (1982), 9; *Letters*, 2.323.

In 1939 W. H. Auden, whose homosexuality would have exempted him from military service, was also unjustly accused of abandoning his country by emigrating to America. In the *Spectator* of 1940, the Dean of St. Paul's wrote in bitter doggerel:

> "This Europe stinks," you cried—swift to desert
>   Your stricken country in her sore distress.
> You may not care, but still I will assert
>   Since you have left us, here the stink is less.

Quoted in Humphrey Carpenter, *W. H. Auden: A Biography* (Boston, 1981), p. 291.

13. *Letters to Curle*, pp. 112–113. Hemingway's *A Farewell to Arms*, Graves' *Good-bye to All That*, Aldington's *Death of a Hero* and Remarque's *All Quiet on the Western Front* were all published in 1929.

14. E. D. Morel, *Red Rubber* (London, 1907), p. 46; Herman Melville, *Typee* (1846; London, [1907]), p. 13; J. A. Hobson, *Imperialism* (1902; Ann Arbor, 1965), p. 214; William Cornwallis Harris, *The Wild Sports of Southern Africa* (1838; London, 1852), p. 288.

15. A passage from Saul Bellow's *Mr. Sammler's Planet* (New York, 1969), p. 137, suggests the connection between *Heart of Darkness* and the greater horrors of the twentieth century: "Over a similar new grave [Adolf] Eichmann had testified that he had walked, and the fresh blood welling up at his shoes had sickened him. For a day or two, he had to lie in bed."

16. *Youth*, 16.48. See Rudyard Kipling, "The Man Who Would Be King" (1888), *Works*, Outward Bound Edition (New York, 1907), 5.44: "They are the dark places of the earth, full of unimaginable cruelty." *Youth*, 16.50; Cornelii Taciti, *De Vita Agricolae*, ed. R. M. Ogilvie and Sir Ian Richmond (Oxford, 1967), p. 111.

17. Henry David Thoreau, *Walden* (1854; New York, 1956), pp. 142–143; *Youth*, 16.115.

18. Carl Jung, "The Psychology of the Unconscious," *Collected Works*, ed. Herbert Read and Michael Forham (New York, 1953), 7.18; Carl Jung, *The Undiscovered Self*, trans. R. F. C. Hull (New York, 1957), p. 93.

19. *Youth*, 16.151–152; *Letters*, 2.417; V. S. Naipaul, *A Bend in the River* (New York, 1980), p. 53.

20. Stanhope White, *Lost Empire on the Nile: Stanley, Emin Pasha and the Imperialists* (London, 1969), p. 137; Henry M. Stanley, *In Darkest Africa* (New York, 1890), 2.230, 1.446. See also Olivia Manning, *The Remarkable Expedition* (London, 1947).

21. *Letters*, 2.284; *Notes on Life and Letters*, 3.252.

22. *Typhoon*, 20.4; *Lord Jim*, 21.113; Ernest Hemingway, Introduction to *Men at War* (New York, 1942), p. xxvii.

23. *Lord Jim*, 21.50; 66.

24. *Lord Jim*, 21.214; *Under Western Eyes*, 22.10; *Within the Tides*, 10.85; *'Twixt Land and Sea*, 19.143; *Letters*, 2.302–303.

25. *Letters*, 2.428; Ford, *Joseph Conrad*, pp. 243–244; *Youth*, 16.298. See Sophocles, *Oedipus the King*, *Greek Tragedies*, ed. David Grene and Richmond Lattimore, trans. David Grene (Chicago, 1960), 1.176: "Count no mortal happy till / he has passed the final limit of his life secure from pain."

26. *Letters*, 2.163; 194.

Chapter Twelve: J. B. Pinker and *Nostromo*

1. In the end, Unwin, Methuen and Dent published six works each, Heinemann three, Blackwood two, Smith Elder, Harper and Eveleigh Nash one each.

2. *Letters*, 2.195; Frank Swinnerton, *Background with Chorus* (London, 1956), p. 128; *Letters*, 3.60. Frederick Karl, *Joseph Conrad*, p. 488, says Pinker was Jewish, but there is no evidence for this.

3. *Letters*, 2.318; 370–371; Quoted in Najder, *Joseph Conrad*, p. 337; Jessie Conrad, *Conrad as I Knew Him*, p. 22.

4. Quoted in Najder, *Joseph Conrad*, p. 302; *Letters*, 3.335; 154.

5. Wells, *Experiment in Autobiography*, p. 530; *Letters to Garnett*, pp. 25–26.

6. Conrad, *Lettres françaises*, p. 84. During the last two decades I have attempted to trace the missing essay that Conrad sent to *Outlook*, a weekly journal edited by Percy Hurd at 69 Fleet Street, London EC4. Conrad's publisher J. M. Dent could tell me nothing about it; it was not in the major collections of Conrad's papers at the New York Public Library, Yale University or the Rosenbach Foundation. Conrad's son Borys, the Kipling scholars Charles Carrington, Elliot Gilbert and Thomas Pinney, and the Conrad scholars Jocelyn Baines, Thomas Moser, Bernard Meyer, Norman Sherry, Frederick Karl and Zdzislaw Najder did not know where it was. And neither V. S. Pritchett, a former contributor to *Outlook*, nor Douglas Hurd—the British Foreign Secretary and son of Percy Hurd, who examined his father's papers at the family home in Wiltshire—could locate it. If the essay survived in the files of *Outlook* until 1940, it was probably destroyed when the Nazis bombed Fleet Street during the London Blitz. Paul Kirschner's "Conrad's Missing Link with Kipling," *Notes & Queries*, 217 (September 1972), 331, convincingly refuted an erroneous attribution to Conrad, of a short article on Kipling, by Theodore Ehrsam in *A Bibliography of Joseph Conrad* (Metuchen, New Jersey, 1969), p. 277.

7. Charles Carrington, *The Life of Rudyard Kipling* (Garden City, New York, 1955), p. 261n; *Letters*, 1.369–371; *Critical Heritage*, p. 9.

8. *Letters*, 2.207; Ford, *Joseph Conrad*, p. 241; Retinger, *Conrad and His Contemporaries*, pp. 124, 54.

9. Letter about Kipling from Thomas Pinney to Jeffrey Meyers, May 15, 1989; *Familial Eyes*, p. 162.

10. Max Beerbohm, "Enoch Soames," *Seven Men* (London, 1919), pp. 4–5; Rothenstein, *Men and Memories*, 2.41–44, 157–158; Hugh Wal-

pole, quoted in E. V. Lucas, *The Colvins and Their Friends* (London, 1928), pp. 350–351.

11. Ford, *Return to Yesterday*, pp. 190–191; *Letters*, 3.132.

12. *Letters*, 3.184; 293; *Nostromo*, 9.372.

13. Jessie Conrad, *Conrad as I Knew Him*, p. 118; *Typhoon*, 20.34; *Notes on Life and Letters*, 3.190–191.

14. Conrad scholars have discovered that the main sources for *Nostromo* were Alexandre Dumas, ed., *Garibaldi: An Autobiography* (1860); Edward Eastwick, *Venezuela: or Sketches of Life in a South American Republic* (1868); George Frederick Masterman, *Seven Eventful Years in Paraguay* (1869); Frederick Benton Williams, *On Many Seas: The Life and Exploits of a Yankee Sailor* (1897), which describes the theft of a boat full of silver.

15. George Barringer, "Joseph Conrad and *Nostromo*: Two New Letters," *Thoth*, 10 (1969), 24; *A Personal Record*, 6.100, 98–99.

16. Quoted in Mizener, *The Saddest Story*, pp. 90–91; *Letters*, 3.158, 165.

17. *Nostromo*, 9.84; 221–222.

18. *Nostromo*, 9.171; 261, 263, 275.

19. *Nostromo*, 9.498; 292; 552 (italics mine).

20. Barringer, "Conrad and *Nostromo*," p. 22; *Nostromo*, 9.417–418.

21. *Nostromo*, 9.511; 521.

22. Jessie Conrad, *Conrad as I Knew Him*, p. 120; *Critical Heritage*, p. 177.

Upton Sinclair's perverse Marxist criticism in *Mammonart* (Pasadena, 1925), p. 375, completely missed the point of the novel and argued that Conrad had sold out to shipping interests and taken as his God "the capitalist ownership and control of marine transportation."

Chapter Thirteen: Capri, Montpellier and *The Secret Agent*

1. *Letters*, 3.209; 241; Retinger, *Conrad and His Contemporaries*, pp. 120–121; Norman Douglas, *Looking Back* (London, 1931), p. 416.

In *Proust: The Later Years* (Boston, 1965), p. 227, George Painter states: "Humières's silent and self-effacing wife, with her infant daughter, seemed . . . 'to carry in secret the burden of a vast, disappointed illusion.' [Robert de] Montesquiou wrote, in one of his venomous little couplets:

'With Humières you've left your son?
Better make sure the light's still on.'

Overwhelmed by an impending scandal Humières demanded to be
posted to a Zouave regiment in the front line, and took the first
opportunity of charging to his death."

2. Quoted in Mark Holloway, *Norman Douglas: A Biography* (London,
   1976), pp. 39, 102; D. H. Lawrence, Introduction to Maurice Mag-
   nus' *Memoirs of the Foreign Legion* (London, 1924), p. 12; Quoted in
   Charles Doyle, *Richard Aldington: A Biography* (London, 1989), p.
   144.

3. Jean-Aubry, *Life and Letters*, 2.67–68; Quoted in Edward McDonald's
   A Bibliography of Norman Douglas (Philadelphia, 1927), p. 73; Norman
   Douglas to G. Jean-Aubry, November 30, 1924, quoted in Conrad,
   Letters to Warrington Dawson, p. 57; Norman Douglas, review of Rich-
   ard Curle's *Joseph Conrad, English Review*, 17 (July 1914), 569.

4. Letter from Mark Holloway to Jeffrey Meyers, June 12, 1989; Quoted
   in Holloway, *Norman Douglas*, p. 185; Jean-Aubry, *Life and Letters*,
   2.133–134.

5. Robin Douglas, "My Boyhood with Conrad," *Cornhill Magazine*, 66
   (January 1929), 23; Quoted in David Holmes' bookseller's catalogue,
   The Raymond Sutton Collection of Joseph Conrad (Philadelphia, 1985),
   part II, p. 9. For an account of the Cerio family, see *An Impossible
   Woman: The Memories of Dottoressa Moor*, ed. Graham Greene (Lon-
   don, 1957), pp. 118–120.

6. *Letters*, 3.227; *Notes on Life and Letters*, 6.83–84, 90–91, 86, 89.

7. *Letters*, 3.246–249; 259.

8. *Letters*, 3.287; 315; Henry James, *A Little Tour in France* (1884; Oxford,
   1984), p. 118; *Letters*, 3.316.

9. *Letters*, 3.343; 403; 444.

10. *Letters*, 3.420–421; 460, 462.

11. Jessie Conrad, *Conrad and His Circle*, p. 104; In *The Truth about My
    Father* (London, 1924), p. 74, Leon Tolstoy reports that though his
    father liked to instruct his children in mathematics, he was also an
    impatient and terrifying teacher: "He set us problems to solve, and
    woe betide those of us who did not manage them. On such occa-
    sions he grew angry, and wept and fell into fits of despair. His anger
    had the effect of making our minds a complete blank."

12. Quoted in Karl, *Joseph Conrad*, p. 47; Jean-Aubry, *Life and Letters*,
    2.135; Quoted in Ottoline Morrell, *Memoirs*, p. 236; John Conrad,
    Joseph Conrad, p. 165.

13. *Letters*, 3.470; Jean-Aubry, *Life and Letters*, 2.64; Quoted in Baines, *Joseph Conrad*, p. 347.

14. *The Secret Agent*, 13.262; 181; Jessie Conrad, *Conrad as I Knew Him*, pp. 53–54; Jessie Conrad, *Conrad and His Circle*, p. 122.

15. *The Secret Agent*, 13.6, 153; 159–160; Jessie Conrad, *Conrad and His Circle*, p. 90; Fyodor Dostoyevsky, *Crime and Punishment*, trans. Jessie Coulson (New York, 1964), p. 56.

16. *The Secret Agent*, 13.33; 31; 303; George Orwell, *Collected Essays, Journalism and Letters*, ed. Sonia Orwell and Ian Angus (New York, 1968), 3.389.

17. *Letters to Curle*, p. 114; *Critical Heritage*, p. 21; Jean-Aubry, *Life and Letters*, 2.65.

18. Moser, *Ford Madox Ford*, p. 93; John Conrad, *Joseph Conrad*, p. 74; Ford Madox Ford, *It Was the Nightingale* (1933; New York, 1984), pp. 207–208; Quoted in Mizener, *The Saddest Story*, p. 156.

19. Jean-Aubry, *Life and Letters*, 2.65; Thomas Hardy, *Collected Letters*, ed. Richard Purdy and Michael Millgate (Oxford, 1987), 6.282. Their second meeting is mentioned in Florence Hardy, *The Later Years of Thomas Hardy* (London, 1930), p. 124, which was actually written by Hardy himself.

20. Retinger, *Conrad and His Contemporaries*, p. 89; Norman Douglas, *Alone* (London, 1926), pp. 138–140; Perceval Gibbon, "Conrad," *Bookman*, 42 (April 1912), 27. See also his equally enthusiastic "Joseph Conrad—An Appreciation," *Bookman*, 39 (January 1911), 177–179.

21. Jessie Conrad, *Conrad and His Circle*, pp. 144, 132; Jean-Aubry, *Life and Letters*, 2.112. See also Jessie's "A Personal Tribute to the Late Perceval Gibbon and Edward Thomas," *Bookman*, 78 (September 1930), 323–324.

22. Borys Conrad, *My Father*, p. 61. Many of Conrad's letters to Gibbon, and all of Gibbon's papers, were destroyed during the Nazi occupation of Guernsey in World War Two. For further information on Gibbon, whose importance to Conrad has not been recognized (Karl, p. 677, says "they were not even close friends"), see his entry in *Who's Who* (1926); his obituary in *The Times*, June 1, 1926, p. 19; Lucas, *The Colvins and Their Friends* (1928); David Garnett, *The Golden Echo* (1953); *Cassell's Encyclopedia of World Literature*, ed. John Buchan-Brown (New York, 1973), p. 538; Holloway, *Norman Douglas* (1976); *Dictionary of South African Biography*, ed. D. W. Krüger and C. J. Beyers (Capetown, 1977), 3.324–325; and John Conrad, *Joseph Conrad* (1981).

23. Jean-Aubry, *Life and Letters*, 2.66; *A Set of Six*, 18.280.

24. Mikhail Lermontov, *A Hero of Our Time*, trans. Vladimir Nabokov (New York, 1958), p. 180; *A Set of Six*, 18.266; Borys Conrad, *My Father*, p. 57.

25. Quoted in Douglas Goldring, *South Lodge* (London, 1943), p. 24; Quoted in Karl, *Joseph Conrad*, pp. 654, 658–659; Jessie Conrad, *Conrad and His Circle*, p. 131.

26. David Garnett, *The Golden Echo*, p. 129; Wells, *Experiment in Autobiography*, p. 526; Quoted in Doyle, *Richard Aldington*, p. 34; Richard Aldington, *Death of a Hero* (Garden City, New York, 1929), p. 132.

27. David Garnett, *The Golden Echo*, p. 183; Lawrence, *Letters*, 1.170. In 1915 Violet dedicated *The House of Many Mirrors* to Conrad.

28. Quoted in Jean-Aubry, *Life and Letters*, 2.98; Quoted in Karl, *Joseph Conrad*, pp. 665–667.

29. Jean-Aubry, *Life and Letters*, 2.101; Quoted in Baines, *Joseph Conrad*, pp. 350–351; Edward Nehls, *D. H. Lawrence: A Composite Biography* (Madison, 1958), 2.412–413.

30. Moser, *Ford Madox Ford*, p. 98; Quoted in Najder, *Joseph Conrad*, p. 488.

Chapter Fourteen: Breakdown and Success

1. *Nostromo*, 9.x; Quoted in Najder, *Joseph Conrad*, p. 355; Quoted in Baines, *Joseph Conrad*, pp. 359–360.

2. Jean Aubry, *Life and Letters*, 2.64–65; James Joll, *The Anarchists* (1964; New York, 1966), p. 96. See also Edward Carr, "The *Affaire Nechaev*; or the First Terrorist," *The Romantic Exiles* (1933; Boston, 1961), pp. 290–310; "Nechaev, Sergei Gannadievich (1847–1882)," *Great Soviet Encyclopedia*, ed. A. M. Prokhorov, 3rd ed. (New York, 1978), 17.406; and Philip Pomper, *Sergei Nechaev* (New Brunswick, New Jersey, 1979). "One of us" appears in *Under Western Eyes*, 22.208 and 271.

3. *Letters*, 3.89; *Under Western Eyes*, 22.141, 288; 134–135. A comparison of the opening paragraphs of *Under Western Eyes* and Thomas Mann's *Doctor Faustus* (1947) reveals that the self-effacing, pedantic tone of Serenus Zeitblom, the deliberately imperceptive narrator of Mann's novel, is taken directly from the professor of languages.

4. *Letters to Garnett*, p. 234; *Polish Background*, p. 170 and note. For Conrad's other denials, see *Letters to Garnett*, p. 248, Jean-Aubry, *Life and Letters*, 2.336 and Retinger, *Conrad and His Contemporaries*, p. 95. For similar reasons, Conrad had always told Borys that he could

speak only a few words of German, but when they crossed the frontier from Austria to Italy in 1914, he spoke German with great fluency.

5. *Notes on Life and Letters*, 3.47–48; Jean-Aubry, *Life and Letters*, 2.77; Baines, *Joseph Conrad*, p. 372.

6. Vladimir Nabokov, *Lectures on Russian Literature*, ed. Fredson Bowers (New York, 1981), p. 104; *Letters to Garnett*, p. 240.

7. Quoted in Paul Kirschner, *Conrad: The Psychologist as Artist* (Edinburgh, 1968), p. 253 n3; Ralph Matlaw, "Dostoevskij and Conrad's Political Novels," *American Contributions to the Fifth International Congress of Slavists* (The Hague, 1963), 2.213. For a discussion of Dostoyevsky's influence, see Baines, *Joseph Conrad*, pp. 360–361, 369–371 (noting verbal echoes); Morton Dauwen Zabel, Introduction to *Under Western Eyes* (Garden City, New York, 1963), pp. li–lii; Karl, *Joseph Conrad*, pp. 678–679.

8. *Letters to Garnett*, pp. 232–233; Arthur Symons, *Selected Letters, 1880–1935*, ed. Karl Beckson and John Monro (Iowa City, 1989), p. 217.

9. Quoted in Baines, *Joseph Conrad*, p. 373; Jessie Conrad, *Conrad and His Circle*, pp. 142–144; Joseph Conrad, *Letters to William Blackwood and David S. Meldrum*, ed. William Blackburn (Durham, North Carolina, 1958), p. 192.

10. Jean-Aubry, *Life and Letters*, 2.109, 113.

11. Francis Meynell, quoted in *Agnes Tobin: Letters—Translations—Poems, With Some Account of Her Life* (San Francisco, 1958), p. xvii. This volume contains a sketch of Agnes by Augustus John on p. xiii and a photograph by Julia Cameron on p. 3; W. B. Yeats, *Letters*, ed. Allan Wade (New York, 1955), pp. 458–459; Yeats to Lady Gregory, July 3, 1906, quoted in David Greene and Edward Stephens, *J. M. Synge* (New York, 1959), p. 211; Quoted in Karl Beckson, *Arthur Symons: A Life* (New York, 1987), p. 238; Arthur Symons, *Confessions* (New York, 1930), p. 61. For other information on Agnes, see Edward O'Day, "Agnes Tobin," *Varied Types* (San Francisco, 1915), pp. 286–288; Celia Tobin Clark's obituary, "Agnes Tobin," *San Francisco Monitor*, February 25, 1939, p. 10; and Lorna Strachan, "Agnes Tobin, Translator of Petrarch," unpublished master's thesis, St. John's University, Brooklyn, New York, 1953.

12. André Gide, *Selected Letters of André Gide and Dorothy Bussy*, ed. Richard Tedeschi (Oxford, 1983), p. 77; André Gide, *Travels in the Congo*, trans. Dorothy Bussy (Berkeley, 1962), pp. 14, 292–293; André Gide, *Journals*, trans. Justin O'Brien (New York, 1949), 3.94.

13. Quoted in Frederick Karl, "Conrad and Gide: A Relationship and a Correspondence," *Comparative Literature*, 29 (1977), 168 n14; Robin Douglas, "My Boyhood with Conrad," p. 20; Otolia Retinger, quoted in Najder, *Joseph Conrad*, p. 383.

14. Jean-Aubry, *Life and Letters*, 2.87; See Busza, "Conrad's Polish Literary Background," pp. 224, 241.

15. Quoted in Karl, *Joseph Conrad*, p. 675; Basil Hall, *The Log of the Cutty Sark*, 3rd ed. (Glasgow, 1928), p. 357; Quoted in Sherry, *Conrad's Eastern World*, p. 254; *Letters to Garnett*, p. 243.

16. *Letters to Garnett*, p. 231; *'Twixt Land and Sea*, 19.194, 205–206.

17. Adam Curle, "Memoir of the Author," in Richard Curle, *The Last of Conrad* (Farnham, Surrey, [1975]), p. 1; *Letters to Curle*, pp. 63, 80.

18. Katherine Anne Porter, *The Leaning Tower and Other Stories* (New York, 1970), p. 159. After an adventurous life during the 1920s and 1930s, Retinger achieved significant political influence as personal aide to General Wladyslaw Sikorski, the prime minister of the Polish government in exile during World War Two. In 1944, at the age of fifty-six, he parachuted into Nazi-occupied Poland. In *Poland's Place in Europe: General Sikorski and the Origin of the Oder-Neisse Line, 1939–1943* (Princeton, 1983), pp. 196n–197n, Sarah Terry writes:

> As a friend and advisor to Sikorski since the early 1920s, they appeared to have seen eye to eye on many issues and in particular on the question of federation, of which Retinger was a fervent advocate. To the extent that he was involved in Polish politics, his ties were with the PPS [Polish Socialist Party] and the trade union movement, but his real interests were international. Well-connected in British Labour circles . . . he was indispensable to Sikorski in the early years of the war, when the prime minister was still unsure whom else he could trust.
>
> It was Retinger who arranged his most confidential meetings with British leaders—including his dramatic first meeting with Churchill in June 1940, as well as his several meetings with [Ernest] Bevin; again Retinger seems to have been the only other Pole who knew that Sikorski had given a copy of his secret report on his trip to Russia to the Foreign Office. Retinger appears to have played a less important role after the middle of 1942, possibly because of his support for the evacuation of the Polish Army from the Soviet Union. Much of the

suspicion and mystery surrounding his role was likely due to his radical pro-labor leanings and to his adventurous approach to life, from which at one time or another he found himself *persona non grata* in Germany, France, Britain, and the United States (where for a time the State Department viewed him as a "Mexican agent" and "a most undesirable and suspicious character").

For other information about Retinger's political career, see Stanislaw Kot, *Conversations with the Kremlin and Despatches from Russia* (Oxford, 1963), pp. 2, 13, 47, 161, and Joseph Retinger, *Memoirs of an Eminence Grise*, ed. John Pomian (Brighton, Sussex, 1972).

19. Wells, *Experiment in Autobiography*, p. 525; Morrell, *Memoirs*, p. 232; Osbert Sitwell, *Laughter in the Next Room* (Boston, 1951), p. 18; Morrell, *Memoirs*, p. 233.

20. Quoted in Ronald Clark, *The Life of Bertrand Russell* (New York, 1976), p. 212; Quoted in Russell, *Autobiography, 1914–1944*, p. 201.

21. Quoted in Najder, *Joseph Conrad*, p. 374; Henry James, "The New Novel" (originally called "The Younger Generation"), *Selected Literary Criticism*, ed. Morris Shapira (London, 1963), pp. 333, 338. On the dust jacket of *Chance*, an officer in naval uniform is putting a shawl around a woman who is seated in a deck chair, her hat tied down by a scarf and her legs wrapped in a blanket.

22. Thomas Moser, "Conrad, Ford and the Sources of *Chance*," *Conradiana*, 7 (1976), 215; Quoted in Karl, *Joseph Conrad*, p. 666; *Chance*, 2.233.

Chapter Fifteen: Return to Poland and *Victory*

1. *Notes on Life and Letters*, 3.110; Quoted in Curle, *Last Twelve Years*, p. 171; Jean-Aubry, *Life and Letters*, 2.161.

2. Retinger, *Conrad and His Contemporaries*, p.149; *Notes on Life and Letters*, 3.166; Jessie Conrad, *Conrad as I Knew Him*, p. 68; Vio Allen, "Memories of Joseph Conrad," p. 89.

3. Jean-Aubry, *Life and Letters*, 2.158; Quoted in Reid, *The Man from New York*, p. 361; *Notes on Life and Letters*, 3.178. See Penfield's obituary, *New York Times*, June 20, 1922, p. 19.

4. Jean-Aubry, *Life and Letters*, 2.163; 162, 168; Letter from Dame Veronica Wedgwood to Jeffrey Meyers, September 23, 1989. See Sir

Ralph Wedgwood's obituary, *The Times*, September 6, 1956, p. 15.

5. J. F. van Bemmelen and G. B. Hooyer mention two Sourabaya hotels—the Wynveld and the Simpang (proprietor: Mr. Brinkman)—in their *Guide to the Dutch East Indies* (London, 1897), p. 71, but discourage visitors from lingering in the town that "cannot boast of many places worth visiting. The climate is not exactly unhealthy, though very hot. They have not succeeded in digging artesian wells and the surface-water is bad. . . . Therefore we would advise travellers to stay no longer in Soerabaja than is necessary." Conrad modeled Zangiacomo's Ladies' Orchestra on the unconventional English orchestra of the Ranee of Sarawak, which was established in 1903 in order to secure suitable wives for her sons. See Jeffrey Meyers, "The Ranee of Sarawak and Conrad's *Victory*," *Conradiana*, 18 (1986), 41–44.

6. *Victory*, 15.199–200; *Lord Jim*, 21.387.

7. Quoted in Bernard Meyer, *Joseph Conrad: A Psychoanalytic Biography* (Princeton, 1967), p. 325. Conrad also told Hastings, with comparable ambiguity, that Jones *may* himself be frightened of women but is certainly frightened of women for Ricardo (unpublished, undated letter in Colgate University Library).

8. Morgan, "Conrad's Unknown Ship," p. 190, wrote of the *Falconhurst*, in which Conrad sailed in 1886: "He met the redoubtable Captain Jones, lieutenant in the Reserve, who had got rid of two second mates on each of his last two voyages." Conrad may have taken his villain's name from Captain Jones and attributed his "lieutenant of the Reserve" manner to Schomberg.

9. *Victory*, 15.197.

10. *Victory*, 15.308.

11. *Victory*, 15.210–211.

12. *Victory*, 15.212.

13. *Victory*, 15.199–200.

14. *Victory*, 15.400.

15. *Victory*, 15.401.

16. *Victory*, 15.160.

17. The death of Lena is an intensely visualized and somewhat sentimental scene, modeled on the Pietàs of the dead Christ, and on the historical paintings of the death of Admiral Nelson by A. W. Davis (1806) and Benjamin West (1808), both of which Conrad must have seen in the Nelson Room of the Greenwich Museum. See Jeffrey Meyers, "Lord Nelson and Conrad's *Victory*," *Papers on Language and Literature*, 19, (1983), 419–426.

Chapter Sixteen: Jane Anderson

1. Jean-Aubry, *Life and Letters* and *The Sea Dreamer*, and Jerry Allen's *The Thunder and the Sunshine*, do not even mention Jane; Baines gives her one paragraph, Meyer one sentence. Karl devotes two pages (out of 913) to Jane, Najder four pages (out of 495).

2. Quoted in Halverson and Watt, "Notes on Jane Anderson, 1955–1989," *Conradiana*, 23 (Spring 1991).

   Jane Anderson has striking similarities to Esther Andrews, who became emotionally involved with D. H. Lawrence in 1916. Both were young, extremely attractive and unconventional American journalists. Both had rather theatrical personalities and hoped to become professional actresses. Both were loosely tied to another man. Both were literary headhunters, knew many famous writers and had numerous lovers. Both adored the famous novelists, lived in their houses for an extended period of time and aroused their interest in America. Both novelists became very fond of the tall, slim, glamorous, lively, witty and amusing women. Both women provoked the jealousy of the stout, matronly wives, who eventually prevailed against their young rivals. Lawrence and Conrad both portrayed Esther and Jane in their fiction. See Jeffrey Meyers, *D. H. Lawrence: A Biography* (New York, 1990), pp. 199–204, 414–415, which includes a photograph of Esther Andrews.

3. There is considerable uncertainty about Jane's birth date and about many other details of her life. Numerous facts, recycled and unsubstantiated by many writers, are either inconsistent or flatly contradictory. Mary Lane of Piedmont College and Jane Anderson Jenkins (the daughter of Kitty Crawford) believe she was born in 1888. Other writers give dates between 1890 and 1893.

   Jane's passport application of October 15, 1924, at the Department of State says she was born on January 6, 1893. But this information was supplied (without documentation) by Jane herself, who had reason to make herself seem younger than she actually was. Since no birth records exist in Atlanta for the period before 1919, this date cannot be verified. However, since Jane entered Piedmont College in 1903 and published her first stories in *Harper's Weekly* in 1910, it is unlikely that she was born in 1893. The information about Jane in the unnumbered 446-page FBI file is extremely repetitious and filled with uncorroborated statements offered by many anonymous informants.

4. Kitty Barry Crawford, "About Jane Anderson," p. 5, unpublished typescript, courtesy of her Estate; Retinger, *Memoirs of an Eminence*

Grise, p. 38; Quoted in Jess Hayes, *Sheriff Thompson's Day: Turbulence in the Arizona Territory* (Tucson, 1968), p. 26.

5. Isabel Chrisler, *Demorest in the Piedmont* (Privately printed, 1968), p. 25; Letter from Mary Lane, Archivist of Piedmont College, to Jeffrey Meyers, March 13, 1990; Letter from the Arizona Historical Society to Jeffrey Meyers, July 28, 1989.

6. Kitty Crawford papers. Jane also told Kitty: "I have recently accepted an order from the *Atlantic Monthly* to do a learned article on ants." This may have been published as Beebe's "With Army Ants Somewhere in the Jungle," *Atlantic Monthly,* 19 (April 1917), 514–522.

7. Jane Anderson and Gordon Bruce, *Flying, Submarining and Mine Sweeping* (London, 1916), p. 13; Jane Anderson, "Submarine's Fine Achievement. Voyage Home After Being Mined. 300 Miles of Peril," *The Times,* May 18, 1916, p. 3; Jane Anderson, "A Woman's Flight Over London. 'Looping the Loop.' Mile-and-a-Half Above Hyde Park," *The Times,* June 2, 1916, p. 6.

8. Quoted in Halverson and Watt, "Notes on Jane Anderson"; Quoted in John Edwards, "Atlanta's Prodigal Daughter: The Turbulent Life of Jane Anderson as Expatriate and Nazi Propagandist," *Atlanta Historical Journal,* 28 (1984), 26.

   Hemingway, who married Mary Welsh in 1945, once contemptuously accused her of "fucking generals in order to get a story for *Time* magazine" (quoted in Jeffrey Meyers, *Hemingway: A Biography* [New York, 1985], pp. 392, 394).

9. *The Inheritors,* 5.35, 19; *Letters to Cunninghame Graham,* p. 194.

10. See "Hyde Park Regulations Charge Against Sir Leo Money," *The Times,* April 25, 1928, p. 13; "Hyde Park Case. Sir Leo Money Acquitted. Magistrate and Police Methods," *The Times,* May 3, 1928, p. 13; Leading articles on May 19, 1928, p. 15 and May 22, 1928, p. 17; and "Sir Leo Money Fined. Alleged Incidents in Train. Shop-Girl in Assault Charge," *The Times,* September 12, 1933, p. 6.

11. John Conrad, *Joseph Conrad,* pp. 108–109; Robin Douglas, "My Boyhood with Conrad," p. 25.

12. Quoted in Najder, *Joseph Conrad,* pp. 411–412; Halverson and Watt, "Notes on Jane Anderson"; Kitty Crawford papers. For the photographs, see Borys Conrad, *My Father,* opposite p. 96.

13. Joan Givner, *Katherine Anne Porter: A Life* (New York, 1982), p. 121; Jessie Conrad, *Conrad and His Circle,* pp. 204–205.

14. *Letters to Curle,* p. 44; Quoted in Karl, *Joseph Conrad,* p. 790; Conrad, *Letters to His Wife,* pp. 21–22, 19.

15. Jessie Conrad, *Conrad as I Knew Him*, p. 3; *Within the Tides*, 10.210; Jessie Conrad, *Conrad and His Circle*, pp. 206–208.

16. *'Twixt Land and Sea*, 19.36; Quoted in Najder, *Joseph Conrad*, p. 421.

17. Halverson and Watt, "Notes on Jane Anderson"; Curle, *Last Twelve Years*, p. 55; Unpublished letters of July 5, 1915 and April 20, 1917; these and all others courtesy of Frederick Karl and Laurence Davies.

18. Ford Madox Ford, *Some Do Not* (1924; New York, 1964), p. 19; Richard Curle, quoted in Vincent Brome and Douglas Cleverdon, "Recollections of Joseph Conrad," unpublished transcript of BBC Third Programme, November 29, 1957, courtesy of Ian Watt; Richard Curle, quoted in Halverson and Watt, "Notes on Jane Anderson"; Graham Greene, "The Domestic Background," *Collected Essays* (New York, 1969), p. 186.

19. Interview with George Seldes, August 21, 1989; George Seldes, *Witness to a Century* (New York, 1987), p. 56.

20. Jessie Conrad, *Conrad and His Circle*, p. 205; Borys Conrad, *My Father*, p. 118; Quoted in Najder, *Joseph Conrad*, p. 421.

21. Borys Conrad, *My Father*, pp. 120–122; Givner, *Katherine Anne Porter*, p. 151; Retinger, *Conrad and His Contemporaries*, p. 98.

22. *The Arrow of Gold*, 1.164; Jessie Conrad, *Conrad and His Circle*, p. 196; *The Arrow of Gold*, 1.91; 210; 158; 57. The telegrams are in the New York Public Library. For the later life of Jane Anderson, see Appendix I.

Chapter Seventeen: The War Years

1. Quoted in Karl, *Joseph Conrad*, p. 781n; Ford, *Letters*, p. 79.

2. *Suspense*, 25.20; Casement, "The Congo Diary," in Singleton-Gates and Girodias, *The Black Diaries of Roger Casement*, p. 189; Jessie Conrad, *Conrad and His Circle*, pp. 103–104.

3. Quoted in Reid, *The Man from New York*, pp. 234–235; Retinger, *Conrad and His Contemporaries*, p. 49. This appeal was signed by Bennett, Chesterton, Conan Doyle, Galsworthy, Masefield and many others.

4. Quoted in Reid, *The Man from New York*, p. 360; Unpublished letter to John Quinn, July 15, 1916; Quoted in *Familial Eyes*, p. 248.

5. Quoted in René MacColl, *Roger Casement: A New Judgement* (London, 1956), p. 268; *Typhoon*, 20.222. For a thorough discussion of Casement, see Jeffrey Meyers, "Roger Casement," *A Fever at the Core: The Idealist in Politics* (London, 1976), pp. 59–88.

6. Quoted in Karl, *Joseph Conrad*, p. 780; Admiral Sir Douglas Brown-rigg, *Indiscretions of the Naval Censor* (London, 1920), p. 64; *Notes on Life and Letters*, 3.211, 209.

   Borys Conrad, *My Father*, pp. 111–112, ignoring the evidence of Conrad's essay, emphasized his eccentricity and improved the story by stating that Conrad stubbornly refused "to be parted from his bowler hat when he went for a flight over the North Sea . . . but finally agreed to anchor the bowler by passing his silk scarf over it and then tying it under his chin."

   For a comparative description of Hemingway's first flight, a few years later in September 1922, see "A Paris-to-Strasbourg Flight," *Dateline: Toronto*, ed. William White (New York, 1985), pp. 205–207.

7. Jean-Aubry, *Life and Letters*, 2.177; 179; Quoted in Jessie Conrad, *Conrad and His Circle*, p. 203; *Tales of Hearsay*, 26.80; John Conrad, *Joseph Conrad*, p. 139.

8. Quoted in Holloway, *Norman Douglas*, pp. 229, 231; Mark Holloway, Notes on his interview with Borys Conrad, January 1, 1969; Quoted in Najder, *Joseph Conrad*, p. 421.

9. Quoted in Baines, *Joseph Conrad*, p. 421; Quoted in Wilfred Parting-ton, *Forging Ahead: The True Story and Upward Progress of Thomas J. Wise* (New York, 1939), p. 211.

10. Quoted in Edel, *The Master*, p. 407; Quoted in Hart-Davis, *Hugh Walpole*, pp. 168; 286.

    The fourteen works dedicated to Conrad trace the history of his friendships and include: Galsworthy's *Jocelyn* (1898), Constance Gar-nett's translation of Turgenev's *A Desperate Character* (1899), Cun-ninghame Graham's *Progress* (1905), Ford's *The Fifth Queen* (1906), Gibbon's *Margaret Harding* (1911), Reynolds' *How 'Twas* (1912), Ed-ward Thomas' *Walter Pater* (1913), Violet Hunt's *The House of Many Mirrors* (1915), Symons' *Figures of Several Centuries* (1916), John Pow-ell's musical composition *Negro Rhapsody* (1918), Galsworthy's *In Chancery* (1920), Curle's *Wanderings* (1920), Walpole's *The Cathedral* (1922) and Dawson's *Adventure in the Night* (1924).

11. Valery Larbaud and G. Jean-Aubry, *Correspondance, 1920–1935*, ed. Frida Weissman (Paris, 1971), p. 12. Conrad dedicated all the books published during his lifetime (except *A Personal Record* and *Notes on Life and Letters*) to family and friends, but there were no dedications to the memory of his parents, to his son John, to Colvin, Crane, Doubleday, Ford, Gide, James, Marwood, Pinker, Poradowska, Quinn, Retinger, Rothenstein or Walpole. Crane and Marwood died early; Conrad was in awe of James; had some sort of *contretemps* with

Poradowska; quarreled with Ford and Retinger; and had commercial relations with Pinker, Doubleday and Quinn.

12. John Conrad, *Joseph Conrad*, p. 205; Halverson and Watt, "Notes on Jane Anderson"; Quoted in Najder, *Joseph Conrad*, p. 423.

13. Conrad, *Lettres françaises*, p. 151; Borys Conrad, *My Father*, p. 108; Quoted in Vio Allen, "Memories of Joseph Conrad," p. 78; Frederick Watson, *The Life of Sir Robert Jones* (Baltimore, 1934), pp. 283–284.

14. *Within the Tides*, 10.211; 85; Jean-Aubry, *Life and Letters*, 2.164

15. Quoted in Sherry, *Conrad's Eastern World*, p. 317; *The Shadow-Line*, 17.132. Ford adopted Conrad's thematic phrase for the title of the third volume in his *Parade's End* tetralogy: *A Man Could Stand Up* (1926).

16. Jean-Aubry, *Life and Letters*, 2.271; Quoted in Najder, *Joseph Conrad*, p. 426.

17. Conrad, "Mr. Conrad Is Not a Jew," *New Republic*, p. 109. The rumor that Conrad was a Jew may have started with Ford's satiric portrayal of him in *The Simple Life Limited* (London, 1911), p. 69, as Simon Bransdon, who is "possibly Polish, possibly Lithuanian, possibly Little Russian Jew."

    Frank Harris, not mentioned in the published letter, is identified in Thomas Wise, *A Bibliography of the Writings of Joseph Conrad (1895–1921)*, Second Edition, Revised and Enlarged (London, 1921; 1964), pp. 117–118. Harris was the editor of the *Saturday Review* when Wells published his favorable reviews of *Almayer's Folly* and *An Outcast of the Islands* in 1895–96. Conrad first met him in October 1910.

18. See Baines, *Joseph Conrad*, p. 374; Meyer, *Joseph Conrad*, p. 352; Adam Gillon, "Joseph Conrad: Polish Cosmopolitan," *Joseph Conrad: Theory and World Fiction*, p. 55.

19. *Nostromo*, 9.449; See Davies, *God's Playground*, p. 257, and Adam Mickiewicz, *Pan Tadeusz*, trans. George Rapall Noyes (London, 1917), pp. 95, 326; *Tales of Hearsay*, 26.39.

20. *Critical Heritage*, p. 232; Jean-Aubry, *Life and Letters*, 2.136; See Robert Speaight, *The Life of Hilaire Belloc* (London, 1957), p. 253. Conrad met Belloc in 1908 at Garnett's Tuesday luncheons at the Mont-Blanc restaurant.

21. *Letters to Cunninghame Graham*, p. 179; "Joseph Conrad: Some Polish Documents," in *Joseph Conrad: Centennial Essays*, p. 124; Quoted in Najder, *Joseph Conrad*, p. 430; Ford, *Joseph Conrad*, p. 59.

22. Lloyd George, quoted in *Hansard*, November 11, 1918; Jean-Aubry, *Life and Letters*, 2.211. D. H. Lawrence shared Conrad's fears and at

an Armistice Day party told Edward Garnett's son, David: "I suppose you think the war is over and that we shall go back to the kind
of world you lived in before it. But the war isn't over. The hate and
evil [are] greater now than ever. Very soon war will break out again
and overwhelm you." (Quoted in David Garnett, *Flowers of the Forest*, p. 190.)

23. Jean-Aubry, *Life and Letters*, 2.237.

Chapter Eighteen: Fame and America

1. Jean-Aubry, *Life and Letters*, 2.110.

2. *The Mirror of the Sea*, 4.123; *A Personal Record*, 6.5; Karl, *Joseph Conrad*,
   p. 259; Borys Conrad, *My Father*, pp. 32, 49.

3. Robin Douglas, "My Boyhood with Conrad," pp. 24–25; *Critical
   Heritage*, p. 193; Quoted in Jean-Aubry, *The Sea Dreamer*, p. 259.

4. Jean-Aubry, *Life and Letters*, 2.209. John Gordan, *Joseph Conrad: The
   Making of a Novelist* (Cambridge, Mass., 1941), p. 211, states that
   Conrad "had progressed at least as far as twenty-four manuscript
   pages of part four when he stopped work in February, 1899." Conrad, describing a manuscript page of *Almayer's Folly* in *A Personal
   Record* (6.69), notes that "it contained about two hundred words and
   this proportion of words to a page has remained with me through
   the fifteen years of my writing life." Karl, contradicting Conrad,
   says his "holograph was rarely more than 100–150 words per page"
   (p. 638). A hundred and fifty words per page would be 3,600 words
   into part IV and 200 words per page would be 4,800. Though there
   is no exact correspondence between the original unrevised manuscript and the printed version of *The Rescue*, the manuscript seems to
   conclude at the end of part IV, chapter 4.

   The only comparably protracted fictional composition was Thomas Mann's *Felix Krull*, which he began in 1911 and completed,
   maintaining a seamless style and tone, in 1954.

5. Thomas Moser, *Joseph Conrad: Achievement and Decline* (Cambridge,
   Mass., 1957), p. 68; *Letters*, 1.381; 2.191; F. N. Doubleday, "Joseph
   Conrad as a Friend," *World Today*, 52 (July 1928), 145; *The Rescue*,
   12.x; 453.

6. *Suspense*, 25.123. Irwin, *Nineteenth-Century Borneo: A Study in Diplomatic Rivalry*, pp. 1–2, confirms the riverine reality of the novel:
   "Some of the larger rivers are navigable for hundreds of miles, but
   with one or two exceptions their mouths are blocked by sand bars,

which permit entrance only at high tide, and then only for vessels of shallow draught."

7. *The Rescue*, 12.319; Quoted in G. Jean-Aubry, "Conrad and Music," *The Chesterian* (London), 6 (November 1924), 41; *The Rescue*, 12.300–301; 412.

8. Katherine Mansfield, *Novels and Novelists* (1930; Boston, 1959), p. 217; *The Rescue*, 12.431; 116; *Letters to Blackwood*, p. 44.

9. Quoted in Carolyn Heilbrun, *The Garnett Family* (London, 1961), p. 118; *Letters to Garnett*, p. 271.

10. *Letters to Curle*, p. 88; Jean-Aubry, *Life and Letters*, 2.250; Najder, *Joseph Conrad*, p. 456; Neill Joy, "Catalogue of a Memorial Exhibition of the MSS, Letters, Editions and Memorabilia of Joseph Conrad," *Philobiblion* (Colgate University), 10 (1974), 17.

11. "The Strong Man," pp. 13, 27, courtesy of Colgate University Library.

Though Famous Players–Lasky turned down Conrad's scenario, it did make the first two (of eighteen) films that were inspired by his works, and that had a profound influence on his readers and his reputation: *Victory* (1919), *Lord Jim* (1925), *The Silver Treasure* (based on *Nostromo*, 1926), *The Road to Romance* (based on *Romance*, 1927), *The Rescue* (1929), *Dangerous Paradise* (based on *Victory*, 1930), *Sabotage* (based on *The Secret Agent*, directed by Alfred Hitchcock, with Oscar Homolka and Sylvia Sidney as the Verlocs, 1936), *Razumov* (based on *Under Western Eyes*, directed by Marc Allégret, with Jean-Louis Barrault as Haldin, 1936), *Victory* (with Cedric Hardwicke as Jones, Fredric March as Heyst and Betty Field as Lena, 1940), *An Outcast of the Islands* (the best Conrad film, directed by Carol Reed, with Trevor Howard, Robert Morley, Ralph Richardson and Wendy Hiller, 1951), *Face to Face* (the first episode of which was based on "The Secret Sharer," with James Mason, 1952), *Laughing Anne* (1954), *Lord Jim* (with Peter O'Toole, 1964), *The Rover* (1967), *The Shadow-Line* (directed by Andrzej Wajda, 1976), *The Duellists* (based on "The Duel," 1977), *Apocalypse Now* (based on *Heart of Darkness*, 1979) and *Devil's Paradise* (based on *Victory*, 1986). Robert Bolt has written a screenplay for *Nostromo*, which is now being filmed by David Lean.

12. Jean-Aubry, *Life and Letters*, 2.233–234, 238; R. L. Mégroz, *Joseph Conrad's Mind and Method* (1931; New York, 1964), p. 25.

13. Jessie Conrad, *Conrad and His Circle*, p. 85; Jean-Aubry, *Life and Letters*, 2.287; Bennett, *Letters*, 1.317.

14. Quoted in Hart-Davis, *Hugh Walpole*, p. 195; Quoted in Keating,

Conrad Memorial Library, p. 165: T. E. Lawrence, *Letters,* pp. 843; 301–302; Quoted in Sir Sydney Cockerell, *Friends of a Lifetime,* ed. Viola Meynell (London, 1940), pp. 360–361.

15. Conrad, *Lettres françaises,* pp. 163–164; H. R. Lenormand, "Note on a Sojourn of Conrad in Corsica" (1924), reprinted in *The Art of Joseph Conrad,* ed. R. W. Stallman, pp. 5–6.

16. *The Rover,* 24.17; Ernest Hemingway, *The Sun Also Rises* (1926; New York, 1954), p. 108; *The Rover,* 24.273; 276–277. See Jeffrey Meyers, "Conrad's Influence on Modern Writers," *Twentieth Century Literature,* 36 (Summer 1990), 186–206.

17. Jean-Aubry, *Life and Letters,* 2.265. Though Pinker eventually earned a considerable income from Conrad and left an estate of £40,000, his sons ran the business into the ground. Eric, a sporty type with gambling proclivities, founded the American branch of the firm in the 1930s: "Things went along well with him until E. Phillips Oppenheim could not collect from Eric $100,000 owed in royalties. Eric was sentenced to a term in Sing Sing" for embezzlement. His brother Ralph followed Eric into the firm and into prison. He kept his clients' earnings, was prosecuted for general malpractice and misappropriation of money, and in 1939, when the business went into liquidation, was sentenced to a term in Wormwood Scrubs. See Sybille Bedford, *Aldous Huxley: A Biography* (New York, 1974), p. 396.

18. *Suspense,* 25.189; James Thurber, "Recollections of Henry James," *New Yorker,* 9 (June 17, 1933), 13.

19. Quoted in Reid, *The Man from New York,* p. 244.

20. Retinger, *Conrad and His Contemporaries,* p. 97; Quoted in Hart-Davis, *Hugh Walpole,* p. 203. Eloise Hay, *The Political Novels of Joseph Conrad* (Chicago, 1963), p. 167, speaks of "Conrad's insuppressible antipathy to American politics, institutions, and character"; and Mizener, *The Saddest Story,* p. 157, starkly asserts that Conrad "disliked Americans."

21. *Last Essays,* pp. 254–255, 257; Jean-Aubry, *Life and Letters,* 2.307; Quoted in Richard Veler, "Walter Tittle and Joseph Conrad," *Conradiana,* 12 (1980), 96.

22. Doubleday, "Joseph Conrad as a Friend," p. 146; *Letters to Curle,* p. 143; Christopher Morley, *Conrad and the Reporters* (Garden City, New York, 1923), pp. 47–48; Quoted in Arnold Schwab, "Conrad's American Speeches and His Reading from *Victory,*" *Modern Philology,* 62 (1965), 345–346.

23. Doubleday, "Joseph Conrad as a Friend," pp. 146–147; Eleanor

Palffy, "Drunk on Conrad," *Fortnightly Review*, 132 (October 1929), 534, 536–538; *Polish Background*, pp. 292–293.

24. Quoted in Reid, *The Man from New York*, p. 568; Ford, *It Was the Nightingale*, pp. 309–310.

25. Seymour Leslie, *The Jerome Connection* (London, 1964), p. 147; *Letters to Garnett*, p. 295; Quoted in Cockerell, *Friends of a Lifetime*, p. 325. A list of the major Conrad manuscripts and prices appears in Matthew Bruccoli, *The Fortunes of Mitchell Kennerley, Bookman* (New York, 1986), pp. 153–154.

    On April 28, 1927, at the American Art Association Galleries in New York, Richard Curle sold his collection of books inscribed by Conrad for nearly £8,000.

26. Quoted in "Joseph Conrad's Son Gets Year in Prison for Swindling a Friend Out of £1,100," *New York Times*, July 23, 1927, p. 2 (See also *The Times* [London], July 2, 1927, p. 9, and July 23, 1927, p. 9); Unpublished letter to Richard Curle, July 25, 1922; Jessie Conrad, *Conrad and His Circle*, pp. 255–256.

27. Quoted in Reid, *The Man from New York*, p. 127; Quoted in Karl, *Joseph Conrad*, p. 881; Curle, *Last Twelve Years*, p. 127.

28. Conrad, *Lettres françaises*, p. 193; See Jeffrey Meyers, "The Nobel Prize and Literary Politics," *Dictionary of Literary Biography Yearbook: 1988*, ed. J. M. Brook (Detroit, 1989), pp. 188–192. Both Kipling and Galsworthy were offered the Order of Merit; Kipling refused and Galsworthy accepted it.

29. John Conrad, *Joseph Conrad*, p. 89; Epstein, *An Autobiography*, pp. 74–75, 77. A photograph of Epstein's bust appears between pp. 30 and 31. For other works of art, see Jeffrey Meyers, "Joseph Conrad: An Iconography," *Bulletin of Bibliography*, 47 (March 1990), 33–34.

30. *Letters to Curle*, p. 172; Quoted in Najder, *Joseph Conrad*, p. 490; Borys Conrad, *My Father*, p. 162; Cunninghame Graham, "Inveni Portum: Joseph Conrad," *Redeemed* (London, 1927), p. 171; Edmund Spenser, *The Faerie Queene*, 1.9.40.

    Ford slightly misquoted these lines in the conclusion of *No Enemy* (1929; New York, 1984), p. 292: " 'Rest,' " he said with his heavy tired voice, " 'after toil, port after stormy seas. . . .' " He paused and added after a moment: " 'Do greatly please!' "

    The Times of November 17, 1924, p. 17, reported that Conrad, after all the agonizing worries about money, had left a valuable estate of £20,000. His executors were Richard Curle and Sir Ralph Wedgwood.

    After Conrad's death Jessie relished the role of literary widow. On

August 25, 1927, Ellen Glasgow reported: "Tea with Mrs. Conrad was rather dismal. She has become enormously stout, and so very complacent, poor soul, clinging to the shadow of fame which he shed over her" (*Letters*, ed. Blair Rouse, New York, 1948, p. 88). Jessie named her last home, a little place about a mile from Canterbury, after Conrad's ship, the *Torrens*. She had yet another operation on her knee in February 1929 and bravely told Warrington Dawson: "I have faced the knife just a dozen times now." Seven months later she fantasized: "My idea would be to have some rooms in New York and be at home there to all Conrad's friends and admirers for a month. . . . I might be able to give talks if not actually lecture" (Quoted in *Letters to Warrington Dawson*, p. 113).

In a letter to the *Times Literary Supplement* of December 4, 1924, p. 826, Jessie took on her old adversary, challenged the accuracy of Ford's hastily written and "detestable book," *Joseph Conrad: A Personal Remembrance*, and damaged his reputation—though Ford's version of his relations with Conrad, not Jessie's, has finally prevailed. In 1926 she published the seriously flawed but still valuable *Joseph Conrad as I Knew Him* and in 1935 expanded her memoir in *Joseph Conrad and His Circle*. Reviewing the later book, Graham Greene (a great admirer of Ford) said that Jessie's mind was "peculiarly retentive of injuries" and that her book made "rather repellent reading" ("The Domestic Background," p. 185). And Edward Garnett, who (like Curle) had always detested Jessie, discharged a lifetime of venom in his savage letter to her about that work: "I think it is the most detestable book ever written by a wife about her husband. You have exposed Conrad & yourself to ridicule by your petty vindictiveness & treasuring up of all the incidents of his bad temper & outbursts which you suffered in his lifetime; & the complacency & conceit with which you show yourself always superior to him are both amusing & painful" (quoted in Jefferson, *Edward Garnett*, p. 266).

On December 6, 1936, Jessie died in Guy's Hospital in London at the age of sixty-three.

Appendix I: The Later Life
of Jane Anderson

1. Interview with George Seldes; Letter from Joan Kennedy Taylor to Jeffrey Meyers, October 26, 1989; Beebe's letter in the Kitty Crawford papers.

2. Givner, *Katherine Anne Porter*, p. 121; Katherine Anne Porter, *Ship of Fools* (Boston, 1962), p. 107.

3. John Pomian, in Retinger, *Memoirs of an Eminence Grise*, p. 38; Givner, *Katherine Anne Porter*, p. 152.

4. William Ewer, quoted in Halverson and Watt, "Notes on Jane Anderson."

5. Quoted in Edwards, "Atlanta's Prodigal Daughter," p. 31. The photograph of Jane and her husband is in the Kitty Crawford papers.

   The woman who had twice been deserted by her father was involved with at least eleven men: Deems Taylor, Lord Northcliffe, Sir Leo Money, Joseph Conrad, Joseph Retinger, Gilbert Seldes, William McCombs, Stephen Austin, Dai Ballusek, the Canadian Boyer and Cienfuegos.

6. Rebecca West, quoted in Halverson and Watt, "Notes on Jane Anderson"; Letter from Dr. Ian Gibson (the biographer of García Lorca) to Jeffrey Meyers, February 6, 1990.

7. Quoted in Eoin O'Duffy, *Crusade in Spain* (Dublin, 1938), p. 73; H. Edward Knoblaugh, *Correspondent in Spain* (New York, 1937), p. 194; William Schofield, *Treason Trail* (New York, 1964), p. 219.

8. Quoted in "Lady Haw-Haw," *Time*, 39 (January 19, 1942), p. 30 (the title alludes to the British radio traitor William Joyce, known as Lord Haw-Haw, who broadcast Nazi propaganda and was executed after the war); Quoted in Edwards, "Atlanta's Prodigal Daughter," p. 33.

   The FBI file contains several other anonymous condemnations of Jane's unscrupulous greed: "the greatest liar he ever heard," "mercenary and ambitious for power," "an adventuress who threw herself into any scheme for which she thought she might realize some money." The FBI agent concluded that she "is emotional to an extreme . . . and capable of changing her mind overnight."

9. *The Goebbels Diaries, 1939–1941*, trans. and ed. Fred Taylor (New York, 1983), pp. 26, 357.

10. Charles Rolo, *Radio Goes to War* (New York, 1942), p. 105; Quoted in Derek Sington and Arthur Weidenfeld, *The Goebbels Experiment: A Study of the Nazi Propaganda Machine* (New Haven, 1943), pp. 187–

188; Quoted in Harold Ettlinger, *The Axis on the Air* (New York, 1943), p. 53; Quoted in Edwards, "Atlanta's Prodigal Daughter," p. 36.

11. Quoted in *Time*, January 19, 1942, p. 30; Quoted in "Germany: Sweets and Cookies," *Time*, 39 (April 6, 1942), p. 32.

12. Katherine Anne Porter, "A Letter to the Editor of the *Saturday Review of Literature* [about Ezra Pound]," *Collected Essays* (New York, 1973), pp. 212–213; Letter from Joan Kennedy Taylor to Jeffrey Meyers.

Bibliography of Conrad

Aubry, G. Jean. *Joseph Conrad: Life and Letters.* 2 vols. Garden City, New York, 1927.

———. *The Sea Dreamer: A Definitive Biography of Joseph Conrad.* Trans. Helen Sebba. 1947; Garden City, New York, 1957.

Baines, Jocelyn. *Joseph Conrad: A Critical Biography.* London, 1959.

Conrad, Borys. *My Father: Joseph Conrad.* London, 1970.

Conrad, Jessie. *Joseph Conrad as I Knew Him.* Garden City, New York, 1926.

———. *Joseph Conrad and His Circle.* New York, 1935.

Conrad, John. *Joseph Conrad: Times Remembered.* Cambridge, England, 1981.

Curle, Richard. *The Last Twelve Years of Joseph Conrad.* London, 1928.

Ehrsam, Theodore. *A Bibliography of Joseph Conrad.* Metuchen, N. J., 1969.

Ford, Ford Madox. *Joseph Conrad: A Personal Remembrance.* London, 1924.

———. *Return to Yesterday.* 1932; New York, 1972.

Gordan, John. *Joseph Conrad: The Making of a Novelist.* Cambridge, Mass., 1941.

Guerard, Albert. *Conrad the Novelist.* Cambridge, Mass., 1966.

Karl, Frederick. *Joseph Conrad: The Three Lives.* London, 1979.

Keating, George. *A Conrad Memorial Library.* Garden City, New York, 1929.

Lohf, Kenneth, and Eugene Sheehy. *Joseph Conrad at Mid-Century.* Minneapolis, 1957.

Meyer, Bernard. *Joseph Conrad: A Psychoanalytic Biography.* Princeton, 1967.

Moser, Thomas. *The Life in the Fiction of Ford Madox Ford.* Princeton, 1980.

Najder, Zdzislaw. *Joseph Conrad: A Chronicle.* Trans. Halina Carroll-Najder. Cambridge, England, 1983.

——, ed. *Conrad's Polish Background: Letters to and From Polish Friends.* London, 1964.

——, ed. *Conrad Under Familial Eyes.* Trans. Halina Carroll-Najder. Cambridge, England, 1983.

Retinger, J. H. *Conrad and His Contemporaries.* New York, 1943.

Sherry, Norman. *Conrad's Eastern World.* Cambridge, England, 1966.

——. *Conrad's Western World.* Cambridge, England, 1971.

——, ed. *Conrad: The Critical Heritage.* London, 1973.

Watt, Ian. *Conrad in the Nineteenth Century.* Berkeley, 1979.

Wise, Thomas. *A Bibliography of the Writings of Joseph Conrad (1895–1921).* Second Edition, Revised and Enlarged, London, 1921.

Bibliography
of Jane Anderson

I. Works by Jane Anderson

"Editorial: Enterprise," *Kidd-Key Journal* (Sherman, Texas), December 1, 1908, p. [1].

"With Long Distance [Calls] From 7 to 9 p.m.," *Kidd-Key Journal*, December 1, 1908, pp. 13–14.

"Story," *Kidd-Key Journal*, December 1, 1908, pp. 17–20.

"The Keeper of the Well," *Harper's Weekly*, 54 (April 23, 1910), 17.

"The Burying of Lil," *Harper's Weekly*, 54 (August 13, 1910), 18–19.

"The Gift of the Hills," *Harper's Weekly*, 55 (October 21, 1911), 24–26.

"The Spur of Courage," *Harper's Weekly*, 56 (January 13, 1912), 16–18.

"El Valiente," *Harper's Weekly*, 56 (June 22, 1912), 16–17, 24.

"Red King," *Harper's Weekly*, 56 (July 13, 1912), 16–18.

"The Reckoning," *Collier's*, 49 (July 13, 1912), 16–17, 27.

"Bob-o-loo," *Harper's Weekly*, 56 (December 14, 1912), 19–20.

"Children of the Dust," *Munsey's Magazine*, 48 (January 1913), 577–583.

"Forbidden Road," *Harper's Weekly*, 57 (February 8, 1913), 16–18.

"Son of Hagar," *Collier's*, 50 (March 8, 1913), 18–19, 35.

"Mr. Warner," *Harper's Monthly*, 127 (June 1913), 18–27.

"Ich Dien," *Munsey's Magazine*, 49 (August 1913), 786–793.

"Submarine's Fine Achievement. Voyage Home After Being Mined. 300 Miles of Peril," *The Times*, May 18, 1916, p. 3. Also in *DailyMail*.

"A Woman's Flight Over London. 'Looping the Loop.' Mile-and-a-Half Above Hyde Park," *The Times*, June 2, 1916, p. 6. Also in *New York Tribune, Globe, Sketch, News of the World, Pall Mall Gazette, Westminster Gazette, Standard, Chronicle, Express, Daily News* and *Daily Mirror*.

and Gordon Bruce. *Flying, Submarining and Mine Sweeping: In the "Daily*

Mail," the "New York Tribune" and the "New York Sun." London, 1916.
36 pp.

"Human Interest Stories. Sacrifice of People in War. Most Emphasize Women's Role in War," *Daily Mail*, June 14, 1916.

"The Lost Legion," *The Winnie Post* (a spoof newspaper), London, June 14, 1916, p. 1.

"Our German Prisoners. How We Treat Them," *Daily Mail*, June 28, 1916.

"Over the North Sea in a Messroom Chair," *New York Tribune Magazine*, August 27, 1916, pp. 1, 8.

"They Keep Their England Merry Still," *New York Tribune Magazine*, October 1, 1916, pp. 1, 6.

"A Woman in the Trenches," *Daily Express*, December 27, 1916.

"My Day in the Trenches. Thunderous Waves of Firing That Never Ceased. The Awful Business of War," *Daily Express*, December 28, 1916.

"English War Workers. An American Point of View," *The Times*, no date.

"I Came to Scorn But I Stayed to Marvel. How Visit to England Changed an American Girl's Views," *Daily Mail*, no date.

"The English Way. An American View," *Daily Mail*, no date.

"The Golden Hart. One British Village in War Time," *Daily Mail*, no date.

"The Leave Train and the Brave Women of England," *Daily Mail*, no date.

"The Boy on the Farm. A Ten-Year-Old Man," *Daily Mail*, no date.

"The Happiest Man in the World," *Century*, 99 (January 1920), 330–343.

"Horror in Spain," *Catholic Digest*, 1 (August 1937), 69–74.

II. Unpublished Material on Jane Anderson

Kitty Barry Crawford papers, courtesy of her Estate.

Joan Givner papers, courtesy of Professor Givner.

Deems Taylor papers, courtesy of Joan Kennedy Taylor.

FBI file. 446 pages.

Letter from Mary Lane, Piedmont College, Demorest, Georgia.

Letters from Dr. Ian Gibson, Madrid, about Jane's second husband, the Marqués de Cienfuegos.

III. Published Material on Jane Anderson

"Germans' Lady Haw-Haw Is Native of Atlanta," *Atlanta Journal*, January 20, 1942.

Boelcke, Willie. *Die Macht des Radio: Weltpolitik und Auslandsrundfunk, 1924–1976*. Frankfurt, 1976. Pp. 379–380, 383–385.

Carlson, John Roy. *Under Cover*. New York, 1943. Pp. 457, 469.

————. *The Plotters*. New York, 1946. P. 279.

Chrisler, Isabel. *Demorest in the Piedmont*. Privately printed, 1968. Pp. 25–26.

Conrad, Borys. *My Father: Joseph Conrad*. London, 1970. Pp. 117–122.

Conrad, Jessie. *Joseph Conrad and His Circle*. New York, 1935. Pp. 195–197, 204–208.

Conrad, John. *Joseph Conrad: Times Remembered*. Cambridge, England, 1981. Pp. 107–109.

Conrad, Joseph. *The Arrow of Gold*. London, 1919.

————. *Letters to His Wife*. London, 1927.

"Free 3 Who Broadcast for Hitler," *Daily Worker*, October 28, 1947, p. 3.

Douglas, Robin. "My Boyhood with Conrad," *Cornhill Magazine*, 66 (January 1929), 24.

Drake, Frank. "Lady Haw-Haw's Girlhood Recalled by Atlanta Kinsmen," *Atlanta Constitution*, January 20, 1942, p. 2.

Edwards, John. "Atlanta's Prodigal Daughter: The Turbulent Life of Jane Anderson as Expatriate and Nazi Propagandist," *Atlanta Historical Journal*, 28 (1984), 23–42.

Ettlinger, Harold. *The Axis on the Air*. New York, 1943. Pp. 52–53.

Givner, Joan. *Katherine Anne Porter: A Life*. New York, 1982. Pp. 114–115, 117, 120–123, 146, 151–152, 157, 160, 229, 360, 415, 523–524.

The Goebbels Diaries, 1939–1941. Trans. and ed. Fred Taylor. New York, 1983. Pp. 26, 357.

Halverson, John and Ian Watt. "Notes on Jane Anderson, 1955–1989," *Conradiana*, 23 (Spring 1991).

Hayes, Jess. *Sheriff Thompson's Day: Turbulence in the Arizona Territory*. Tucson, 1968. Pp. 24–25.

Knoblaugh, H. Edward. *Correspondent in Spain*. New York, 1937. P. 194.

Neville, Charles. "The Georgia Peach Who Became Lady Haw-Haw," *New York Journal American*, May 5, 1943.

"U.S. Drops Treason Charge Against Hitler's Lady Ha-Ha [sic]," *New York News*, December 10, 1947.

New York Times, October 11, 1936, p. 35.

New York Times, October 15, 1936, p. 2.

New York Times, February 28, 1938, p. 3.

New York Times, January 14, 1943, p. 1.

New York Times, July 27, 1943, pp. 1–2.

New York Times, September 20, 1945, p. 10.

New York Times, October 19, 1946, p. 7.

New York Times, October 28, 1947, p. 27.

O'Duffy, Eoin. *Crusade in Spain*. Dublin, 1938. P. 73.

"These People Joined [Merwin] Hart in Crying 'Communist,' " *PM*, June 12, 1941, p. 16.

Porter, Katherine Anne. "A Letter to the Editor of the *Saturday Review of Literature*" (1949). *Collected Essays*. New York, 1973. Pp. 212–213.

————. *Ship of Fools*. Boston, 1962. Pp. xii, 105, 107, 114–116, 117–122, 171–173.

————. *Letters*. Ed. Isabel Bayley. New York, 1990. P. 354.

Retinger, J. H. *Conrad and His Contemporaries*. New York, 1943. P. 98.

Retinger, Joseph. *Memoirs of an Eminence Grise*. Ed. John Pomian. Brighton, Sussex, 1972. Pp. 37–39, 45.

Rolo, Charles. *Radio Goes to War*. New York, 1942. Pp. 105–106.

Schofield, William. *Treason Trail*. New York, 1964. Pp. 25, 202–222.

Secor, Robert and Marie. *The Return of the Good Soldier: Ford Madox Ford and Violet Hunt's 1917 Diary*. Victoria, B.C., 1983. P. 71.

Seldes, George. *Witness to a Century*. New York, 1987. Pp. 53–57.

Shirer, William. "The American Radio Traitors," *Harper's*, 187 (October 1943), 397–404.

Sington, Derek and Arthur Weidenfeld. *The Goebbels Experiment: A Study of the Nazi Propaganda Machine*. New Haven, 1943. Pp. 187–188.

Thrapp, Dan. *Al Sieber: Chief of Scouts*. Norman, Okla., 1964. Pp. 390–391.

"Lady Haw-Haw," *Time*, 39 (January 19, 1942), 30.

"Germany: Sweets and Cookies," *Time*, 39 (April 6, 1942), 30.

"Death Penalty Urged for U.S. 'Haw-Haws,' " *Washington Post*, August 27, 1942.

"1943 Charges of Treason Dropped Against 3 Americans," *Washington Times Herald*, December 10, 1947, p. 5.

Weekly People, January 24, 1942.

Weyl, Nathaniel. *Treason: The Story of Disloyalty and Betrayal in American History*. Washington, D.C., 1950. Pp. 374–376.

Winchell, Walter, *Daily Mirror*, January 22, 1942.

Index

—Compiled by Valerie Meyers